Negotiating Reproductive Rights

The International Reproductive Rights Research Action Group (IRRRAG) is a consortium of women's health movement activists, researchers and physicians in Brazil, Egypt, Malaysia, Mexico, Nigeria, the Philippines and the United States. IRRRAG country teams conduct research and work locally, regionally and internationally to promote women's empowerment and transform women's reproductive and sexual rights into concrete policies and programmes.

INTERNATIONAL REPRODUCTIVE RIGHTS RESEARCH ACTION GROUP (IRRAG)

Negotiating Reproductive Rights

WOMEN'S PERSPECTIVES ACROSS COUNTRIES AND CULTURES

EDITED BY

Rosalind P. Petchesky and Karen Judd

Zed Books

LONDON AND NEW YORK

Negotiating Reproductive Rights was first published by
Zed Books Ltd, 7 Cynthia Street, London N1 9JF, UK, and
Room 400, 175 Fifth Avenue, New York, NY 10010, USA
in 1998

2nd impression 2001

Distributed in the USA exclusively by Palgrave, a division of
St. Martin's Press LLC, Room 400, 175 Fifth Avenue,
New York, NY 10010, USA

Editorial copyright © Rosalind P. Petchesky and Karen Judd, 1998
Individual chapters copyright © authors, 1998

Cover designed by Andrew Corbett,
Laserset by Long House, Cumbria, UK.
Printed and bound in the United Kingdom by Biddles Ltd
www.biddles.co.uk

A catalogue record for this book
is available from the British Library.

ISBN 1 85649 533 3 Cased
ISBN 1 85649 536 1 Limp

Contents

CONTENTS

Acknowledgements

Besides the authors, editors, and researchers listed in these pages, many organizations and individuals contributed to the realization of this book. The research was supported throughout by the Ford Foundation's Reproductive Health Program and by the John D. and Catherine T. MacArthur Foundation's Population Program, without which a project of this scope would not have been possible. We especially want to thank Margaret Hempel from Ford and Carmen Barroso and Leni Silverstein from MacArthur, who gave us invaluable intellectual and moral as well as material support. Along the way we also received partial support from the World Bank's Development Grant Facility and especially Tom Merrick, the Netherlands Foreign Ministry, the Ford Foundation offices in Lagos and Mexico City, the Moriah Fund, the Norwegian foreign ministry, the Rockefeller Foundation and its Bellagio Center, the United Nations Population Fund (UNFPA) offices in the Philippines and Brazil, World Vision, and personal gifts from Lillian M. Danziger and Roberta Pollack. To all these angels, we are very grateful.

As an offshoot of local and international women's health and rights movements, IRRRAG has received incalculable backing from many NGOs – backing that encouraged and inspired our work and sometimes helped pull us through financial crises. We owe deep thanks to CEPIA (Cidadania, Estudos, Pesquisa, Informação e Ação), the Coletivo Feminista Sexualidade e Saúde, ECOS (Equipe de Comunicação em Sexualidade), FALA PRETA-Organização de Mulheres Negras, SOS-Corpo Cidadania, SOF (Sempreviva Organização Feminista), and the Fundação Carlos Chagas in Brazil; the New Woman Research Centre, the Coptic Evangelical Organization for Social Services and the Population Council in Egypt; Casa de la Mujer Rosario Castellanos, the Centro de Sonora para la Atención de la Mujer, the Programa Universitario de Estudios de Género de la UNAM, the Programa de Salud Reproductiva de El Colegio de México, and the Population Council in Mexico; the Asian Pacific Resource and Research Centre for Women (ARROW) in Malaysia; the Girls' Power Initiative (GPI), Empowerment and Action Research Centre (EMPARC) and Women's Health Organization of Nigeria (WHON) in Nigeria; WomanHealth, the Center for Women's Resources (CWR), the Women's Resource and Research Center (WRRC), and KALAYAAN in the Philippines; the Women's Studies Program at Hunter College, the Reproductive Rights Education Project at Hunter College, and the National Black Women's Health Project in the United States.

In addition, many individuals from these organizations gave us advice, resources, and vital logistical support. We particularly thank Maria Jose Araújo, Maria Betania Ávila, Regina Barbosa, Sonia Corrêa, Maria Luiza Heilborn, Jacqueline Pitanguy, Leila Linhares Barsted, Albertina de Oliveira Costa, Edna Roland, Cecília Simonetti, and Mary Jane Paris Spink in Brazil; Rosamaria Roffiel and Claudia Hinajosa in Mexico; Adepeju Olukoya and Adetoun Ilumoka in Nigeria; Marilen Dañguilan and Ana Maria Nemenzo in the Philippines; and Debbie Bell, Rebecca Cook, Rhonda Copelon, Joan Dunlop, Lynn Freedman, Adrienne Germain, Jodi Jacobson, Monica Rocha, Ragnhild Utheim, and Susan Wood in North America.

Enormous thanks go also to IRRRAG's team of research consultants – Iris Lopez, Sylvia Marcos, Carla Makhlouf Obermeyer, Tola Olu Pearce, Rayna Rapp, T. K. Sundari Ravindran, Beth Richie, and Joanna Gould Stuart – for their help and encouragement in the early stages of field research and data analysis. A number of them as well as other friends and colleagues also kindly read parts of the manuscript and shared their wisdom. In particular, we want to thank Marge Berer, Sonia Corrêa, Zillah Eisenstein, Carla Obermeyer, Vera Paiva, Richard Parker, Tola Pearce, Sundari Ravindran, and Beth Richie, as well as Pat Harper and Louise Murray at Zed Books. The book is better for their suggestions, but certainly they bear no responsibility for its flaws. Finally, and most of all, the IRRRAG project is hugely indebted to the hundreds of women and men who so graciously shared their stories and perceptions with us and to the grassroots organizations and communities from which they come.

In loving memory of Guadalupe Musalem, of the IRRRAG team and the Casa de la Mujer Rosario Castellanos in Mexico; Expedita Lima, member of the Movimento da Mulher Trabalhadora Rural in northeast Brazil; and Esther Onyilo, of the IRRRAG team in Nigeria. Up to the moment of their tragic deaths, all three worked to further women's empowerment and reproductive health and participated actively in IRRRAG's research. They remain in our hearts.

1 Introduction

ROSALIND P. PETCHESKY*

The Origins and Global Context of IRRRAG

> Through travelling to other people's 'worlds' we discover that there are 'worlds' in which those who are the victims of arrogant perception are really subjects, lively beings, resistors, constructors of visions even though in the mainstream construction they are animated only by the arrogant perceiver and are pliable, ... classifiable. (Lugones 1990)

The International Reproductive Rights Research Action Group (IRRRAG) was born out of the premise that, until we know more about the local contexts and ways of thinking in which women in their everyday lives negotiate reproductive health and sexual matters, we cannot assume that reproductive and sexual rights are a goal they seek and therefore one that has universal applicability. Nor can we know how a concept of reproductive and sexual rights might have differing meanings for women according to their age, place in the life cycle, marital status, economic conditions, religious and ethnic identity, or other social circumstances. To bring this concept down from the lofty plane of abstract principle, we need to situate it within direct testimonies about the daily constraints and relationships through which women – across a variety of countries and cultures – engage in reproductive and sexual transactions.

The participants in this project – some as researchers, some as health providers, all as feminist activists of some sort – have been engaged in work around a variety of reproductive and sexual health issues in our own countries.[1] Through our experiences in our local settings and in regional and international debates, we became convinced that it was both historically

* For their helpful readings and comments on this introduction, thanks to Marge Berer, Zillah Eisenstein, Rayna Rapp, the Egyptian IRRRAG team, Rashidah Abdullah (Malaysian team), Adriana Ortiz Ortega (Mexican team), participants in IRRRAG's meeting in Mexico, May 1996, and Mercy Fabros of the Philippines team, who contributed much to the substance of IRRRAG's conceptual framework and its formulation below.

I

timely and politically urgent to look at the diverse meanings of reproductive rights from the ground up. All of us subscribe to a view of human rights rooted in the concept of 'cultural citizenship' and the mandate that we 'listen to women's voices' in order to build a culturally and situationally appropriate definition of what reproductive and sexual rights should entail (Benmayor, Torruellas and Juarbe 1992). Illuminating the perspectives of grassroots women who are not ordinarily part of these debates is important, not only to generate more useful policies and programmes but also to expand our own visions and develop our organizing capacities.[2]

Established in 1992, IRRRAG emerged in a context in which feminist health and women's rights movements and networks had long been a vital force for social and legislative change, in countries and regions of the global South as well as North. By the early 1980s, these movements were already exerting a critical impact on debates about population growth and fertility rates. For one thing, the perspective of women's health activists (based on years of practical experience providing popular education and alternative services) challenged demographic assumptions that attribute poverty and environmental degradation to women's high fertility and, in turn, women's high fertility to an absence of information or methods. Whilst women in all countries surely seek safe, effective methods of contraception and abortion, they also want healthy conditions for childbearing, sexuality free from violence and disease, food security, skills and incomes of their own, and dignity and respect as service recipients and human beings.

Target-driven population control programmes fail to take into account women's own perceptions of their health needs and how they fit within a larger set of aspirations for social and economic empowerment (Batliwala 1994). Too often heavy-handed or coercive, denying necessary information and counselling, such programmes frequently meet the resistance of women, who drop out, stop using the methods, or in some cases organize vocal movements against certain technologies perceived as harmful to their health (see Barroso and Corrêa 1995; Dixon-Mueller 1993; Hartmann 1995; Ravindran 1993 and 1996; *Reproductive Health Matters* 1993–97; and Women's Global Network for Reproductive Rights 1990–97). But feminist health activists in many countries have also opposed mainstream population and family planning programmes on ethical and political grounds: that their failure to treat women's health and wellbeing as ends in themselves (rather than as means toward lowering or raising numbers) and their disregard for women as reproductive decision makers constitute violations of women's human rights.[3]

Although the origin of the term 'reproductive rights' may be traced to movements that initially surfaced in North America and Europe, similar yet distinct movements on behalf of women's reproductive health and rights rapidly formed during the early-to-mid 1980s in Latin America and the Caribbean, Asia and Africa.[4] As Garcia-Moreno and Claro (1994:48) have observed, while the principles embedded in reproductive and sexual rights are often labelled a byproduct of Western culture, this view distorts both history and the varieties and local roots of feminist movements: 'While Western ideas have played a role, women in Southern countries have generated their own analyses, organizations, and movements, with and without exposure to the West, and there has been considerable cross-fertilization of ideas – across many countries and continents'. Women's and gay and lesbian rights movements in countries where the Catholic Church is powerful – such as the Philippines, Brazil, and Mexico – have struggled to legalize abortion, reduce maternal mortality and educate about safer sex and condom use. In Bangladesh, women's organizations have publicly countered brutal attacks on women accused by Islamic religious tribunals of transgressing sexual norms (Amin and Hossain 1995). In Africa and the Middle East, campaigns by women's groups against female genital mutilation (FGM) have focused both on the procedure's suppression of women's sexual pleasure and on its severe risks to their health (Toubia 1995; Tambiah 1995).[5] Women-of-color organizations in the United States, like women's groups in India, have vigorously opposed sterilization abuse and the coercive or nonconsensual promotion of long-acting contraceptives by family planning programmes (Fried 1990; Hathi 1996; Srinivas and Kanakamala 1992; United States Women of Color Delegation 1994).

These practical campaigns and theoretical reconceptions nourished the forcefulness of the women's coalitions at the World Conference on Human Rights in Vienna in 1993, the International Conference on Population and Development (ICPD) in Cairo in 1994, and the Fourth World Conference on Women (FWCW) in Beijing in 1995. Representing women from both the global South and the North, those coalitions worked to replace the old population-and-family-planning discourse with a broad concept of reproductive and sexual health and rights that links sexual and reproductive freedom to women's human rights.[6] At the core of that concept lies a principle that as recently as the mid-1980s, in nearly all countries and political systems, was widely deemed unacceptable if not unthinkable: that even the most intimate areas of family, procreative and sexual life are ones where women's human rights to self-determination and equality must prevail. This principle, and the success of women's movements in gaining international recognition for it, is embodied in a historic paragraph adopted by government delegates in Beijing:

> The human rights of women include their right to have control over and decide freely and responsibly on matters related to their sexuality, including sexual and reproductive health, free of coercion, discrimination and violence. Equal relationships between women and men in matters of sexual relations and reproduction, including full respect for the integrity of the person, require mutual respect, consent and shared responsibility for sexual behaviour and its consequences.[7]

Yet, while Southern women and women of colour in the North in the 1980s and 1990s affirmed the critical importance of women's control over their fertility and sexuality, they were pushing for a much broader approach. That approach would integrate issues about abortion, contraception, childbearing and sexuality – the politics of the body – into a larger framework that emphasizes 'the transformation of state social, demographic and economic development policies to incorporate women's social and economic rights'. As DAWN's platform puts it, 'women's reproductive health must be placed within a comprehensive human development framework that promotes all people's well-being and women's full citizenship' (Corrêa 1994:64).[8] This suggests that the concept of reproductive and sexual rights must be seen through a double lens, and that its personal and social dimensions, rather than being in conflict, are mutually dependent.

On the one hand, a double perspective on reproductive and sexual rights embraces the feminist ethics of bodily integrity and personhood that permeates the Cairo and Beijing documents and directly challenges the moral arsenal of Christian, Islamic and other fundamentalists. Such a feminist ethics requires not only that women must be free from abuse and violation of their bodies but also that they must be treated as principal actors and decision makers over their fertility and sexuality; as the ends and not the means of health, population and development programmes. And it applies this imperative not only to states and their agents but to every level where power operates, including the home, the clinic, the workplace, the religious centre, and the community. On the other hand, this feminist perspective links the rights of the body and the person directly with the social, economic and political rights – the enabling conditions – necessary to achieve gender, class and racial–ethnic justice (Batliwala 1994; Corrêa and Petchesky 1994).

Having achieved considerable success at the level of theoretical visions and United Nations rhetoric, feminist activists in all the world's regions now face the problems of turning reproductive and sexual rights into concrete realities in women's everyday lives. In so doing, they confront several major obstacles. First, in most countries, due to hegemonic capitalist markets and the declining role of the state, the availability and quality of public health services continue to deteriorate, especially burdening low-income women. For women's reproductive and sexual rights to be implemented in practice will require not only supportive laws and policies (still to be enacted within most countries) but also a thorough transformation of existing global, regional and national economic structures (Bandarage 1997; Corrêa 1994; Desai 1994; Sen forthcoming; Sparr 1994). Individual women cannot exercise their reproductive and sexual rights without the necessary enabling conditions for their empowerment. These include both material and infra-structural supports (such as reliable transport, child care, and jobs as well as accessible and adequate health services); and cultural and political supports

4

(such as access to education, self-esteem, and political power). In turn, such conditions for the vast majority would require a reordering of international and national economic policies to abandon debt servicing and militarism in favour of social welfare and primary health care (Corrêa and Petchesky 1994). Yet economic and social policies in all seven IRRRAG countries, reflecting global trends, continue to move in the opposite direction: towards structural adjustments that dictate privatization and reduction of social services, deference to corporate interests and transnational capital, and high levels of military spending.

Second, resurgent fundamentalisms in many countries, claiming ultimate authority over religious doctrine and moral values, actively challenge the recognition of reproductive and sexual freedom as a basic human right. Whether Christian, Hindu, Islamic, Buddhist or Jewish, these fundamentalist currents reinforce traditional patriarchal views of women's 'natural' subordination and the primacy of a male-dominated, procreative, hetero-sexual family form. Despite their religious facade, the impact and aims of today's fundamentalist movements are overwhelmingly political: to influence or take over state power, to buttress the authority of religious laws and courts over all family and sexual relations, and to reshape national policies and international norms in a conservative mould. During the mid-1990s, the Vatican and its Catholic state allies formed an outspoken alliance with Islamist regimes in order to influence the Cairo and Beijing conferences – and especially to oppose the notions of reproductive and sexual rights, individual rights, and diversity of family forms. Although they lost the contest over words in the United Nations documents, these forces continue to wield considerable power and to influence governments, legislation and popular opinion in all the countries of IRRRAG's research as well as many others (Amin and Hossain 1995; Catholics for a Free Choice 1995; Freedman 1996; Women Against Fundamentalism 1995).

Finally, these economic and political obstacles to realizing reproductive and sexual rights are reinforced by the deep cultural and social roots of gender inequality. The misbelief (going back to Aristotle) that women are mainly private actors incapable of, or uninterested in, public debate acts as a brake on the power of many women in all societies to articulate and embrace their rights and make claims on public agencies to enforce them; that is, to act as citizens in defence of their own bodily integrity and personhood (Peters and Wolper 1995; Nelson and Chowdhury 1994). For reproductive and sexual rights to become practical realities for all women, such rights must be fully integrated into the agendas of social justice and democratization movements. In the first instance, this means mobilization of women's groups into strong alliances and actions that can secure government and international enforcement mechanisms; in other words, that can stimulate political will where such will is lacking.

Ultimately, however, political action can be effective only if masses of women believe in and own their rights. They must have a conviction that they are entitled to be treated as primary decision-makers over their own bodies and reproductive capacities. It is this level of women's aspirations and consciousness that the IRRRAG research aimed to address.

Conceptual Framework

IRRRAG derived the critical conceptual tools that informed our research from the feminist ethical perspective described above and its emphasis on linking personal and social rights. However, despite its widespread use since the Cairo conference, the concept of reproductive rights is by no means universally accepted among feminist groups around the globe. For some, it evokes a highly Westernized and narrow frame of reference that reduces reproduction at best to fertility control and at worst to the single issue of abortion; or it evokes an even more devious scenario that masks racist and eugenic population control behind 'a feminist face' (Akhter 1994; Hartmann 1994). For others, any rights discourse is suspect if not objectionable, either on philosophical and political grounds (because of its association with individualistic, privatized, adversarial meanings derived from Western law and ethics); or on pragmatic grounds (because of its lack of any meaning to grassroots women). Still other feminists are troubled by the focus not on rights but on reproduction, insofar as it may reinforce the ideological bias that reduces women to one aspect of their being and occludes other aspects, particularly (nonprocreative) sexuality (Pateman 1988; *WGNRR Newsletter* 1993).

At IRRRAG's founding meeting in 1992, it quickly became apparent that similar doubts persisted within our own group, requiring critical investigation of how we ourselves were using the concept. For one thing, the term 'reproductive rights' as well as several ancillary terms in English have no equivalent in certain national languages (for example, there is no word for 'reproductive' in Arabic or Malay and none for 'empowerment' or 'entitlement' in Portuguese or Spanish[9]). Although women's groups in some of our countries had been using some version of the term for the previous decade in their organizing and advocacy, in others it had far less currency. Participants from Nigeria and the Philippines preferred to use a discourse of 'health' or 'wellness', which they felt would have more meaning to their grassroots constituencies than would a rights discourse. Other participants, however – especially those from Mexico and Brazil, where women's movements have associated reproductive autonomy with citizenship rights; and from the US, where the African American civil rights movement has nourished a long tradition of community-based rights – argued just as strongly on behalf of retaining 'reproductive rights'. They pointed out how progressive movements around the world have embraced a human rights agenda associated with struggles for equality and justice, not only of women, but of many other oppressed groups. And participants from Egypt and Malaysia noted that, despite the lack of an exact equivalent in their languages, feminists and even ministry of health officials in their countries were now using the term.

Although our initial meeting did not resolve this debate, it was precisely in order to give the concept of reproductive rights a more culturally grounded definition that the project had come into existence. We thus decided to retain it until such time as we could see whether the research findings would give us reason to discard it. Indeed, as Sonia Corrêa observes, 'health' and 'rights' as strategies 'are not mutually exclusive' but, rather, have been used simultaneously by women's movements in both the North and the South:

> Women may or may not construe their decision [to terminate a pregnancy] as having anything to do with gender relations or 'rights'. Just the same, a woman's decision represents a balancing of her own, her family's, and sometimes her community's needs. This decision – whether taken alone or in dialogue with significant others – represents a critical marker of a woman's reproductive autonomy and her right to health. (1994:69)

Despite the debate over language, we reached consensus that women should have control over when, whether and with whom they have children, and access to the enabling conditions that make such control possible. All participants agreed that, especially for the majority of women who are poor and marginalized, achieving reproductive self-determination would ultimately require fundamental changes, not only in the quality and availability of services, but also in the structural conditions and state policies that support an unjust economic and social order. But tensions persisted over not only the language but also the content of reproductive rights. In particular, some country teams in 1992 were still reluctant to acknowledge freedom of sexual expression or orientation as both integral to reproductive rights and health and basic to the inquiry on which we were embarking. Due to both the work of lesbian feminist and AIDS activists and the worldwide pandemic of HIV/AIDS and its growing prevalence among heterosexual women, the concept of 'sexual rights' subsequently became encoded in the Beijing document (see above). Though still in its infancy, that concept is now high on the agenda of many women's and reproductive health organizations, and both its negative and positive dimensions (freedom *from* sexual abuse and risk, freedom *for* sexual pleasure) have been embraced by all the IRRRAG teams.

In recent years, numerous well-documented studies and journals have explored diverse feminist perspectives on reproduction in an international context, laying a solid analytical basis for further empirical and cross-cultural research.[10] Building on these, IRRRAG's research attempted to (a) gather primary ethnographic data, (b) filter it through a comparative and cross-cultural lens, and (c) ask a distinct set of questions related to women's reproductive and sexual awareness and decision-making strategies. Although our research posed many interrelated questions, two above all motivated the country studies: How do women across diverse countries, cultures and generations arrive at and negotiate a sense of entitlement with regard to their reproductive and sexual health and wellbeing? In what life circumstances and through which terms, codes, and strategies do they begin to take charge of their reproductive and sexual bodies? From the outset, then, our research was centrally concerned with issues of moral and political agency and women's formulation and pursuit of claims to decision-making authority. We were especially interested in how and when such claims arise within the so-called 'private' arenas of family and sexual relations but also in their resonance within more 'public' domains – the state, the clinic, the religious institution, and the community – that become the local gatekeepers of women's reproductive and sexual behaviour. Beyond this micro-political level, we were also interested in knowing when state policies concerning health and population act to reinforce traditional norms of female sub-ordination and when they actually help to empower women in challenging those norms.

Thus our inquiry travels back and forth between two levels of social reality. One is that of *perceptions* – how women articulate their entitlements and aspirations in light of both community norms and their own (and their children's) most urgent material and emotional needs. The other is that of *power relations and enabling conditions* – how they negotiate relations with parents, husbands and other sexual partners, clinicians, religious and public authorities, as well as scarce resources and services, in order to translate such needs into deliberate claims of right or justice. A shared observation of all the country studies, based on the research findings, is that women engage in such negotiations as active agents rather than passive victims, even though circumstances and those with more power may defeat their efforts:

> [Women] have always attempted, from their traditional positions as workers, mothers, and wives, not only to influence their immediate environment but also to expand their space. However, the prevailing patriarchal ideology, which promotes the values of submission, sacrifice, obedience, and silent suffering, often undermines even these attempts by women to assert themselves or demand some share of resources. (Batliwala 1994:129–30)

The aim of IRRRAG's research was to uncover and enhance the conditions for women to overcome these barriers to 'challenging existing power relations and ... gaining greater control over the sources of power' (Batliwala 1994).

At IRRRAG's founding meeting in 1992, we adopted a set of broad questions to frame the research, organized around four conceptual matrices: (1) concept of entitlement; (2) reproductive decision making; (3) resistance and accommodation; and (4) social, political, legal and economic conditions.

In the course of our research, however, we not only discovered considerable overlap among the questions but also realized that the concepts underlying them required continual deconstruction and reconstruction, as we tried to apply them to different contexts and situations in the field. Only after revisiting these concepts in our collective discussions and using them concretely in our fieldwork and data interpretation over a period of three years did we begin to understand their nuances and their utility for decoding the speech and actions of the women we interviewed.

Reproduction

Virtually all the country teams, through their experience in local and regional women's health movements, brought to the project a view of reproduction as denoting a far broader sphere of activity than mere fertility management. We agreed that reproductive health includes not only access to safe contraceptives and obstetrical and prenatal care but also services relating to the menarche and menopause; safe, legal abortion; services to prevent and treat reproductive tract infections (RTIs), HIV/AIDS, infertility, and gynaecological cancers; protection against sexual violence, female genital mutilation, and other harmful traditional practices; full information and respect for women's decision-making capacities; and access to good-quality primary health care across the life cycle. Further, the Egyptian team reminded us that reproduction and motherhood are social functions and not just an individual right or responsibility; and the Brazilian team, drawing from its research among domestic and rural workers, continually emphasized that social reproduction involves activities that span a woman's life cycle and not only her so-called reproductive years.

The view of women's reproductive activities as socially determined and useful labour truly came alive in the experiences of the women we spoke with in all our research communities.[11] It became evident that the array of issues clustered around biological reproduction was, in the daily lives of the women, intimately interconnected with the tasks of social reproduction. Social scientists and demographers have long understood that women make decisions about whether or not to bear children with reference to their position within or outside paid work, their access to childcare resources, the demands of husbands or other kin, etcetera. We soon realized, however, that the 'reproductive career', including child care and household tasks, is not only socially determined. In the male-dominated context of many societies today, it is lifelong and highly gender-specific – continuing from the time when young girls are expected to perform as 'little mothers' into old age. Moreover, the bearing and care of children are themselves experienced by many women, not as biological events, but as forms of social labour done for others and demanding considerable organization, energy and skill. This perception had important implications for our methodology and research design; it meant that, in studying women's expressions of entitlement regarding reproduction and sexuality, we had to inquire as well into how they understood their entitlements with regard to the division of labour and power relations within the wider arenas of marriage, work and family.

Rights

Since the 1970s, women's movements have played a leading role in securing recognition for matters of personal and bodily integrity, health and reproduction in international instruments. They have also helped to promote the principle of the indivisibility of such 'personal' rights from the more established civil and political as well as economic, social and cultural rights.[12] Early documents such as the founding Charter of the World Health Organization (1946), the Universal Declaration of Human Rights (1948), and the International Covenant on Economic, Social and Cultural Rights (1967) contain language inscribing 'the enjoyment of the highest attainable standard of health' and the right to 'life, liberty and security of the person' as fundamental human rights. The American Convention on Human Rights (1970) and the African Charter on Human and People's Rights (1982) also refer to the inviolability of the person and mental and physical integrity; while the Convention on the Elimination of Discrimination Against Women (Women's Convention, 1979) prohibits its signatories from discriminating against women with regard to all the established rights including access to health care, education and information, employment, freedom in marriage and reproductive decision making.

More recently, thanks to the work of women's international coalitions mentioned above, the Vienna Declaration and Programme of Action (1993), the ICPD Programme of Action (1994) and the FWCW Declaration and Platform for Action (1995) extend these basic human rights principles to specific aspects of women's reproductive and sexual freedom. Thus the international human rights vocabulary now includes not only 'the basic right of all couples and individuals to decide freely and responsibly the number, spacing and timing of their children and to have the information and means to do so' but also freedom from 'violence against women and all forms of sexual harassment and exploitation', including 'systematic rape, sexual slavery, and forced pregnancy'; freedom from genital mutilation; the 'right to make decisions concerning reproduction free of discrimination, coercion and violence'; and the right 'to have a satisfying and safe sex life' (Cook 1995; Leary 1994; Otto 1995).

But a major problem with such formal documents is that, given the continued weakness and divisions plaguing international organizations, they depend for their enforcement on existing governments, which are often corrupt, unstable and uncommitted. Although the series of parallel NGO (nongovernmental organization) forums held during the 1990s United Nations conferences were tentative steps toward creating an 'international civil society' that might pressure governments to honour their human rights commitments, reliable enforcement mechanisms through which sub-ordinated groups and individuals can bring claims on their own behalf are still a rarity. More important, formal statements of women's rights are not only unknown to the vast majority of women; they are also very distant from the constraints burdening poor women and the conditions IRRRAG researchers typically encounter in the field. For most people, codified expressions of rights in national laws and international agreements are very removed from the ways they envision rights and wrongs, justice and injustice, needs and deprivations, in their daily lives – for at least two reasons.

First, the term 'rights' is commonly associated with formal arenas and mechanisms of law, whether of the state or of religious institutions. Yet many people in the countries where we did our research consistently experience the authorities charged with enforcing rights (police, government officials, hospital and clinic personnel) as oppressive, corrupt and routinely ready to disregard national laws and international principles, or even common decency. As a result, they view formally constituted rights as inapplicable to them, particularly if they are poor and female. We discovered among the respondents in some of our countries (particularly Brazil, Mexico, and the US) a very sharp distrust of bureaucrats, courts and law enforcement officials and, by association, of any notion that this formal system would protect their rights or interests. In these contexts, to speak of 'reproductive and sexual rights' means little except to those who are already politicized and involved in organized struggles that presume the possibility of exacting justice.

Second, although human rights procedures do function theoretically to hold states and state agents (police, military, officials, public health and family planning personnel) accountable, perpetrators of violations against women's reproductive and sexual rights also include 'private' parties, such as parents or other kin, husbands and sexual partners. Actually, as some of the IRRRAG country studies included in this volume suggest, a sense of entitlement to assert one's rights or decision-making authority may be easier for many women to feel in relation to more distant authority figures – doctors, religious leaders, the mayor – than to persons with whom they are intimately involved, such as husbands. Especially for women, whose lives are still in many countries and cultures locked within domesticity, assertions of human rights must penetrate the 'private' sphere where everyday violations of their bodily integrity and personhood – marital rape, FGM, virginity codes for women, customary repudiation of birth control – occur. 'Public' actions of the state and its agents – for example, laws prohibiting or restricting abortion, or rape of civilians by soldiers and police – reinforce such daily life intrusions and, with them, form a continuum of systemic abuse (Copelon 1994; Romany 1994). Breaking down the artificial barrier between 'public' and 'private' spheres has been a principal aim of feminists organizing for women's human rights throughout the 1970s, 1980s and 1990s (Bunch

1990; Freedman and Isaacs 1993; Corrêa and Petchesky 1994; Obermeyer 1994). Yet their efforts have only begun to generate new forms of struggle and language that resonate at a local, grassroots level.

The absence of trust in formal mechanisms for securing legal rights does not, however, mean that people are passive or unwilling to stake claims and take forceful actions in order to get what they believe is right or necessary for themselves and their children. Such claims may be grounded in fundamental principles of justice or equity even if they have not yet been realized in legal terms. Moreover, effective strategies for their achievement may include not only public or institutional means, such as legal actions, lobbying or strikes, but also less formal group protests, self-help measures, and even more subtle forms of individual resistance or 'private' subversion. By viewing rights and strategies for achieving them in this inclusive way, we reached an understanding that is more politically dynamic and open with regard to the so-called private or personal realm than are conventional human rights models.

Entitlement

Even before we arrived at this understanding of rights and possible remedies to their violation, we were aware of our need for a more flexible terminology that would take into account not only the everyday ways in which women express their sense of necessity, fairness, or self-determination in regard to their bodies but also the informal and even surreptitious ways in which they act on that sense. In order to capture our respondents' own perception of their needs and just claims (whether on husbands, parents, medical providers, or the state), beyond what may exist juridically, we adopted the concept of 'sense of entitlement'. Through this notion we hoped to illuminate the subjective component of rights (what women *feel* entitled to), and our central research question thus became: when, where, and under what circumstances does such a sense of entitlement emerge in regard to reproductive and sexual decisions and choices?

It is important to distinguish the way in which IRRRAG's framework interprets 'entitlement' from more familiar uses of the concept in public policy discourse. In the history of the European welfare state, the term 'entitlement' emerged after World War Two in recognition of the idea that every individual possesses a set of 'birthrights' and that governments have an obligation to enable marginalized or economically disadvantaged persons to enjoy such birthrights (Marshall 1975). Conceded as a way to secure social stability and mitigate the harsher effects of a capitalist economic system (such as chronic unemployment) rather than to transform that system, the welfare state also recognized that entitlements, even if based on economic and social rights, depended on statutory mandates for their legitimacy.[13] The well-known 'entitlement approach' developed by Harvard economist Amartya Sen follows in this welfare state tradition. In order to explain the fact that famines occur, and people starve, even when plenty of food is available, Sen interprets entitlement as a lack or failure: some people get no food because they are unable to access the existing legal, political, economic and social structures of entitlement in a given country – 'the law stands between food availability and food entitlement' (Sen 1981; 1984:348). In other words, the existing system of entitlements fails to honour birthrights.

IRRRAG's subjective approach to a 'sense of entitlement' focuses more on women's moral claims, especially on partners, kin and caregivers, than on their perceptions of what the law or state owes them. Our basic hypothesis in developing this concept was that many women, including those who are poor, lacking formal education, or from cultures where rights discourse may be alien, will act consciously to secure their own or their children's needs, including in the realm of reproduction and sexuality. Sense of entitlement goes beyond the concept of 'needs' insofar as it entails a conviction of the moral rightness of one's claim, without perhaps the formal public or legal acknowledgement that 'rights' imply. It thus denotes the space in between a felt sense of need and an articulation of right. 'Entitlement' in this under-standing is meant to signify those actions of speech, metaphor, or even unspoken behaviour that represent both (1) an aspiration to change one's own or one's children's situation, a hope for a better life; and (2) a sense of authority to effect these changes through one's own words or actions.

Clearly such a broad, and in many ways philosophical, research objective poses difficult analytical and methodological problems that this project only began to address. Assuming that the terms in which people justify their own ('private') behaviour or decisions will often differ from the more 'public' forms of legitimation that activists may invoke, it becomes necessary to develop careful ways of listening to grasp the expressions, local codes and even silences that may signal a sense of entitlement. This suggests a second problem, familiar to much qualitative research but particularly urgent in research dealing with the most intimate – and often camouflaged – matters of sexual and reproductive relations: how to distinguish between the *normative* and the *behavioural*, between *what people say and think they ought to do* and *what they actually do*. In fact the problem is more complicated than this, since the normative terms people may use to justify – or even condemn – their own actions (for example, secretly getting an abortion under conditions of illegality and community censure) may not fully articulate how they justify those actions to themselves in light of their immediate circumstances. Thus, for purposes of analytical clarity, we need to reconfigure the concept of entitlement through several normative levels: (1) codified national and international law, that is, formal rights (both what they are and what respondents think they are); (2) custom/tradition (dominant religious or other norms that govern people's values and/or behaviour in the community); (3) practice (what people actually do in everyday life, apart from legal and normative values); and (4) vision (what respondents believe ought to be, ways they feel their sense of entitlement and aspirations are unrecognized or unfulfilled in reality).[14]

In the midst of the research, preliminary reports from the field offered us more nuanced understandings of the culturally grounded cues and images that may invoke a sense of entitlement for poor women. For example, the Brazil team's research in Pernambuco found that the rural women they interviewed tended to associate entitlement with 'freedom to come and go', to leave the house and go to the land. Women in a small rural town in the southern US used almost the same words – 'to do what I want to do and go where I want to go' – to signify the achievement of adult status and the beginning of entitlement. Likewise, women respondents in Egypt saw public proof of their virginity upon marriage as a ticket to walk freely in the streets. (See chapters 2, 3 and 8.) Sometimes women's expressions of entitlement took a negative rather than a positive form: for example, when a respondent would voice regret or a feeling of unfairness about having been sterilized, prevented from working outside the home, denied sexual information, or forced into early marriage and childbearing. Often such regret evolves into women's determination that their daughters will enjoy more freedom than they had, or *inter-generational entitlement*.

Finally, the responses we were getting in the field prompted us to view the sense of entitlement as emerging not from a fixed 'self' or isolated subject (the 'individual' of classical liberal thought), but from a social context of norms and relationships that are continually changing and contested. The Philippines team helped us to develop this understanding through its careful formulation of the idea of 'negotiated, or situated, entitlement'. Associating 'sense of entitlement' with the Filipino term *sana*, or 'aspirations and expectations', the Philippines analysis emphasizes the multi-layered dimensions of entitlement as it intersects with family and sexual dynamics, socioeconomic conditions, availability of medical and family planning services, as well as a woman's place in the life cycle. It points out that, for grassroots women (thus, most of the women in our seven country studies), 'the desire for entitlement largely stems from a relational or situational condition rather than a clear notion of bodily integrity'. A woman's decision regarding her fertility and sexuality will depend not only on her class position, occupation, household structure, education, access to reproductive health services, and other such socioeconomic variables, but also on her own perceptions, as her 'notion of her "self" evolves and changes through her life stages'. Before she marries, a woman 'may have more aspirations for herself'; after marriage, she is more likely to project her aspirations towards her family, especially her children. In sum:

> The fulfilment of a woman's aspiration is a product of the interaction of what the woman says she wants and needs, on the one hand, and what she believes her family and society can realistically give her as well as what she actually does for herself, on the other. It can be said, therefore, that the pursuit of entitlement is

always *under negotiation*. Negotiation takes place within the woman herself – typically between competing demands or values – and between herself and the external world, with the family as the first layer.[15]

As this relationally grounded analysis makes clear, IRRRAG's approach to the concept of entitlement as a form of rights discourse is more complex and multi-layered than conventional Western notions of 'privacy' and 'individualism'. Rather, we invoke a subversive tradition of autonomy and self-ownership that exists in popular European, African American and many non-Western cultures, one that postulates the self as *both* individual *and* constructed through ongoing interaction and interdependency with others (Corrêa and Petchesky 1994; Petchesky 1995b; Collins 1990; Eisenstein 1988). For a woman to assert her authority or agency to make decisions over reproduction and sexuality because it is her own body or health at stake, or because she is a mother who has the major responsibility for what happens to her children, is not the same as being 'selfish' or acting only for one's own interests. In fact, as the studies in this book confirm, women often present themselves as acting or deciding on their own (that is, apart from husbands or in contravention of dominant community norms) out of a sense of duty to others, usually their living children. In this way, they both carry out their intentions and reconcile them normatively with centuries of patriarchal culture and socialization that define women as caretakers who ought to think of everyone else's needs before their own.

This initial impression prompted a debate within IRRRAG as to whether a feminist ethics implies a kind of hierarchy in which acting for oneself is in some way superior to, or more politically aware than, acting for others (the traditional role of women). Yet, with more careful probing, the data from our research suggest that women in their everyday deliberations over matters of fertility, sexuality, work, and child care do not necessarily experience their own entitlement and that of their families, especially their children, as operating on different or conflicting levels of decision making. Rather, they interweave the self–other relationship in their moral calculations all the time, rooting their individual identity in family and community. For example, in the eyes of rural Nigerian women, to rest and conserve their bodies after pregnancy seems necessary for competent mothering, for the sake of their children as well as themselves. Similarly, for urban Brazilian mothers, to give their daughters greater sexual and reproductive freedom than they had as young women will enhance their (the older generation's) own dignity and self-worth. Thus 'negotiated entitlement' implies a concept of the self that 'reaches far beyond the notion of bodily integrity [to encompass] ... the context of all significant family, cultural, social and economic relationships' (Corrêa 1994:77).

Body and Self
Even while IRRRAG researchers agreed that 'the decision-making self must

remain at the core of reproductive rights' (Corrêa 1994:77), philosophical differences arose around the tension between 'the self' as moral agent and 'the body', with its sexual connotations. During an informal presentation made by IRRRAG members in 1995,[16] Turkish feminist sociologist Nilüfer Göle remarked, 'I'm surprised that none of you has mentioned the focus it seems to me your work is all about: women's bodies, their self-determination over their bodies'. Our country coordinator from the Philippines rejoined that grassroots women in the Philippines would feel alien from any 'body' talk; culturally, they would speak not of the body but rather of 'the self'. Did this response reflect religious teachings stigmatizing the body and associating it with sexuality? or a continued hesitancy – including among our researchers in the field – to link reproductive and sexual rights with an *affirmative* assertion of sexuality, as opposed to a defence against sexual abuse or disease? (Petchesky forthcoming) On the other hand, our Egyptian team members rejected the body–self dichotomy from the standpoint of a cultural context in which the two terms are closely associated and the self is understood as an integral unity of body and soul.[17]

With regard to the concept of entitlement, this question of the relationship between body and self is theoretically important because of the issues it raises about whether that concept implies a sense of *owning* and therefore of one's body as somehow separate from oneself. According to some feminist theorists, to apply any notion of proprietorship (or, in the language of Lockean liberalism, a 'property in one's person') to women's relation to their bodies is to invoke an instrumentalism and radical dualism that originated in a bourgeois culture and is anathema to feminist thought. In this view, the idea of 'control over one's body', by invoking property, may countenance the commercial alienation of one's body, for example, through prostitution or so-called surrogate motherhood contracts (Akhter 1990; Pateman 1988).

Yet one can also argue that notions of self-ownership partake of a long tradition of popular resistance movements, both in Europe and in a variety of non-European cultures, on behalf of sexual autonomy as well as bodily integrity for women and oppressed or enslaved groups. This has been true historically and continues to be true today – witness the widespread affirmation of the idea of women's 'right to control over their bodies' among women's movements in the global South as well as the North – precisely because, for women particularly, our bodies have been so routinely appropriated by others for their sexual and reproductive ends and therefore are both separate from us and part of our selves at the same time. Thus, for women collectively, to speak of our right to self-determination over our bodies expresses 'a fundamental condition for women's development and strength as a social group and thus for their full participation as citizens' (Petchesky 1995b). With regard to sexuality as well as pregnancy, our research findings suggest that many women do experience their bodies as both belonging to them and alienated from them at the same time, depending on the circumstances. Yet the extent to which IRRRAG's conceptual framework and consequently our research findings were able fully to address women's sense of entitlement to sexual pleasure and satisfaction across a range of sexualities and life stages remained fairly tenuous and incomplete (see Chapter 9).

Accommodation and resistance

If sense of entitlement represents women's consciousness of their rights or authority to make decisions, the cluster of strategies we have called the 'accommodation–resistance nexus' represents how entitlement gets manifested at the level of behaviour and speech. In our early deliberations, we imagined accommodation and resistance as a dichotomy, the former reflecting passive compliance with dominant norms and the latter active opposition. Implied in this model was a moral and political judgement that saw women's concessions to traditional forms of gender subordination as always one-dimensionally self-destructive. As our fieldwork progressed, however, we found that the two extremes of outright resistance and passive accommodation are much rarer than the kinds of complicated, subtle reproductive and sexual strategies that most of our respondents adopt in order to achieve some degree of autonomy and at the same time maintain their place in the family and community. We thus began to think in terms of a continuum model in which accommodative and resistant acts are linked by a large grey area in between, reflecting the specific cultural and material circumstances in which our respondents find themselves. To interpret whether a particular behaviour constitutes resistance or possibly just a resilient way of surviving or coping with necessity, we need to look carefully at the particular context in which the behaviour takes place as well as the woman's own understanding of it. An action that is accommodative in one context may be oppositional in another (for example, running away to a neighbour's house to escape domestic violence); an action that appears resistant may be in conflict with the woman's own moral judgements about it (for example, the decision to seek an abortion despite one's conviction that it is a 'sin' or forbidden). To add to the complexity, though a woman's actions and words may appear to conflict in such cases, she herself may see no contradiction whatsoever in both acting against a particular norm and speaking in deference to it. Indeed, accommodation in practice often means a nonconfrontational or conciliatory way of achieving one's wishes or sense of right.

Seen from this nuanced perspective, the meanings of 'traditional practices' also become more complicated. Members of IRRRAG's Brazil team have suggested that certain forms of popular resistance are actually traditional even though they may not be conventionally recognized as such. Thus poor rural women of the Brazilian Northeast draw on a longstanding history of popular opposition to Catholic Church teaching on abortion when they commonly regard their first-trimester abortions as 'trading with God'. Liberation theology provides them with an alternative vision – that of a merciful, kind deity who helps women through hard times and understands their needs – to justify the women's transgression. Conversely, women in Nigeria frequently act as guardians of cultural tradition (for example, performing and enforcing FGM or widowhood rituals) in an ambiguous positioning that both enhances their power in the community (especially over younger women) and perpetuates patterns of male domination. In interpreting what are called 'harmful traditional practices', the anthropologists among us have urged that we see women's reproductive and sexual decisions 'through their own logic'. That logic may condone beliefs and practices that are deeply disturbing to our political values as feminists and remind us that our respondents' views of their own needs and entitlements may be different from how we see their situation. On the other hand, traditional practices do not always follow a simple 'oppression' model; women may deploy them strategically to reinforce their power or position within their community or to assert a specific national, cultural or religious identity.[18]

Confronted with such ambiguous cases, how then can we define resistance or identify strategies of reproductive and sexual decision-making that are clearly and consciously in opposition to dominant norms or expectations? In several, albeit infrequent, cases in IRRRAG's research, we could locate clear, overt markers of such resistance – for example, when a woman's nonconformist behaviour is publicly visible (as opposed to clandestine or secret); when she shows obvious willingness to risk likely punishment or disapproval; and, above all, when she articulates an ideology or discourse that justifies her action or belief in terms of right, justice or fairness (as opposed to having no choice). On the other hand, we were quite aware that an informant's response in an interview contending that her action was 'wrong' or 'a sin' but that she had no choice does not necessarily tell us the whole story about her beliefs in the matter. Surely there are deeper layers of moral value embedded here, however unverbalized or difficult to plumb; and most often these layers demonstrate women's willingness to defy prevailing secular or religious law (though usually in secret) in order to carry out the practical moral and social imperatives of their reproductive work.

To help navigate these difficulties, the Egyptian team developed a useful analytical tool in their articulation of four different strategic postures among their respondents: 'in the nature of things' (fatalism, nonquestioning of received norms); 'painful but necessary' (acting transgressively while conceding traditional disapproving beliefs, or the reverse – complicity in traditional practices accompanied by overt complaints or regrets); 'resistance and resistance in disguise' (subterfuges and subversions); and 'no is no!' (direct confrontation to assert an entitlement or right). The crucial element this analysis contributed was that of trade-offs or strategic accommodations. We became more attuned to such trade-offs in the discussions of preliminary findings from the field, where we learned, for example, that wives among the Philippines respondents will typically comply with their husbands' desire for sex, contrary to their own wishes, in order to derive certain other strategic benefits, such as help with domestic chores or the deflection of conflict in the home. Similarly, some women among the Egyptian respondents expressed compliance with the traditional wedding night defloration ritual (*baladi dokhla*) as a trade-off to achieve greater freedom and mobility. They would say, 'Since I have proved my chastity, I should be able to work outside the home and come and go as I please.'

Thus we began to realize that women often *choose* to go along with traditional expectations they dislike, even ones that blatantly violate their own sense of bodily integrity or wellbeing, in order to gain other advantages under existing domestic and community power relations in which their manoeuvrability is constrained. In the end, the view of accommodations and resistances as interactive and overlapping rather than dichotomous reminds us that the strategies women adopt to express or act on their sense of entitlement almost always exist in a context of domination, subordination and limited power or resources. (Indeed, the very concept of 'resistance' implies this reality; see MacLeod 1991, and Scott 1990.) Feminists reject most accommodative strategies, since they tend often to reinforce traditional gender relations in the long run (Corrêa 1994; Molyneux 1985). Yet this continuous process of negotiation, through the most limited and compromising circumstances, also reminds us that, for many women, success means an ability to get beyond the position of victim to that of survivor.

Ultimately, however, we need to ask whether and how women's strategies within the accommodation–resistance nexus begin to change existing power relations within the household and beyond it. The strategic accommodations that respondents in the IRRRAG studies most often use to negotiate their reproductive and sexual entitlements are still reactive rather than transformative. In this context, it is interesting to note that active assertion of rights or entitlement is very often linked to economic activities, which in turn are seen as part of the burdens and responsibilities of motherhood; in almost all the research sites, personal growth and leisure, as well as claims on behalf of a woman's sexual self-determination and pleasure, come last. This ordering may be attributed to the fact that in low-income households, economic survival is the woman's most urgent need. But it would also seem that in many cases resistance in the name of economic necessity or survival is more socially acceptable, since the woman is generally perceived as resisting not for herself but for her family. In other words, this behaviour conforms to notions of women's domestic role that prevail in the larger society, while more 'personal' claims are perceived as 'selfish', in violation of patriarchal tradition.[19]

When a woman argues (as many of our respondents did), 'I am the one who should decide about contraception, because I am the one who bears the burdens and responsibilities of motherhood,' she is definitely asserting a type of ethical claim on behalf of her own entitlement as reproductive decision-maker. For some of our respondents, indeed – especially in Mexico, the Philippines and Nigeria, and for the Dominican and African American groups in the US – motherhood becomes the overarching category that not only orders their economic activities but forms their identity as social citizens or adults. For many, too, motherhood is the domain where they experience the only real gratification and sense of authority they know. But this stance may also imply a belief that the harsh burdens and gender and class inequities of motherhood as it exists are somehow in the nature of things; that poverty, lack of education and the absence of social supports keep any different, more 'public' identity beyond motherhood virtually out of reach.

To the extent that the concept of 'agency' connotes self-determination, it points to a vision of a transformed set of relations and a transformed society, in which women act as full citizens and empowered decision makers both within the home and in public life. With Development Alternatives for Women in a New Era (DAWN), IRRRAG participants agree that 'when cultural practices only consolidate women's subordination and damage women's physical integrity or their freedom to make decisions about their own lives, we must question them' (Corrêa 1994:82). At the same time, IRRRAG's conceptual framework insists on the importance of the in-between: at this juncture in history and social development, women may evidence a sense of entitlement even in the absence of any concrete vision of a more just family and society or of any practical remedy for the compromises they make to their bodily integrity. It is this tenuous, ambiguous, but still promising place where the women we encountered through our research now find themselves.

Process and Methodology:
IRRRAG's Model for International Collaborative Research

In the initial conceptualization of the IRRRAG project, our idea was to develop and implement a model for research about the cross-cultural meanings of reproductive rights. This model's unique contribution would be its multi-country scope, its ethnographic and comparative methodology, and its feminist ethics and objectives. The latter implied that research, to be ethical, must be linked to positive action and lead to empowering changes in the lives of those who are both its subjects and its agents. This agenda contained within it the seeds of an unavoidable tension. Where is the line between maintaining a set of political values and action-oriented goals (the 'feminist ethics and objectives') and 'listening to women's voices' (the unbiased stance of the researcher)? What if women's voices tell us things we would rather not hear, or simply cannot hear – because they express values and priorities that are different from those we espouse? To what extent do unacknowledged motives or assumptions lie hidden within even a feminist research project aimed at improving women's lives, especially when wide gaps of education and class separate the researchers from their respondents?

This problem of the contradictions inherent in research that seeks to be 'feminist' and 'participatory' is much debated among ethnographers (for example, Abu-Lughod 1994; Behar 1993; Benmayor 1991; Patai 1991). However, it becomes compounded in a project explicitly geared to the arenas of advocacy and social change. Further, the challenge of overcoming divisions between researchers and subjects was mirrored in IRRRAG's efforts to learn and benefit from, even as we struggled with, differences among and within the country teams and between the teams and the international coordination – differences of political perspective, economic and political conditions, culture, orientation toward activism or research, access to technology, and even personal style. What would it take to make research truly participatory and to make international collaboration truly democratic?

From the start, the project was burdened by a major structural issue: the differential positioning of our seven countries, and especially the international coordination located in New York, with regard to the power dynamics of global capital, donor countries and donor agencies.[20] Locating IRRRAG's international coordination in the US potentially recreated a global pattern in which financial and organizational decisions, links with donors, and other aspects of power would once again be concentrated in the North. In large and small ways – from how and where we got our funding, to our ability to access information, to where and what we ate in restaurants – we were constantly reminded that, even with the best of will, international feminist collaborations must contend with the hierarchical power structures that now exist, in a world in which we are differently situated. Our different degrees of access to resources and privilege within those structures may affect our relative stakes in transforming them as well as our ability to trust one another. Thus, collectively developing a process that would nourish trust was critical to IRRRAG's ability to work together.

Several criteria were applied in selecting countries where the research would be carried out. First, while recognizing the impossibility of representing all the world's regions and cultural groups, we aimed to include a diversity of regions, ethnic and religious traditions, and political and social systems. Second, we sought countries where there existed women's movements or organizations with tested experience in researching and advocating about reproductive rights as well as enthusiasm about furthering such work. Third, we expected that some social-science-based research on issues related to reproductive health would already have been conducted in the country, so the teams would not be starting from zero and would be able to find informed local consultants. Finally, we hoped to find countries with a well-established coordinating organization, capable of handling international and intra-country communications with relative efficiency. Including the US was not expected to yield a true North–South comparison; rather, focusing on communities of colour in the US would be useful, as the US team later continued to remind us, in order to illuminate the often neglected 'South within the North'.

While the specific composition of the country teams was left largely up to the local coordinator or core group, guidelines were provided to ensure that every country team encompassed the following areas of knowledge: social-science-based research skills previously applied to reproductive health/rights issues; strong links with women's advocacy and community-based organizations; and experience in direct service provision in health or reproductive health care. In reality, neither the criteria for selecting countries nor those for selecting team members were followed with complete consistency. Yet the very absence of consistency – the disparities among political contexts and research team composition across the seven countries – has proved one of the most interesting variables shaping the process and the outcomes of IRRRAG's research. Certainly the seven IRRRAG countries and the research–action teams assembled in each of them by no means begin to approximate the tremendous range of differences among the world's women or among women within each country. Yet the diversity of conditions and backgrounds they represent is none the less significant, a fact that enhances the richness of the country studies contained in this volume while it complicates any intra-country or cross-country comparisons we might draw from them (see Chapter 9).

At our first international meeting, held in Kuala Lumpur in November 1992, IRRRAG participants agreed on several procedures aimed at maximizing the collaborative, consultative aspects of our process and maintaining a democratic method of decision-making. These included collective policy-making, so that the international meetings in effect became IRRRAG's governing body; rotating chairs and meeting sites, to share leadership and responsibility; and careful reporting and record keeping, to ensure that all important decisions were truly consensual and all viewpoints were represented. In this way, we built up a common body of internal policy and procedures as well as documenting the evolution of our thinking over time.

A tension inherent in the project from its origins was that between international consensus and local autonomy. While such a tension has obvious implications with regard to the kinds of power differences discussed above, it also raised complicated issues for how we defined our research methodologies and our conceptual framework. Where should the line be drawn between the need for cross-country comparability and the need to respect local priorities and specificities? At our first international meeting we adopted common ground rules for the research methods to be used in the field and the selection of research sites and subjects. In keeping with the primarily subjective focus of our inquiry on grassroots women's own understandings of their reproductive and sexual entitlements, we agreed that a qualitative, ethnographic approach was the most suitable for our purposes. Such an approach, involving in-depth interviews with relatively small numbers of people in carefully selected sites, could best illuminate the local meanings of reproductive decision making, reveal women's own ways of seeing those meanings, and enable us to use the research process itself to empower the women participating in the study.

This did not mean that qualitative methods would be used to the exclusion of quantitative methods or a variety of secondary and statistical sources, but rather that the latter would be used to validate and reinforce our qualitative findings. Country teams would be free to choose among a number of qualitative interviewing techniques (group interviews, in-depth individual interviews, role playing, etcetera); but all would contextualize the interviews with background research relevant to the economic, social, cultural, legal and health status of women in their countries and make this context integral to their interpretation of the local findings. While country teams would develop their own instruments and analyses appropriate to the local contexts, these would be guided by our common framework questions. Together, the framework questions, common themes (sexuality, marriage, fertility control, childbearing), and overlapping methodologies would provide a reasonable basis for comparability among the studies.

In addition to the methodological parameters, we agreed on guidelines for selecting research sites and subjects. These included the provision that our research would focus primarily on low-income women to carry out our purpose of giving voice to women who are not ordinarily heard in international debates about reproductive health and rights.[21] In addition, we agreed that each country study would include at least one urban and one rural site, and would encompass a diversity of subjects by ethnicity, race (where relevant), religion, age, and marital status. Although there was no realistic way such a small-scale study could be representative of the women of any country or of any class or group within the country, we felt it was necessary to gather data that might reflect significant social differences even within our small sample.[22] Initially we also decided to exclude men from the study, at least at the present stage, because of concerns that women's responses might be muted by knowing that men in the community or family were also being interviewed. Finally, to compensate for our researchers' inability to reside in the research communities for an extended period, we decided to seek groups of respondents based on their affiliation with community, labour or health organizations with whom we had some connection and who could provide us with a basis of entry and trust within the site or group.

In practice, many of these decisions were revised along the way, or modified by different country teams as their particular circumstances seemed to require (see Table 1.1). With regard to research methods, most country teams used a combination of three approaches: unstructured group interviews (sometimes loosely referred to as 'focus group discussions'[23]); in-depth individual interviews of a smaller number of respondents chosen from among the group participants and based on more structured questionnaires; and background research (including secondary national surveys as well as primary community profiles). In addition, several countries supplemented these methods by recording individual life histories (more open and unstructured than the individual interviews); interviewing key informants in the community (such as health providers and community, union or religious leaders, who often included men); conducting more large-scale surveys using questionnaires; or using psychodrama or role-playing techniques.[24]

Concerning the focus of the research, an initial decision to concentrate on just two aspects of reproductive health – contraception and childbearing – turned out to be inconsistent with both the broader goals of the project and the kinds of qualitative, open-ended methodologies we had chosen. The aim of contextualizing women's reproductive decisions and seeing them in all their situational complexity led all the teams to investigate a much wider range of issues. Moreover, in both group discussions and individual interviews, the respondents themselves did not conveniently stick to such discrete topics as contraception but rather disclosed a matrix of interrelated issues and themes that interwove fertility, sexuality, economics, gender and kin relations, work and child care. In other words, the very process of our research as much as the findings affirmed that fertility control cannot be isolated from other aspects of women's lives.

The greatest variations in the teams' research designs had to do with the composition of their respective respondent groups. Both the Egypt and Brazil teams decided to include a certain number of men among their group interview respondents in order to compare their views with those of the women. In contrast, the Philippines team chose to illuminate the dimension of generational differences and commonalities in a particularly intimate way through a research strategy of conducting in-depth interviews among selected pairs of mothers and daughters. Finally, the country teams differed in their approach to our original decision to seek research subjects through their involvement in some type of community or workplace organization. Thus teams in Malaysia, Egypt and the Philippines selected respondents based on their neighbourhood or residence, reflecting the reality that most women in those societies are not organized in formal ways but derive their identities primarily from kin groups and religious or residential communities. By contrast, teams in Mexico, Brazil, and the US – where women's participation in popular organizations is a key part of civil society and social change – not only selected their respondents based on their organizational affiliation but looked at organizational membership and community activism as a major factor in analysing the data.[25] Thus methodological strategies were necessarily adapted to reflect particular conditions in the local political landscape.

Diverse political cultures among the national women's movements represented in IRRRAG, as well as variations in the balance within each team between activists and academics, no doubt affected each team's location on the continuum between 'objective' and 'participatory' research. While everyone accepted in principle the responsibility to 'give back' something to the research communities and contribute to women's empowerment, not all the country teams have had the necessary organizational resources or base to take on this responsibility to the same degree or in the same ways. Beyond the practical problems of moving from research to action, however, more basic questions of research ethics and values remain. In attempting to transmit 'women's voices', particularly in languages that are not their own, how can we avoid the risks of distortion and misinterpretation that come from multiple layers of translating, editing, rewriting, and decontextualizing? And how should we balance the two different goals of reproducing 'women's voices' (however imperfectly) and transforming their conditions?

Although we never resolved these questions, they stimulated many fruitful dialogues throughout the nearly five years of work leading to this volume. The Egyptian team (sobered by battles over and the prevailing acceptance of FGM in their country) emphasized the challenge to researchers' own preconceptions and values posed by women informants who do not share their view that certain practices violate women's rights. Are researchers able to see respondents' situations through respondents' eyes rather than their own? Members of the Brazil team argued that this tension in our work between reproducing women's realities and changing them is inevitable, that our purpose is to analyse women's own logic in order to interpret it and intervene in appropriate ways, and that just because our informants judge a practice or tradition to be good or natural, does not mean we must judge it so. Others pointed out that, while we must try to remain nonjudgemental, the data we gather are always necessarily mediated by our analysis and interpretation, as we select certain issues and responses and put those responses within a larger social context. As engaged researchers, we cannot avoid the double responsibility of *both* trying to understand our informants' situation through their eyes *and* working to realize our own vision of women's empowerment and full human rights.

In reality, however, IRRRAG's experience has shown that the dilemma is more easily solved in theory than in practice and is further complicated by our commitment to a conceptual framework grounded in the ethics of entitlement or rights. The temptation to trade the researcher's hat for that of the community organizer or educator was very great at certain moments: for example, when some women respondents matter-of-factly defended FGM as socially beneficial for themselves and their daughters, denying its health and sexual harm to women; or contended that sex on demand was a husband's prerogative. Yet a climate of instability and uncertainty about the

Table 1.1 Profile of IRRRAG Respondents

RESPONDENTS	BRAZIL[a]	EGYPT[b]	MALAYSIA	MEXICO[a]	NIGERIA[a]	PHILIPPINES[a]	US
Number (total)	182[c]	130	71	141	354	334[c]	130
individual	45	12	71	29	72	28	32
group	104	130	0	141	354	39	101
Include men	Yes	Yes	No	No	No	No	No
Urban	59%	79%	38%	44%	35%	36%	73%
Rural	41%	21%	62%	56%	65%	64%	27%
Married or cohabiting	58%	63%	68%	61%	53%[d]	93%	42%
Never married	31%	35%	24%	25%	28%	0	40%[e]
Divorced, widowed, or separated	11%	2%	8%	14%	19%	7%	13%
Employed	84%	61%	68%	64%	65%	71%	84%
Unemployed[f]	16%	39%	32%	36%	35%	29%	16%
Age							
Under 21	13%	36%	19%	0	25%	3%	11%
21–44	46%	61%	62%	86%	49%	39%	65%
45+	41%	3%	19%	14%	26%	57%	24%

a. Percentages include only individual interview respondents.
b. Percentages include women respondents only.
c. Includes some respondents to the questionnaire only (not interviewed).
d. Of these 33% polygamous.
e. Includes welfare (public assistance) clients with undeclared partners.
f. Includes students and retirees as well as housewives.

26

future, involving personal pressures and dislocations sometimes as severe for (middle-class) researchers as for (working-class and poor) respondents, has if anything intensified since 1992, when our research began. Without minimizing the class and educational differences often separating our researchers from the women they met in the field, we have become aware, through changes experienced in our own lives during the years of this study, that the economic and political crises wrought by neoliberal capitalism in many ways bring us closer to our respondents rather than further apart. Travelling to other women's worlds has enabled us not only to discover their subjectivity and vision but also to re-animate our own.

Negotiating Reproductive Rights presents seven country studies that illuminate women's strategies for achieving reproductive and sexual dignity, if not authority, in very distinct and diverse contexts of culture, nation, region, religion, and life cycle. Yet, as the twentieth century closes, many of the life experiences presented in the following chapters and the social conditions limiting them speak to women across these differences and across the globe.[26]

Notes

1 Clearly there are many definitions of the term 'feminist' and many varieties of feminist practice. For purposes of consistency and clarity in this book, we in the IRRRAG project have agreed on the following definition of feminism: *A concern in theory and practice with the conditions of women, and a commitment to transform gender oppression along with and in relation to the systems of domination that divide women by class, race, ethnicity, region, nationality, religion, sexual orientation and age. This definition implies a questioning of all hierarchies and power relations, including those within the research process itself, and a general commitment to achieving social justice throughout the world. It also implies recognition that women's movements, geared toward 'the political action of women' on many issues, may not always be self-defined as feminist in this sense, and that the accepted meanings of feminism in our different national and cultural contexts may vary.* For a broad overview of these variations, see Basu (1995), especially Introduction and chapters on Brazil, Nigeria and the Philippines.

2 In this text we often refer to 'grassroots women' to indicate IRRRAG's research focus on non-elite, usually low-income women – both urban and rural, of diverse age and ethnic groups and marital and occupational situations, some involved in local community groups and others whose reference points are mainly their families.

3 Numerous feminist critiques of neo-Malthusian population theories and policies have been published in the 1990s. See, for example, Bandarage 1997; Batliwala 1994; Corrêa 1994; Dixon-Mueller 1993; Greenhalgh 1996; Hartmann 1995; Pitanguy and Petchesky 1993; and Sen, Germain and Chen 1994.

4 In the US, the Committee for Abortion Rights and Against Sterilization Abuse (CARASA) was formed in 1977 and the Reproductive Rights National Network (R2N2) in 1978. In Europe, the International Campaign for Abortion Rights, which became the International Campaign on Abortion, Sterilization and Contraception (ICASC) was also founded in 1978. In 1984 (just prior to the World Population Conference in Mexico City), at the prodding of groups of activists from the global South, it became the Women's Global Network for Reproductive Rights

(WGNRR), with a broader mandate to address all women's reproductive health issues, not only those involving fertility control. (See Petchesky and Weiner 1990; Corrêa 1994; and Garcia-Moreno and Claro 1994.)

During the 1980s and early 1990s, national and regional networks and campaigns formed around a wide range of reproductive and sexual rights issues in Latin America and the Caribbean, South and Southeast Asia and the Pacific, and many countries in Africa and the Middle East. Among the international organizations formed during this period and embracing reproductive and sexual rights as part of their agenda were Isis International, DAWN (Development Alternatives for Women in a New Era), the Latin American and Caribbean Women's Health Network, the East and Southeast Asia–Pacific Regional Women and Health Network, Women in Law and Development and the Society for Women and AIDS in Africa, and Women Living Under Muslim Laws Network.

5 Female genital mutilation (FGM), involving the removal of parts or all of the external female genitalia, can result in long-lasting physical and psychological trauma, pain during intercourse, and severe complications during childbearing (see Toubia 1995 for a comprehensive overview).

6 Both the ICPD Programme of Action (Para. 7.2) and the Beijing Declaration and Platform for Action (Para. 95) define 'reproductive rights' as '[resting] on the recognition of the basic right of all couples and individuals to decide freely and responsibly the number, spacing and timing of their children and to have the information and means to do so, and the right to attain the highest standard of sexual and reproductive health. It also includes their right to make decisions concerning reproduction free of discrimination, coercion and violence, as expressed in human rights documents.' For fuller discussion of women's organized efforts to impact on the conferences, see Boland 1997; Center for Women's Global Leadership 1995; Copelon and Petchesky 1995; DAWN 1995; Germain and Kyte 1995; Hartmann 1994; Hodgson and Watkins 1997; Petchesky 1997 and forthcoming; and Rashidah/ARROW 1995.

7 United Nations, Fourth World Conference on Women, Beijing, September 1995. *Declaration and Platform for Action*, Para. 96, United Nations, New York.

8 For other examples of feminist analyses linking reproductive health and rights issues to questions of development and the global economy, see Bandarage 1997; Committee on Women, Population and the Environment 1994–97; DAWN 1995; Kabeer 1994; Petchesky 1995a; Sen 1997; and US Women of Color Delegation 1994).

9 The direct translation of 'reproductive rights' into Arabic is *al-hoqouq al-ingabiah*, which literally means 'the right to give birth'.

10 See Corrêa 1994; Dixon-Mueller 1993; Ginsburg and Rapp 1995; Greenhalgh 1995; Hartmann 1995; Sen, Germain and Chen 1994; Sen and Snow 1994; *Reproductive Health Matters* 1993–97; and *WGNRR Newsletter* 1987-97. When IRRRAG began, we were unaware of any similar international collaborative research efforts. Subsequently we have been pleased to see a number of projects emerge that, while organized under very different institutional arrangements, have similar research – and in some cases action – goals. For example, the GRHPP (Gender, Reproductive Health and Population Policy Project, formerly known as INDRA-HAIN), based in Amsterdam and Manila and encompassing eleven countries in several global regions, has been using qualitative methods to investigate user perspectives on different types of reproductive health and family planning services. The International Center for Research on Women has commissioned studies in many countries to look ethnographically at how women negotiate sexuality in relation to HIV/AIDS. The

Women's Studies Project of Family Health International has developed qualitative research programmes in eight countries to look at women's needs and perspectives regarding family planning programmes and methods. And several existing international networks – Women Living Under Muslim Laws, Women and Law in Southern Africa, ARROW, and RAINBO (Research, Action and Information Network on Bodily Integrity, focused primarily on female genital mutilation) – have added a substantial research component to their international advocacy work. In addition, the journal *Reproductive Health Matters* publishes a compendium of similar research and analysis, usually based in single countries, in two volumes a year.

11   This view has been the subject of a vast sociological and feminist literature. Among others, see Afshar 1991; Agarwal 1988; Collins 1990; Dixon-Mueller 1993; Eisenstein 1978; Engels 1972; Ginsburg and Rapp 1995; Kelly 1984; Kuhn and Wolpe 1978; Mies 1986; Mies, Bennholdt-Thomsen and Von Werlhof 1988; Ruddick 1989; and Yuval-Davis and Anthias 1989. This literature, much of it growing out of a Marxist-feminist perspective, critically analyses the ways in which husbands, kin groups, communities, and states appropriate women's capacities as childbearers and household sustainers for their own economic and political purposes. It also urges recognition of women's bio-social reproductive labour as valuable, necessary to community survival, and laden with its own set of knowledges and skills.

12   For fuller discussions of this interconnective approach to human rights, see Boland, Rao, and Zeidenstein 1994; Cook 1994 and 1995; Copelon 1995; Copelon and Petchesky 1995; Corrêa and Petchesky 1994; Freedman 1995; Freedman and Isaacs 1994; S. Fried 1994; and Schuler 1995.

13   In the US in the 1930s Depression, struggles around unemployment, poverty, labour rights, housing and other issues resulted in legislative enactments that came to be known as 'entitlements' – most notably, the Social Security Act and Aid to Dependent Children (later, Aid to Families with Dependent Children), popularly known as 'welfare'. In the 1960s, the Medicaid and Medicare programmes were enacted, creating health entitlements for the poor and the elderly respectively. In the 1980s and 1990s, these and many other 'entitlement' programmes to assist the poor, disabled, and immigrant populations came under a barrage of attack from right-wing conservatives promoting a return to *laissez-faire* 'free market' values. In the wake of global privatization, similar movements have occurred in many European countries and Canada, with various degrees of success.

14   Beth Richie of Hunter College in New York, one of our research consultants, provided this useful categorization.

15   These excerpts come from the 1995 draft of the Philippines team's country report.

16   This took place at the Rockefeller Conference Center in Bellagio, Italy, where we held a nine-day work meeting.

17   Members of the IRRRAG Egyptian team pointed out that the Arabic word used in Egypt for 'self', in relation to physical and sexual matters, is the same as that for 'soul' (*nafsek*). This word is sometimes used to evoke chastity – for example, when a mother tells her daughter to 'take care of herself', meaning to keep her body sexually pure.

18   Cf. Trinh (1990): '… when women decide to lift the veil one can say that they do so in defiance of their men's oppressive right to their bodies. But when they decide to keep or put on the veil they once took off they might do so to reappropriate their space or to claim a new difference in defiance of genderless, hegemonic, centered standardization.' Feminist anthropologists have made the same point; see Ginsburg and Rapp 1995, Göle 1996, Pearce 1995, and Sanday 1981.

19   The ideas in this paragraph are derived largely from an earlier draft of the Philippines chapter, 'Negotiated Entitlement in Reproductive Decision-Making: Toward a

Definition of Reproductive Rights among Grassroots Women in the Philippines', by Mercedes Lactao-Fabros and Maria Teresa Guia-Padilla (July 1995).

20 Local economies, politics and daily life in Nigeria, Mexico, Egypt and the Philippines have been driven by the pressures of the international financial institutions (IFIs) as well as the transnational corporations that dominate world markets, both of which are based largely in the US and Europe. Only Malaysia among IRRRAG's Southern countries, like other economically prospering countries in Asia, remained relatively free, until the economic problems of 1997, of these external pressures behind which the contemporary neo-liberal economy often masks forms of neo-imperialism. (See Cavanagh, Wysham and Arruda 1994; and Sparr 1994.)

21 IRRRAG members attempted to realize this purpose in part through panel presentations of our findings at the NGO Forums in Cairo (1994) and Beijing (1995) and the Eighth International Women and Health Meeting in Rio de Janeiro in March 1997.

22 We did not require a common or minimum number of respondents for each country study, although given the qualitative, in-depth methods chosen we anticipated the total number would be small. In practice, including both individual and group interviews and surveys, the average per country was 197; including only individual in-depth or life-story interviews, the average was 41 per country. In total, 1,376 persons, from 32 distinct communities, were involved as research subjects through all the methods combined.

23 These were not technically 'focus groups' insofar as the latter are conventionally made up of individuals selected randomly from different 'walks of life'; whereas our groups were deliberately composed of friends, neighbours, co-workers, etc., based on common residency or membership in a union or community group, and were sometimes defined by common age cohort, marital status or gender as well.

24 There were significant variations in how country teams approached these method-ologies. For example, one team (Mexico) used group discussions more as a way of gauging the local cultural context and identifying individual respondents than as sources of primary data; another (Egypt) relied on group interviews as its primary source of data, only supplementing them with a small number of individual interviews (12); while one (Malaysia) dispensed with group interviews altogether, concentrating exclusively on individual interviews. The Philippines mainly concentrated on individual interviews with 19 mother–daughter pairs, but supplemented these with both focus groups and a much larger survey (354 respondents) done through a questionnaire.

25 The Nigerian team also selected respondents based on their membership in grassroots organizations, but these tended to be more traditional groups, such as associations of market women or church groups; this selection was less an analytical strategy than an activist one of developing a community base to facilitate future interventions.

26 The more detailed story of IRRRAG's history, organizational process and methods, as well as lessons we want to share with other researcher-activists, may be found in a separate publication, *Both Catalysts and Messengers: Lessons from a Cross-Cultural Project on Women's Reproductive and Sexual Rights* (1998), available from IRRRAG's international office. The seven chapters that follow are all condensed versions of longer, more detailed country study reports. Names used for respondents in the following chapters are all pseudonyms, used to protect their confidentiality.

2 Not Like Our Mothers
Reproductive Choice and the Emergence of Citizenship Among Brazilian Rural Workers, Domestic Workers and Housewives

SIMONE GRILO DINIZ, CECÍLIA DE MELLO E SOUZA,
AND ANA PAULA PORTELLA*
(TRANSLATED BY JONES DE FREITAS AND CECÍLIA DE MELLO E SOUZA)

For Brazilian women, reproductive activity is woven into the larger fabric of gender subordination in the workplace and the household, domestic violence, representations and practices regarding marriage and sexuality, and a continually deteriorating healthcare system. The new Brazilian constitution, adopted in 1988, established health as a universal right and a state responsibility, but in practice the full implementation of this right and of health reform has been impeded by financial instability and mismanagement. Meanwhile, Brazil's fertility rate has declined almost 50 per cent since 1970, from 5.6 to 2.5, despite the government's *laissez-faire* policy regarding family planning (BEMFAM/DHS 1997); yet this 'demographic miracle' has not been accompanied by the anticipated 'economic miracle' for a significant percentage of Brazilians who remain trapped in poverty. Poor women in both urban and rural areas – particularly black and mestizo women – have the worst-paid and least-valued jobs, without childcare centres or other public facilities and with almost no male help with domestic chores.

In this context, it is not surprising that the women in our study, who belong to the rural and urban poor, do not easily separate the different spheres of work, reproduction and sexuality. For them, the body is a working instrument with which to labour in the fields, clean someone's house, raise children or have sexual relations. None the less, some of these women have begun to question and transform the unjust burdens that reproductive work imposes on them as women. This is the case of women involved in social and labour movements that, while not identifying themselves as feminist, fight for women's rights and the improvement of their daily lives.

* In addition to the three principal authors, this chapter could not have been produced without the dedicated work of the other IRRRAG team members in Brazil: Margareth Arilha, Cassia Carloto, and Maria Dirce Gomes Pinho in São Paulo; Maria Betania D'Avila in Pernambuco; and Helena Bocayuva and Carmen Guimarães in Rio de Janeiro. Many thanks also to our researchers: Silvia Marques Dantas, Josineide de Oliveira and Vanete Almeida in Pernambuco, and Maria Lucia da Silveira in São Paula.

IRRRAG's Brazil team carried out our study among three groups representing Brazilian women's most frequent activities: rural workers in the Northeast, domestic servants in Rio de Janeiro, and low-income housewives active in the popular health movement in São Paulo's outskirts. Despite geographic separation and differences in their working and living conditions, important commonalities link the three groups. Many of the Rio domestic workers and the São Paulo housewives and their families are themselves migrants from the Northeast, so that many of the women in all three groups share a common cultural and economic background. Similarities also appear in their strategies to acquire decision-making power over reproduction and sexuality and their desires to transform their own pain and hardships into a better life for themselves and their children. Above all, a good number of our respondents have consciously sought a life beyond reproduction, through paid work outside the home and political participation in the trade union and popular movements. Such involvement has been an important step towards developing awareness of their own value, capacities, and social, reproductive and sexual rights.

The Brazilian Socioeconomic and Political Context

Occupying half the area of Latin America and ranking ninth among capitalist economies in gross domestic product (GDP), Brazil has one of the most unequal distributions of income and resources in the world. The Southeast, the country's richest and most developed region, where almost half the population is concentrated, is largely industrialized and urbanized, accounting for 80 per cent of industrial output and more than 75 per cent of farm goods production. In this region, we carried out our study among women from Brazil's two largest cities, Rio de Janeiro and São Paulo. The Northeast, which includes our third research site in the *sertão* (semi-arid hinterland covering most of the Northeast) in the state of Pernambuco, remains a mostly rural region where large landed estates and informal wage labour still prevail (Soares *et al.* 1996). By all social indicators, this region lags far behind the Southeast, with illiteracy rates three times as high, infant mortality rates nearly three times as high, higher fertility, lower life expectancy, and a median wage of less than half that in the more prosperous Southeast (FIBGE 1996; FLACSO/CEPIA 1993).

Intersecting these economic and regional disparities are those of ethnicity and race. Brazil is a multiracial society whose population is 45 per cent mestizo and black (FIBGE 1996). Moreover, over 70 per cent of Brazil's black and mestizo population live in the Northeast, where working and living conditions are far more precarious and marginal than in other regions. Black and mestizo women have the lowest education and income levels among all women and are most likely to be employed in the low-paid informal sector or as domestic workers. Thus structural racism compounds the gender and class oppression experienced by the women of this region and those who have migrated to escape its hardships. Rural employment in Pernambuco (like the rest of the Northeast) remains largely unregulated, at below minimum wages, and in violation of national maximum hour and safety requirements. A whole set of rights that have been granted to male and female workers in other sectors in Brazil, including maternity leave, on-site child care, and breastfeeding at work for women, still lies outside the grasp of agricultural workers.

In the *sertão*, land conflicts are only the most visible aspect of an extraordinarily violent social context that includes political persecution, noncompliance with labour laws, slave and child labour, inhumane working conditions, and domestic violence as daily aspects of rural life. In addition, periodic droughts force whole populations to relocate in search of work and food. Since rural women are skilled only in agricultural work and domestic labour, when they migrate to the city fleeing drought or poverty they are typically employed as domestic servants, performing household chores in exchange for wages, food, and often housing as well.

In the Southeast, Rio de Janeiro, the second largest city and the national capital until 1960, remains a national economic and cultural centre as well as an internationally known tourist mecca. Both Rio and São Paulo are comparable to major urban centres in developed countries in their tech-nological and cultural resources, despite the huge pockets of poverty in their surrounding *favelas* (slums, or shantytowns). Both experienced an increased flow of migrants in search of jobs and better living conditions from the 1960s on. Rural women workers from the Northeast have migrated in significant numbers to the Southeast, where they work as domestics or their spouses work in industry. (See Minayo 1995.)

From 1964 until 1985, Brazil experienced a military dictatorship whose most repressive period (1968–74) coincided with intense industrialization and economic growth. But the so-called 'economic miracle' was achieved at the cost of a huge foreign debt, political and economic exclusion of the masses of Brazilian people, and a widening income gap between rich and poor. In the 1980s, recession, inflation, high unemployment, a decline in social investment and a deterioration of public services exacerbated the gap and the domestic burdens borne by poor women. At the same time, industrialization and urbanization in the 1960s and 1970s triggered profound changes in the structure of the labour market, in family relations, and in the position of women. As a result, today over 39 per cent of all women, and 50 per cent of women aged 20–49, participate in the labour force (as compared with 75 per cent of all men) (FIBGE 1996; Bruschini 1994). In addition, a huge contingent of women work in the informal labour market and are not officially counted among the 'economically active'.

The reasons for this massive increase of women workers are primarily economic, and include declining salaries for male workers, rising consumer expectations, and expanding job markets. Still, women's earnings have not increased relative to men's (even though as a group they receive more years of formal schooling), mainly in consequence of the persistence of gender segregation in Brazil's labour market (FLACSO/CEPIA 1993). Most women still work in the least prestigious, lowest-paying jobs, the largest urban contingent in domestic service. The domestic workers we interviewed were typically migrants, mostly black and mestizo, earning between US$112 and $224 per month. Most of them have not completed elementary school, and their literacy rate is very low. Female domestic servants in Brazil are estimated to number 10 million, of whom 350,000 are located in the state of Rio de Janeiro.

Although military rule persisted, the early 1980s were a transition period known as the *abertura* (opening), when political parties were reorganized and many social movements emerged. Elections were held for state and federal legislative and executive positions, culminating in the presidential election of 1989. The new constitution that went into effect in 1988 is considered one of the most progressive in the world; it not only guarantees gender equality in civic affairs, work, and family relations but also makes the 'practice of racism' a federal crime punishable by imprisonment.[1] Moreover, the Brazilian government has signed several conventions, treaties and agreements since 1948 concerning women and their rights, including the Universal Declaration of Human Rights, the Cairo (ICPD) Programme of Action and the Beijing (FWCW) Platform for Action.[2] Tremendous gaps still exist, however, between the democratic principles of the Federal Constitution and their enforcement and implementation, especially in regard to nondiscrimination by social class, gender, race, ethnicity and sexual orientation. Most of the women in our study – who are predominantly women of colour, domestic workers, rural workers, and informal sector workers – fall within these gaps, where equality exists on paper only. In 1972, domestic workers became entitled to a formal contract and to some benefits, such as one day off a week, paid vacations, access to social security and maternity leave; with the 1988 constitution, rural workers won some social security benefits, such as a retirement pension. Yet both categories of worker are still denied maximum-hour protection and job security, and only in 1995 did women rural workers win the right to maternity leave (CFEMEA 1994).

Outside the workplace, all working women in Brazil suffer from the failure of men to share in domestic tasks, despite women's participation in the labour force; thus, in addition to their paid work, women are left with the major burdens of housework and child care. Nor have social policies been put into place to provide education and day care centres for children up to six years old, even though such benefits are prescribed in the 1988 constitution. Between 1982 and 1990, the proportion of female-headed households in Brazil – which have lower incomes than those headed by men

– increased from 16.6 to 20.3 per cent.[3] Moreover, the lack of adequate child care or other supports for reproductive work, plus the illegal but common practice of requiring a pregnancy test or tubal ligation as a condition of hiring, help to explain why fertility has declined despite limited social policies to support motherhood[4] (CFEMEA 1993).

Like employment, health care under Brazil's Federal Constitution receives formal protections that go well beyond those of many countries, defining health as a universal right entailing the state's duty to guarantee universal access. The public health care system, open to all, is composed of public health centres, emergency centres, hospitals and private health centres associated with the Ministry of Health. The constitution also considers family planning to be a universal right based on the free decision of couples. In 1983 the Ministry of Health, prompted by feminist women's health advocates and academics, created the PAISM, or Programme of Integrated Assistance to Women's Health. This programme recognizes the need for action and services directed especially toward women to assist them from childhood to old age, with special emphasis on the reproductive years. The PAISM, conceived of as an alternative to traditional maternal and child health programmes, mandates that the state should provide preventive and educational services to meet a wide range of needs, including prenatal care, delivery and post-partum care, infertility treatment, contraception, prevention and treatment of breast and cervical cancer and STDs, and treatment of disorders related to menopause (Pitanguy 1994; CFEMEA 1994).

In practice, however, the implementation of these services has suffered from the serious resource allocation problems that affect many areas of social expenditure in Brazil. Privatization and the deterioration of public services in the health sector generally have combined with cultural and religious pressures in Brazilian society to constrain the practical realization of women's reproductive rights. Despite constitutional guarantees, despite the PAISM, and despite a public policy endorsing universal access to family planning, the government has long been reluctant to translate these rights into action. Although state authorities in the 1960s and 1970s encouraged private family planning services,[5] it was only in 1983 that the government officially launched PAISM, and it never gave its comprehensive reproductive health programme the necessary resources. In addition, abortion remains illegal in Brazil except in cases of rape and when a woman's life is at risk; thus most abortions can only be obtained illegally through the private sector. Even women who are eligible for legal abortions are usually denied public hospital services by physicians and the courts, who delay the process until it is too late.[6]

Thus, despite the broad vision of PAISM, the range of reproductive health methods and services to which Brazilian women have access remains in practice quite limited. Even the rising demand for and use of birth control in the 1980 and 1990s have not been accompanied by equal and free access to the full range of safe, effective contraceptive methods. The most recent national data on contraceptive use reveal that nearly 77 per cent of women aged 15–49, whether married or cohabiting, and 55 per cent of all women, were using contraception. However, contraceptive use patterns are dominated by female sterilization, which by 1996 had become the method adopted among 40 per cent of women countrywide living with a partner, followed by hormonal methods (mainly the pill) among 22 per cent. Female sterilization rates also vary by region: 44 per cent of women living with a partner in the Northeast, 46.3 per cent of those in Rio, and 33.6 per cent of those in São Paulo have been sterilized (BEMFAM/DHS 1997). Sterilization, despite being the most widely used contraceptive method in Brazil, had an ambiguous legal status before 1997. Until then, it was not officially provided by public health services, yet doctors and women found strategies for performing sterilizations routinely, the most common being to combine tubal ligation with a Caesarean section. Indeed, 60 per cent of all tubal ligations were performed in this way.[7]

Maternal mortality is still very high throughout Brazil, but especially in the Northeast, notwithstanding the recent fertility decline. According to the revised estimates of the World Health Organization (WHO) and the United Nations Children's Fund (UNICEF), the national ratio per 100,000 live births was 220 maternal deaths. Poor women continue to die from pregnancy-related causes for reasons that are avoidable and treatable; unsafe illegal abortions, hypertension, curable illnesses, haemorrhage, and post-partum infections are responsible for over 90 per cent of these deaths. This fact points to the failure of the public health services, especially in prenatal and obstetric care, despite their expansion in the 1980s. Unsafe abortion is thought to account for 12 per cent of Brazil's maternal deaths. Given that abortion is an illegal practice and given the difficulty of collecting reliable information, data on its prevalence in Brazil must be interpreted carefully. However, data derived from hospital records indicate that abortion rates in the country as a whole rose steadily throughout the 1980s and early 1990s, particularly in the Northeast and Rio de Janeiro, where they accounted for over one-third of all pregnancies (Singh and Sedgh 1997).[8] The Ministry of Health estimates that 800,000–1,200,000 abortions occur every year in Brazil by a variety of methods, ranging from the safer ones performed in private clinics to those performed through traditional and home remedies.

Abortion is clearly a widespread procedure among women of all social classes, despite the difficulty in obtaining proper care for resulting complications. The main reason for its high incidence is the poor quality of reproductive health services and the lack of access through public facilities, especially for poor women, to safe, nonpermanent contraceptive methods (Singh and Sedgh 1997). In the late 1980s women began using the abortifacient misoprostol, available over the counter in the form of the drug

Cytotec (prescribed for ulcers). Cytotec has offered Brazilian women a relatively easy and private way to obtain abortions in an overall context of illegality and religious condemnation (Arilha and Barbosa 1995, see note 28).

Along with a high rate of STDs generally, Brazil accounts for an estimated 50 per cent of all persons known to be HIV-positive in Latin America, and São Paulo accounts for 57 per cent of all registered AIDS cases in Brazil. As elsewhere in the world, women are becoming infected far more frequently and sick more rapidly; the ratio of female to male AIDS cases has shrunk in the last decade from 1:40 to 1:3 (Brazil Ministry of Health 1996). Married women, especially from low-income groups, are at present the most exposed to HIV and other STD infections, in a cultural context of gender inequality that creates obstacles to education and prevention, including negotiating safer sex. While women are held to a standard of heterosexual monogamy, many married men still have multiple sexual partners and often homoerotic relationships that alter neither their sexual identity nor their position as head of the household (Barbosa and Villela 1996; Guimarães 1996).

These socioeconomic conditions, particularly the deficiencies of health and reproductive health services in Brazil, have helped to galvanize an unusually dynamic and widespread women's movement, much of whose focus has been on issues of reproductive and sexual rights.

The Women's Movement and the Development of Reproductive Rights

Since the decline of the dictatorship in the late 1970s, women's movements in Brazil have been allied with other popular movements to end human misery and injustice and to advance democratization and *cidadania* (citizenship rights). Among diverse women's groups – some connected to the Church (for example, the parish-based mothers' clubs), some to the Catholic Base Communities (CEBs), some to neighbourhood organizations seeking health services or child care, some to labour unions or opposition political parties – 'over four hundred self-professed feminist organizations were formed during the 1970s and 1980s' (Alvarez 1990:10; Barroso and Bruschini 1989; Soares *et al.* 1996). While feminist groups are located mainly within the urban centres, the majority of women's groups (who do not necessarily identify themselves as feminist) are active in the urban peripheries and *favelas*, small rural communities, and labour unions (Carloto 1992).

It is ironic that during the period of political repression, women had more latitude than men in grassroots social movements, the reason being the common view of women as domestic and apolitical. It was then that the popular, neighbourhood-based sector of the contemporary women's movement, composed mostly of poor housewives and some working women, emerged from domesticity to organize publicly around their concerns as family caretakers – protesting against the military regime and rising prices and demanding better government services. Feminist groups in Brazil have formed only one segment of a larger and increasingly diverse women's movement that has created many opportunities for women's political participation. The movement's focus on *cidadania* signifies the recasting of individual rights as social rights through the creation of political subjects who learn to exercise their decision-making capacity, to formulate policies expressing community interests, and to monitor state actions. Their emphasis on daily life needs, including reproductive and sexual rights, forms the common ground connecting the various streams within the Brazilian women's movement, both feminist and nonfeminist.

Perhaps more than any other institution in Brazil's civil society, the Catholic Church has had a crucial yet contradictory impact on the development of the women's movement, providing not only spaces for women's organizing but organized opposition to feminist campaigns. The Church was present at the start as a stimulus and base of support for most of the women's movements of the last decades, including the groups that are analysed in this research. Through the CEBs and various pastoral movements, the Church provided a legitimate channel for women's activism outside the domestic sphere and a space where issues of social justice and equality were constant topics of conversation. At the same time, the hierarchy has absolutely opposed any official family planning policy and feminist demands concerning legal abortion and contraception. Yet women in church-based movements have often resisted church teachings and practices on these issues and undertaken many joint activities with feminist groups, especially in the arena of health (Soares *et al.* 1996; Barroso and Bruschini 1989). Indeed, the strength of their alliance with church-based women may help to explain the remarkable effectiveness of feminist campaigns in some areas.

Women's reproductive rights are integral to the political agenda of the feminist movement in Brazil. During the democratization period in the 1980s, Brazilian feminists formulated an ethical and political understanding of reproductive rights as an essential part of *cidadania*. The demand for 'woman's right to control her own body' and feminist critiques of many abuses and deficiencies in prevailing health and population policies and practices came to occupy an important place in public debates. Campaigns to increase women's access to safe legal abortion have been crucial to these efforts (Alvarez 1990; Ávila 1993; Barroso and Bruschini 1989; Barroso and Corrêa 1995; Barsted 1992; Dixon-Mueller 1993; Martine 1996; Pitanguy 1994).

The approach of Brazilian feminists (and of this study) to the notion of reproductive rights contains two analytically separate levels, the first encompassing reproductive experiences directly related to women's bodies (sexuality, STDs, fertility, contraception, pregnancy, abortion, childbirth, breastfeeding) and the second involving domestic tasks related to the social reproduction of human life (child care, housework, care for the family's health, etcetera). On the first level, thanks to feminist movements it is now possible in Brazil to think of reproduction as a sphere of social responsibility where rights are being shaped. The second level is less frequently perceived as a locus of social and state responsibility, with some exceptions such as the powerful struggle for day care centres (Movimento de Luta por Creches) in São Paulo in the 1970s (Alvarez 1990). Thus there is a long way to go in order to broaden the concept of reproductive rights to encompass women's unpaid work in social reproduction.

Methodology, Process, and Groups Studied

Members of seven organizations – one in Recife, one in Rio de Janeiro, and five in São Paulo – participated in the IRRRAG research team in Brazil. Among these organizations, six have been involved in advocacy, research and education; one has been an institutional catalyst for research on reproductive health and rights issues throughout Latin America; and three have worked for years in service provision and with the movements described below in their respective locales.[9] All have been at the forefront of Brazil's feminist health movement. We chose the three constituencies of domestic workers, agricultural workers and urban housewives as our focal points not only because they represent the three largest occupational groups of women in Brazil but because we already had a history of cooperation with them, which would ease communication and future implementation activities. On the basis of our members' prior work and established connections with the three popular movements, the team selected the research communities. The sample of 182 individuals (158 women and 24 men) who participated in the investigation was selected using a snowball method starting with contacts among community leaders who then referred us to individual participants from their movements.[10]

Table 2.1 Respondents, By Occupation

OCCUPATION	%
Not participating in the formal market (housewives)	25.3
Domestic workers	29.6
Rural workers	11.0
Male small landowners	11.6
Female small landowners	20.7
Male health workers[11]	1.8
Total	100.0

The IRRRAG Brazil study selected our informants from the ranks of three organizations representing the three occupational groupings: the

Sindicato dos Trabalhadores Domésticos do Município do Rio de Janeiro, (Domestic Workers' Union of the City of Rio de Janeiro); the Movimento da Mulher Trabalhadora Rural do Nordeste (Movement of Women Agricultural Workers of the Northeast, MMTR); and the Movimento de Saúde da Zona Leste (Health Movement of the Eastern Zone, MSZL) in São Paulo. The occupational composition of the respondents selected from the three groups is shown in Table 2.1.

Domestic workers

Besides limited labour protection and an extremely isolated work environment, the social relations of domestic work set it apart from other occupations. It is one of the few work relations that take place between two women, as determined usually by their different class and racial conditions (Rollins 1985). Because as women they share subordination and daily intimacy within the domestic realm but have unequal power (one supervising, the other performing tasks), the employer–employee relationship here is particularly tense and conflictual (Souza 1980; Mello e Souza 1989). Thus, the extent to which domestic workers have organized in Rio de Janeiro is all the more remarkable. The Rio Domestic Workers' Union was founded as an association in 1961 by eighteen women, under the auspices of the Young Catholic Workers (JOC) movement; only in 1989 did it achieve union status. Currently the union has over 2,000 members, who come from all three types of domestic labour regime: day workers (*diaristas*), who are paid by the day and work in different homes each week; monthly nonresidents (*mensalistas não-residentes*), who work every day in the same household for monthly wages but commute to work; and monthly resident workers (*mensalistas residentes*), who live at their workplace, are paid monthly, and get one and a half days off at weekends. With work days as long as twelve hours and frequent abuse of their right to time off with pay, this last group suffers more violations of their rights than any other.[12] For a variety of reasons, however, reflecting changes in the economy and the desire of domestic workers for greater freedom with higher pay, live-in workers are declining in relation to nonresidential domestics. Our sample is composed of daily workers working in different locations and of residents who have been at the same job for many years. The leaders of the Rio de Janeiro union belong to the latter.

Rural workers

Women small producers, landless villagers, day labourers and employees on the large plantations have been transforming the political and social scene in Brazilian agriculture, demonstrating their militant role in the struggle to assert a new social identity (Soares *et al.* 1996). Until the early 1980s, the number of unionized female rural workers was extremely low, a fact that prompted the organization of the MMTR in 1981. Throughout its existence, this movement has been independent from the unions, although it works closely with them, prepares women to assume leadership positions, and influences the political agenda of the unions to include women's demands. Its main objective is to organize rural women workers, reinforce their identity, and help them to assume decision-making positions in all spheres of society. Today the MMTR has a national presence, with strong connections to other Latin American rural movements.

Rural labour in Brazil is characterized by very differentiated social relationships. In addition to the wide gap between owners of large estates (*latifúndios*) and peasants, the latter group contains many different strata.[13] Our sample includes two types of rural workers: small landowners who raise subsistence crops and develop links with local markets; and male and female wage workers in the export-oriented fruit agribusiness. While small landowners are considered self-employed and thus have minimal access to labour rights and social benefits, wage workers on export farms are generally protected through rigorous union monitoring of labour laws affecting them. But neither labour laws nor the unions have prevented the violation of women workers' reproductive rights by companies determined to hire childless and sterilized women. Confronting this lack of protection, women farm workers in the São Francisco region, where we conducted our research, demonstrated their militancy in 1994 by demanding and winning an important clause in the collective agreement between the union and the companies granting them the right to two days' rest during their menstrual period (FETAPE 1994).

Urban housewives

The MSZL, the third group included in our research, was formed by women from the mothers' clubs and the CEBs of the Catholic Church and is typical of the popular, peri-urban women's movements described earlier. It originated in 1973 in the eastern working-class district of São Paulo as an alternative vehicle for demanding better health care during the military regime, when normal institutional channels were blocked. With the support of health workers, the movement organized mass demonstrations, set up health commissions to pressure the government to open clinics and hospitals and hire more personnel, and demanded participation in the monitoring and managing of health services through local councils. The MSZL's coordinating committee is made up of twenty-five participants, all women, who now (with the creation of a Women's Health Commission) lead its activities around these issues.

The women interviewed in São Paulo consider themselves housewives and political activists who fight for the community's wellbeing. Most of them have lived in the region for many years after migrating from rural areas, especially the Northeast. They have raised families in São Paulo, and achieved a better standard of living than they could in the interior, and they do not consider returning to their home state. Their husbands are predominantly workers in the industrial region of the state known as ABC Paulista, Brazil's greatest industrial centre.[14] As such, they have attained the highest level of organization, the highest salaries and the best labour and economic conditions of all Brazilian workers, evident in comparisons with the families of the two other groups. (See Citeli 1994.) Family benefits, however, as we shall see below, are not always converted into benefits for women.

Although the contact points for the research were organized social movements, the degree to which individual respondents could be considered activists in these movements varied. Informants ranged from leaders who had participated in the movement for decades, sometimes even having a regional or a national presence, to women whose affiliation with their organization had just begun at the time of the research and in some cases was motivated by a labour dispute. Despite such variations, we recognize that our respondents are atypical among low-income rural and urban groups in Brazil, insofar as their union or movement affiliation signals a certain degree of political awareness or consciousness of belonging to a collectivity, and therefore a prior disposition to think about group claims or rights. We thus decided to include a small number of non-activist women (10 per cent of the total), who were not engaged in the movement's activities in an ongoing way, as a control group for comparative purposes. Throughout the data analysis, we shall refer to 'activists' and 'nonactivists', with the understanding that the former range from leaders to rank-and-file members.

All three research sites used the same instruments: (1) a sociodemographic questionnaire (with questions specific to each region), (2) focus groups, or group interviews, and (3) in-depth interviews (among women only). Methods for conducting the group interviews varied somewhat from one site to another, depending on the availability and needs of the participants. Our 45 in-depth interviews (total for all three sites) included both participants and nonparticipants of the focus groups. In Pernambuco and Rio de Janeiro, these interviews used the 'life history' technique, while in São Paulo they used semi-structured questions within a lifecycle framework. All three sub-studies attempted to interview people across a wide spectrum of ages, roughly divided into three generational categories: below 21 (12.5 per cent of total), 21–44 (46.3 per cent of total), and 45 and over (41.2 per cent of total).[15]

In addition to seeking generational diversity, we also attempted to vary respondents by race, taking into account the complexity of racial classifications in Brazil.[16] Echoing the considerable confusion attending race as a social and political discourse in Brazil at present, the men and women interviewed often used language to describe themselves that reflects the society's current preoccupation with shades of skin colour – for example, *morena* (brunette), *escurinha* (little dark one), or *amarelo* (yellow). We chose to avoid these categories, instead classifying respondents as 'Amerindian', 'black' (all nonspecified respondent references to dark skin), or 'white', reserving this 'white' category only for those cases where respondents explicitly made this reference to themselves. Within this classification, it is noteworthy that the overwhelming majority of respondents in Pernambuco and Rio de Janeiro were black, while nearly two-thirds of those in the São Paulo site were white. In addition, those in São Paulo tended to be somewhat older and more affluent than respondents in the other two groups. As we shall see, however, while social conditions differentiate the groups' relation to the labour force and to work generally, social activism brings many of the urban housewives closer to the other two groups, from whom they differ by class and race, when it comes to their attitudes about gender and reproduction.

Table 2.2 Participants by race and site (per cent; total per site = 100)

RACE	PERNAMBUCO	RIO DE JANEIRO	SÃO PAULO
White	12	18	60
Black	85	82	36
Amerindian	3	–	4

Negotiating Public and Private Space: Work, Activism, and *Cidadania*

The distinction between the private and the public spheres – including both the labour market and political/social activism – is deeply ingrained in Brazilian culture and becomes a necessary reference point in discussing *cidadania*. In the framework of *cidadania* as it emerged in the 1980s, only the public domain is associated with a sense of entitlement and rights language as the currency for transacting claims. In the private world of household or patron–client relations, on the other hand, the language of rights is rarely applied; issues of domestic space are most often articulated as needs to be met or personal problems to be resolved within the private sphere.

While recognizing the continued ideological force of the public–private dichotomy in the dominant culture, IRRRAG's findings in Brazil call into question the very distinction between public and private as it has often been understood. Among the women we studied, this distinction bears little relation to daily life. For urban groups, spatial permeability between the public and the private results from the very configuration of cities, with their immense circulation of people, better access to the media and public services, and neighbourhoods enmeshed in public debates (over allocation of resources, police brutality, etcetera). For rural groups, private space itself is a continuum linking different houses and fields on the same property. Conditions of work in agriculture and domestic service also conflate dimensions of the public and private, where workplace and home, social space and intimate space, often intersect.

Not only the environmental but also the interpersonal experience of our respondents contradict the usual assumptions about a division between public and private. Above all, the great majority of our female respondents, like Brazilian women generally, are both working outside the home and caring for family members (see Table 2.1). Through their jobs and/or political activity, the women we interviewed crossed the domestic threshold and came to view public space as an avenue for developing both a new personal project and a collective political vision. Among activists in Pernambuco and São Paulo, there came a moment when they realized their whole life had been dedicated to caring for other people. (One of our São Paulo respondents had been so confined to her domestic boundaries she did not even possess a key to her own house.) Their self-image changed from that of housewife – politically and socially unaware, financially dependent, lacking autonomy – to that of social actor and citizen. One São Paulo leader in the popular health movement recalled: 'when I started to participate I was Mary Nobody, who was not aware of anything; a woman who looked after her husband, had to hand him his clothes, his slippers. Here in the movement I became conscious that we have to struggle for our rights, for our space, and to think about tomorrow.' And another: 'We learn a lot ... a woman who only stays home ... seems to regress. The woman who gets out, participates, she gets ahead, sees the world as it is.'

Men, however, particularly in the rural areas, may not share this view. One male union leader in Pernambuco (small producer, forty-eight years old) expressed a more traditional perspective on women's place: 'For a woman to get off the truck with a bag of beans on her head – don't you see that nowadays? It doesn't look good. People will say, "Doesn't she have a husband?"' Such an attitude contrasts sharply with that of our female respondents, for whom the home signifies restrictions on women, dependence on husbands and fathers, and the burdens of housework and child care. Amara, a 26-year-old mother of four, explains her inability to participate in public life: 'I have no one to leave the kids with. My husband ... says: "you wanna go, I will not get in your way, but I will not stay with the kids for you to go out."'

Household work has played a key role in the development of a concept of injustice among our respondents. Many describe domestic labour as repetitive, time-consuming, solitary and servile. It is performed for other people who, for this very reason, feel free to give orders. It is invisible and unpaid (except in the case of hired domestic workers), therefore socially devalued. These realities turn the house into a place from which one wants to escape, at least some of the time. When given the choice of work inside or outside the home, most women chose the latter, for reasons like those stated by this rural worker from one of the Pernambuco focus groups:

> I prefer to work in the fields because you see the work done. At home you do something and then you do not see the product of your work. If you wash, it gets dirty again. In the fields we work all day long, and at the end of the day you see your production; and after eight, fifteen days it adds up.

Paid work gives women autonomy and mobility, providing them with the freedom to come and go (*ir e vir*) as well as the expansion of their world. Spatial mobility and increased social contact open new possibilities of access to information and other points of view. The extension of one's social network is particularly relevant in Brazilian culture since social contacts operate as the means towards problem resolution and achievements. For some, work provides their first direct contact with money, freeing them from dependence on partners, husbands, or other male relatives and enhancing their self-esteem. Fully 84 per cent of our female respondents were working outside the home in either the formal or informal sector.

Being part of a work-related social movement or a union also brings women directly into negotiations involving *cidadania*. Rural and domestic workers, nonactivists as well as activists, demonstrate an enhanced sense of entitlement and greater knowledge about their rights as a result of belonging to the only two occupations not entitled to the full range of labour protection. At the same time, they evidence a sense of pride and awareness about labour laws that have been won by domestic and rural workers' organizations. As a result, activist and nonactivist domestic workers and activist rural workers indicate that they are more likely to make demands on their employer, to refuse certain work conditions or, when necessary, to seek out the union to take a labour complaint to court. This is not to romanticize the working conditions that most women in our study have to contend with. Isolation, long work hours for the live-in domestic and long commutes for the *diarista* make it difficult for domestic workers to meet each other, discuss their work issues, organize around them and even create a work identity. Yet for many of the women we interviewed, it was precisely these inhumane and 'slavery'-like conditions that led them to the union and to develop a strong sense of injustice and rights.

Significantly, most activists in the domestic workers' union are live-in workers who have worked in the same household for over ten years and are likely to have sacrificed families of their own. In contrast to nonactivists, activists demonstrate a strong work identity and commitment to their occupation, proudly continuing to work as domestics while also holding office in the union. The collective endeavour has merged with their individual life projects, to the point where union activism becomes their primary route to self-fulfilment. Nonactivists, on the other hand, whose age range was between twenty-five and thirty-five years, perceive domestic service as arduous but temporary, a job to be held while striving to move on to something better. For them, domestic work is a passing stage in a personal project of upward mobility during which they seek better employment opportunities as well as trying to further their studies and training to enable them to escape domestic work. Moreover, if they have children of their own, they dream of a different life for them. This is apparent in 31-year-old Cila's comment about her daughter:

> I wish a wonderful future for my daughter. One thing I will tell you, which I have said to my friends as well. I do not want my child ever to be a domestic worker. Never, ever, ever. I will do anything, with or without him [her husband] ... for her to be somebody. But never a domestic, because I have seen it. I know it is the saddest profession in the world – the most distressing, the most discriminated against.

The women in the MSZL (São Paulo) are even more likely to project onto their daughters this sense of entitlement regarding work and 'being somebody', since most of them were in the paid labour force only briefly if at all or perform home-based work on an irregular basis. As Maria, a 61-year-old leader of the movement, observed: 'When I was raising my daughters, I took in sewing, I worked like a slave so they could study.... I used to tell them, you can't depend on a husband.' While many of these women had worked in the industrial or service sectors before marriage, they faced numerous obstacles to continuing work outside the home after marriage, such as the opposition of husbands, lack of childcare services, and employer policies that discriminated against working mothers (for example, of pregnancy tests, dismissal when pregnant, or the requirement of a tubal ligation certificate). Now, attempting to re-enter the labour market, they find themselves lacking the necessary experience and skills and victimized by age discrimination – a double injustice.

Nonactivist rural workers, though seeing their suffering as unjust, seem more resigned to their situation and unable to envision change for themselves or their daughters. Lourdes, a smallholding peasant and mother of ten, teaches her daughters that their lives will always be separate from men's. Amara describes the dreary repetitiveness of labour in house and field:

> I had no youth because I got married at eighteen and life became routine. Work, heat your belly at the stove and chill it at the sink. That is all you learn. Move, chicken! Shut up, boy! Today many things are changing, but for me nothing changed. It is always the same – field, home, kids, wash.... I take a basin of clothes on my head, a kid in my arms, another on my belly, and another walking slowly beside me with my skirt clutched in his hand. Every day is like the day before.

Activists transform such conditions through participation in tasks defined and valued by the movement rather than by their brother, father or husband.

With their frame of reference expanded beyond the family circle, they no longer feel the need to follow the traditional pattern of gender behaviour for wives and daughters. Miraceia, a 38-year-old activist and mother of seven, now has her husband do housework when she is away at political meetings: 'If I am not home and it is necessary he will do it. He gets the boy at school, helps with homework, punishes the kids, all that. These are *parents'* obligations' (emphasis added). Miraceia's expectation that her husband will share the responsibility for child care is an example of how notions of social justice and equality that originated in connection to work or activism have permeated other arenas of these womens' lives, including gender roles and relationships within the domestic sphere.

Among domestic workers, both paid work and political activism facilitate the development of a sense of entitlement and a public discourse to express it, though in Pernambuco activism was a more significant factor. Participation in church and movement groups was the great opening for many women in all three of our research sites. Once involved in their community, church or union, they found themselves no longer thinking and speaking only of family and children but starting to speak for their class and women as a group. They acquired new information, skills and horizons through access to meetings, seminars and travel – opportunities ordinarily denied to semi-literate women by their class, gender and race. For domestic workers, involvement in the union provided a space for socializing with their peers, making up for the gaping emotional and personal void in their private and work lives.

However, the road to activism is not an easy one. Activist women meet resistance from husbands, family members and neighbours, who accuse them of violating prescribed gender norms. It is thus not surprising that in all three research sites most activists initiated their community participation after their reproductive work had diminished, in the life stage when marriage and motherhood were no longer central preoccupations; in Rio activists have been mostly single women. Usually after age forty, they either have fewer childcare and housework tasks or have shifted these to their older daughters, freeing themselves for activities outside the home. Thus begins a process of confronting new ideas and questioning the past, including how their sexual bodies have been constructed and suppressed.

Our data suggest, then, that gender is an important mediator of how notions of public and private are perceived. The women's responses call into question anthropological analyses of the dynamics of public and private that identify the first as negative (impersonal relations, the suspicious stranger, mistrust and danger) and the second as positive (intimacy, loyalty, trust, protection) (DaMatta 1987). In all three of our research sites, women frequently associated the 'public' world of workplace or organization with such values as freedom, mobility, empowerment, self-discovery, personal growth, sociability, and meaningful relationships. In contrast, they often described the 'private' household in negative terms: as imprisoning, violent, burdensome, a source of exhaustion, pain and suffering.

Sexuality, Marriage and the Family

The unknown and silenced body

Lack of information or misinformation about bodily functions, sexuality and reproduction constitutes one of the main obstacles to women's development of a sense of entitlement over their bodies. For all three of our research groups, this denial of information is intricately tied to socialization about gender roles and is carried out in the first instance by older female relatives.[17] Rural and older women acquired a sense of the body as an unknown entity, not to be talked about. Instructing a young unmarried woman to 'take care of her body' meant protecting the virginal and untouched body, maintaining its purity and guarding it from shame. The only time when a limited transfer of knowledge regarding the body would occur across generations was the first menstruation, but this information was usually inaccurate and incomplete. (Compare Desser 1993 and Leal 1994.)

Our interviews show that older women during their childhood and adolescence had to search on their own for answers to their questions about changes in their bodies. Some turned to books, magazines and friends; others only learned about these taboo matters from their first sexual partner. In this context, menstruation was a very relevant milestone. Mariana, a 46-year-old São Paulo housewife, conveys the symbolic confusion typical among her generation, in which the arrival of menstruation became intermeshed with the dread of losing her virginity: 'On the first day I menstruated I was so terribly shocked, the blood started to flow down and I thought that I had lost my virginity.... I got so scared and I didn't know if I should tell my mother or not ... I cried, "Oh, I am lost today."' The advice she received from her mother is even more revealing of the silence and shame that surrounded menstruation:

> When my mother got home, I worked up the courage and told her. Then she called me to her room and said, 'You will do the following – go make a lining in your panties ...' and she gave me some pieces of cloth, 'and you will not tell anyone about this, you won't let the blood appear, you won't let anyone see this. And do not even tell your sisters ... wash your panties carefully, because this is ... very shameful, if anyone knows about this, it is very shameful for a woman.'

Among rural women, gender roles, representations of the body and sexuality are all permeated by rules and taboos justified by the naturalized difference between men and women as well as the key notion of feminine honour. An honourable woman protects her body from the masculine gaze and from sex. She should keep to the restricted family space, moving from her parents' household, where she obeyed her parents and brothers, to her own household, where she is to obey her husband. Virginity, the fundamental symbol of honour, is inscribed on the woman's body, which must not be touched, even by herself. It is a social currency that buys the woman's future, and it is an indispensable requirement for marriage, whose ultimate goal is procreation. This social code guarantees the reproduction of the family, the basic unit of production, while its transgression threatens the survival of the family, inheritance and honour (Quintas 1987).

From childhood, bodily contacts between boys and girls are discouraged in order not to arouse sexual desire. In rural Pernambuco, control is stronger than in the urban Southeast, as is the severity awaiting those who transgress the norm. For rural women, sexual experience before marriage may lead to social ostracization through sanctions that force them into prostitution, migration or seclusion in their parents' home, where they are subjected to humiliation and violence. Among our older rural respondents, loss of their virginity was the one condition that meant losing their status as rural workers, demonstrating the extent to which sexuality and production are intimately related. As adolescents and young adults, older women who grew up in the Northeast lived constantly under the threat of 'losing themselves'. Even the most tentative initiatives in search of bodily pleasure, such as a boy's advances, a kiss or caress, provoked enormous anxiety and the fear of losing their honour. Ines, a 45-year-old vendor in São Paulo, recalled an incident when her boyfriend started holding her 'a bit tighter, and then I thought, my God! am I still a virgin?' In a similar vein, one of the older women in a São Paulo focus group described the circumstances provoking her marriage:

> I had been going out with a young man for some time. One day he kissed my forehead; I didn't expect it and I almost died right there.... [I thought,] I've got to marry this bastard right now, if I want to break up I can't, because he'll tell everybody that he kissed me.... Dad will kill me, and I won't accept to be kissed and dishonoured.

Thus the masculine touch on the woman's body defined female honour and morality for these women and ended up determining their future. Marriage with the man who 'dishonoured her with a kiss' is the only way to preserve the woman's morality.

Most of our respondents were angry about the lack of information, mis-information and silence about sexuality and reproduction that had surrounded them. Aside from inhibiting their sexual life, they perceived lack of know-ledge as having undermined their ability to make informed decisions about their reproductive health. Personal stories reveal the anguish, loneliness and helplessness many women experienced when they gave birth, some having had no idea what to expect and no one to talk to about it. Men, especially in the rural areas, were often as ill informed as women about reproduction and thus of little or no help to their wives. João, a 61-year-old health movement activist, said that he had 'never had any explanation about diseases or about the body because this was taboo. No one ever talked about this on the farm.'

When it comes to their own children, however, our data show a strikingly different sensibility from that which the respondents themselves experienced as adolescents and young adults. Increasingly, it seems, issues concerning sexuality and reproductive decision-making in Brazil are no longer considered taboo, contaminating, or unspeakable for young people but rather are seen as a 'part of life'.[18] There is no doubt that the HIV/AIDS epidemic and growing awareness about it, particularly in the cities, have played a crucial role in this attitudinal shift (Daniel and Parker 1993; Parker and Barbosa 1996). Yet our data also reflect a strong sense of regret among the older women about the silences veiling their own budding sexuality, which they apply in a positive way to their adolescent daughters. The activists in São Paulo were especially forthright in accepting the sexuality of their daughters while urging them to protect themselves against AIDS, other STDs and unwanted pregnancy; above all they want them to become self-reliant in their lives. Even those who are nonactivists reject the old norms of feminine purity and passivity for their daughters. 'I don't have anything to do with this notion of virginity,' says Fernanda, a 36-year-old mother of three, 'but I want [my daughter] at least to finish high school, to have a more open mind, to get through adolescence.' One São Paulo mother's report of her advice to her daughter indicates a dramatic transformation in the traditional meanings associated with the term 'good girl':

> You have to obey your mother and be a good girl. Even if you have sex, do it carefully, use a condom. Know what you are doing ... because if afterwards you have a child, who will take care of your children? There are so many ways to avoid it.[19]

Our few interviews with adolescents suggest that the shift in social attitudes about sexuality has had a direct effect on younger women. Reflecting a degree of self-determination their mothers lacked at their age, these younger women seek information concerning the body and sexuality and, when they meet with resistance from older women, challenge them. In contrast to the women of all generations, however, our male respondents were relatively unconcerned about their lack of sexual and reproductive information. Typically for them, initiation into sexual knowledge came through contact with prostitutes, and the only worry was sexually trans-mitted diseases. Older men seemed most reluctant to change their personal behaviour and attitudes about sexuality with regard to either their children or current wives or partners. Echoing the attitude responsible for the drastic rise in heterosexual HIV transmission in Brazil, João admitted:

> We don't use any method, no condom, we don't use anything. She says that I go out with other women and I could contaminate her, but I don't use anything.... My partner said that she gave a condom to her daughter. I said, You have the courage to do this? You don't think that you are encouraging the girl to have sexual relations?

Our findings thus disclose signs of changing moral values and women's willingness to address their daughters as autonomous sexual subjects, though men seem to be lagging behind. Among women interviewed, the concept of taking care of the body for adolescents nowadays includes preventing unwanted pregnancy, avoiding early motherhood, and instead building an autonomous life plan and financial independence, and preventing AIDS and other sexually transmitted diseases (Guimarães 1996). This new vision is especially pronounced among the São Paulo respondents, whose activism focuses on health, whereas those in Pernambuco direct their rethinking of sexual values more toward future generations of girls and boys. While virginity may not have disappeared as a value, its importance has diminished in the face of social and medical realities and the impact of contemporary urban life – which feminism both influences and reflects – on today's moral ethos in Brazil.

Marriage and sexual relations

Women in this study had two conflicting languages for referring to sex: as a marital duty and a kind of work on the one hand, and as a source of pleasure and a healthy activity on the other. The latter discourse – which emerged among all three research groups – was partly associated in some cases with exposure to women's groups and the stronger sense of self that work and activism generate. Even more pronounced among our respondents, however, was the association of pleasurable sex with single or post-marital life; and conversely, in São Paulo and Pernambuco, of sex as burden or violence, with marriage. More than sexual relations with men or traditional norms of honour and virginity, the most oppressive obstacle to realizing their sense of entitlement and aspirations for equality for many of the women we interviewed was marriage.

Younger, nonactivist domestic workers in Rio de Janeiro talk about the right to pleasure, choice over sexual intercourse, and equality in sexual relations: 'I think there should be pleasure for both of us.' Surprisingly, some of the strongest expressions of sexual autonomy and freedom from the bonds of marriage came from these young women *diaristas*, who exhibit a clear sense of entitlement to sexual rights *vis-à-vis* their companions. But we also found that older women activists – those forty years or older who had been involved either in the rural workers' union, the women's movement or both – have developed a clear idea of a right to sexual pleasure for themselves. Some had experienced consciousness-raising within women's groups. Perhaps even more significant, many had separated from their first husbands, often to escape domestic violence (see below), and had the opportunity to meet other partners. In their speech we find sexual pleasure linked to physical and mental health as well as positive experiences of condom use: 'There's nothing better than sexuality, when it is done with someone you like and when you need it. It's the best therapy for a woman. It involves every part of her body.' Or:

[Condoms] don't make a difference, uh-uh. Because it's such a thin thing, it's very sensitive, and it's smooth at the same time.... It's just an oily little skin that isn't different at all.... If you knew how good it is, you'd never give it up.

Sometimes speakers in the rural women's focus groups stressed individual freedom regarding sexuality to such an extent that we began to hear their speech as genuinely feminist. One woman over forty-five asserted: 'because she owns her body, she doesn't need to ask for any permission. It's her own body and she does whatever she wishes with it.' And another, also a farm worker, somewhat younger, pronounced:

it's a matter of choice. If someone feels better with a man, she should keep to him ... if I like a woman, it's my business. I've got to think of myself, not of what others may say.... Everyone has the right to choose what is right for herself.

Yet the cultural bias dictating that women are supposed to be sexually available and compliant for their partners, at whatever risk to themselves, seems to die hard. Josefa, a 51-year-old black movement leader and house-wife from São Paulo, conveys this traditional notion: 'When I married him, ... an older woman advised me, "Whether you're sick or dying, you always have to be ready and sweet-smelling for him," and I do this faithfully. Once I had a uterine inflammation; when we had sex, I almost died from the pain. But I never told him this.' If exposure to women's groups was the final catalyst evoking liberal ideas about sexuality, it did so within an overarching context of constraint and disappointment in marriage.

With regard to decision making about whether to marry, when and whom, women in all three research sites said they had had very little choice. In the rural areas, only men exercised choice in this domain, looking for an appropriate woman to marry and approaching her by first asking her parents' consent. Women are left in a position of reacting: checking out if the man will make a good husband, if he works hard, has no addictions, is a good son. Most married the first man who proposed to them. As one participant in a Pernambuco focus group put it, 'I didn't wish to marry. I married to obey my parents.' Black women respondents in São Paulo also experienced intrusion by their families in their choice of a marriage partner, through the distorting lens of race. Internalizing the equation of lighter skin with upward mobility, some black parents refused to let their daughters go out with black men, encouraging them to seek lighter partners 'to improve the race'. Several nonactivist domestics in Rio de Janeiro were compelled into marriage by out-of-wedlock pregnancy.

Despite these constraints, our interviews suggest that many of the women entered marriage with strong expectations of not only *reciprocity* (a gender division of labour in which each carries out his or her prescribed role) but also *equality*. Many of the older women in all three groups saw marriage not only as a culturally prescribed mandate but as an escape from the control of parents and the endless chores that good daughters were expected to perform in rural households, even, as Marta (a 38-year-old divorced woman who migrated from a rural area to São Paulo) put it, as a way to 'see places' and 'have fun'. But their expectations in this regard were sadly destroyed by the realities of married life, characterized by men's violence, alcoholism, philandering, and absence from household labour. They feel cheated and blame the men for not upholding their end of the contract. Disappointment with marriage was a salient theme among all three groups of women respondents. Almost unanimously, both activists and nonactivists voiced nostalgia for their single (premarital) days as the favourite time in their life; after marriage, they lost the few advantages they previously had had. Joséfa typifies this disillusionment: 'When I married, I thought he was choosing me as his wife. [In fact] he was choosing me to be his maid, but I only see this now, after I joined the Workers' Party (PT).' Selma, a 27-year-old white *diarista* who, unlike Josefa, is not an activist, also voices an awareness of marriage as having limited her freedom:

> If I had to start it all over again, I would not marry. I would *namorar* [stay in a long-term romantic relationship].... But we would not live together. Personally, when I am alone at home, I feel better. You have your own space, freedom to think, to listen to music. You are more at ease and more self-determined.

The ultimate expression of gender inequality in sexual and emotional relationships, especially marriage, is male violence against women. We heard numerous testimonies in all three research sites of wives who had been battered, frequently as a result of men's resentment of their participation in work or political activism. In Pernambuco, domestic conflicts leading to violence are a common occurrence, but separation results only when the violence becomes extreme, that is, when the woman's life is actually under threat. In these cases, the family and sometimes also the women's movement become involved, establishing solidarity networks to protect the woman. A 46-year-old leader in the MMTR recounted a long history of violence and abuse she endured from her husband. Finally, with the support of the local women's groups, she was able to leave him and rebuild her life.

For this woman as for many others, the pattern of violence began with pregnancy. During a first pregnancy, especially among rural workers, men often start to reject their wives sexually and to pursue other women or to beat their wives.[20] Apart from its psychological motivations, such violence is related to the unequal division of labour that assigns to women the multiple burdens of wife, mother, rural worker, and household maintainer. With children, the fulfilment of all these tasks becomes increasingly difficult, particularly when there is no auxiliary arrangement for child care. Husbands react to getting less attention and to women's absence from their 'obligations', and from then on violence emerges as a regular practice, resolved only by separation. One focus group participant conveys the horror of this situation:

I was beaten every day. I would say ... I can't leave him so I will take poison. 'Poison is worse because you will go to hell' [they would tell me], and I would say that it would be better than to live with that son of a bitch.... There were only two solutions. To kill him was not a choice ... his family is also not easy and I am sure they would kill me. The last time we separated ... I had six kids. He beat me, dragged me on the floor. I was nursing my baby. I left only with this little one and left four behind. One had died. I left with this boy, barefoot, my hair pulled out and lived for two years and two months in my father's house.

Younger women, consciously seeking to avoid the brutality they witnessed in their mothers' and grandmothers' lives, expect to delay marriage and to meet a man who will not oppress them. The adolescents we interviewed in São Paulo attempt to evade parental control, secretly dating and prolonging their status as single women. When and if they marry, they fully expect to choose their own partners.

Live-in domestic workers are at an extreme disadvantage when it comes to sexual relations. Isolated in middle-class homes where it is difficult to meet people, lacking the time and availability to form relationships, they typically refer to sexual relations as 'a thing of the past'. They tell stories of how their employers, jealous to have their domestic's full attention for themselves, discouraged or openly sabotaged their relationships with men. Yet, while some complain about their condition, others – particularly the more militant unionists – have clearly chosen marriage to the union over life with a man. As one ex-president of the union put it:

After I became conscious of my life and what I wanted, everything became easier. I couldn't stand having a husband. I love my freedom. I work as a maid, it's always the same work; there's a time when you get tired and you have to see things your way. That's why working in the union is so important. And sex and the presidency, both are not possible. A woman doesn't just live for a man ... she can live on her own. It's not just through sex that she feels fulfilled.

The increase in the numbers of single mothers, separations, and female heads of households is a growing reality in Brazil, suggesting that women's disillusionment with marriage may represent a wider social phenomenon that extends beyond feminist ideology. In Pernambuco, a forty-year-old activist in the agricultural union chose to be a single mother and managed still to achieve respect and social legitimacy in the community: 'I am a single mother. I chose the best thing for my son. I might make mistakes in his upbringing, but I hope to do things right and to build a different world from the one around us.'

Reproductive Health and Social Reproduction

Motherhood and childbearing

When they speak of reproduction, the women in our study tell a story reaching from childhood to old age. Child care and housework start when girls replace their mothers so that the mothers can do other work inside or outside the home; these tasks end only with disability or death, since, at the other end of the life cycle, grandmothers are now expected to fill in for their daughters. Pressed by necessity, in the context of government failure to implement childcare legislation and the increasing erosion of state schools, mothers rely on female child labour, repeating within mother–daughter relationships the pattern they criticize as domestic workers and wives.[21] But among the rural women there is a clear difference between nonactivists, who accept the traditional gender division, and activists, who are consciously trying to transform it through their own childrearing practices. Nonactivists in the focus groups reported that their sons 'helped the father in the fields' while they themselves had taught their daughters 'since they were small to look after the house'. In contrast, Miraceia – union leader and full-time rural worker – exacts equal cooperation from both her activist husband and her sons:

> I taught my sons. They wash clothes, mend their own clothes, get clothes from the clothesline.... When they want to go out, they iron their own clothes.... Do you think I am going to slave by myself without sharing the work with my sons? ... Before [I joined the movement], they had everything done for them. I didn't feed them because that would be too much, but I set the table, put lunch on the table, and they would say 'I'm tired, bring it over here,' and I would. Not anymore. If they are tired, I am too. 'You work, I work, so go to the stove and get it yourself.' This is how I educate my kids and my husband too.

Nonactivist (and nonresident) domestic workers, who are more likely than resident domestics to have husbands and children, are the ones to push for gender equality in their households. Selma's insistence on sharing the housework led to serious confrontations:

> [My husband] wouldn't pick up a glass ... wherever he sat to eat something, he would leave it. One day I went crazy and said, 'If I find one glass, I'll smash it, I won't wash it, I'll throw it out.' Then I did it. Never again ... today he washes, tidies up, makes the bed, cleans the bathroom; he gives me lots of help. My mother-in-law said he used to be even worse. She said, 'Don't be dumb – rights should be equal....' [Now] the only thing he does not do is iron.

Domestic workers present the special case of an occupation that imposes the tasks of social reproduction while inhibiting biological reproduction. Many report having greater difficulties finding work if they are married and have children. Both activists and nonactivists, as well as their employers, are clearly aware of pregnancy as a condition that can mean losing their job; many get unsafe, illegal and even unwanted abortions for this reason. While numerous domestics do become wives and mothers, they do so at great cost. Those who sleep at their job must hand over their family care to others, seeing their spouses and children at weekends or even less frequently. *Diaristas* have long and strenuous commutes in order to go back to their families every night.

Thus caring for another woman's family in effect means giving up one's own.

Reproductive labour involves not only domestic tasks but countless negotiations in the public arena, in a context made increasingly stressful by poor quality in health and other public services, long distances and waiting times, as well as disrespect and mistreatment by personnel. (See Diniz 1996, and D'Oliveira 1996.) Marta, a black divorced mother of two who works as a domestic in São Paulo, spoke of 'hating' to take her children to the local health clinic because 'they treated us so badly. I lost so many days of work in order to get prenatal care and also care for the children.' Others complained of lack of access in addition to poor quality of care. But the most bitter accounts related to women's experience of gynaecological and obstetric services. Amelia, a 63-year-old health movement leader with three children, cringes at the impersonality of public gynaecological services: 'Suddenly you arrive there and you have to take your clothes off for a guy you've never seen before to start touching you.... To me ... this type of gynaecological consultation is violent.' Another São Paulo woman observed the following incident of abusive treatment in childbirth: 'The young woman was yelling in labour; she said, "Doctor, help me!" The doctor looked at her and said, "You're not my mother, my sister or my wife, why should I help you?" He just turned his back on her and left.'

Adoption of new cost-saving procedures in hospitals has increased the risks of childbearing by curtailing women's already limited time for rest, such as postpartum recovery. An older rural woman in Pernambuco deplores this regression from the old ways:

> In my time, the woman had her baby at home. The mother would spend I don't know how many days with her daughter after birth. It would take around fifteen days for her to wash her hair for the first time. It was a whole month of rest, wasn't it? Now, within twenty-four hours the woman leaves the maternity ward and goes home to do everything herself.

Traditional customs of two weeks' rest or more enabled rural women to refrain from domestic chores and to recover their energy from childbirth. Today, when rural women are expected to do all the domestic work without family help plus participate in agricultural labour, the postnatal recovery period has all but disappeared, with serious health consequences.

Poor women pay a high price for motherhood. In the rural Northeast, testimonies speak of pain, incapacity to meet marital obligations, and deterioration of reproductive health ultimately leading to tubal ligation or hysterectomy. Some of the older women had had as many as twenty pregnancies, which added up to fifteen years of their lives. A fifty-year-old movement leader who currently lives with her young granddaughter in the *sertão* exemplifies the suffering and continual medical interventions associated with the reproductive lives of women in this region (see Scheper-Hughes 1992):

I had my first daughter. In eleven months a boy was born. Then I couldn't take it any more and started to use [birth control] ... I had lots of bleeding ... I bled for sixteen years. I was treated, got better and became pregnant again.... I had seven [children]. I've done three electrocauterizations, three cervical cauterizations, one cervical amputation [*sic*] ... and curettage ... because I had a cervical infection and an abortion. At thirty-eight I had a full hysterectomy.

If pregnancy must always be viewed as a socially constructed experience, in Brazil it is one not only of increasing medicalization but, even more, of increasing surgicalization. For most women, to have children or to avoid them means to undergo surgery, as evidenced by the very high number of Caesarean sections (52 per cent of all births) and tubal ligations (see above, Mello e Souza 1994, and BEMFAM/DHS 1997). As suggested earlier, however, reproductive health is not a uniform experience throughout the country but is mediated by distinct regional differences, which are also differences of race and class. Prenatal care, for example, reaches only 42 per cent of women in the North and Northeast, as opposed to 75 per cent in other regions. Moreover, the quality of public system prenatal care is very poor, with most appointments lasting no more than five minutes (Berquó, Araújo and Sorrentino 1995).

For all these reasons, childbearing and motherhood become experiences fraught with danger and anguish rather than joy. As Lenice, a 46-year-old black domestic worker, laments: 'From the time you conceive, you have worries. You worry about birth; after it is born, you worry about its health.... You can no longer be happy after you have a child.' Continual assaults on the body in reproduction – both medical and spousal – lead these women to the realistic perception of maternity as a risk to their health; in rural areas, it is more likely to be perceived as life-threatening. If having children means dying a little, having fewer children is equivalent to survival. One MSZL activist gasped, 'Can you imagine a woman here in São Paulo having twenty-three kids like my mother? She wouldn't even be alive!' But perceptions of risk are relative. Selma reflects on her own situation: 'My mother-in-law used to think that one should have just one child. When I had my third one, she pressed a hand to her forehead and said, "Woman, you're killing yourself." She had had seven.'

These pessimistic views of marriage and reproduction do not mean that the women in our study are rejecting motherhood, which they still value highly. But they are striving to make it more compatible with work, school, economic independence, community activism, and their own health and wellbeing. The result for older women is increasing use of contraception, sterilization and abortion, and in some cases separation or divorce; and for younger women, greater efforts to postpone marriage and motherhood and to become self-determined in their sexual lives.

Controlling Fertility

Despite the social changes documented in our research showing the diminishing place of reproduction in respondents' life course, most of the women seldom seek methods of birth control before their first child. Only the younger domestic workers, encouraged to avoid pregnancy by their boyfriends as well as fearing reprisals from parents and employers if they became pregnant, reported such efforts prior to marriage and a first pregnancy. Generally, women from all three regions move from an attitude of passivity regarding pregnancy to a growing urge to take charge of their fertility. With each child born, their efforts and concerns increase. At first they rely inconsistently on the pill; once they feel they have reached their physical limits, they go to great pains to get sterilized. Thus the common pattern is that fertility control methods – above all sterilization and the pill, backed up frequently by abortion – are used as a means to stop rather than to space or postpone childbearing.

Our findings confirm the regional differences discussed earlier in total fertility as well as in infant and maternal mortality rates in Brazil. Thus respondents in Pernambuco had had an average of eight pregnancy and infant losses and six living children, while the averages for São Paulo and Rio de Janeiro were significantly lower – 4.1 and 3.1, and 3.4 and 3.1, respectively. In other words, the women in the Pernambuco group terminate or lose twice as many pregnancies and infants, and raise twice as many children, as those in São Paulo and Rio de Janeiro. Women in the Northeast are paying through their bodies, anguish and lives as a result of both the greater poverty and the lesser access to health and family planning services than in the other regions.

As might be expected, we found an inverse correlation between age and number of children, particularly in the Southeastern urban sites, with women who had had five or more children being in the older age cohorts (late forties to sixties). This pattern was less true in Pernambuco, where several women in their thirties had five or more children. But for most younger rural respondents, lower fertility is a direct response to subsistence needs. Declining fertility generally in Brazil, as suggested earlier, is a function of economic conditions, women's rising labour force participation, urbanization, and a new ethos disseminated by the media, whose impact is greatest on younger generations. Yet it is also noteworthy that increasing numbers of women of all ages are now ready and willing to say openly, 'I want no more children',[22] they feel entitled to regulate their fertility, and are acting on this sense of entitlement. Our respondents clearly demonstrate this attitudinal shift, but the methods they use to exercise their entitlement are limited and often risky.

As noted earlier, sterilization is by far the most frequently used method of contraception among Brazilian women, followed by the pill and supplemented heavily by induced abortion. The respondents in our study generally follow this pattern but with significant differences, since the proportion who have been sterilized is lower, and that currently using no contraceptive method is higher, than the most recent national data show for the three regions.[23] Although relatively few of our respondents were using the pill at the time of the study, many more had tried it at some time during their childbearing years. Numerous women in all three groups, however, voiced complaints about the pill's side effects and, in some cases (more so in Rio de Janeiro and Pernambuco), its efficacy. These problems were often used as justification for tubal ligation – by the women, their doctors, or both. Women's stories, particularly in the Northeast, express fears of infection, cancer, or 'wasting away' due to pill use, making sterilization appear harmless in contrast. While in certain cases their fears may have been based on ignorance, they more often reflect real experiences (their own as well as those of friends and neighbours) and the compounded effects of general poor health and malnutrition.

In all three research sites, the condom was repeatedly cited as a preferred method of contraception, particularly for younger women, to avoid HIV/AIDS and STDs. However, very few women in the study actually use this method, claiming refusal by their husbands or partners. On the other hand, the testimony of the male respondents in Pernambuco and other qualitative studies indicate that women are not only deferring to men but in reality also dislike the condom and are simply declining to insist on its use (compare Barbosa and Villela 1996 and Badiani *et al*. 1996 and 1997). In São Paulo, where AIDS is the prime cause of death among women aged 20–35, this finding is particularly troubling. Sterilized, menopausal and pregnant women (as well as women who rely on the pill, rhythm or abortion) are not using any method of protection against HIV or other STDs. This disturbing tendency among our research participants has also been found in other studies of Brazilian women (Barbosa and Villela 1996; Guimarães 1996). Yet, as we saw, the same older São Paulo women who are reluctant to take care of and demand safer sex for themselves are insisting that their daughters do so by using condoms.

The reasons why poor women in Brazil are more likely to use sterilization or abortion rather than nonpermanent methods to control their fertility are many and complex. Mainly they involve the larger context of poverty, work, and lack of child care; inadequacies and distortions in existing reproductive health services; and the recalcitrant attitudes of men – all of which are far more extreme in the Northeast. Though less frequently in Rio, many women we spoke with in all three sites had to contend with the resistance of husbands and partners to their efforts to avoid pregnancy. Especially in Pernambuco, men would often show indifference or openly sabotage such efforts. One participant in the focus groups reported that her husband 'used to snoop in my things' until he eventually found birth control pills hidden in a suitcase:

He knew what they were for. The label had all this. He asked me, 'What do you have these for? Don't you want to live with me anymore?' I said, 'Yes, because you are the father of my children and you must help me raise them.' ... [Then] he took the pills, put them in water, dissolved them and buried them, saying, 'If I see these pills again you will pay me.' Now, 'pay me' means he will beat me.

Problems with use of safe, nonpermanent methods of contraception among women in our research sites also derive from inadequacies in the health care system: the inaccessibility of public reproductive health services that offer a wide range of contraceptive methods, information and counselling; as well as the pressures and gender biases of doctors. Medical approaches are so taken for granted by men and women that 'the pill' is a term used synonymously with 'birth control'. With regard to both fertility control and childbearing, medical providers in Brazil tend to negate women's role as decision makers, especially if they are poor, and to promote methods (tubal ligation and the pill) that they consider more 'efficient' for such women (Gonçalves 1992). Moreover, the prevailing medical culture in Brazil favours surgical and invasive methods. One of the men who participated in the Pernambuco focus groups spoke of the standardization of medical procedures in the public healthcare system: 'doctors tell every woman who goes to the hospital to have her tubes tied, have a cauterization ... and now they all have to have a perineum plastic insert to lift their bladder. They say it has to be done.' Yet doctors appear to be just as resistant as most men in Brazil to vasectomies,[24] as this report by a woman in the São Paulo focus groups suggests: 'Then I made a big effort to convince my husband to get a vasectomy. When we got there, that bastard of a doctor told him, "I'm already going to open her belly [to perform a Caeserean section delivery], why would I operate on you?"'

The disrespectful attitudes and behaviour of medical providers are significant factors pushing women to avoid clinic visits whenever possible and thus to make contraception a one-time proposition, through sterilization. In addition, the rural women in Pernambuco have a much more difficult time accessing services, whatever their quality, since stocking up on contraceptives means making a trip to town to seek medical services and a pharmacy. Sterilization thus becomes the most practical and least onerous alternative, helping women to avoid the worst costs of contraception, including the harassment and violence of husbands. Yet female sterilization, even when voluntary, is not without its own negative consequences for women. Respondents in both São Paulo and Rio de Janeiro expressed concern about an association between tubal ligation and sexual problems; those in Pernambuco, on the other hand, viewed frigidity resulting from tubal ligation more serenely, since they were eager anyway to get rid of the burden of unwanted sexual intercourse. In Pernambuco and Rio de Janeiro, tubal ligation is experienced by most women as salvation, while in São Paulo it brings a mixture of relief and regret, particularly among women who form new relationships or experience child loss (Vieira and Ford 1996). One activist in her mid-forties told a story that resonated with others in the same group. After having been sterilized at the age of twenty-eight, on the birth of her only son, the infant suddenly died: 'I couldn't accept that I had lost my son, the only one I had, and that I couldn't have another one.... I went crazy.'[25]

The same social conditions that impel women towards sterilization and undermine their use of nonpermanent forms of contraception also motivate their frequent recourse to abortion. We found abortion common in all three of our research sites despite its illegality, as it is among Brazilian women generally (Singh and Sedgh 1997). Approximately 15 per cent of all our women respondents admitted to having undergone one or more induced abortions, although many more had undergone miscarriages. The incidence of abortions was much higher among the Rio domestic workers (with 31 per cent reporting having had an abortion), probably because of their greater likelihood of not being in a domestic relationship and the risk of losing their job if they are pregnant. In Pernambuco, we suspect that an undetermined proportion of events reported as 'miscarriages' (aborto espontaneo) were actually induced, given the common practice in the region to use abortive teas 'to bring on menstruation' as well as the ambiguity of the language (the same word in Portuguese, aborto, means both 'abortion' and 'miscarriage'). This cultural understanding came up in a focus group session on contraception, when a nonactivist woman said: 'We've got to use the medicine at the beginning, not to let the baby grow; take it when one is in doubt, after one month of pregnancy. Then the menstruation comes and it's not abortion.'[26] This was a consistent view among all our rural participants, both men and women.

In Rio de Janeiro, nonactivist women resorting to abortion had no qualms and could generally count on a support network that referred them to medical assistance and helped them financially. Among the São Paulo women, the Catholic Church is more influential and the issue is intensely polemical, yet the focus is on the concrete risks of an illegal abortion rather than on morality. Many times women we interviewed rationalized their abortions in terms of their communion with a forgiving and compassionate God, in a direct negotiation that notably bypasses the clergy.[27] As one São Paulo leader said in the focus groups: 'When I was there with my daughter, bleeding profusely, I begged God for everything to be okay; I asked for much forgiveness because I knew it was a sin. But I knew only God could understand my need.'

This belief in a forgiving God, who steers women through their abortions rather than condemning them, is present among the rural women as well. A nonactivist rural worker in the Pernambuco focus group of women over forty-five told about her induced abortion, which lasted for four days and ended in severe haemorrhage and hospitalization: 'It's a sin to kill. I had already had one abortion. At the drugstore they gave me a very strong medicine to abort, I had a haemorrhage, I almost died. I was afraid of dying and leaving my daughter. But I think God forgives.'[28]

These stories tell us the lengths to which women are willing to go in order to control their fertility in the context of illegality and religious and moral condemnation. Indeed, what is striking is not so much the influence of religion but rather the inventiveness of women in navigating around it. While they acknowledge the labelling of abortion as a sin, women's acceptance of abortion as a part of reproductive life is implicit in their routine practice of it. And, while some seem to accept the barriers and hardships put in their way (for example, severe haemorrhaging) as a form of penance, others express great anger at the costs to women's health and lives of illegal abortion. More than anything, this anger is directed at the callousness of health providers. As one focus group participant in São Paulo exclaimed:

> So many women die, they have a hemorrhage, arrive at the hospital and [the staff] don't care, they don't give a damn. Then, what happens? That bleeding woman will die for lack of medical attention in the hospital, and this happens every day.

The majority of women interviewed in São Paulo favoured voluntary and safe abortion, stressing their revulsion at the violence women who have had illegal abortions suffer at the hands of the health services. In Pernambuco as well, many women criticized the inhumane manner in which incomplete abortions were handled in the public health system. Although none of them appeared to favour legalization, it seems that class and gender have a stronger influence than religious norms in shaping rural women's attitudes toward the realities of abortion. This was evident in comments by agricultural workers in the focus groups: 'Many doctors are opposed to it. If they know the woman induced the abortion, she is in for it. Maybe if you are paying, things change, but when it is free ...'; 'If you are rich they do not scold you, but if you are poor they do'; 'If I am rich I can have an abortion, but if I am poor I can't?'

Conclusion

The three groups we studied are part of the struggle for *cidadania,* and as such, their sense of entitlement and notion of rights in regard to reproduction and sexuality tend to be strongest in connection to the public sphere, as shown in their complaints about the public healthcare system. But the steps between a sense of entitlement or injustice and a perceived capacity to make claims on public agencies to ensure enforcement of established rights, or to assert new rights, remain elusive. Many of the women we interviewed, especially the rural and domestic workers, still feel confined to seeking individual solutions to the injustices they experience in their reproductive and sexual lives.

None the less, we found the majority of our respondents to be anything but passive in the face of obstacles to their reproductive self-determination presented by medical providers, husbands, and the Church. Rather, their testimonies reveal heroic efforts to gain some control over their fertility and sexuality, despite the disproportionately high price they often pay. They seek out help among their personal relations or in the movement to secure money for an abortion or tubal ligation, someone to look after their children or a place to live; they make demands for shared domestic labour on their spouses and children; they defy religious prejudices against abortion by calling on a woman-friendly deity; and they encourage their daughters to be more sexually enabled and informed – all in the hope of actively improving their lives and the lives of future generations. Having suffered the consequences of poverty, traditional gender roles, poor health care (or its total absence), and the virginity myth that kept them ignorant of their own bodies and sexuality, the older generations of women hope their own daughters will have an education and a profession, marry later, have fewer children, and achieve full status in the public sphere of paid work and *cidadania*. New, more liberal attitudes about sexual education for young people not only spring from fears of the HIV-AIDS epidemic but also reflect the impact of feminism, urbanization, the media, and women's desire for a freer life.

In nearly all cases, we found that women's participation in social movements tends to increase their sense of reproductive and sexual entitlement by strengthening their self-esteem, increasing their access to information, and facilitating their development of social and political awareness and skills in regard to the larger community. Yet some nonactivist women too were unusually assertive with regard to such issues as the division of household labour and child care, traditional virginity norms, or their right as women to sexual pleasure in a relationship. The most important factor triggering their sense of entitlement, we found, was their engagement in paid work outside the home. In its more positive aspects, such work offers women mobility, access to information, new social relations, and some degree of economic independence. Nonactivist women workers not only have a sense of their status as rights bearers through employment legislation; they also learn the meaning of exploitation on the job. Some of the nonactivist domestic workers we interviewed had applied a notion of equality and fairness emerging from their sense of themselves as equal workers and family providers in order to challenge traditional gender arrangements within the family and make demands on their husbands or partners and children. Some of the rural workers laid strong claim to the notion that sexuality is healthy and positive, that a woman's body is her own.

While activities in community organizations and work facilitate women's development of a sense of entitlement, however, the tasks and responsibilities of reproduction serve as obstacles to its realization. All the women in our study began participating in the tasks of social reproduction as young daughters and continue to be engaged in such work well beyond menopause or sterilization as mothers, grandmothers, aunts, and domestic workers. Their experience indicates the complexity of reproductive work, and the inadequacy of the concept of 'reproductive years' as biologically determined, since reproduction ends for masses of Brazilian women in sterilization instead of menopause.

Despite the cultural idealization of the maternal role, in practice motherhood brings material, social, political and health deficits for women. As wives, mothers and workers their daily life is characterized by an overload of work that is detrimental to their health, especially their reproductive health. This problem is most severe for rural workers, whose socioeconomic conditions are most precarious and who have more children, more pregnancy and child losses, and the least access to adequate health care. Perversely, older women's health problems justify the maintenance of such arrangements for girls, who take over their sick mothers' domestic obligations. Thus, domestic life is marked by unrewarded effort and gender inequality at all stages of women's life cycle.

Pernambuco and São Paulo women in particular feel unappreciated and exploited by their children and spouses, with little room for negotiation in decision making. Although women point to their children as what is most important to them, their descriptions of daily life and family relations are permeated by the loneliness of motherhood, the oppressiveness of household work, and the all-too-frequent risk of spousal violence and abuse. Reproductive labour and the lack of child care limit women's mobility and, for some, their possibility of participating in social movements or work outside the home. Most of the São Paulo women had left the formal job market once they had children, whereas most of the domestic workers in Rio de Janeiro found it necessary to forgo sexual relationships and the opportunity to raise children of their own. It is thus no accident that, among the women in our study, activists were mainly childless women or women with grown children who were free from the obligations of childrearing. Nor is it surprising that many of our married respondents look back nostalgically on their single years and that single motherhood is becoming a growing lifepath for Brazilian women.

A combination of barriers – spousal opposition, religious taboos, a hostile medical culture and inadequate health services – inhibits the women we interviewed from regular use of contraception as a means of postponing or spacing children. As the burden of biological and social reproduction increases with age, they become more active in determining both their fertility and their sexuality, enduring the difficult side-effects of the the pill and health risks of illegal abortions, leaving abusive marriages, and sometimes finding more satisfying relationships. Sterilization, perceived as the definitive solution to their reproductive problems, epitomizes the pattern that associates fertility control with an end to childbearing. The medical system offers women this 'final solution' in a context of few alternatives (a context the medical system itself helps to create).

Reproductive hardships are enhanced by women's lack of access to information regarding their body, sexuality and reproduction, which increases their vulnerability and fear. All the women we encountered in this study recognize the importance of sexual education and medical information for themselves and their daughters to exercise sexual and reproductive rights. In many ways this yearning for reproductive and sexual knowledge transgresses traditional notions of femininity that derive from Catholic religious teachings that extol virginity and maternity. Whether through appealing to the beneficent personal God of popular religion to justify their abortions or arguing in favour of their right to touch and take pleasure in their own bodies, many women we interviewed are clearly breaking with established religious norms concerning reproduction and sexuality. If not for themselves then surely for their daughters, if not through their words then through their actions, they are claiming authority over their reproductive and sexual lives. Gender and class intersect here in motivating the anger of women in all three sites against the insults and injuries they confront from the healthcare system. Gradually, as they learn to act as reproductive and sexual agents, Brazilian women engaged in social movements are transforming an ethic of suffering and penitence into one of entitlement and citizenship.

Notes

1 The women's movement in Brazil has succeeded in winning codification of many significant rights that now provide a formal basis for transforming gender relations. With regard to work, the constitution prohibits gender discrimination in hiring, promotion and wages; guarantees paid maternity leave without risk of job loss for up to 120 days, as well as paternity leave for up to 5 days; and gives women the right to own and use land in both urban and rural areas. In addition, it declares equal rights and obligations for men and women in marriage (Alvarez 1990; Pitanguy 1994). For the recent history of democratization, see Stepan 1989.

2 Brazil is also a signatory to the Interamerican Convention on Women's Civil Rights (1948), the Interamerican Convention on Women's Political Rights (1948), the Convention on Women's Political Rights (1952), and the Convention for the Elimination of All Forms of Discrimination Against Women (1981).

3 While the average monthly household income of families headed by men in 1990 was US$705.60, that of female-headed families was only $291.20 (PNAD 1990, cited in Berquó, Araújo and Sorrentino 1995).

4 In fact, recent scholarship makes clear that the rapid fertility decline since 1970 was not the result of an aggressive, deliberate population control strategy but rather of modernization and socioeconomic change, economic pressures, urbanization, and the unintended outcomes of public policies – all of which have resulted in higher costs of raising children and thus a lowering of family size preferences (Martine 1996). Moreover, these changes in economic and social conditions have both contributed to and been reinforced by important changes in the domain of popular culture, including

mass dissemination of television images that encourage consumerism and small family size. In turn, the massive growth in the numbers of industrial and service workers has vastly increased the numbers of people who are both exposed to the commercial media and constrained by economic circumstances, thus amenable to a capitalist ethic favouring fewer children (Faria 1989).

5 In 1965, the International Planned Parenthood Federation established BEMFAM (Civil Society for Family Welfare in Brazil), a private institution to provide free family planning services and conduct advocacy (Barroso and Bruschini 1989).

6 Only a handful of hospitals provide this service, always after long and difficult negotiations. The struggle to convince public services to provide legal abortions is a major focus of the women's movement. On 20 August 1997, the Constitution and Justice Committee of the Congress approved a legislative proposal to regulate provision of legal abortions by health care services in those instances required by the Penal Code (risk of life to the pregnant woman and rape).

7 Before 1997, a tubal ligation could be performed legally and recorded in official medical records based on medical testimony that another pregnancy would endanger the woman's health or life, in which case the state pays for the surgery. See Berquó 1993; Barros et al. 1991; Faúndes and Ceccatti 1991; and Vieira and Ford 1996. The Constitution of 1988 mandated family planning as a basic right, but only in 1997 did this become part of the ordinary law establishing clear rules for counselling and service provision regarding sterilization.

8 Estimates based on hospitalizations for complications indicate that the abortion ratio (per 100 pregnancies) for Brazil overall in 1991 was 31.2; for Rio de Janeiro, 38.5; for São Paulo, 32.5; and for the Northeast, 37.9 (Singh and Sedgh 1997, Table 1).

9 The seven organizations are, in Rio de Janeiro, CEPIA (Cidadania, Estudos, Pesquisa, Informação e Ação), which has long worked with the domestic workers' union; in Recife, SOS CORPO, which has a longstanding relation with MMTR-NE; and, in São Paulo, the Coletivo Feminista Sexualidade e Saúde, the Equipe de Comunicação em Sexualidade (ECOS), FALA PRETA-Organização de Mulheres Negras, Sempreviva Organização Feminista (SOF), which has worked for years with the MSZL, and the Fundação Carlos Chagas, a social science research centre whose PRO-DIR Programme sponsors research throughout Latin America on reproductive rights and health.

10 A total of 75 respondents (54 women and 21 men) participated in Pernambuco; 54 women in Rio de Janeiro; and 50 women and 3 men in São Paulo.

11 Three men interviewed in São Paulo, affiliated with MSZL.

12 Portella's data indicate that the working conditions of domestic workers in Rio de Janeiro are similar to those elsewhere in Brazil (Portella 1993).

13 Peasants include the landless (sem terra), both those who lost their property and those who never owned any; proletarianized agricultural workers, hired for wages to work on great plantations and in extraction fields; small landowners who work in subsistence agriculture, in commercial cooperatives, or as independent producers directly for the local market; and 'integrated' farmers (integrados), who sell their entire production to a single industry.

14 The region formed by the cities Santo André, São Bernardo and São Caetano, containing much of São Paulo's metallurgical and mechanical industries. It is also the place where the new union movement in Brazil emerged and the Workers' Party, the main leftist group in Brazil today, was originally formed.

15 There were no participants in the under-21 age category among the Rio domestic workers.

16 According to FIBGE, the Brazilian population is composed of blacks, whites, pardos

(mestizos) and *amarelos* (yellow-skinned). The self-perception of the individuals interviewed for demographic research determines to which of these groups they belong. There has been much criticism aimed at this classification system and its definitions based on perceived skin colour. Its impact is to dilute the social importance of the black race, making it one end of a continuum that leads to increasing degrees of whiteness. This ideological process of 'whitening' the black race challenges the social construction by blacks of their own identity. The category *amarelos*, on the other hand, ends up mixing all indigenous groups with Asians, which is also very confusing and denies the distinct realities of those groups. To avoid these complexities and their ideological baggage, we adopted the simpler classification used in Table 2.2.

17 One of the first qualitative feminist studies of Brazilian women's reproductive and sexual life histories in the early 1970s, conducted by Grupo CERES (1981), presented an extensive analysis of the silence surrounding the female body. For more recent analyses of how Brazilian women negotiate sexuality and their bodies, see Desser 1993; Guimarães 1996; Heilborn 1996; Parker and Barbosa 1996; Quintas 1987; and Victora 1995.

18 Data from several recent national opinion surveys confirm the testimonies of our respondents that attitudes of Brazilian parents, especially mothers, toward the importance of sex education for young people have undergone dramatic changes. According to the results of a 1994 study conducted in São Paulo and three other state capitals by the Data Folha Institute, increasing numbers of parents support sex education in the schools or through health clinics, though they feel unable to provide this information to their children themselves.

19 Council members, who represent the most politically active of our respondents, had complicated reasons for worrying about a daughter's possible pregnancy. In addition to their concern about their daughters losing ground in education or professional development, they also were worried about being criticized socially for not being 'good' mothers, for not having protected their daughters sufficiently.

20 In analysing the links between domestic violence and women's reproductive health, Lori Heise suggests that the increased risk of battering during pregnancy is a pattern existing in many parts of the world (Heise 1995).

21 In rural areas (and to a lesser extent in urban areas too), the work of social reproduction traditionally incorporated female kin, neighbours and godmothers; children circulated among houses of relatives and neighbors. More recently, migration, urbanization, family dispersal, the schooling of girls, the instability of conjugal arrangements, and the entry of women of all ages into the labour market (formal and informal) have limited such possibilities. Thus the circle of available female kin to help with household labour has narrowed to include only young daughters and nonworking grandmothers, but children still circulate widely among relatives and neighbours.

22 In 1986, the main argument for tubal ligation in Brazil was 'health reasons'. By 1992, this motive had lost ground in a number of states to 'I already have all the kids I want' (Berquó, Araújo and Sorrentino 1995:99).

23 Twenty-six per cent of the respondents in Pernambuco have had tubal ligations as compared with 27 per cent of those in São Paulo and 16 per cent of those in Rio de Janeiro. The majority in all three sites reported they were currently using 'no method' of (nonpermanent) contraception. This fact may reflect not only reliance on sterilization and abortion but also the relatively high number of older and post-menopausal women included in our study. In the case of the Rio respondents, the high percentage (relative to Rio generally) who are neither sterilized nor using any method of contraception also reflects the occupational situation of domestic workers,

discussed earlier, many of whom are virtually celibate.

24 None of the male respondents or partners of women respondents in the communities we studied had had vasectomies. This mirrors national patterns, where vasectomies are rare; see Berquó, Araújo and Sorrentino 1995.

25 We suspect that such feelings of regret among women in São Paulo reflect the influence of feminist groups with whom they have come into contact and who are critical of the prevalence of sterilization among poor and black women in Brazil, as well as the focus of the MSZL on health issues.

26 Leal and Lewgoy (1995), in their study of the social construction of abortion and personhood in Porto Alegre, found quite similar views.

27 This pattern has been noted in previous studies (Ávila 1993; Nunes 1994; Ribeiro 1994). An aspect of liberation theology, it reflects a longstanding popular tradition among the poor in Brazil, who interpret God as a personal saviour who understands their situation.

28 As both these quotes indicate, the use of Cytotec to induce abortion can be risky. Acquired in drugstores – actually through the black market, since government regulation of its distribution was introduced in 1991 – at exorbitant prices, the drug's most frequent result is to turn unwanted pregnancy into unfinished abortion, often with very heavy bleeding requiring subsequent hospitalization (Arilha and Barbosa 1993).

3 Women's Wit Over Men's
Trade-offs and Strategic Accommodations in Egyptian Women's Reproductive Lives

AIDA SEIF EL DAWLA, AMAL ABDEL HADI
AND NADIA ABDEL WAHAB*

The challenges to Egyptian women's reproductive rights can be understood only when placed in the larger cultural, political and historical context that comprises the realities of Egypt and Egyptians today. Foremost among these realities is the cultural and moral commonality that unites Egyptian women, deriving from a shared language, Arabic, and a common historical experience. This commonality of values transcends geographic and cultural divisions between urban and rural, the Delta (north) and Upper Egypt (south), Muslims and Copts (Egyptian Christians), and underlies the many points of contention and conflict our chapter will discuss.[1]

Yet differences among Egyptian women do exist that made this research for us a tedious and long journey. Carrying out the IRRRAG mandate meant intruding into the very private and difficult lives of many women too burdened with the tasks of day-to-day existence to name the strategies of survival and transgression they use. Moreover, as researchers we were faced with a dilemma when certain traditions that we ourselves perceive as harmful or degrading for women received a very different response from many of the women we interviewed. Not only are some of those traditions (in particular,

* The coordinating organization for the Egyptian IRRRAG team was the New Woman Research Centre in Cairo, founded in 1984. In addition to the three listed writers, we would like to acknowledge the participation of all team members: Aida Seif El Dawla, project coordinator and co-author of a background paper on the health context; Amani Kandil, fieldwork coordinator and author of a background paper on the political context; Mona Zulficar, author of a background paper on the legal context; Hala Shukrallah, author of a background paper on the socioeconomic context; Nadia Abdel Wahab, author of a background paper on the cultural context and leader of group discussions; Amal Abdel Hadi, co-author of a background paper on the health context and leader of group discussions; and Barbara Ibrahim, Mawaheb El Mouelhy, and Moushira Gazairy. We would also like to thank our research consultant, Carla Makhlouf Obermeyer. We were very lucky to have a consultant who was a woman from our region, who understood many of the underlying dynamics, and whose concern was to see more of the iceberg than its tip.

female circumcision) very deeply rooted, but they also serve a social function by appearing to provide protection and a sense of dignity for women, who thus may not seek to change them or be able to imagine an alternative way of life. It was a valuable if painful learning process for us to see the logic in practices antithetical to our own beliefs.

Our research probed into the meanings and experiences of the female body; that body which has been the excuse for women's oppression but also at times the source of their pride and strength. We had to ask about their sense of their rights and entitlements in reproductive decision-making, even though many of the women we interviewed are not even aware they are entitled to certain basic rights they do not yet fully enjoy. The reason for this lack of knowledge is not only deficient information but a whole cultural arrangement that both privileges tradition and allows for many breaches, provided they remain covert and do not challenge established power relations. Thus we found that our respondents rarely exhibit the two extremes of overt resistance or complete compliance in their reproductive and sexual behaviour. More frequently, they interweave elements of both; the outward image of accommodation acts as a cover for subtle mechanisms of subversion or transgression.

The very concept of 'reproductive rights' is not as resonant or clear in Arabic as it is in English. The Arabic equivalent (*al-hoqouq al-ingabiah*, referring literally to rights of giving birth) does not bear any significant meaning for most Egyptians; thus the term itself is not a slogan around which we can mobilize women. Rather, the concept implies a constellation of rights that women's and other groups in Egypt advocate under a variety of different issues and terms. To render it more relevant in the Egyptian context, the Egyptian IRRRAG team tried to translate the concept of reproductive rights in a way that would relate these rights to real problems as identified and reconstructed by Egyptian women. We understand reproductive rights as basic human rights which include the political right to free, uncoerced choice and the real possibility of exercising such choice. They also imply fundamental economic rights of access to health care, education, employment opportunities, welfare, property, and legal services. In other words, we do not posit reproductive rights only within the narrow confines of the female body; rather we conceptualize them at the macro as well as the micro level through historical, societal, political, and economic conditions. These wider spheres determine the limits within which reproductive rights may be formulated, violated, exercised, and/or transformed.

The National Context

The social and economic situation

Changes in social and economic conditions have opened the way for the renegotiation of gender relations and relations of power generally in Egypt.

The slow but determined erosion of welfare state reforms enacted under the Nasser government have on the one hand burdened families with insurmountable financial problems but at the same time challenged traditional gender roles and forced families into reconsidering and contesting these roles. In Egypt as elsewhere, structural adjustment programmes (SAPs) – adopted by successive governments since the 1970s in response to pressures from the International Monetary Fund (IMF) and the World Bank – first struck at basic services, hitting health and education most heavily. SAPs have brought changes in national policy encouraging widespread privatization in health, education, social services and employment. These changes have had a disproportionately negative impact on women, especially the urban working-class and middle-class women who in the 1960s were the primary beneficiaries of state sector employment and benefits (Hatem 1994). Health care, previously provided through free public facilities that prioritized maternal and child health, is now becoming an unaffordable luxury for poor Egyptians.

The gender-related hardships incurred through SAPs have affected women both as housewives and as workers. Soaring food prices due to the withdrawal of government food subsidies intensify the burdens they face daily in food provision and household budgeting. In addition, privatization of both industry and social services and imposition of stringent neoliberal employment policies have resulted in endemic high unemployment. In the 1960s and 1970s, fully half the female labour force in Egypt was employed in the state social services and manufacturing sectors, as opposed to one-quarter of the male labour force; thus cutbacks in these sectors have affected women twice as heavily as men (Hatem 1994). As growing numbers of both men and women are forced to join the high-risk, low-benefit private sector or fall into unemployment or casual work, Egyptian households are increasingly reliant on the labour of women and even of children to avoid destitution. One recent study shows that three-fifths of all households nationwide are now living on two incomes (Korayem 1991).

A proportion of married women in Egypt have always worked for wages, either outside or within the home; but with the decline in public sector jobs they have had to rely more and more on informal, low-paid and marginal jobs. Official figures show that women's participation in the formal labour force has increased from 4.2 per cent in 1966 to an estimated 22 per cent in 1994 (UN 1995a, Table 11; Moghadam 1993). When the definition of work is broadened to include their participation in the informal domestic sector, however, the figure expands significantly, already reaching an estimated 35.4 per cent by the early 1980s (Zaalouk 1985). Other studies suggest an even greater disparity between official figures and reality, especially in agriculture, where women are doing more work than men.[2]

Compounding the social disruptions introduced by SAPs, labour migration to oil-rich countries has redefined economic relations in Egypt and profoundly affected gender roles on several levels. First, those women left behind were forced to replace absent male labour power and so had to enter the workforce. Second, they now had the responsibility of being heads of households, a role previously unfamiliar to many women who until then had lived in the shadow of male authority. According to a recent study, at least 16 per cent – and possibly as many as 22 per cent – of Egyptian households are now headed by women (Badran 1995). Moreover, migration often means a move to urban centres, exposing rural women to new forms of social organization that deprive them of traditional kin networks and support systems (Zaalouk 1985).

Despite the need for female income and labour, women who work for wages are not allowed to do so in peace. The gender bias of the workplace, state policies actively discouraging women from working, and the prevailing social conservatism – reinforced more recently by Islamist rhetoric – all converge to place women in a double bind. In the public sector, long the largest single employer of women, officials target women – viewed by all as secondary earners – as the obvious candidates to lose their jobs in a campaign of downscaling. A new unified labour law, drafted by government officials in consultation with private businesses and government-controlled unions, overturns the existing labour and reproductive rights of women workers. Designed to free business from worker protections enacted under the Nasser regime, the new law among other things limits women to no more than two maternity leaves during their working lives. An explanatory appendix admits that the law 'neglects some humanitarian aspects' but claims it is intended to 'encourage the state's population policy'. From the government's perspective, driving women out of the formal workforce is aimed both at securing positions for displaced male workers and addressing the strong exhortations of Islamists that women's 'natural place' is in the home. Women, on the other hand, find themselves caught between their need and that of their families that they continue working in the formal sector and their desire – and basic right – to have the number of children they want.[3]

With respect to education, the picture is decidedly mixed. On the one hand, girls' enrolment in primary and secondary education improved dramatically during the 1980s (from 54 per cent to 81 per cent) (UN 1995a). Nevertheless, government subsidies for education, as for health, declined under SAPs; the rate of adult female literacy remained among the lowest in the world; and the gender gap in school enrolment persisted, most severely for rural areas (UNDP 1996). When education becomes economically inaccessible, girls are the first to be held back because of cultural influences favouring education of sons. According to the UNDP's Egypt Human Development Report for 1995, 62.5 per cent of all rural girls aged 6–15 years were enrolled in primary school as opposed to 80 per cent of rural boys in the same age group. This and other recent trends – such as the reappearance of child domestic workers ten years old and younger – suggest that untold numbers of Egyptian girls are falling through society's net, exploited and forgotten by statistics, doomed to remain at the margins with little known about their problems or suffering.

The political situation

During the past two decades, Egyptian women have been fighting to retain political and civil rights previously won, at least on paper, and now threatened on more than one front. In 1956, we became the first national group of women among Arab countries to be granted the right of parliamentary participation. However, despite decades of struggle begun in the 1920s by Egyptian feminists seeking women's equality, in that same year, 1956, the Nasser government dissolved political parties, independent political organizations, and the Egyptian Feminist Union (in existence since 1923) (New Woman Research and Study Centre 1996; Badran 1994). This meant that, while women and men had equal political rights to stand for parliament and vote, both had actually lost the right to independent political organization. In 1976, the government of President Anwar Sadat began to reintroduce a limited multiparty political system, but these parties were mainly a formalistic veneer remote from community concerns and thus from the prospects and problems of women. Two decades later, the situation had not changed dramatically: political parties remain elite organizations addressing a narrow audience.

The most popular political trend in today's Egypt is the Islamist movement, which is still prohibited by law from forming itself into a political party.[4] During the 1980s, this movement gained significant popularity and wider representation in the parliament, but it did so at the expense of women as a political force. In 1979 a new election law had been passed setting a quota of 30 seats for women in the Egyptian People's Assembly and thus raising the percentage of female members from 2 to 9 per cent (Megahed 1994). The first move of Islamist groups in parliament was the exertion of pressure on other members to abolish the women's quota – a compromise of women's rights to which the government and opposition parties acceded. In 1986 the Supreme Constitutional Court ruled that a minimum quota of seats for women violated the constitution; in subsequent elections the proportion of women holding seats in parliament thus dropped to 2.2 per cent, or 10 out of a total of 444 seats (Mossa'ad 1996; Zulficar 1994).

Feminist organizations working in Egypt face a variety of obstacles on all sides. Along with other organizations that work for human rights, democratic participation, and radical social change, they must contend with state repression through emergency laws that give the government wide policing powers and the right to suspend civil liberties. At the same time, feminists are also attacked by Islamist groups, who use women's issues as a battlefield on which to test their power *vis-à-vis* the state, sometimes even colluding with the state against feminist positions. A prime example of this tenuous relationship followed the success of women's health and rights nongovernmental organizations (NGOs) at the International Conference on Population and Development held in Cairo in 1994 in publicizing the issue of female circumcision, or female genital mutilation (FGM).[5] Succumbing to pressure from Islamist and other conservative groups, the Minister of Health issued a regulation reauthorizing the practice of FGM in public hospitals, where it had been prohibited for thirty-five years. Following a series of conflicting religious opinions, or *fatwas*, on the subject,[6] and persistent protests by feminists, the Minister of Health issued a new decree in 1996 prohibiting FGM generally, whether in public or private facilities. At the end of 1997, the high constitutional court in Egypt ruled in support of the ministerial ban. This ruling was a defeat for the conservative Islamist position on FGM and a positive statement signalling that Egypt now legally prohibits the practice. However, the law leaves dangerous loopholes in relation to medical 'indications' and could still be subjected to challenges in the courts, so women's rights activists in Egypt remain wary.

The legal context

Egypt was the first Arab country to ratify the Convention on the Elimination of All Forms of Discrimination Against Women (Women's Convention). Yet it did so with several serious reservations, above all objecting to the equal rights of women and men within marriage and divorce proclaimed in Article 16. The first Egyptian personal status law, based on *shari'a* (Islamic jurisprudence), was issued in 1925. In 1979 amendments were introduced granting a wife the right to divorce where her husband takes a second wife and the right to keep the marital house as long as she has custody of the children.[7] In 1985, however, Islamists in parliament managed to abolish those reforms. In theory, Egyptian law requires the consent of the bride to conclude a marriage contract or to authorize her father to sign such a contract on her behalf. At the same time, it does not allow women to marry without the agreement of their male guardian unless they were previously married or have reached the age of twenty-one. Moreover, despite a legal minimum age at marriage of sixteen for women (eighteen for men), the tradition of marrying off very young girls has remained prevalent, especially in rural areas.

Despite enlightened interpretations of Islamic *shari'a* that restrict men's right to polygamy (Musallam 1983; Obermeyer 1992 and 1994), Egyptian law at present allows polygamy and gives the husband a unilateral licence to divorce his wife. For a wife to obtain a divorce is a far more onerous process. The principles of *shari'a* recognize marriage as a civil contract and admit the wife's right to include a condition in the contract giving her the right to divorce. However, in practice precedents demonstrate that proving damage before a court is extremely difficult for a wife. She must establish at least one of the following grounds: that her husband has ceased to support her financially, that he has deserted her for more than one year, or that he suffers from sexual impotence or a chronic incurable disease she was unaware of at the time of the marriage. This process takes an average of five to seven years and often does not succeed (Zulficar 1994 and 1995).

Efforts to improve women's legal situation in personal affairs regarding marriage, divorce and motherhood are central to the activities of women's groups in Egypt. The new Personal Status Law, passed in 1985, imposes a legal obligation on the husband and the *maazoun* (official responsible for registering marriage and divorce contracts) to notify the wife if her husband divorces her or if a second marriage occurs (in the past, she was often left uninformed). At least this minimal guarantee assures her knowledge of such events and protects her financial and legal rights. Currently some women's groups are advocating a new marriage contract that would introduce optional conditions, including divorce on demand for the wife if her husband takes another wife (Bahey El Din 1997).

Induced abortion is presently prohibited under Egyptian law except when the continuation of pregnancy would endanger the woman's life or health. The penal code provides harsh penalties for any person, including a doctor or other professional, who intentionally causes abortion. Women who voluntarily undergo an abortion may also be penalized by up to three years in prison. The issue of voluntary induced abortion has been subject to much debate in Egypt between those who support continued legal restriction and those who advocate decriminalization during the first three months of pregnancy, in keeping with a major trend of Islamic doctrine (Omran 1992). Major differences in Islamic religious opinions regarding the legitimacy of abortion create a climate of moral confusion for Egyptian women who face unwanted or risky pregnancies.[9]

Religious and cultural constructions of gender and power

Most women in Egypt, whether Muslims or Copts, are religious insofar as they are believers who pray and fast regularly. Yet religious differences and opinions seem to have little effect on the reality of everyday life or on how women make the most basic decisions, including those regarding fertility. In the last analysis, tradition is the locus of the most salient norms by which most Egyptians judge women, and the prevailing cultural portrayal of women is much more determined by patriarchal vestiges than by religion.

Traditional views of women, and their reflections in popular culture, are highly contradictory. On the one hand, women are seen as influential members of households who use cunning, patience, endurance and enormous inner strength to maintain their families and ensure their survival and wellbeing. A familiar saying goes, 'Women's wit wins out over men's wit.' Even the passivity of some women is construed as an act of strength or as the only way of weathering a terrible storm. On the other hand, the culture also contains strong patriarchal tendencies signifying women's economic and social dependence on men, as suggested in this proverb: 'Shade of a man is better than shade of a wall.' This patriarchal tradition gets reinforcement from the currently dominant Islamist discourse, which focuses on women's subordination as a major tool of struggle for political power. Although Islamists' interpretations of religious texts hold women to be moral agents responsible for their actions, they clearly regard them as inferior to men in value and moral capacity. According to these interpretations, women's natural place is the home and their main duty is to care for their husband, see to his comfort, and raise their children according to religious teachings.

One crucial aspect of patriarchal tradition that survives in popular culture is the value placed on young women's virginity and honour – a non-negotiable matter for Egyptian women of all classes and religious backgrounds. The persistence of practices like showing a bloodstained towel after the first wedding night (sometimes referred to as 'showing the honour'), or its more drastic form, the *baladi dokhla*, is an obvious reflection of this pervasive code of values.[10] It is a public declaration that the woman has cherished her virginity and protected herself until the day of her marriage, thus preserving the family's honour and proving her sexual purity. Though nowhere sanctioned by religion – in fact, some religious leaders deplore the practice – the *baladi dokhla* is strongly accepted among many rural and urban working-class Egyptian women.

But in other respects popular culture directly undercuts Islamic religious teaching. For example, while polygamy is a right granted to Muslim men by the Q'uran under certain conditions, most Egyptians disdain it, and popular culture ridicules the practice.[11] We collected twelve proverbs about polygamy, of which only two were permissive. The rest clearly scorn polygamy, for example: 'You who take the husband of another woman, you are publicly ridiculed (*maskhara*)'; 'He is a loser who makes them [his women] his trade'; 'The gown of a second wife is bitter, whoever wears it is shameless,' and many others. This contradiction of religious doctrine represents one of several examples where religion and tradition do not agree, yet people find no difficulty in believing in both.

Egyptian society celebrates fertility and big families. This pronatalist tendency is deeply rooted in the culture, but Islamic religion plays a major role in encouraging it. One of the Prophet's sayings is, 'Marry and reproduce, I shall boast your numbers on doom's day'; and a second, 'The best of your women is she who has many births.' These sayings are frequently quoted by people who wish to have more children. One important reason for high fertility and ideal-family-size norms, especially among rural and less educated women and men and despite difficult economic circumstances, is the preference for sons. Having sons is considered an economic asset for the family, particularly given the privileged status of males in inheritance. Since males get twice the share of females, the birth of a son guarantees that any property will remain inside the family. Women when they marry move to their husband's household and, in the absence of a son, a share of the inheritance will go to the uncle or his sons. Therefore, a strong economic interest lies behind the perpetuation of patrilineal tradition.

Yet, alongside these pronatalist influences, many popular sayings discourage excessive childbearing: 'The more the children the fewer the resources'; 'The best offspring are a boy and a girl'. Some proverbs even ridicule women who have many children: 'A sour watermelon has many seeds'. Interestingly, these proverbs assume that it is women who are responsible for deciding on the number of children; men are nowhere mentioned as having any role in the matter. This is consistent with recent research showing that Egyptian women often exert substantial influence over household decisions about reproduction and fertility even when they may lack power in other domains (Naguib 1994; Nawar, Lloyd and Ibrahim 1994; Kishor 1995). Yet the cultural underpinnings of their reproductive power and sense of entitlement may not be sufficiently strong to offset the deficits that come from increasingly inadequate and inaccessible health services.

Health/reproductive health services

According to Article 10 of the 1956 constitution, one of the important responsibilities of the state is to guarantee health care for all citizens. The new health policy implemented in the 1960s created a country-wide network of rural health units, maternity and infant care centres and delivery and medical services to the mother and child at home (MCH), with family planning services as a central component (Egypt, Institute of National Planning 1994; Hatem 1994). This system, though comprehensive in scale, was limited in scope, since the centres provide their services only to married women and do not address the needs of adolescents or of adult women's general health outside the realm of MCH and family planning. Yet the initial impact on women's and children's health was beneficial, with maternal mortality declining by 50 per cent in the pre-1970 decades and infant mortality by 62 per cent (from 150 to 57 per 1,000 live births) between 1970 and 1990 (Hatem 1994, citing CAPMAS).

The introduction of SAPs in the 1970s brought a serious decline in public expenditure on health in Egypt and, with it, a sharp deterioration in the quality and accessibility of care. Cost recovery programmes in the health sector have been implemented with ruthless vigour, converting many previously free or low-cost services in public hospitals and clinics into paid services available only to those who can afford them. The past two decades especially have witnessed growing inefficiency in health care; a variety of factors are responsible, including shrinking government outlays and inequitable allocation of resources in relation to the majority population's real health needs. This is aggravated by the decentralized structure of the Egyptian health system, where different institutions operate side by side with little coordination.[12]

Although the MCH services described above continue to be provided by the state, theoretically free of charge, the availability of services is offset by their poor quality. Even with regard to family planning and the government's population control policy – promoted by international donors like USAID and the World Bank since the 1960s – services are not delivered effectively. While two-thirds of all married women in rural areas have access to family planning in their local village and 96 per cent of women live within 5 kilometres of a family planning provider, only 48 per cent of married women in Egypt overall, and 40.5 per cent of rural married women, were using any sort of contraceptive in 1995. In fact, surveys show that over two-thirds of the intrauterine devices (IUDs) in the country are dispensed through urban and private facilities (IUDs are the most prevalent method among current contraceptive users). Further, many women who rely on the pill, especially those who use government facilities, appear to be using it incorrectly, in part as a result of lack of instruction (EDHS 1992 and 1995; Trottier *et al*. 1994). Problems of access for rural women are reflected not only in their lower contraceptive use rates but their higher fertility, shown in Table 3.1.

Table 3.1 Total Fertility Rate and Contraceptive Use Among Ever-married Women

LOCATION	TOTAL FERTILITY RATE	CONTRACEPTIVE USE (%)*
Urban	3.0	56.4
Rural	4.2	40.5
Lower Egypt	3.2	55.4
Upper Egypt	4.7	32.1
Overall	3.6	48

*Currently married women ages 15-49, currently using contraception.
Source: EDHS 1995

Evidence suggests that underuse of the services is related to poor quality of care, which hinders actual accessibility. According to a 1992 study, reproductive health services suffer serious limitations as a result of technical incompetence and lack of training of providers, limited choice of family planning methods, lack of information and counselling given to clients, absence of follow-up mechanisms, and bad management (Egypt, Institute of National Planning 1994). Another study done in the same year showed that the majority of respondents would prefer to travel up to 30 kilometres if necessary to buy these services from general hospitals or private clinics, delaying visits until they have saved up the money (Cairo Demographic Centre 1992). One important reason women are avoiding the free or low-cost government services may be the disrespectful treatment they receive there. Doctors in the public health care system in Egypt tend to trivialize women's complaints about the most common side effects of medical contraceptives – for example, menstrual pains, headaches and irregular bleeding. They also dismiss or even ridicule women's sexual complaints, especially if the complaining woman is in her post-reproductive years (Seif El Dawla 1996). Medical providers, moreover, are typically insensitive and unaware about women's feelings of shame regarding a gynaecological exam (Younis *et al.* 1993). The medical profession – hierarchical, increasingly market-driven and hindered by undertrained and underpaid doctors – has little time or motivation to learn about women's perceptions of their well-being.

That *de facto* inaccessibility and poor-quality services have had dire consequences for women's reproductive health in Egypt seems evident based on several indicators. First, although maternal mortality declined in the 1960s, it remains today at 170 per 100,000 live births, putting Egypt in the medium range of developing countries (see Table 9.1). Second, contributing to maternal mortality and morbidity, 75 per cent of pregnant women in Egypt suffer from anaemia, 61 per cent receive no antenatal care, and nearly 64 per cent give birth unattended by any medical personnel[13] (UNDP 1996; EDHS 1995). Moreover, even in Cairo, where health facilities are more abundant and accessible than elsewhere in the country, many women suffer silently from high rates of maternal and gynaecological morbidity that often goes undiagnosed[14] (Younis *et al.* 1993; Khattab 1992).

But also contributing to maternal mortality and morbidity in Egypt is undoubtedly the persistence of illegal, unsafe abortion. No reliable data exist allowing accurate estimates of the incidence of illegal abortions in Egypt.[15] None the less, it is safe to assume that a prime result of the legal and moral ambiguity described earlier is a high proportion of such abortions – 46 per cent according to one source – that are either self-induced or performed by lay healers. These abortions use traditional and often dangerous methods, for example 'beating or violent massage of the abdomen, introducing plants, a catheter, feather or wire into the uterus, injecting substances into the uterus, drinking herbal preparations or taking various drugs' (El Mouelhy 1993: 114).

In sum, although Egyptian health officials have coopted the language of 'reproductive health', especially since the ICPD, in practice health services, whether public or private, still do not provide much beyond the bare minimum of family planning methods, and only to married women. Full access to reproductive rights remains a far-off and mostly disregarded ideal in Egypt.

Methodology and Description of Research Sites

Our field research was carried out in seven locations: two neighbourhoods in Cairo (Boulaq and Sakakini); three sites outside Cairo in the Delta region

(Lower Egypt), two urban and one rural; and two, one urban and one rural, in Upper Egypt. Communities where the research was conducted were all lower or lower-middle class. The capital city of Cairo, with a population of around 12 million by night and 16 million by day, hosts the extremes of wealth and poverty, sometimes literally abutting one another in adjacent neighbourhoods. Ongoing clearance of slum areas from the centre towards the periphery has now come to form a poverty belt surrounding the city. Inhabitants of these poor districts are mainly migrants from rural areas in Upper and Lower Egypt who either reside permanently in Cairo or come as day wage labourers working in construction and all kinds of odd jobs.

The division of the country into Upper Egypt (Sa'aid) and Lower Egypt (Delta) is both historical and cultural. Very broadly speaking, Delta Egyptians are known to be more outgoing and liberal in their worldview. Although Upper Egyptians also work traditionally in agriculture, it is the Delta people who are usually called peasants. Upper Egyptians are thought to be more politically and culturally conservative, their image associated with stubbornness, strict adherence to local tradition, vendettas and honour killings. Upper Egypt has long been considered difficult to change, despite the fact that the majority of the country's development projects take place there, especially in Menya, the governerate where we undertook our fieldwork. Today Upper Egypt is both the home of the majority of Egyptian Copts and the region where Islamists are strongest.

The Egyptian IRRRAG team is composed of women activists, professionals, scholars and researchers who share a concern for human rights and a particular interest in matters relating to women's health.[16] In the first phase of our process, we discussed the concept of reproductive rights in the Egyptian context as well as the difficulties of airing certain sensitive issues such as those related to sexuality, religion, or private strategies women use in their daily lives. The personal experiences of the team members became one important reference point in these exploratory discussions. To gain access to a socially and geographically mixed sample of women we had to rely on intermediaries, who were mostly NGOs working in the areas where we conducted our group discussions. These bridge groups, particularly the Coptic Evangelical Organization for Social Services (CEOSS), played a major role in facilitating our entrance into the local communities. Their field staff had the confidence of the men and women in the areas of research and so could bring a climate of rapport and trust to the group discussions, which was essential to the integrity of the research.

Research data were generated from 19 group discussions, 13 with women (85 participants) and 6 with men (39 participants), as well as 12 loosely structured in-depth interviews (women-only). Informants for the in-depth interviews were selected from both within and outside the focus groups (6 were nonparticipants in focus groups).[17] Focus groups were useful as a source of normative values and community expectations, whereas in-depth interviews tended to reveal more about actual behaviour and attitudes that might deviate from the dominant norms. Besides the differences between urban and rural and Muslim and Copt, both female and male respondents included a range of educational levels, age groups, and work experience as well as both married and unmarried individuals. Marital status even more than work outside the home or education seemed to be the most relevant indicator affecting women's perceptions of reproductive rights. In Egypt an unmarried woman is referred to as a 'girl' (*bint* in Arabic), irrespective of her age. The assumption is virtually universal that a woman who has never been married is by definition a virgin and that sexual experience is possible only within the parameters of marriage. Therefore, in the Egyptian context, marital status is the most critical differentiating factor when one is discussing how women perceive their bodies, sexuality and reproductive experience. Among our female urban respondents who were over nineteen at the time of the study, 14 out of 66, or 21 per cent, were unmarried, including 2 who had been married but were currently separated. Among the rural women over nineteen years (twenty years and older), only 2 out of 25, or 8 per cent, were unmarried.

One focus group was conducted with female medical students in the city of Mansoura in Lower Egypt. These educated young women are all associated with the Islamist political movement and as such are highly politicized. Though unrepresentative of Egyptian women as a whole, they do represent an important ideological and social presence in the current development of attitudes on sexuality, gender and society. We also convened a focus group of diversely situated men from each of the six communities where we conducted group discussions and interviews with women.[18] Our purpose in working with male groups was to compare women's perceptions of men's roles and attitudes with those of men themselves. Since men's views form a major component of the social environment in which women experience their reproductive rights or the absence thereof, we felt they should be part of the data.

Listening to Egyptian Women in Context

Socialization about gender and sexuality

From the day of her birth, an Egyptian girl's destiny is coloured by the popular tradition of son preference. This tradition is embodied in many proverbs and folk songs, as illustrated in the following lyrics: 'When they told me it was a boy, I felt strong and powerful and was given peeled eggs with a lot of butter/ But when they told me it was a girl, the house felt closed-in around me and I was given unpeeled eggs cooked in water.' Yet folk culture in Egypt also contains a double message about the worth of a girl child: on the one hand, she may bring shame to her family, but on the other it is the daughter who provides tenderness and support for her mother in old age.

Participants in both the group discussions and the in-depth interviews reflected this ambiguous theme. On initial inquiry, the majority of women respondents, both married and unmarried, asserted that there was no discrimination between boys and girls in their upbringing. More detailed questions, however, uncovered significant gender divisions. Most of the married women recited a long list of restrictions imposed on girls and women because of their sex, which they felt were reasonable or 'natural'. For example, a boy will not be blamed by the community for what he does but a girl will bring shame to her family if she does something wrong, since the girl carries the family's honour. An average Egyptian girl is expected to play and mix freely with her siblings, cousins and neighbours of both genders until puberty, when the mixing and play must be curtailed so that girls can prepare for womanhood. However, many of the women stated that times are changing and that girls are becoming 'equal' to boys because they are increasingly taking economic responsibility in their families, while boys need more monitoring to keep them out of trouble. Zeinab – thirty-five years old, illiterate, and employed in a sewing workshop – draws from her own experience to justify equal treatment of her two daughters and son:

> I do not discriminate among my children. They all are God's gift. It is true that in old times people used to privilege sons as the son will bring money to the family. Now both girls and boys are suffering. A woman even suffers more; in addition to her work outside the home she has to cope with pregnancy, childbirth and housework. I hope my girls will not have to work [so they can] avoid my agony.

Unmarried women also claimed that their families did not discriminate against them; differences in their chances for education and greater limits on their free mobility were seen as 'natural' because 'the roles are different'. Manar, a student from the urban Delta, stated that she has always been expected to make concessions to her brothers: 'for the older brother because he is older, and for the younger because I should be like a mother to him.' Iman, another student from the same area, bluntly said, 'Equal rights are just slogans.' Yet many accepted this division of roles with reluctance. In the rural sites, young women respondents expressed the wish to be boys in order to be able to have their own projects, travel abroad for work, support their families, and acquire more education. The Cairenes complained that their brothers had greater freedom to go out, have friends, come home late, do what they wanted without parental permission, dress as they pleased, form friendships and talk to the other sex. Most of the urban young women too wanted to be boys in order to have the same freedom as their brothers. Thus it would appear that many unmarried women may not be so accepting of gender discrimination. Wishing they could be men, or believing they would have to change their gender in order to gain more freedom, is a way of expressing dissatisfaction with the gender inequities they experience.

Men in the focus groups generally expressed a belief that they are superior to women, that boys and girls should be brought up differently and boys allowed more space. Men from Upper Egypt agreed with their Cairene counterparts on this, but they felt the girl is entitled to more care within the household because, as a future mother, she needs to have good health and education to be able to bring up her children properly. Also, having an education will assure her an educated husband who would know her value and respect her more. The verbal respect for girls' education among these male respondents contrasts, however, with the low level of schooling and literacy for rural girls cited earlier.

As Egyptian girls reach puberty, they are typically given very little if any information about sexuality and reproduction. Wafa'a, a Cairene, middle-aged married woman originally from Upper Egypt, recalled:

> I got my period when I was twelve years old, [but] no one had ever said anything to me. My mother used to tell me that I should take care of myself and be careful with boys. When I got my period I was so afraid that something wrong was happening. I did not tell anybody. I finally told my mother after nearly a year, although I am sure she knew much earlier. But she was very shy, and such topics are not a matter of discussion among mothers and daughters or sisters, not even friends or neighbours.

Reliable sources of information on sexuality and reproductive health for young unmarried women are practically nonexistent. The Egyptian educational system does not include sex education, nor does the health system provide such information except with regard to maternity. Although Islamic texts are open about sexual issues, in practice they are never discussed before marriage. It would be considered shameful, for example, for an unmarried woman to visit a gynaecologist.

Yet certain generational differences clearly emerged among our female respondents with regard to information on menstruation and sexual matters. Like Wafa'a, most of the married women said they were totally uninformed about menstruation: surprised, frightened, and embarrassed when 'it happened' but aware they were entering a new life phase: 'When I saw it [the menstrual blood] I knew I could no longer play around and run; I had to bear my responsibilities, preparing myself to be a woman.' On the other hand, the majority of unmarried women did know about menstruation before their cycles began. Very few received this information from their mothers, however, but rather from friends and classmates. When asked whether they would provide their daughters with this information, the majority of married women said they did not want 'to open the eyes of their daughters' prematurely; they would do so only at the time of menarche or marriage, 'when the information is necessary'. Unmarried women, however, expressed a more liberal attitude towards the importance of providing daughters with sexual and reproductive information at the onset of puberty.

This included the Islamist women, who felt that sexual and reproductive information before marriage is essential but would prefer it to come from the mother in order to avoid girls' exposure to erotic writings.

The extent to which sexuality is shrouded in mystery and an aura of danger for young Egyptian women, even at the level of information, is nowhere clearer than with respect to the 'secrets of the wedding night'. The majority of our married women respondents were not given any information on this subject before marriage; in only two groups (one in Cairo and one in urban Upper Egypt) did a majority know something about sexuality beforehand. Here too, however, generational differences are striking, since the majority of unmarried women seem to know what to expect on their wedding night. Most of those, both married and unmarried, who did receive this information as younger girls would like to inform their daughters to save them from fears, worries and problems associated with sexual ignorance. The Islamist women were very clear that young women should be informed about sex before marriage, one even suggesting sexual literacy classes for women, but only shortly before the wedding.

Female circumcision (FGM)

'Of course I was circumcised. What do you mean by this question? Do you think something is wrong with me? Everybody does it.' (Donia, forty-year-old domestic worker from Cairo, married twice with three children)

By the time a girl reaches puberty she will most likely have been circumcised, a procedure usually justified as a means to guard her from sexual promiscuity and dishonour. Female genital mutilation, known as *tahara* (literally, 'purity') in Egyptian common language, is a widely prevalent practice throughout the country (Toubia 1995). The results of the 1995 Demographic Health Survey (unpublished) show that 97 per cent of Egyptian women have been circumcised, and they include both Christians and Muslims.[19] Although most Islamic jurists have agreed that FGM is optional and not an obligation, its advocates continue to invoke religion to encourage the practice. Given the common misbelief that the practice is religiously mandated, it is not surprising that many of our women informants asked us about this. But the majority defended FGM as a tradition deeply rooted in their communities.

For most of the women we interviewed, and especially for the younger generations, FGM is a very painful memory. Hoda, a 23-year-old medical student and an Islamist, seemed about to cry while recalling her experience of being circumcised by the *daya* (midwife):

I cannot forget that day … I was deeply humiliated. A woman tied my arms behind my back, and two opened my thighs, and the *daya* was cutting my flesh while talking to attendants. They congratulated my family, since from now on my prayers and fasting would be accepted by God.[20]

Mary, a 50-year-old Christian food vendor from Upper Egypt, was circumcised at the age of six. She too found she 'could not forget that day', more embedded in her memory even than the pains of labour. With a few exceptions,[21] the unmarried women from rural Upper Egypt – all of whom had been circumcised – were mostly resigned to circumcising their daughters, feeling they have no choice. They view circumcision as necessary to comply with the expected norm and to control the sexuality of their daughters, in part to make prospective husbands feel confident should they need to travel abroad or be away from home. Circumcision for girls is a passport into social acceptance and belonging. Soheir is a part-time cleaning woman in a private hospital, thirty-eight years old, married with three daughters. She did not circumcise them because a woman doctor in the hospital advised her not to. But this decision causes her great anxiety:

> I am worried; we are common people and if the girls get married to someone who is [like us] he may find them strange and then be upset with them. I know that doctors do not circumcise their daughters, but then their daughters get married to doctors or architects like them who are used to that. I was going to circumcise them but the doctor told me they may bleed or get infections. I was scared so I did not do it.

It would seem, then, from our research findings, that Egyptian women are having to negotiate the conflicting pressures of religious authorities, medical authorities, class divisions, and above all traditional gender norms when it comes to FGM.

Circumcision was the cause of heated debate among women in the group discussions. Knowing that some of the researchers were physicians, they raised questions about whether practising circumcision is right or wrong. In one of the focus groups a noncircumcised woman claimed that the practice makes women sexually frigid. Others responded that 'it is better to be frigid than to desire her husband', since 'a circumcised woman has less desire [and thus] will not be at the mercy of her husband satisfying her needs. She will be stronger.' In other words, it would be better to cut off the part of her body that could put her at the sexual mercy of her husband than to be needy and vulnerable. This pattern in which women convert a physical and emotional violence into an empowering mechanism is one we encountered frequently.

Male respondents had a position on the issue of FGM quite different from the women's. Some said that it was a *sunna* (teaching of the prophet) while others said it was *haram* (prohibited by religion); but in either case the men seemed to think about the issue more abstractly, in terms of religious teachings, whereas the women's reference points were more often social (the status of daughters in the community, or the bargaining position of wives *vis-à-vis* husbands). The lenient attitude of some male respondents on an issue that so directly involves women's sexuality may be explained by their confidence that circumcision is one tradition that women themselves are committed to carrying out.

Entering marriage and sexual relations

CHOICE OF PARTNER

Decisions about marriage affect the whole life of an individual, especially in a society where it is very difficult for both Christian and Muslim women to get a divorce and where divorce is looked on as bringing shame to the whole family. For this reason, in most marriages the parents, and especially mothers, still play a crucial if not decisive role in choosing the partner. Soheir, like many other mothers we interviewed, wants to allow her three daughters some choice, but also wants to retain control over their decisions:

> I did not choose my husband. We were villagers and not enlightened. But my girls are educated, I should ask them before accepting a husband [for them], but also he should be suitable. I don't want any of them to choose a bad husband and regret her choice in the future, as I do now.

Most of the married women respondents were themselves in arranged marriages, with some variations. Women from the urban settings had more room for manoeuvre; several from the urban Delta site had tried openly to resist arranged marriage, but only a few were successful in managing to impose their decision on the family. Married women from Boulaq had all married of their own free will and rejected any kind of forced arrangement. 'I was in charge of the situation when it came to my marriage' was the clear statement of one Boulaqi woman.[22] Even in the more traditional situations, women may have exercised some hidden choice in the matter. One form of disguised resistance to an unwanted match is blackmail through refusal of marriage proposals. This is a well-known tactic to push the family into a position where they will eventually accept the girl's choice just to prevent her from remaining unmarried and becoming the object of gossip as well as a continued financial burden. Our in-depth interviews also made it clear that some of these arranged marriages had begun as love stories behind the backs of the family but then were put into the traditional formula. As Wafa'a said, 'He was our neighbour. He called on me, and when I felt he was serious, we agreed that he should come to my father. When I was asked, I said yes, I accept him.'

It is interesting to note the different and shifting positions with respect to the right of the girl to have a final say in her marriage. The majority of married women in the focus groups initially said the final decision should be the father's, yet on further probing or in individual interviews many said they will not force their daughter into a marriage even if they are convinced it is for her benefit. As some of the women from Upper Egypt put it, 'Things are changing now. Girls are educated and work outside the home. We will advise them, but the final decision should be theirs.' Among unmarried women the majority agreed that parents should have the final say but insist that girls should not be forced to marry someone they do not like and accept. Educated women were more assertive on this point; for example, Maha, a student from the urban Delta, argued emphatically, 'I have the first and last word over my marriage. I am the one who will live with him, I am the one who might suffer.' Some had already resisted: 'They did not agree to my fiancé at the beginning, but I insisted and now they all love him.' Only the Islamist young women claimed (contrary, ironically, to the Islamic text[23]) that it was the absolute right of parents to decide who and when a girl should marry. They explained, 'The girl cannot disagree with her family,' for, 'if [she] married against her family's will and has any problems with her husband, he will not respect her; if divorced, she cannot go back to her family'. This suggests that, besides patriarchal tradition, Islamist young women adhere to family obedience on the basis also of a practical calculation of future financial security.

In striking contrast to the older women respondents, the majority of men said the final decision about a marriage partner should belong to their daughters. They will try to convince a daughter of their opinion, but if they fail then it is up to her, 'she is free'. Even the minority who said the final decision is the father's would change their mind if the daughter is educated: 'Educated girls should be given more space, they are more able to make decisions.' The only male respondent who insisted on asserting his patriarchal authority in this matter – 'she will marry whom I choose' – was an old illiterate Cairene man who had no permanent job.

THE FIRST WEDDING NIGHT

> I married the ordinary way. The next morning my family asked me about the 'honour' [bloodstained handkerchief]. These things are important for women who go out and work. My husband was not concerned with that issue. He asked me, 'Why do you want to keep it?' But my brother thought I should.

Nour, a forty-year-old married woman with four children, has been working outside the home since she was fourteen, first in a factory and now in a community development association. She, like many women in Egypt, accepts the *baladi dokhla* (BD) ritual, despite the embarrassment and pain it causes her, since it protects her from being exposed to gossip after marriage. Aziza, a 28-year-old Cairene working woman who graduated from a secondary technical school and has been married for twelve years, says:

> It was the decision of my mother and aunts [for me] to have a BD, because I was working with my husband in the same place. My father and my father-in-law objected, but my husband responded to the pressures although he did not want to do it. I remember that night very well, I was very frightened but I was also very sure about my honour. They kept taking towels, and I was falling apart. I could not sleep with him and had to be treated at the clinic for several weeks after.

Our research found an important correlation between adherence to the BD, class, age and gender. The majority of married women in the Delta and

Boulaq–Cairo had not undergone a BD, while the majority in Upper Egypt had; yet the latter unanimously would have preferred not to have had the BD. In fact, the only group in which a majority stated a clear preference for the BD was the women respondents in El Sakakini, Cairo.[24] Like the women from Boulaq–Cairo and the Delta who had had the BD, these were low-income, uneducated housewives who had migrated with their families from Upper Egypt. Their strong adherence to the BD may reflect the need of women uprooted to an alien community to prove their honour, define their identity and protect their traditions and values from being eroded by 'the city'. Defenders of the BD argue that, although it is a cruel and painful experience and they themselves have terrible memories of it, it is better to have it so a woman can avoid gossip and hold her head high among her future in-laws.

Yet a significant number of the married women we interviewed in all the research sites, who themselves had undergone BD, would not have their daughters do it and believe that things are changing now. And apparently their daughters feel the same, for the majority of unmarried respondents preferred the ordinary *dokhla*. The only group that was adamantly against *baladi dokhla* was the group of Islamist students. They all took the position that it is religiously *haram* because it exposes the woman's genitals, which should not be seen by anybody, not even her mother or sister. The overwhelming majority of men too preferred an ordinary wedding night. They felt it is more dignified for women, that the intimacy of the wedding night is a private matter between husband and wife, and that its invasion through the BD ritual may cause future sexual problems and traumas. A few said that it was against Islam, and one even charged, 'it is a kind of rape and murder of the girl'.

It is disconcerting to find that men are the ones defending 'privacy' and women's bodily integrity here, while women grit their teeth and support traditional norms of honour and chastity even if the price is their own pain and humiliation. We have to ask in what ways 'privacy' becomes associated, in the current Egyptian context, with men's control over sexuality in marriage; and in what ways 'honour', in the absence of other forms of power and mobility, becomes the only passport for women to move about freely and 'hold their head high'.

... AND SUBSEQUENT NIGHTS

My husband is nice to me, he usually does foreplay before the intercourse. I enjoy having sex with him, on the condition that the room is darkened. He mocks me [for this] but agrees.... No, I would never ask him for sex. If he had his way, we would have sex every day. But I think once a week is quite enough because I am always tired from work and household chores. Sometimes I feel guilty, because people say it is *haram* [to refuse your husband], but I know that God will forgive me [because] He knows how tired I really am.

Wafa'a's frank description of her sexual relations with her husband reflects the sentiments of many of the married women we spoke with. The majority of both married and unmarried women respondents had no hesitation about acknowledging their entitlement to sexual pleasure in marriage. This includes the Islamist women, who explained that a wife's right to sexual pleasure is mentioned in the Q'uran. They were the only group (among both unmarried and married women) to mention the husband's impotence as a valid reason for a woman seeking divorce. At the same time, the majority of respondents felt 'it is improper that a woman express her desire' directly to her husband. This would shame women, since 'a woman should be wanted by her husband, and not the other way around'. However, as we heard from a few outspoken women in all the group discussions as well as the in-depth interviews, a woman may use a variety of indirect means to signify sexual desire while maintaining female modesty. For example, she can 'give him a sign, wear pretty nightgowns, put on some make-up and perfume, be nice to him....'

On the question of whether she can refuse her husband if he approaches her and she is unwilling, most of the married women initially responded that it is the man's right to have sex with his wife and this right should not be denied: 'It is her job'; 'Why did he marry her?'; 'It is the wife's duty to serve her husband.' Yet, underneath this attitude of devout compliance with unwanted sex lurked some hard practical realities, especially fear of the husband's retaliation. Some said, 'He will make my life miserable' or 'Next day will be a disaster,' hinting at the threat of abuse or violence (see below); while others alluded to the risk that a husband will divorce her and remarry if she does not satisfy his sexual desires. In fact, in all the groups and the individual interviews many women were more assertive about taking care of their own needs. Like Wafa'a, they believed that being tired or ill is a legitimate reason for a wife to refuse sex with her husband and that the husband should accommodate her needs in such a case or else be considered rude. Other inventive tactics mentioned for avoiding unwanted sex included playing sick, sleeping with the children or going to bed early, pretending to be in deep sleep, or even pinching one of the young ones to wake them up.

In contrast to the married women, unmarried women were much more straightforward in their view that the husband does not have an absolute right to sex with his wife, some even calling such a notion *haram*. Yet, like the married women, they seemed aware of the practical obstacles against a wife's asserting her right to refuse unwanted sexual advances from her husband too directly. They too suggested indirect ways of avoiding unwanted sex: 'I would say I have my period or that my back hurts or pretend I am asleep.' The point of such excuses is to refuse sex without either wounding the man's pride or exposing oneself to a quarrel, while making it seem that the refusal has nothing to do with the woman's desire or lack thereof. The Islamist young women were the only group that unanimously expressed their belief in the man's unconditional right to have sex with his wife whenever and wherever he wants, irrespective of her desire. In diametric opposition to their non-Islamist peers, they insisted that it is *haram* for a wife to deny her husband even if she is tired or feeling unwell.

In contrast, the majority of men said they would understand if their wives refused sex because of fatigue, ill health or menstruation. A few even agreed that a woman has the right to refuse sex if she is not in the mood, up to a point, although the majority would first try to discuss with her her reasons. Only a few said they would force their wives to have sex ('Why else did I marry her?'); and only one made the very interesting argument that a wife cannot refuse her husband's desire, because 'This is a tool of punishment to be used by the man, not the woman.' If there was any common ground worth noting in this discussion – across residence, gender, age groups and marital status – it was this assumption that married women are just as capable of and generally entitled to sexual pleasure as their husbands.

MARITAL CONFLICTS AND DIVORCE

Although both religion and tradition declare it a husband's duty to satisfy his wife, financially and sexually, they also designate the man the head of the household and principal decision maker who sets the rules and must be obeyed. Women's endurance of marital conflicts is 'the nature of things'. When conflicts become too difficult, they may leave home temporarily and return to their families, but divorce or permanent separation is not easily accepted, since this would mean dissolving the household and harming the children. A family may willingly host a daughter and her children after a fight with her husband while negotiations are going on to reconcile them and to make demands on the husband. But the same family will try to discourage the woman from divorce, since that would involve financial burdens on them to support her and her children as well as the bad reputation associated with being a divorced woman. Given the very great difficulty of suing for divorce as a woman in Egypt (see above), women are likely to yield to these family and social pressures. They thus frequently face the unhappy choice of either staying within a difficult marriage or leaving their children and returning to their families alone.

In both the focus groups and the in-depth interviews, women described the traits of a good wife in extremely accommodative terms, including tolerance of the husband, patience with him and being contented with what he has to offer. The good wife obeys her husband and gets his permission for many things, especially to work or go out of the house, even to visit her family. In return, the husband should be decent and able to support her and their children. However, some women admitted that things can go wrong, the husband can be violent for example, in which case a woman may leave her house and go back to her family until he apologizes. As Wafa'a explains,

[During a fight] I usually leave the house while he is there, but once he leaves I go clean and prepare food for the children then leave before he comes home. But last time he was terrible and totally wrong, [so] I deserted the house completely and stayed at my mother-in-law's house … [until] his father made him apologize.

Within the theoretical consensus that the man in the family has the final say, as Wafa'a's tactics suggest, there is in practice considerable room to manoeuvre. The married women we interviewed found many ways of getting around husbands' objections, either through persuasion ('talking him into it'), manipulation ('feminine ways'), or fighting it out. Many stressed the art of persuading without appearing to antagonize the man, as reflected in this account by Nour:

Even if [I am] sure that his point of view is wrong … I listen to him to the end … if the matter is not very important I can let him have his way in what is trivial, in order to be able to argue more strongly in more important things. Suppose for example my husband refuses to let me go visit my family. I would not clash or else this will close the matter completely. I would call them without him knowing and tell them to express that they wish to see him.… He will be embarrassed and will let me go or at least will come with me to visit them.

But some husbands remain unsusceptible to persuasion, raising the problem of domestic violence. The most recent EDHS data indicate that 35 per cent of Egyptian wives have been beaten at least once by their husbands, and a somewhat higher percentage of rural women.[25] Just as disturbing are the responses of the women surveyed, 86 per cent of whom agreed that husbands are justified in beating their wives at least sometimes – particularly for refusing sex (70 per cent), answering back (69 per cent), talking to other men (64 per cent) and neglecting the children (51 per cent). This conciliatory attitude among married women toward domestic violence is reinforced by not only patriarchal tradition but also public policy. Specific provisions of Egyptian law are intended to protect women from acts of public violence, particularly those governing rape, the kidnapping of women in conjunction with rape, or any lewd behaviour that offends women's modesty. But husbands' violence against wives is implicitly considered a private affair, especially if the woman is poor or has little or no education.

Yet are Egyptian women actually so accepting of 'private' male violence against them? Our study, covering far fewer women than the EDHS but going into greater depth, suggests that women's feelings, if not their daily realities, are quite the contrary. And subsequent research likewise shows Egyptian women morally and psychologically rejecting spousal violence, although they may lack the practical power to prevent it.[26] Some women in the focus groups stated that the man does have the right to beat his wife 'mildly'; however, when faced with the actual prospect of such behaviour, women in the in-depth interviews revealed much more opposition. The majority of women in the Delta sites expressed clear rejection of wife battering, on a number of grounds: 'it is not his right', 'it is humiliating to the woman, and what then would be left if respect is eroded?', 'it will reverberate on the children', etcetera. A good number of women in Cairo and Upper Egypt also felt that the man who beats his wife is a bad man, unless he is provoked by particularly extreme circumstances – for example, as Zeinab put it, 'if she did not preserve his honour or disclosed his secrets or wasted his money'. But, when considering the issue in more personal rather than abstract terms, Zeinab too voices her strong moral objection:

> The man who beats his wife lacks manhood. My husband did it once and it was for a trivial reason. When I cried he regretted it and promised not to repeat it. Beating could not be a part of the religion. God would not agree that a man should use his strength against the woman who serves him and his children.

Married respondents differentiated between verbal and physical violence. In the case of verbal abuse, they said that it is wisest to let the storm pass and not fuss about it. This does not imply that they like or accept it, which they do not; rather, they believe a woman who knows how to manage her husband will be able to avoid such abuse. So strong is their belief in women's power of manipulation, in fact, that they tend to assume a woman who is victimized by domestic violence must have failed to 'manage' her husband properly. But only the group of low-income housewives in Sakakini, Cairo – who, as we have seen, tend to take more traditional positions on other issues as well – consistently blamed the woman for her husband's battering, assuming she must have done something wrong to deserve it.

The young women respondents, thinking ahead to their own future marriages, would also refuse violence from husbands. Domestic violence, they asserted, would be a reason, not necessarily to seek divorce, but to leave the house and let the family negotiate better conditions. The group of young Islamist women, on initial inquiry, argued that it was the right of the husband to beat his wife: 'Religion granted him this right,' they held, 'provided it is mild and he has tried all other ways of mending the situation, such as involving her family or abandoning her in bed.' Yet, when one of the researchers told an anecdote about a quarrel between a husband and his wife in which he violently pushed her away from him, the women were angered and said, 'this is not his right', 'if this happened I would be very upset', 'this is very insulting, unacceptable'. In the end, refusal, not obedience, was the overwhelming response to abusive husbands.

WORK OUTSIDE THE HOME

In cases of marital conflict, including domestic violence, a working woman with her own income will have a stronger negotiating position *vis-à-vis* her family of origin as well as her husband. Yet whether a wife can leave the house to work is itself an issue that often precipitates a power struggle between husbands and wives. The growing number of Egyptian women who work for wages do so primarily because of economic need, to ensure food, health care and education for their children. Even with the presence of a husband's income many poor women have to work to make ends meet, especially with costs rising in consequence of privatization and SAPs. Work and earnings themselves by no means assure women's equality to men in society or the home, but they do give women additional power and resources in negotiating their relations with husbands and their status in the community. Judging from the testimonies of our respondents, this is a margin of power that women greatly value and aspire to.

Over two-thirds of the married women we interviewed were working women, employed in a variety of occupations, although most of those employed were in the Delta or urban areas. Among these, the most commonly held occupations were those of government worker, sales clerk, community worker, domestic or institutional cleaner, and nurse. Many of those who did not work outside the home expressed their wish to find an appropriate work opportunity, preferably in the neighbourhood. Above all, the majority felt that work is important to a woman. It enhances family income and helps in the education of children; it also gives her money to obtain what she wants and needs – not only (the Cairene women said) for the house but for herself. Work is 'a weapon for the wife in case her husband abandons her', or, as the Boulaq group affirmed, 'work gives women independence'. Some even used the term 'self-realization' and listed work as one of the factors that would give a woman value in her community and 'make people respect [her]', as one Sakakini woman put it.

Yet this implicit sense of entitlement around work comes freighted with very clear elements of accommodation to traditional norms about women's obligations in marriage. The same women in the Cairo groups who voiced the advantage of having 'independence' and the resources to support themselves on their own if necessary also maintained that, for this to become their right, they had to earn it first by fulfilling their role as housewife and mother. This becomes a trade-off: if you do not pay in advance you cannot demand what you want and will not get it. Moreover, the majority of married women respondents in all the groups said that a husband does have the right and ability to prevent his wife from going out to work; if he objects, there is little to be done. They would try to convince their husbands, especially if the family income is low, but he has the final say. Only a few showed some reluctance to concede the man this right, arguing, 'If a woman is fulfilling her duties in the household, then he has no right to prevent her' (this is consistent with the trade-off philosophy). However, women in the in-depth interviews were more assertive. A few women in the rural Delta had open fights with their families (parents, then husbands) and were able to continue their work. Hamida, a 46-year-old illiterate domestic worker with a married daughter and three sons, was one who persisted:

He wanted me to stop working, he even beat me twice, but I continued to work.

I wanted to educate my children, and he wasn't working all the time; finally he stopped. Now I am the one who is paying for everything.

Most of the unmarried women in the research communities do not work at present, some because they are still students at different stages of their education. Yet many are trainees in knitting and sewing classes in community development projects, suggesting the possibility and desire to continue working outside the home in the future. Whereas married women would view economic necessity as the main reason for seeking a job, unmarried women were more inclined to emphasize the values of personal satisfaction and fulfilment. 'It is not the money factor, I should be able to prove myself'; 'Work is more important than marriage'; 'I feel self-satisfaction in teaching others what I have learned', were some of their responses. One young woman told us she had acquired 'a voice inside my family when I started to work and contribute to the family income'. As a result, though she herself was circumcised, she managed to argue successfully on behalf of sparing her younger sister – a striking example of how economic empowerment may support women's claims in regard to bodily integrity and reproductive health.

While all the Islamist young women intend to work after graduation, they stipulated that if there is a contradiction between their work and their household duties after marriage, they will choose to stay at home. The reason for working outside the home is to serve their community, especially to meet the need for women doctors. Although self-realization is a consideration for them as for the other unmarried women, they are clearly more prepared to adhere to a husband's wish that they should stay at home. Like the married women, they used the more traditional argument that a woman may try to persuade, but the final decision belongs to the man.

Although many of the male respondents agreed in principle that women should be able to work outside the home, especially if they are educated, this consent was most often made conditional on economic necessity – if the husband's income is too low or if he dies. Few were willing to acknowledge that women might need to work to realize their own aims, much less to have value and dignity in the community. One man from Upper Egypt stated, 'Life is becoming very hard and it is no shame that a woman helps her husband.' Others, who in the abstract insisted that women's place is to stay at home and serve their husbands and children, when pressed justified exceptions in the case of economic hardship; one such hard-liner admitted that his own wife is working outside the home. Thus, although Egyptian men, judging from our respondents, tend to reject the idea of wage-earning wives, it seems they also need them.[27] Some men (the majority in Sakakini-Cairo), however, were consistent in rejecting the prospect of women working outside the home, regardless of economic constraints. Women 'should serve at home' and devote themselves to childrearing, as one man in rural Menya put it. Some argued that women are different from men and cannot have the same jobs: 'Suppose a woman is mayor and you ask for her, so they tell you the mayor is in labour, what would you do?'

It is doubtful that some of our male respondents would have stressed their superior position in their families so strongly if they were not keenly aware that this superiority is increasingly being threatened, especially as changing economic and social conditions precipitate a shift in gender roles. Faced with such changes, men, like women, tend to accommodate to traditional patri-archal norms; but there is a difference, since men's stance in accommodating tradition is one of proving themselves and defending their own power at the expense of women.[28] Moreover, men on some level are no doubt aware that expanding women's activities and freedom of movement outside the home will surely affect their power and decision-making capacity within it – including with regard to choices about fertility and childbearing.

MOTHERHOOD AND REPRODUCTIVE CHOICES

As all of our respondents, both women and men, attested, children are the main reason for marrying and establishing a family, and bearing children is one of the principal duties of an Egyptian wife. Children are the major source of a woman's value. Once she has them she has gained the power to negotiate and stand up to her husband; without them, she becomes weak and vulnerable to conditions in the marriage of which she does not approve. Children also serve as a kind of insurance against divorce; in times of marital conflict, mothers typically advise their daughters to have another child in order to deflect the problem. The force of the childbearing mandate for women is evident in the consensus among our women respondents that one legitimate ground for a husband to divorce his wife would be her inability to bear children. Indeed, infertility is the single circumstance in which some would make an exception to their nearly unanimous condemnation of polygamy. Wafa'a, who has four children, remarked:

> Of course having children is important for both men and women…. My husband was going crazy when we had been married five months and I did not get pregnant…. If they love each other and are on good terms, maybe they can endure not having children…. If [infertility] was his [problem], I would have tolerated it because he is a good man … [but] if it had been my fault and he wanted to remarry to have children, then that would be his right … we would divorce, but I would never accept a second wife.

These comments reflect a double standard in cases of infertility: A husband is expected to divorce his wife (or perhaps take a second one) if she is infertile; but if he is the one incapable of having children, she will assess how 'good' he is and how much she loves him before determining whether or not to seek a divorce (clearly, she does not have the option of taking a second husband). Despite the high value attributed to childbearing for women, the choice between remaining childless and getting a divorce was presented as a difficult one among the women we interviewed. This may reflect that being married is even more important to women's status and sense of self-worth in Egypt than having children. In addition, if the husband is the one who is infertile, the woman herself cannot be blamed for the couple's childless state. She can then be spared the comments of the neighbours and family and regarded instead as a wife who has sacrificed herself for the sake of not breaking up the marriage.

Paralleling a recent analysis of national survey data in Egypt, the first reaction of most married women respondents in our study to the question of who decides the timing of pregnancy or the number of children was that it is a joint decision between the husband and wife; women's position in reproductive decision-making is one of 'equality rather than autonomy' (Govindasamy and Malhotra 1996).[29] In case of disagreement, the final decision should be in the hands of the man, they would say, 'because he is the one who spends' (that is, controls household budget decisions). Yet further probing revealed a different scenario in reality. If a real or anticipated conflict occurs, many married women in our study appear to be doing what they want without telling husbands – that is, using or stopping contraceptives or sometimes resorting to traditional methods of abortion (see below). One Cairene housewife from Boulaq stated that she would leave home and go to her family if her husband tried to force her to get pregnant or prevent her from getting pregnant, asserting, 'It is my decision, only mine.' All Cairene women interviewed agreed that having children is crucial for women but the number of children is the woman's decision. Zeinab, a skilled seamstress employed in a garment workshop, clearly asserts her authority in this arena: 'No, my husband has nothing to do with this contraception issue.... He wanted children, I bore him children and got the boy; that is it. We can hardly feed ourselves.'

The strong sense of their own entitlement to take charge of reproductive decisions demonstrated by our married women respondents is consistent with other research findings that Egyptian women who work for wages outside the home and have greater freedom of mobility are more likely to practise contraception (Govindasamy and Malhotra 1996). This may reflect the disproportionately high labour force participation rate among our sample of married women relative to national data. Yet our study challenges the assumption that wives in Egypt necessarily prefer joint (husband–wife) decision-making to autonomy when it comes to the issue of controlling fertility, even if the culture generally and they themselves 'support inter-action and negotiation' in many other areas. Most often, however, this sense of entitlement is exercised secretly rather than in the open. In one of the Cairo focus groups, a participant observed that, if she wanted a baby and her husband did not, she could have her IUD removed without his knowing. Another said she could induce an abortion by drinking boiled Pepsi Cola and it would look like a miscarriage. In either case, whether to have an additional child or prevent it, the group offered suggestions as to how women can take control of the situation surreptitiously while seeming to abide by their husband's wish. The most important reasons mentioned for using contraception or terminating a pregnancy were, first, the woman's health; then the family's economic situation, especially if another child would mean giving up her job and needed income; finally, having had a son already and lacking access to child care if she is working.

Unlike the other groups, the Islamist women were opposed to any sort of artificial family planning; the number of children, they argued, should be left to God. One member of the group told a story about a 'sister' who was against limiting the number of children and left the decision to God. God obligingly gave her only four children, after which she stopped getting pregnant without having to use any methods. The only reasons these young women accepted for using contraceptives were to space children during breastfeeding and when the woman's health is in danger. At the same time, they wondered if there might be a method that has no health problems or side effects for the woman, does not interfere with the man's enjoyment of sex, and is clearly approved by religion (such as coitus interruptus or the rhythm method). In other words, their desire to be religiously correct coincides with a wish that they should somehow not have more children than they want. Most of the other unmarried women expect to limit the number of children they will have to two or three and have abandoned the traditional son preference in favour of an ethic of gender equality. 'Life has changed,' they say, 'now a girl is like a boy.' The majority felt that the number of children should be decided jointly by both partners. However, some of them were convinced that women's health and wellbeing should be the main determinant of how many children a woman has and when, even if she has to 'manipulate' her husband.

The men we interviewed also stated a preference that decisions about childbearing and fertility control be joint, determined first by the woman's health and second by the family's economic circumstances. But, as with most other decisions, if mutual agreement is not possible, they would insist that the final say should be the man's, because he is the one in charge of the household economy. Several men argued that a man is entitled to a second wife if his wife cannot bear children, so that his property, no matter how small, can be passed on to his offspring. Only one man objected to this, fearing that the tables could be turned and a wife might then 'have the right to leave her husband if he cannot have children'. In general, however, male informants grounded their claim to ultimate authority over reproductive decisions in their economic power and their status as heads of household. Increasingly, this assertion may be wishful thinking, given two prevalent realities: that wives are gaining some degree of economic independence and are *de facto* making the decisions about fertility and childbearing themselves.

CONTRACEPTION AND ABORTION

While our small sample of respondents is in no way representative of Egyptian women as a whole, and while many of the women we interviewed have not completed their childbearing, a glance at the existing number of children among our married women respondents suggests they are effectively limiting their childbearing. Most of these women, including those from Upper Egypt and rural areas, have between one and four children, with nearly half having none to two; only three of our forty-five married women respondents had had more than four children at the time of the study.

The majority of the married women in our study were currently using or had previously used some form of contraception, though not necessarily a 'modern' or medical form. Those who are not currently using contraception have specific practical reasons; either they are trying to get pregnant, their husband is away, or they are divorced or separated. Interestingly, several women who were or had been using contraceptives believed (erroneously) that religion forbids the use of artificial contraception. This underscores the reality we discovered over and over again when it comes to women's decisions about fertility and childbearing: their own view of practical necessity supersedes either religious belief or patriarchal tradition in guiding their choices.

Yet the sense of entitlement to determine their own fertility may be accompanied by a lack of reliable methods or information. Zeinab, for example, uses contraceptive pills 'when needed' (that is, when she has sex with her husband) because 'it [intercourse] usually happens only once a month'. She is ill-informed about the pill's correct use, and her low level of education makes it harder for her to understand written instructions. Not surprisingly, the ineffective use of contraception leads to attempts at induced abortion, which also may be ineffective. One woman working as a cleaning woman in Cairo reported with evident pride in her resourcefulness:

> I had three abortions; two of them I did myself. I drank boiled Coca-Cola and carried heavy things and jumped around. But my second abortion was very difficult and I had long pains, so when I got pregnant again I went to the *daya* and it was easier. [laughing] Of course [my husband] never knew about any of that.

The commonly accepted norm across the research communities, as revealed by all the focus groups, is that having an abortion is *haram*. Yet more detailed questions and the in-depth interviews revealed a much more complex range of values and experiences, especially when women were asked about what friends and relatives do to resolve an unwanted pregnancy. The majority of both married and unmarried respondents assume that a woman can always find a method for ending a pregnancy without her husband knowing and also without going to a doctor or making the matter public. This means, of course, risky, self-induced methods such as carrying heavy weights, jumping off a bed or sofa, or using folk remedies such as boiled onion leaves, boiled Coca-Cola or other carbonated drinks. She may even insert a knitting needle into the cervix to induce bleeding and thereby gain admission to a public hospital where she can expect the procedure to be completed. But given the poor conditions in Egyptian public sector hospitals, this is truly a measure of last resort.

Whatever the method, the clear implication of such actions as well as the matter-of-fact way in which they were reported is not only that induced abortions among Egyptian women are frequent (whether or not successful) but that they are often regarded as both necessary and on some level justified. In the in-depth interviews, many women admitted that they themselves had had abortions. Some of them said it was *haram* but they had no other choice because they could not afford another baby at that time. Soheir's account of her experience is not unusual and confirms other studies (see Huntington *et al.* 1995):

> I had an abortion once. I was using a loop but I got pregnant. My neighbour advised me to drink boiled Coca-Cola and take an enema. I had bleeding for fifteen days, then I was transferred to the hospital and they did a small operation on me. I never told anybody that I did it to myself, not even my husband. He is a religious man. I was afraid of God's punishment, but at the same time I wonder, does God accept the suffering of the whole family if I have to stop work [in order to breastfeed another baby]?

Implicit in such statements is a practical morality governing fertility and childbearing in which the economic realities of having to feed and care for a family take precedence over both perceived religious doctrine and the tradition of wifely obedience. Moreover, as Soheir's reasoning illustrates, sometimes women may even fashion their own interpretation of God's will that is more congenial than official theology to the needs of reproduction in everyday life.

Conclusion

Our research confirms how the very concept of rights, including reproductive rights, is given meaning by the specific culture, social space and political context in which a right is to be exercised. Egyptian culture does not place the individual above the community. The mere fact that a woman is part of a family, a marriage, a peer group, and a community entails that she voluntarily compromises part of herself for the sake of these affiliations, which in turn promise emotional, material and moral support. Women's relationship to their bodies is shaped by such negotiations among needs, desires and obligations; ownership of the body is both personal and socially determined. Hardly any woman we interviewed would say that her body is actually under the control of anyone other than herself, yet nearly all relegate part of their personal control by submitting to social norms and traditions. This conformity is not perceived by them as self-disownment or servitude but rather as a route to the greater security afforded by community acceptance and solidarity.

But adherence to a communal rather than individual approach to rights does not mean that women in Egypt are willing to be passively obedient. In order to protect their dignity, their material and physical wellbeing and that of their children, Egyptian women will take power over decision-making into their own hands; at times they will transgress tradition, religious opinion and patriarchal authority. One of the most important findings of this study is that religion, while a strong presence in their lives, does not govern the everyday reproductive and sexual choices of most of our women informants. Whether trying to avoid unwanted sex or unwanted pregnancy, they rely on the personal forgiveness of God rather than the opinions of religious authorities. Implicit in their subversive strategies is a practical if not moral conviction about their entitlement to sexual and bodily integrity, even in marriage; as well as their effort to strike a balance between traditional definitions of the obedient wife and their own belief in a forgiving God.

We uncovered four variants in women's reproductive and sexual strategies:

1 *It is just the nature of things.* We identified some areas where women fatalistically perceived their situation as 'the way things are'. For example, in their experiences of gender discrimination in the upbringing of boys and girls, or in deferring to husbands' authority on certain issues (especially around work), many women respondents did not manifest feeling oppressed. In this case 'accommodation' may not be the most accurate term to use, since women felt they were dealing with normal behaviours or attitudes that cannot be changed. Even the few women who were frustrated by such experiences did not suggest rebelling against the situation or trying to manipulate it.

2 *Painful, but necessary.* On certain other issues – in particular, the *baladi dokhla* and female circumcision – many women consented to a tradition for which they saw a positive social function. Despite the pain they suffered while undergoing these practices, they submitted to them as a necessary trade-off to purchase other benefits they value more than 'control over their bodies': respect and acceptance in their communities, honour for themselves and their families, freedom to come and go without gossip. For some women, submission to unwanted sex with husbands fell into this category, as a trade-off to avoid male violence or possibly divorce.

3 *Resistance and resistance in disguise.* Within this spectrum fall a number of verbal and behavioural strategies that women respondents enacted *vis-à-vis* their husbands in daily life, particularly with regard to such issues as childbearing, contraception, abortion, sexual relations, and going out of

the house.[30] In these areas, our research uncovered many tactics and subterfuges that women consciously adopt to take control of the situation – and of their bodies – and turn matters in their own favour: adorning themselves to allure their husbands without seeming to initiate sex; feigning illness to avoid unwanted sex; or secretly getting an abortion or removing an IUD. In describing such strategies, our respondents did not use words like resistance or right but rather talked about wit, cleverness, accurate assessment of the situation, etcetera.

4 *No is no!* Much more rarely, we heard overt statements of resistance or refusal from a few women in both the older and younger generations, especially in relation to domestic violence and forced sexual relations with husbands. We also identified much greater assertiveness, if not resistance, on the part of younger (unmarried) women relative to the older ones with regard to certain issues – for example, demanding more and earlier sexual and reproductive information, refusing an unwanted or arranged marriage, refusing the *baladi dokhla,* and in one case resisting the imposition of FGM on a younger sister. This sense of entitlement may be due to greater opportunities for education and access to (limited) earnings among younger women.

An example of how Egyptian women share the ownership of their 'selves' with society at large is reflected in the high value they give to female chastity, virginity, and avoidance of premarital or extramarital relationships. This is illustrated by the overwhelming acceptance among most Egyptian women (including our respondents) of FGM and, among many, of the *baladi dokhla*. It is the price they feel they must pay in order to prove their modesty and thus secure their entitlement to their reproductive and sexual rights. Given the strength of this feeling, we cannot say that the fight against FGM based on a sense of entitlement reflects the sentiments of the majority of women in Egypt at this point in time. This is not to suggest that this fight should be suspended but that women's rights and health advocates should recognize that FGM has a social function that many young girls and women find compelling – beyond choice. The issue becomes more complex surely when women themselves see such traditions as a tool of empowerment rather than oppression, for example, in reducing their need for sexual gratification. Clearly the challenge is not only one of opposing harmful practices or mobilizing around rights but of publicly deconstructing the ideological and social system – rooted in age-old gender divisions – that makes those practices acceptable and sometimes even desired.

Another example is the high value Egyptian women place on motherhood and their acceptance of the traditional division of labour within the family. Women in our research communities do not consider the expectation that they will have children when they marry coercive or an invasion of their privacy; rather it is part of the bargain by which they secure social, familial and spousal respect. Only if they cannot have children for some reason do they begin to feel coerced and vulnerable, especially if threatened by a divorce or a second wife. For growing numbers of Egyptian women, however, as our research findings confirm, marriage and motherhood are being combined with remunerative work. And the women, unlike their husbands and fathers, see their work as not only dictated by economic necessity but important for their own self-realization and empowerment. Though by no means assuring their equality or liberation, having an income of their own does give women a stronger negotiating position in the household and family, enabling them to compromise less and demand a bit more. The opposition of conservative male elements in society to married women working outside the home is evidence that financial independence, even if partial, can expand women's ability to make their own decisions, transgress traditional norms, perhaps leave an unhappy marriage and live on their own.

In other realms too, practical acceptance of some forms of subordination does not mean unconditional acceptance. A woman does not 'accept' being beaten by her husband, but neither does this mean she will seek separation or divorce the first time her husband lays a hand on her. She is ready, especially if there are children, to forgive or endure a certain level of abuse, but only up to a point, after which she will take matters into her own hands (that is, leave the house). The same applies to decisions about limiting childbearing. Like Egyptian women generally, the women interviewed in our study would rather make those decisions jointly with their partners and try to do so. Being free to decide on their own is not something valued for its own sake. At the same time, compliance with husbands or family pressures (to have another child or to have a son) is itself a conscious choice. At a certain limit, when countervailing pressures impinge – for example, too many mouths to feed, their own health needs, or the absence of child care – they are ready to breach the commitment to joint decision-making and find their own way out of an unwanted pregnancy. They may defy the law, religion and a husband's wishes in order to obtain an abortion, risking their lives with traditional and unsafe methods. Given the declining fertility rate in Egypt, combined with indications that contraceptive use is still often ineffective, our respondents' experience adds to the evidence that Egyptian women are frequently and effectively resorting to abortions to resolve unwanted pregnancies – under conditions of serious health and legal risk.

Women who defer to religious authority in every aspect of their lives are an exception to the above description of women in Egypt. The Islamist women we interviewed are politically informed activists who have decided to create an alternative identity as women based on certain interpretations of Islam. Unfortunately in our view, this alternative identity is riddled with shame, fear, and male domination, prescribing the seclusion and veiling of women, their confinement to the home, and the regulation of their bodies.

Yet, as participants in the Islamist cultural and political project, the women we worked with in Mansoura see themselves as fighting, not against patriarchy or local oppressors, but against the Egyptian government, Western cultural and economic domination, and the global forces that impose harsh economic policies and alien lifestyles. In this they are no different from many women's movements in the Arab world who have willingly subordinated their own struggle to the national and regional political struggle.

At the same time, our group discussions revealed evidence that even these Islamist women want to limit the number of children they have (albeit through 'natural' or God-given means); expect to work outside the home (to serve the community as doctors); and find the prospect of spousal violence toward them personally appalling. We found that the motivations of the Islamist women students were not always strictly religious but sometimes transparently practical and economic: for example, their insistence that parents must approve women's choice of a husband to secure their support in case the marriage falls apart. It may be that, along with political and religious ideology, these young women are also influenced by generational changes and their middle-class and university-educated back-ground. In general, our respondents – across lines of ideology as well as age and gender – expressed the 'modern' belief in education for women and the view that educated women have greater capacity to make their own choices.

Like the Islamist women, the male respondents in our study, though generally more conservative than the women, often seemed motivated as much by economic conditions as by patriarchal tradition and religion. Unemployment, poverty and economic insecurity have created levels of anger and frustration that men direct at women for want of other outlets. The destabilization of their head-of-household status has meant a loss of dignity and compromised manhood that sometimes lead to domestic violence and resistance to women's working outside the home and controlling their own fertility. On the other hand, men's economic anxieties may have an opposite effect: for example, fathers may want their daughters to have free choice of a marriage partner in order to lessen the risk that the marriage will fail and financial responsibility revert to them. In either case, structural conditions strongly influence reproductive values.

Most often we found that the women we interviewed situate themselves somewhere between the two poles of fatalism and resistance. For most of them, whether married or unmarried, equality and sense of entitlement are embedded in a complex mosaic of strategies and negotiations. This fre-quently means trading off an outspoken sense of entitlement to certain rights for a sequence of mechanisms and rationalizations that aim at securing the best of what is available without openly violating the norm or becoming an outcast from the family and community and hence losing their support. Some of the women we interviewed – particularly those in the Islamist group and in Sakakini–Cairo – accept traditional notions of gender divisions and hierarchy. Others, however – especially in rural Upper Egypt and Boulaq–Cairo, and more so among young unmarried women – have a stronger belief in gender equality and the idea that women can do as well or better than men. But even these women generally prefer to employ subtle tactics rather than direct confrontation, to convince men that the final decision is theirs while trying to influence them from behind the scenes.

For all Egyptian women and for us as researchers, the concept of 'reproductive rights' remains sensitive, contentious and complex. This is so largely because of a social context of constraining factors that affect women's ability to act on their rights: economic hardship, the prevalence of male violence, the difficulty of both divorce and survival outside marriage for women, the poor quality of health services, the continued opposition to gender equality among the men in their own families, and the lack of extra-familial organizations and support networks for women (outside the Islamist groups and the largely urban-based, middle-class feminist circles). Younger generations of women appear to be more assertive about their rights than their mothers and grandmothers, in part due to improved access to education. But they too will be unable to make real, informed choices about reproduction and sexuality until these other social conditions begin to change. Until then, Egyptian women's culture of secretly outwitting and strategically accommodating will prevail over some women's outspoken voices.

Notes

1 All Egyptians speak the Arabic language, but minorities living in the desert oases in the west and south and the Nubian population in the south speak both Arabic and their own indigenous language. While the great majority of Egyptians are Muslims, a significant minority (over 10 per cent) are Copts.

2 A sample survey carried out in rural communities in 1988 estimated women's participation in agriculture at 50.7 per cent, compared with 49.3 per cent for men. The same survey showed 70.7 per cent of rural women participating in unpaid economic activity (El Baz 1994).

3 In fact, the law could have an antinatalist effect (discouraging working women from having more than two children); or a pronatalist one (discouraging women from working outside the home and thus indirectly promoting childbearing). In either case, it creates an incentive scheme that constrains women's reproductive choices and goes against the spirit and letter of the ICPD Programme of Action, which the Egyptian government signed.

4 We are using the term 'Islamist' to refer to the militant political groups in Egypt and elsewhere that draw on a particular interpretation of Islam and seek to convert the countries in which they are active into religious states. This term is preferable to the term 'fundamentalist', which has more ambiguous meanings and may be applied to many groups throughout the world that are non-Islamic (Christians, Jews, Hindus, royalists, etc.).

5 For a full definition of female genital mutilation and its variations in Egypt and other

countries, see Toubia 1995.

6 The Sheikh of Al-Azhar, the supreme religious authority in Egypt, issued a *fatwa* approving FGM, in opposition to another from the Grand Mufti (head of the state religious institution) saying that the matter is for medical doctors to decide. This was a further blow to women's rights in Egypt, since it suggested that medical opinion could take precedence over basic rights of bodily integrity. Al Azhar, an ancient Islamic university that once played a crucial role in national struggle, has more recently become the source of very conservative *fatwas*.

7 Women have the right to custody of their children until they reach age ten for boys (extendable by the judge until the age of fifteen), and age twelve for girls (extendable by the judge until their marriage).

8 The latest national statistics show one out of three Egyptian women aged 25–29 were married before the age of 18 (EDHS 1995). A recent study of two rural villages indicates that as many as 40 per cent of women in those areas are marrying before they reach age sixteen (El Hamamsy *et al.* 1996).

9 Abortion after the third month is considered a sin in all Islamic schools of jurisprudence, while before that time it is acceptable to some schools. Some scholars would allow it even without the permission of the husband; others would allow it on certain conditions (e.g., risk to the life of the woman or a breastfeeding baby); and a third group would consider it a sin whatever the reason (*Fatawi Al Azhar*, Vol. 9, No. 26).

10 In the *baladi dokhla* version of this ritual, either the bridegroom, or the midwife in the presence of the bridegroom and other women from the family, uses a handkerchief to deflower the virgin bride manually on the wedding night and then exhibits the bloodstained handkerchief to the gathered guests.

11 The Q'uran allows men up to four wives, but only if they are able to provide for and treat them equitably. According to the most recent national statistics, only 2 per cent of all marriages in Egypt are polygamous.

12 As well as shrinking, public expenditure on health is unevenly distributed over the country's twenty-six governerates, with urban areas eating up disproportionately more than the rural and marginalized areas (Egypt Human Development Report 1994; DANIDA 1994). Egypt's multiple health institutions include: the Ministry of Health, university hospitals, the Health Insurance Authority, curative institutions (military, police and private-sector), each with its own separate facilities, staff and budget.

13 Many women apparently prefer home to hospital delivery because they fear the risks related to the high rate of Caesarean sections (Morsy 1995; El Mouelhy 1987). Only one-third of all pregnant women in Egypt deliver in a medical facility (EDHS 1995).

14 An important study of two rural villages in Giza in Lower Egypt, based on a random sample of ever-married women, found that between 56 and 83 per cent suffered from various genital, uterine or cervical anomalies and 63 per cent were anaemic; a smaller number had malignant cervical cell changes and a few had undiagnosed syphilis. Sixty per cent of the women had two or more morbidities all of which, up to the time of the study, were going untreated – and this in the governerate of Giza bordering on Cairo (Younis *et al.* 1993).

15 One recent study of family planning clients by the Cairo Demographic Centre found that one in eight of all pregnancies, and one in four unwanted pregnancies, among the sample studied, resulted in an induced abortion through some means, not always successful (Huntington *et al.* 1995).

16 Team members come from the following different disciplines: law, medicine, human rights, anthropology, sociology and political science; but all have been doing

interdisciplinary work on women's issues.

17 The core team members conducted the in-depth interviews while trained field researchers (nine women and three men) conducted the focus group discussions. An intensive training process for the field researchers included two focus group discussions on the topic of reproductive rights, conducted by members of the core team, and further work to help them address more sensitive issues (especially abortion and sexual relations in marriage). The focus group discussion with Islamist women was conducted solely by core group members.

18 Since we were using the men as a kind of control group, we conducted fewer group discussions and no in-depth interviews with men. We would have preferred to work with husbands and male kin of the women we interviewed, but this proved to be logistically impossible. Thus the male informants were not necessarily related to the women.

19 Far from being particularly Islamic, the practice was begun in ancient Egypt and later adopted by both Muslims and Copts; it is nowhere mentioned in the Q'uran and does not even exist in many Islamic countries.

20 According to data from the most recent EDHS, *dayas* perform only one-third of female circumcisions today, as compared with nearly two-thirds in the previous generation. Increasingly, as awareness of the severe health consequences of female circumcision grows, the procedure is being performed by doctors.

21 A few of the rural women are determined to spare their own daughters the pains they endured from this procedure. Their unusual position might be due to the long-standing efforts of development work and education against FGM carried out by the CEOSS in this part of Upper Egypt.

22 Boulaq is one of the oldest quarters in Cairo. All the women in this group were working in a community-based development organization, which might explain their more assertive attitude.

23 According to the Q'uran, no one can force a woman or a man into a marriage; in fact, a marriage or an annulment against the woman's will is *haram*, religiously speaking, on the basis of stories from the Prophet's time.

24 Researchers asked, 'Would you do it again if you had the choice?', or 'Do you want your daughter to have a BD?'

25 The latest EDHS collected information on 14,779 ever-married women between the ages of fifteen and forty-nine in 1995 and 1996.

26 The results of the EDHS concerning women's attitudes towards violence by husbands may be coloured by the way the questions were posed; the responses elicited probably reflect women's views about the *causes* of male battering but were not intended to justify such actions. In preparation for the Fourth World Women's Conference in Beijing, the New Woman Research Centre and El Nadim Centre on Violence in Cairo interviewed 500 women about the different forms of violence to which they were exposed in different situations. In response to the question, 'What would a woman find hard to forgive in her husband?', the second most frequent answer (after 'betrayal') was violence. See New Woman Research Centre and El Nadim Centre 1995.

27 Male informants in Upper Egypt link even this grudging acceptance to certain conditions, for example, that their wives be modestly dressed to go out (long skirts and sleeves) and not use public transport.

28 It is important to note that, while these statements reflect an attitude of superiority over women, the bold and defiant way in which they are expressed could be explained as a reaction to the interview. We found that when women felt embarrassed by a question they sometimes kept silent or made statements that sounded more like

slogans than their own views. The men we interviewed, on the other hand, did not usually show embarrassment but did sometimes appear provoked and begin to make macho declarations that would tend to snowball into group resistance against women's empowerment. In psychological terms, we could say that such behaviour represents a reaction formation mechanism whereby men attempt to maintain their dignity and self-image.

29 The data base used in this analysis was the 1988 EDHS.

30 Evidence of transgressive behaviour in these arenas often emerged through an interesting group dynamic in which the first woman to speak usually expressed the norm expected of a proper woman and wife. When, later in the conversation, someone else uttered a possibility of subverting the norm, this would trigger a sequence of similarly subversive comments from the others, including the one who made the first, 'proper' statement.

4 Between Modernization and Patriarchal Revivalism
Reproductive Negotiations Among Women in Peninsular Malaysia

RITA RAJ, CHEE HENG LENG AND RASHIDAH SHUIB*

The National Context

Malaysia is a multiethnic, multicultural and multireligious country often, until the Asian regional economic crisis of 1997, cited as an example of rapid development with a sustained rate of economic growth (UNDP 1996, Box 2.8). Ethnicity and religion are very much intertwined in Malaysia and are the main characteristics that identify individuals and families socially, economically and politically. Yet important differences characterize the three major ethnic groups – Malays, Chinese and Indians – with ethnic Malays having the lowest incomes, the greatest prevalence in rural areas, and the highest fertility rates.[1] Malays, who by definition are all Muslims, make up about 61 per cent of the population; Chinese, who generally believe in Chinese folk religion, comprise 30 per cent; and Indians, who are predominantly Hindus, comprise about 8 per cent (Malaysia Department of Statistics 1992).[2] A small minority among the non-Malays are Christians. Although the state religion is Islam, and Islamic revivalism in recent years has received strong government support, freedom of worship is guaranteed under the constitution.

Since independence from Britain in 1957, the government has carried out a delicate balancing act affecting the distribution of numbers and resources

* In addition to the work of the three principal authors – who were, respectively, co-coordinator and researchers on the Malaysia IRRRAG team – we would like to thank the other team members for their prodigious work on this project: Rashidah Abdullah, co-coordinator; and Roziah Omar, Rajeswari Nagaraja, and Siti Norazah Zulkifli, researchers. We would also like to acknowledge the valuable work of several people who assisted us in the research and compilation of the data: Mastura Adnan, Norisah Che Ahmad, Zuriah Abu Bakar, Zaiton Kassim, Swarna Rekha Kodikara, Kristina Wati Ramlan, Low Paik Swan, Angela Kuga Thas, and Chong Wei Yee; in translation and transcription: Suganeswary and Mrs Usha Ramachandran; and with expert administrative support: Thilaha Nalliah, N. Manimekaladevy and Khatijah Mohd Baki.

among the three major population groups. Economic and social policies in Malaysia have thus become an instrument for resource allocation and political control among the ethnic groups and, according to some commentators, for bringing the rural Malay population into a relatively more advantageous position within the expanding capitalist–industrial economy (Ackerman and Lee 1990; Ong 1994; Ong 1987). These policies both affect and are affected by official attitudes toward the position of women in the economy and the family.

Economic and political conditions

Following communal riots in 1969, the Malaysian government instituted its New Economic Policy (NEP), aimed at eradicating poverty and redressing the socioeconomic imbalances inherited from British colonial rule. The NEP and various national development plans, particularly policies to increase industrialization and wage labour among rural Malays, have resulted in significant improvements in the economic conditions of the rural poor. By 1990, for example, only 15 per cent of all households in peninsular Malaysia were classified as living below the poverty line, compared with 40 per cent in 1976 (Government of Malaysia 1985). This thrust towards industrialization and wage employment, including the establishment of free trade zones (FTZs), has also brought important shifts in the gender division of labour and the relative position of Malay women (Ng 1989). Not only have young men been pulled out from the agricultural sector; young women too have been encouraged to enter the rapidly expanding manufacturing and service sectors. Ong describes the new 'army of working daughters' generated, perhaps unwittingly, by government policy to expand labour markets and create a skilled workforce:

> For the first time in Malay history, a large number of [young] women had the money and social freedom to experiment with a newly awakened sense of self. Many came to define themselves, through work experiences and market choices, as not materially or even morally dependent on parents and kinsmen. (Ong 1994:30)

As a result of the rapid development of the manufacturing sector, and to a certain extent the service sector, the labour force participation rate for women in the formal labour market has increased from 37.2 per cent in 1970 to 47.1 per cent in 1995; by 1995 women comprised 33.7 per cent of the total workforce (Malaysia Department of Statistics 1995). They form the majority of the workers in some industries situated in FTZs (especially electronics and textiles), which exploit young women as a source of cheap, hard-working and compliant labour. These economic trends have clearly had negative as well as positive outcomes for Malaysian women. Gender differentials in wages still persist, especially in the private sector, with female production workers earning 83 per cent of male earnings (Ng and Chee 1996) and women who perform the same jobs as men on private plantations being paid lower wages.[3] Moreover, the economic restructuring promised by Malaysia's Vision 2020, a long-term projection of the fully developed nation, may not necessarily overturn existing gender hierarchies to the extent that it emphasizes high-tech industries with skilled job opportunities for men, while women will continue to be largely confined to unskilled employment (Jamilah 1994).

While the government urges women to take a full part in education and the industrialization process, it has not provided the necessary social supports to facilitate this participation. Instead of childcare services and progressive family laws, various government agencies offer 'family development' courses such as cooking, sewing and handicrafts. In 1984 the country's prime minister alarmed feminists by publicly expressing the view that married women's work outside the home was a temporary palliative; women whose husbands could support them should stay at home and have at least five children (Chee 1988). The ambiguity in women's economic position reflects the contradictory pulls of state policy: on the one hand towards economic modernization and on the other towards traditional patriarchal views of gender divisions in the family. Whilst women were and are needed as part of Malaysia's human resource development strategy, their inclusion has been motivated more by capitalist self-interest and profits than by any commitment to women's empowerment or to gender equality. Thus the National Policy on Women, adopted in 1989 and intended to incorporate women fully into the national development plan, remains on the back burner even though funds have been allocated. In the context of these deepening contradictions, Malaysian women find their daily lives becoming more complicated as they try to juggle conflicting roles.

Culture, law and religion

Islamic revivalism, and with it the resurgence of the most patriarchal Islamic values and practices, began to emerge in Malaysia in the late 1970s *dakwa* (missionary) movement, stimulated by events in Iran and elsewhere in the Middle East (Nagata 1984; Ong 1994). As in many countries with emergent neo-religious and fundamentalist movements, Islamic revivalism in Malaysia may be read in part as a counterfeminist posture about gender, the meanings of tradition, and the need to control the sexuality, reproduction and social mobility of women.[4]

For Malays, one of the most powerful factors shaping women's and men's relative positions in society is the interaction between *adat* (customary practices) and Islam. Under the *adat* system, neither women nor men in traditional *kampung* (village) society were free to marry when and whom they chose, nor did women have a choice about motherhood as their ultimate goal. At the same time, women were not bound to the household, nor were they completely dependent on their husbands for economic survival. In contrast, Islamic revivalism invokes a more rigid gender hierarchy. While the *adat* practices gave women a certain degree of autonomy, revivalist interpretations of Islam define a man by the control he exerts over his wife and daughters and by the ability to provide for his entire household. The Islamic requirement of female chastity and its emphasis on modesty in women's behaviour and dress further symbolize control by fathers and husbands over women's sexuality (Ong 1994; Roziah 1994; Wazir-Jahan 1992).

The state's response to the Islamist resurgence has been one of both accommodation and containment: on the one hand endorsing official Islam's moral constructions of the ideal Muslim woman and wife (for example, through government-sponsored family life education programmes); and on the other trying to curb extreme Islamic revivalism and to encourage liberalism in Islamic thinking (Norani 1994). These conflicting strands of Islamic understanding at the top policy levels of the state create a confusing context for the average Malaysian Muslim. For example, young women in secondary school are encouraged to go into the fields of science and technology, now dominated by males, and are told by educators that they have the same intellectual capacities as males. Yet state-sponsored Islamic television programmes promote images of the self-sacrificing mother and obedient wife; so what are young women being trained for? Modernization and an attempt to reassert both traditional male authority and Malay ethnic ascendancy coexist uneasily through the regulation of women's status (Ong 1994).

Certainly, within Malaysia's multiethnic context, Hindu culture and religion, Chinese folk religion and Christianity play an important part in shaping the social structure and life ways of their respective adherents. Each of these religious groups has lately experienced a resurgence in religious observance. Yet Islamic revivalism has sought to have a broader reach, beyond the Malay community, through influencing not only government policies and programmes but also daily life – for example, in the prayers and sermons by Muslim religious officials routinely broadcast over radio and television and pronounced at public functions. Pressured by the rise of Islamism, the state has adopted policies that constrain women's reproductive and sexual rights as well as re-emphasizing the patriarchal family. Thus the Malaysian government delegation sided with the Vatican-led fundamentalists in opposing provisions of the Cairo Programme and the Beijing Platform that recognize women's reproductive rights and their right to control over their sexuality (Ng and Chee 1996). And the government's pronatalist population policy (see below) conveys a maternalist discourse of womanhood that limits the horizons of all Malaysian women.

With regard to formal law, the Federal Constitution of Malaysia declares that 'all persons are equal before the law and entitled to the equal protection of the law'; however, it omits the word 'sex' in the clause stating that 'there shall be no discrimination against citizens on the ground of religion, race, descent or place of birth in any law' (Article 8). Women and men have formal equality in regard to civil rights (voting, property rights, contracts), but in areas of family law such as divorce, child custody and inheritance, the legacy of colonialism and Islamic influence still result in overt discrimination on the basis of gender and different applications of the law to Muslims and non-Muslims. The Marriage and Divorce Act of Malaysia, implemented in 1982, abolishes the practice of polygamy, expands the grounds for divorce for both women and men, and secures better protection for women and children in the event of a divorce; however, the act applies only to non-Muslims. Muslim women are governed by *syriah* law through the jurisdiction of the individual states.[5] Under *syriah* law a man may have four wives, provided he can support them equally and obtains permission in writing from the religious court (Mehrun 1988). A husband may terminate a marriage by pronouncing a *talaq*, a declaration in the presence of a witness, to dissolve the marriage. New laws have attempted to regulate this unilateral right to divorce by requiring efforts at conciliation before certifying the divorce, but the husband's decision is still final. Nevertheless, this formal discrimination may be offset by cultural practices: Malay families have higher divorce and remarriage rates, and sometimes give greater support to women who wish to divorce, than do the other ethnic communities in Malaysia (see data below).

The women's movement

The resurgence of patriarchal values in Malaysia, of which the Islamic revival is perhaps more a symptom than a cause, has called forth a variety of responses from organized women's groups. Malaysian feminist writers have criticized recent state policies for legitimizing 'archaic and patriarchal forms of the subordination and control of women' (Norani 1994:123; Chandra in Norani 1994). In addition to theoretical critiques, Malaysian women have launched various forms of activism and protest against such policies. These organized efforts have been as much an outgrowth of postcolonial modernization and recent social and economic changes in women's lives as a reaction to the patriarchal and fundamentalist currents. As suggested earlier, the expansion of the labour market under the NEP brought significant advances for younger generations of women in Malaysia. For middle-class women, higher education has meant an opportunity to come into contact with new ideas and movements, including feminism: 'Women who were students in the 1970s both at home and abroad, and who were influenced by international feminist trends, either joined existing women's organizations or more often started new autonomous women's groups' (Ng and Chee 1996:6).

The various women's groups that emerged in Malaysia in the 1960s, 1970s and 1980s grew out of these developments. The National Council of Women's Organizations (NCWO), formed in 1963, has focused mainly on lobbying and legal reforms in both civil and Muslim family law to end discrimination against women. Like most NGOs in Malaysia, the NCWO is controlled and monitored closely by the government, and tends to be non-confrontational and reformist, working through mainstream institutions and respecting existing social hierarchies. By the mid-1980s, however, more activist coalitions were formed, such as the Joint Action Group Against Violence Against Women (JAG) and the National Women's Coalition – a cluster of many organizations that began to come together in the 1990s to bring a gender perspective to human rights, land, labour and other grassroots issues and to mobilize for the FWCW in Beijing (Dairiam 1995; Ng and Chee 1996).[6]

At the same time, more religious or traditional women have also found a public voice to express their concerns. Rural Malay housewives have demanded government allowances and enforcement of traditional male obligations to provide family support. Urban female university students in sizeable numbers have joined the *dakwa* movement against Western and consumerist culture and have voluntarily donned the *tudung* (headscarf) or even the fuller *hijab* and face veil (Ong 1994). In quite a different vein, the group Sisters in Islam emerged in the late 1980s to provide an alternative voice within the Muslim community to the prevailing conservative Muslim ideology. Originally concerned with the discriminatory treatment of women under *syriah* law in regard to divorce, maintenance and domestic violence, Sisters in Islam has more recently become part of an international movement of Muslim women seeking to reinterpret the Qu'ran from a women's perspective (Rashidah 1996).

More than any other issue, the aim of combating various forms of violence against women has galvanized the energies of women's groups in Malaysia, which have followed the lead of those in India and the Philippines. Beginning with the establishment of a shelter for battered women in 1982, the Women's Aid Organization (WAO) brought a feminist vision and leadership to this movement. Through public forums, media campaigns and mass demonstrations, WAO and the other organizations within JAG succeeded in creating a genuinely multiethnic women's movement and in raising public consciousness about the issues of rape and domestic violence against women and girls. Their efforts resulted in significant legal and judicial reforms, in the form of amendments to the rape laws and a new domestic violence bill that expands criminal sanctions against spousal abuse under the penal code and takes domestic violence out of the Islamic religious courts (Dairiam 1995; Ng and Chee 1996; Rashidah, Raj-Hashim and Schmitt 1995).

As in many countries, feminist actions in Malaysia to combat violence against women reflect a broader vision of women's right to control their bodies with regard to more affirmative domains, including fertility and sexuality. Malaysian women participated in the international meeting of activists in Amsterdam in 1984 where the term 'reproductive rights' was officially adopted (see Chapter 1). In the national context, some of the same women's groups that formed JAG also attempted in the mid-1980s to initiate public debates about the New Population Policy (see below) and to call attention to the need of women in all classes and ethnic groups for greater access to safe, effective contraceptive methods and services and to sex education. But these efforts had no practical results, and no organization has thus far emerged in Malaysia that focuses primarily on women's health and reproductive rights (Rashidah 1993). This lack becomes increasingly evident as women's groups contend with the government's pronatalist population policies and the official discourse of women's natural maternalism.

Population and health policies

Like other rapidly industrializing societies, Malaysia in the 1960s and 1970s experienced a declining fertility rate that helped to slow its annual population growth rate. This decline was due not only to women's rising education and labour force participation, later age at marriage, urbanization and improved living standards but also in part to the government's deliberate policy of promoting family planning, health and family welfare services as an integral part of national development (Leete 1996). In 1984, however, the Malaysian government introduced its New Population Policy with a distinctly pronatalist objective: to stabilise the total population at 70 million by the year 2100 and to create 'a larger consumer base with increasing purchasing power to generate and support industrial growth' (Government of Malaysia 1985). Its strategies to offset the decline in fertility include encouraging more women to marry and have children, strengthening marriage and family stability, and implementing incentives for childbearing through increased maternity leave and tax credits.

In reality, the government's recent pronatalist policy seems to have had little success, since the fertility rates of all three major ethnic groups, including Malays, have continued to decline. According to the government's Population and Family Survey for 1990, the total fertility rate for Malays was 4.1 (down from 5.1 in 1970), that for ethnic Indians was 2.6 (down from 4.8) and that for ethnic Chinese was 2.3 (down from 4.6). The higher rates, and slower decline, among ethnic Malay women was probably influenced as much by the Islamic revival beginning in the 1970s, and by the greater tendency of Malays to use traditional rather than modern contraceptive methods, as it was by the new policy (Leete 1996; Leete and Tan 1993). Further, the ethnic difference may have been abetted in the short run by anxiety among government family planning providers to avoid offending local religious sensitivities in predominantly Malay rural areas. Although contraceptive use varies among the three ethnic groups (it is highest among the Chinese and lowest among the Malays), it has been rising among all three as fertility has declined. Apparently, then, development policies have overridden population policies in influencing Malaysians' family planning decisions (Rashidah 1993; Tey 1993).

Yet the pronatalist policy may still have an ideological and psychological impact, reinforcing the notion that women's primary role is to stay at home and bear children and thus exacerbating feelings of conflict, guilt and confusion among the increasing majority of women who take a different path. Moreover, the policy has apparently affected women's access to safe, legal abortion. Abortion in Malaysia is legal if carried out by a registered medical practitioner who judges that 'the continuance of the pregnancy would involve risk to the life of the pregnant woman, or cause injury to the mental or physical health of the pregnant woman, greater than if the pregnancy were terminated' (Johan 1993:28). Despite this narrow language, prior to the New Population Policy government hospitals and family planning clinics as well as private practitioners had been providing abortions 'fairly liberally since the mid-1970s' (Rashidah 1993). After the new pronatalist policy was instituted, however, government centres, which serve mainly low-income people, became much more restrictive in applying the abortion law (Rashidah 1993).

In relation to other aspects of reproductive health, however, Malaysia's health care system has played a positive role. Through its maternal and child health (MCH) programme, the government has adopted specific strategies to reduce maternal mortality and morbidity. An extensive network of health centres, MCH clinics and mobile teams offers the bulk of the rural population a wide range of public health programmes: family health, home-birth midwifery, home visiting, MCH services, and family planning services. In the cities, health care is dispensed through government general and district hospitals and polyclinics, but increasingly urban health services are undergoing privatization, with the construction of many new private hospitals and clinics that mainly serve people with the means to pay for them. The plantation sector, privately owned, does not come under the purview of the government health services, although its workers may obtain public health services if they are able to travel to the clinics (Kanidah 1993).

In combination with overall development and higher standards of living – and, so far, in spite of the trend toward privatization – the expansion of the health infrastructure, especially in the rural areas, has meant significantly improved reproductive health outcomes for Malaysian women and their children. Thus infant and maternal mortality rates have declined rapidly since the 1960s, according to official government figures, with the infant mortality rate falling from 30 per 1,000 live births in 1960 to 11.6 in 1992 and the maternal mortality ratio plummeting from 240 per 100,000 live births to 20 during the same period (Malaysia Ministry of Health 1992).[7]

With regard to HIV/AIDS, the incidence of female infection in Malaysia is still relatively low compared with that of men: in October 1996, there were 788 women known to be HIV positive and 37 known to have AIDS, compared with 17,373 HIV positive men and 585 AIDS cases among men.

In order to curtail transmission of the HIV virus, the Ministry of Health has mounted an active campaign under its Healthy Lifestyle Programme making use of mass media, public exhibits and talks, and the dissemination of informational materials. Working through the Malaysian AIDS Council, several NGOs are also involved in AIDS prevention activities, doing counselling and outreach to drug users and prostitutes, as well as public education. Recently the government lifted a previous ban on the advertising of condoms in the mass media and began to encourage more sex education among adolescents. In consultation with people with HIV/AIDS, NGOs and religious groups, and sex workers, it also launched a Malaysian AIDS Charter laying out individual and group rights and responsibilities with regard to HIV/AIDS (Norazah Zulkifli et al 1996).

These positive developments suggest the need for a degree of cautious optimism in interpreting the contradictory situation in which Malaysian women currently find themselves. On the one hand, the dominant patriarchal ideology still perceives women's reproductive activity as their main occupation and sees their income-generating jobs as secondary, both to motherhood and to their husbands' work. On the other hand, development policies and their material effects have encouraged increasing numbers of women to become permanent members of the labour force, to marry later, to lower their fertility, and to raise their expectations about being fully contributing members of society beyond the domestic sphere. IRRRAG's research in Malaysia (presented below) confirms that, for younger women – the primary beneficiaries of economic development and gender equality in education – a growing desire to make decisions for themselves about marriage and childbearing may be an irreversible pattern, notwithstanding mainstream society's adherence to patriarchal codes and the state's accommodation of religious and fundamentalist revivalism.

Profile of the Malaysian Research: Methods, Sites and Respondents

The Malaysian IRRRAG team[8] decided to conduct our qualitative field-work primarily by using the life history method, which enabled us to explore the sequence of events and dynamics of women's lives from the time of puberty to the present. Based on a research design that mapped the various components of reproductive health and reproductive rights and the factors influencing them, we identified a list of key issues and formulated guidelines for broad, semi-structured interview questions. The issues included education, work, premarital sexuality, marriage, divorce, polygamy, domestic violence, childbearing and fertility regulation, including contraceptive methods and abortion. Researchers pre-tested and recast the questions before doing the actual interviews; the researchers also recorded information on local demographic data, infrastructures and services; and collected summary information on respondents' socioeconomic backgrounds. This information was helpful in identifying key players in the community as well as economic and social variables that may have influenced respondents' reproductive and sexual values and choices.

We selected five low-income sites, all in peninsular Malaysia, for this study: two rural villages (Sekmai, Chinese, and Kampung Pulau, Malay); a rural plantation (Sungei Linggi estate, Indian); and two urban communities (KL Flats, Chinese, and Kampung Liri, Malay). Selection of the sites was based on previous research or personal contact with the site by a member or associate of the research team. Respondents were chosen on the basis of introductions by key informants in the community, with the exception of the plantation, where they were chosen from a household survey. In total, we selected 71 women for reproductive life-history interviews, including single, married and previously married women ranging in age from fourteen to fifty-eight years. Each respondent was interviewed two to five times, depending on her availability, in her first language (later transcribed into English), to elicit her own understanding of her reproductive history. All were interviewed in the privacy of their homes, without husbands present, with the exception of some of the Indian respondents, who were interviewed in the estate clinic (see below) in order to assure privacy from crowded households.[9]

KL Flats[10] (Chinese urban), a public low-cost residence, is in the capital city of Kuala Lumpur, which has a population of just over 1 million. In this community, the average family income is approximately RM1,500 (US$600) – an amount just sufficient for both everyday living costs in the city and children's education. Husbands of the married respondents are mostly semi-skilled workers, while the sixteen respondents themselves are a mixture of housewives and women who work outside the home, for example as waitresses or saleswomen. The other Chinese site, **Sekmai**, a rural new village,[11] is located about 25 kilometres from Ipoh, a city on the northwest coast of peninsular Malaysia. It consists of about 180 households (around 800 people, almost all of Chinese origin) among whom we likewise interviewed twelve married and four single women. Except for a few spouses from outside the village, there are very few in-migrants. The people in Sekmai are factory workers, drivers of heavy machinery and lorries, agricultural workers, vegetable and tapioca farmers, rubber tappers, smallholders, petty traders and hawkers. The income range is very wide, but most households have an average monthly income of RM1,000 (US$400) to RM 2,000 (US$800) and include the husband's parents.

Unlike KL Flats, where residents have access to both the government health clinics and the private clinics and hospitals in the capital, the only health service available in Sekmai is the government mobile clinic, which visits once a month. Many residents use this service for common illnesses and for immunization of children. Several private clinics are available about 3 to 6 kilometres away, while the government hospitals are about 10 to 25 kilometres away. For antenatal check-ups and family planning, Sekmai residents either use the private clinics and nursing homes or the government hospitals.

Kampung Liri (Malay urban) is a complex of six apartment blocks on the outskirts of Kuala Lumpur, where we interviewed eight married and three single women. A total population of 2,280 people, the majority of them Malay, resides in these five-storey walk-up flats. The majority of the adult residents of Kampung Liri work in the nearby industrial area where the multinational companies and food processing factories are located. Some housewives work part-time in the factories or as cleaners in a nearby hotel. Kampung Liri residents are mainly low and low-to-middle income, although there are some who earn over RM1000 (US$400) per month. Residents have access to three government clinics near the area as well as private clinics in the nearby town and to the university hospital for more serious problems.

The fishing village of **Kampung Pulau** (Malay rural) is located about seven kilometres from Kota Bharu, the capital of Kelantan state.[12] Its population numbers about five hundred, with an average of seven children per family and a total of about seventy households, among whom sixteen women (ten married, two divorced, and four single) were interviewed. Until recently fishing was the major form of employment; however, the number of fishermen has declined rapidly in recent years as the young men have left the village for more lucrative work in the cities, especially Kuala Lumpur and Singapore. Some young women are employed at the garment and ceramic factories in an industrial area about 13 kilometres away (thirty minutes by bus). Many Kampung Pulau residents are employed in local cottage industry, especially batik printing and painting. This is an especially common form of income generation for village housewives, who receive the materials from the batik owners, who live near the village. All respondents in this study are clients of the MCH clinic located about 2 kilometres from the village. Among the informal village leaders who have an important influence on women's reproductive health and decisions is the *bidan kampung* (traditional birth attendant). Her services are still highly sought-after, despite the presence of the government midwife at the MCH clinic.

Sungei Linggi Estate (Indian rural), an oil palm plantation owned by a Malaysian group of companies, is located in the state of Selangor, 85 kilometres from Kuala Lumpur. We interviewed twelve women there – six married, two single, two separated, and two widowed. The plantation has a resident population of 1,562, mostly of south Indian origin, who still maintain the caste system, especially in relation to marriage, job opportunities and social life. The main economic activity, including for the twelve women interviewed, is the planting and processing of palm oil. An underused hospital on site functions only as an outpatient clinic, providing primary medical care through a resident hospital assistant, a nurse, and the infrequent services of a visiting medical officer.[13] Preventive services such as immunization, antenatal care, family planning and health education are only available at the government health clinic 1 kilometre away. Any worker needing hospitalization is transported to the nearest government hospital located about 40 kilometres away.

Although all the five sites are considered low-income, the income levels both within and among these communities vary considerably. Consistent with the national picture (see above), the two Chinese communities in our study have higher income levels than either the Malay or Indian communities, however, they are lower than those of other Chinese communities in Malaysia. Similarly, the urban groups in this study have higher income levels than the rural ones, but they are considered low-income relative to the rest of the urban population.

Internal migration and vibrant ties between urban and rural areas play an important role in shaping the lives of residents in most of the communities. In Kampung Pulau, young men migrate to cities to seek employment while their wives and children remain in the village. In Sekmai, many young unmarried women as well as men have found employment elsewhere; the husbands of most of the women hold jobs outside the village and visit their homes only at weekends or less frequently. The women interviewed in Kuala Lumpur, those living in the outskirts in Kampung Liri as well as those living in the centre of the city (KL Flats), have roots in rural areas outside Kuala Lumpur. The urban Malay women maintain especially strong links with their families in the villages, visiting them during holidays, going back to deliver babies, and sending their children back home for child care. They themselves are recent migrants to the city, having moved there after finishing school to look for jobs or to follow their husbands. In part because of these migration patterns, nearly all respondents were living in nuclear family households; only the rural Chinese women were living with their mothers-in-law.

Malaysian Women Speak – Stories from the Field

Education and employment: 'If you are working you are not afraid...'
Among the generational differences characterizing the women interviewed in this study, across all ethnic groups and sites, none is more striking than the level of education. Since the 1970s, the concept of universal education promoted by the government's modernization policies has permeated all levels of Malaysian society. Although our respondents do not utter the word 'right', their attitudes reflect their strong belief in education as a means of empowerment for women as well as for men. Most of the older women (in their late forties and fifties), especially from the rural areas, had no education at all or only a few years of primary school, having deferred to younger brothers or dropped out because of poverty. These women had accepted their situations; only one mentioned her resentment at that time (Hoi

Chiew, fifty-nine, rural Chinese), while others accepted the family's expectation that they should help parents with work or household chores. Yet when it comes to their own daughters, these same women are firmly committed to the importance of finishing their education.

In contrast to the older women, the younger generation experiences education as an integral part of growing-up. In the Chinese and Malay sites, the majority of the women in the younger age groups have had at least nine to eleven years of schooling; in fact, two have attained post-secondary education.[14] This pattern is consistent with national population census data for 1991 indicating that, among 20–24-year-old women, only 6.3 per cent had never attended school, compared with 35.5 per cent in the 45–49-year-old cohort. Yet we also observed a more disturbing trend among some of the younger women, who tend to drop out after the minimum years of education legally required in order to work or marry or because of bad grades or peer group pressure, even when parents would like them to continue. This may be a response to the double message young women in Malaysia are receiving from the media and religious influences: *get an education, but above all get married and have children.* Yet the drop-out compromise may also invoke later feelings of regret. As Siti, a 25-year-old rural Malay woman, observed: 'If I had continued schooling, I wouldn't be in a situation like this … with two children and no job.' This regret in itself is a sign of significant generational change in women's feelings of entitlement to more dignity and social value.

Overall, the majority of the respondents (48 out of 71, or 68 per cent) are working for an income, either part-time or full-time, in the formal or informal economy. Among them, the most frequent occupations are factory worker and agricultural worker; other women work as seamstresses, batik workers, street vendors, shopkeepers, schoolteachers, clerical and adminis-trative workers, and childminders. In Sekmai, two women in their fifties have retired from employment but spend their time taking care of the household and their grandchildren. Four are full-time housewives, while the rest may consider themselves full-time housewives but either work outside the home or do income-generating work at home. Lai Yin, for example, takes in sewing from a garment factory and integrates this with housework, supervising her school-age children and taking care of a baby. Pek Siew cultivates tapioca, rears fish and plants vegetables, all for sale. Likewise, in Kampung Pulau, most married women are involved in part-time work to earn additional income for their families, typically doing batik painting at home or making cakes to sell at the nearby stalls.

A similar pattern exists in both urban sites. In Kampung Liri, only one student and two older women (those with the least education) among those interviewed are not employed. All the others are involved either in home-based work (such as selling textiles or other merchandise) or work outside their homes. KL Flats has the largest number of respondents claiming to be full-time housewives, but here too the greater number are working for wages. For the rural Indian respondents more than for any of the other groups interviewed, waged work is an intrinsic part of life as much as it is for their husbands. Most of the Indian women are daily wage-earners, employed as fruit-pickers or field workers; of the seven field workers, three also work in the afternoons as operatives in nearby factories. Two with considerably more education than the others are employed as teachers. But all the Indian women worked full-time outside the home.

All the married women in the study were working before their marriage, but even those who had stopped or shifted to part-time work did so only at the birth of their children. Lack of adequate childcare arrangements is one of the main reasons for quitting jobs. Although mothers and mothers-in-law remain important supports, with migration and the loss of nearby extended families both urban and rural women are finding it more difficult to cope. In Sekmai, where patrilocality is the practice, women do receive childrearing support from mothers-in-law or mothers. On the palm oil estate, the Indian women are able to continue working because the management, which has a vested interest in keeping up productivity, provides an on-site childcare facility, albeit of poor quality. In the other communities, however, home-based work, as in Lai Yin's case, becomes the solution for lack of child care.

Work is thus a very important feature in the lives of the respondents, motivated by a range of interacting variables: husbands' low incomes, aspirations to achieve a higher standard of living, access to jobs or informal earning opportunities for women, availability (or not) of child care, and women's own desire for a degree of financial independence. More than anything, the aim of having a better life and securing the family's wellbeing seems to have superseded traditional notions of wives as dependants and husbands as breadwinners. Sarala, a 31-year-old Indian widow who does field and harvesting work on the estate, may speak for others when she says:

> If what he earns is enough then we can sit at home and look after the house. But if his earnings are not enough then it is better for me also to earn. Only then can we bring up the family. We can buy land and live happily.

For the low-income women interviewed in this study, the idea of work is not generally framed as a path to individual career development but rather is constructed out of a complex sense of personal identity that is part familial responsibility, part realism, and part self-worth. This complex understanding is expressed by younger as well as older women – for example, Aini, age eighteen, and Wan Ros, nineteen, from Kampung Pulau, pay lip service to the traditional view of men as primary breadwinners, but assume that they too will work to secure financial stability before marriage and to support their families afterward. Above all, such young women associate work with the capacity for economic independence from parents and husbands, giving them a safety net against potentially abusive or unhappy relationships. As sixteen-year-old Sai Leng (rural Chinese) puts it:

> It's better to work after marriage. If you stay at home your husband may bully you. If you are working you are not afraid, you are supporting yourself. Even if you are staying with your husband's family, you can afford to move out whenever you like. Unless the wages are very low ... in which case, I would not work.

One formula for resolving the tension between the economic reality and the dominant patriarchal ideology of women's work is through the definition of married women's earnings as 'supplementary', as 'extra', or as benefits to the husband. Thus Zai (thirty-five, urban Malay) – echoing the language of many of our respondents – speaks of her right to work but qualifies this by saying she is merely supplementing her husband's income so the family can live more comfortably in the city. The discourse of the supplementary or auxiliary wage serves as a mechanism of accommodation to bridge the gap between the desire for economic resources and autonomy on the one hand and the risk of social stigma or marital conflict on the other.

Another means of accommodating this tension is achieved by women who work at home, or work secretly, in order to acquire earnings while avoiding the opprobrium of husbands, in-laws or community. Because of economic hardship, most husbands do not try to stop their wives from working for pay, especially since wives continue to combine waged work with housework and child care. Yet some women must still contend with husbands who are more traditionally domineering. Che Ton (rural Malay) felt compelled to quit her job not only because of the children but also because her husband demanded that she do so. Meanwhile she still seeks small-business opportunities behind her husband's back, thus openly accommodating his demands while earning money for herself on the sly. Likewise, Lia (thirty-one, urban Malay), despite eleven years of education, had to stop work because her intensely jealous husband forbade her to go out without his permission. She now sells textile fabrics from home through her friends.

In order to keep peace in the household or to placate cultural norms, these women thus adapt their working conditions to spousal or parental demands without, however, giving up the possibility of economic self-determination. A very different case – a kind of resistance in reverse – is that of Pek Siew (forty-five, rural Chinese), who used to work outside the home but stopped as a form of retaliation when she found out that her husband was womanizing:

> If you work, he will give you less money, so I decided not to work. You only work yourself to death. So I do not work.... Even if I have money, I will tell him that I do not have enough to use. If I can get more money from him, I will do so.

While perhaps gaining her some financial leverage in the household, unfortunately Pek Siew's resistant behaviour did not succeed in stopping her husband's extramarital affairs.

Single women also confront scrutiny from parents or neighbours over the 'respectability' of their work choices. Aini left her job at one of the fast-food outlets in town after only one month because of family and community pressures. She ended up working at one of the garment factories where several other women in her village, including her older sister, are working, and where women's employment is more acceptable to the community. Aini's story, like those of Che Ton and Lia, suggests a determination among Malaysian women, across ethnic and age groups, to maintain a work identity and economic independence separate from husbands and other kin, even if through accommodation or subterfuge. For some women the aspect of reclaiming a sense of self and a social identity may even supersede that of financial reward, so that going outside the home to work, even for a low-income job, becomes preferable to the daily routine of a full-time housewife. Yit Meng, forty-two, a vegetable seller, vividly conveys this attitude:

> It's too boring to stay home and not do anything. Who will talk with you? If you go out to work, the days will pass quickly. Otherwise, what will I do at home? After work, have dinner, then it's late, and soon it's another day; quickly the days pass.

To the extent that increasing numbers of Malaysian women share this aspiration for a social identity outside domesticity as well as for economic independence, acquired through education and work, it may provide an important grounding for their sense of entitlement with regard to reproductive and sexual decision making as well.

Marriage and divorce: 'better to be blind in one eye'

In all the sites and ethnic groups we studied, marriage represents a desirable norm, a natural phase in one's life, and a protection against loneliness. In addition, marriage is tied to the wish for children, who are valued not only for security in old age and for extending the family's lineage but also as a source of enjoyment (see section on 'Childbearing and Fertility Regulation', below). Among the Indian respondents, marriage also signifies a young woman's moral value. If young girls do not get married, the community assumes they have committed some wrong or sin in a previous life (for example, ill-treatment of parents, child abuse, or general trouble-making) that is being punished in this life. On the other hand, for some women, particularly among the older groups, the social pressure to get married may have weighed less heavily than the restricted mobility they experienced as unmarried women, expected to remain confined in the home and to assist with household duties (Jones 1994). These women wishfully viewed marriage as an escape route to greater freedom. Karuthama (forty-six, rural Indian), who at the age of fourteen lived with her elder sister and her eight children, accepted a marriage arranged by her grandparents to a thirty-year-old widower. She explains: 'At least if I married him I could see the outside world. I thought by marrying him I could go out and he would buy things for me.'

Younger women in Malaysia are forthrightly rejecting the custom of arranged marriages and asserting their right to marry whom they please when they please (see below). But a few still-exceptional women among our respondents go further, resisting marriage altogether. Oki (rural Malay) is a single woman of thirty who supports herself as a seamstress and has had thirteen years of schooling – more than any of the other respondents in Kampung Pulau. Although labelled by the villagers an 'old maid' and 'too difficult', she holds out, saying the time is not yet right for her; her family supports her resolve. Yati, an urban Malay woman in her late twenties who works as an administrative officer, is even more assertive, projecting an attitude toward marriage that she herself recognizes as deviating from 'the Islamic point of view':

> I feel women can survive without a man.... I never worry about not getting married, because I feel I can survive on my own.... Before actually getting married, we imagine the best – happiness, kids. But it's always the reverse. That's what I don't want.... I'm surrounded by more unhappy than happy marriages; this greatly affects my views.

Yati and Oki express a clear sense of entitlement to live their own lives. Crucially underpinning this stance, of course, is the material situation of both women, who are well educated and have stable jobs. However, since other young women among our Malay respondents were also employed and educated yet succumbed to the pressure to marry, we must conclude that Yati and Oki represent an unusual degree of self-determination in the Malaysian context.

Table 4.1 Distribution of Respondents by Age at Marriage (by site)

AGE AT MARRIAGE	CHINESE URBAN	CHINESE RURAL	MALAY URBAN	MALAY RURAL	INDIAN RURAL	TOTAL
	22.2*	22.1*	20.7*	18.9*	19.5*	
14 years				1	1	2
15–19 years	2	1	3	5	3	14
20–24 years	7	9	4	3	5	28
25–29	2	2	1	2	1	8

* Average age at marriage, 1991 census.
Note: For three respondents, age at marriage was unknown.

At the same time, many other women in Malaysia today, especially among those in their teens and twenties, are moving beyond traditional norms to expand their claims in certain areas of reproductive and sexual entitlement. This is particularly true with regard to the issue of age at marriage and choice of marriage partner. Table 4.1 shows that our respondents follow the national pattern, revealed in demographic research and 1991census data, of ethnic differences in women's age at marriage (Tey *et al.* 1995; Khalipah 1992). The Chinese women, both urban and rural, tend to marry two to three years later than the Malay and Indian women; only among the rural Malay and Indian respondents do we find marriages of women in their mid-teens, the youngest at age fourteen.

Yet perhaps as important in the long run as ethnic differences in determining age at marriage are generation, education and employment. Most of the women among our respondents who married at young ages (fourteen to eighteen) are in their late forties or fifties; these women also had little or no education. The few in the younger age groups (under twenty-five) who married at age eighteen or younger tend to be those who dropped out of school prematurely or were forced to marry to legitimize transgressive sexual behaviour. On the other hand, the majority of our married respondents from all ethnic groups who are now in their twenties or thirties (the cohorts who grew up since the NEP came into effect) were married after the age of twenty and tend either to have at least ten years of schooling or a history of steady employment, or both. Thus our study's respondents appear to confirm a well documented trend among younger Malaysian women, across ethnic groups and rural and urban areas, to postpone marriage to pursue educational and work opportunities[15] (Malaysia Department of Statistics 1991). In turn, women's decision to marry later than their mother's generation is reinforced by societal and parental acceptance of young women's need to complete their education and acquire job skills before marrying.

Similar generational changes emerge around the question of choice of marriage partner among both rural Malay and rural Indian respondents; in the Chinese community choice of marriage partner has been well established for all generations interviewed, among both rural and urban groups. Most of the older Malay and Indian women were married through arrangement by their families, having had no say and, in some cases among the rural Malays,[16] even being coerced despite their protests. Latifah, a 46-year-old woman from Kampung Pulau, recalls: 'I was not willing but father got angry. That was the olden days. The old people, they got angry. Even when their children were not willing, they would still force them.' Similarly, Eton (now forty-six) was told by her parents that she must marry a divorced man nineteen years her senior who already had children. It never occurred to her to object. Like Karuthama, she could not imagine a more desirable future for herself. Today, however, even among Malays in rural areas, arranged marriages are increasingly becoming a thing of the past (Jones 1994; Rudie 1994). Across all research sites and ethnic groups, the younger respondents, especially those not yet married, indicate that they want and expect to choose their own partners. For example, Kui Meng (eighteen, rural Chinese) reasons:

> If my family decides, and they choose someone who treats me badly after marriage, then I will be blaming them. If I decide on my own, then whatever the outcome, I will bear the responsibility.... If I cannot find someone to marry, I would not get married. Matchmaking is weird ... nobody does it nowadays.

Similarly, Wan Ros (nineteen, rural Malay) asserts: 'who has the right to decide? We do, after all we're the ones who want to get married.' This desire to choose one's partner and the ability to carry out that choice is a reflection of the social and economic changes in Malaysia, as well as of 'girls' exposure to a range of ideas, due to education, greater geographic mobility, ... the media (especially television) and movies' (Jones 1994: 144).

The strong defence of personal choice about when and whom to marry does not necessarily mean that young Malaysian women are seeking to defy their parents. Many respondents express a desire both to make their own decisions and to obtain their parents' support and approval. In part this reflects the traditional value of respect for parents, but it also signifies practical concerns. Although Wan Ros insists on her right to decide, if her parents were to oppose her choice of marriage partner she is ready to compromise in order not to hurt their feelings. She might even agree to their choice if she gets to know the man and he meets her criteria for a good husband. Young women may also factor into their calculations the value of their parents' emotional and financial support, in case the marriage does not work out. Such support eluded Janaki, who eloped with a man her parents did not approve of and then was unable to turn to them when her marriage broke up:

> They say that I am a 'runaway girl' and why should I visit their house.... I am very sad. If I had listened to my parents, I would have got married to a good man. Because I ran away I am suffering a lot. If my parents got me married, and if I had many problems, my parents would still help me. But because I chose this life, who would I ask? These things disappoint me. (Janaki, twenty-eight, rural Indian)

Although parent-arranged marriages still occasionally take place, these are based on consultation and consent of the children and mostly occur only with regard to daughters who have dropped out of school and are not working (Rudie 1994). Eli (twenty-five, rural Malay) had eleven years of schooling but dropped out because of poor grades in the national examination. Living with her parents and unemployed, she lacked occasions for meeting young men on her own and thus became a likely candidate for a parent-arranged marriage. Yet this exceptional reversion to traditional roles in the case of dependent daughters merely demonstrates the general trend: young Malaysian women of all classes and ethnic groups who achieve a certain level of education and economic self-sufficiency are perceived, and perceive themselves, as acquiring a clear entitlement to choose when and whom they marry.

When it comes to premarital sexuality, however, religion and culture still play a strong role in shaping the norms and morals of Malaysian society, superseding even the value of education. Young women in all three ethnic groups may find themselves under pressure from parents to marry if they have a boyfriend, but this pattern seems especially prevalent among rural Malays. One young respondent, Noraini (twenty-three, rural Malay), had to marry at the age of sixteen, while she was still in school, because she violated the cultural norm prevailing in Kampung Pulau by going out secretly with a man one evening. When her family found out, Noraini and her male friend were forced to marry immediately.[17] Lamenting the hopelessness of her predicament, she exclaims: 'What could I do? I cried because I was still in school. What would I do if I were to pass the exam? It would be such a pity.' Siti, also from Kampung Pulau, was likewise forced by her angry parents to marry after she stole off to Kuala Lumpur with her boyfriend for the weekend and was caught. These incidents illustrate both the persistence of traditional sexual codes in rural Malay communities and the willingness of some young unmarried women to risk the consequences of transgressing them.

Power within marriage for women seems to involve a delicate balance between verbal deference to traditional gender norms and practical manoeuvring to control and accumulate resources. Regardless of age, level of education or ethnic group, most of the women in this study, like Malaysian women generally, have been active contributors to the welfare and sustenance of their households: engaging in domestic chores, taking care of children and younger siblings, working in production either at home or outside, before and after marriage, and contributing significantly to their families' incomes. Yet, as suggested earlier, both married and single women adhere to the normative ideal of the husband as principal breadwinner and decision maker, the wife as subsidiary earner. The positive side of this conventional gender ideology is the strong sense of entitlement it generates among women of all three ethnic groups: that it is their right to be provided for by their husbands. The negative side is a continued tendency for married women to denigrate their own work and decision making in the household. Lai Yin (thirty-nine, rural Chinese) communicates this complex set of expectations:

> Most of the household decisions, the small things, regarding children and schooling, for example, are made by me. The big decisions, regarding work, for example, are made by my husband. But whether or not I want to work is my own decision. Even if I don't work, he has to support me, it is his responsibility.

In practice, however, women's power to decide about both extra-household and intra-household matters seems to be linked to their economic resources as well as to their social status and age. Yit Meng, aged forty-two, evokes the greater decision-making power in the household that older rural

Chinese women tend to have: 'Usually I am the one to make the decisions in this household. He will say, "You decide."' Karuthama (forty-six, Indian) has been able to expand her role in defiance of her husband because she has managed to save and invest in some properties and livestock and is no longer financially dependent on him. After years of tolerating her husband's demanding and uncaring attitude, she now assumes the responsibility of taking care of the children and making decisions for them even regarding their marriages, normally a matter decided by fathers. In this case, access to economic resources has clearly made her more independent.

But control over finances can be a double-edged sword if it means assuming all the household responsibilities. Latifah's husband gives her almost all his earnings, keeping only pocket money. Her control over household finances has enabled Latifah to decide many family issues (including those related to her reproductive health) yet has also increased her burdens, not only of budgeting the money but also of finding money if it runs out:

> I do everything, everything is on me. Clever or not it all falls on me ... children's schooling. They don't ask money from him because I'm the one who manages to buy this and that.... In order to pay for exam fees or to pay for anything at all, I'm the one who went to pawn my jewellery bit by bit. (Latifah, forty-five, rural Malay)

Married women with children who lack such control or resources find themselves completely dependent on their husbands. As Sai Leng already perceives at age sixteen, without their own safety net such women are more vulnerable to intimidation or to having constantly to accommodate a husband's demands. Developing strategies and diplomatic skills to placate husbands and ensure the marriage's stability becomes a matter of survival. Thus Nora, an urban Malay housewife with four children, explains that if her husband is angry, she will keep quiet; when he is nice, she will be good to him. She accommodates his moods and does not argue because she does not want to expose the children to quarrelling:

> If we fight in front of our children, we will be in trouble. We have to win our husband's heart. We also have to keep in shape. Just like what people used to say, we [women] not only need to serve food but we need to serve everything.

Due to their economic dependence on husbands and the perceived needs of children, divorce is an action that the respondents will take only as a last resort. Because of their low skills as well as gender discrimination in the labour market, most of these women would not be able to earn the kind of money their husbands bring home. Despite much suffering, then, many stay in their marriages. In the rural Chinese community, it is understood that a 'bad' husband is one who does not provide for the family; infidelity or even physical abuse may be tolerated so long as the husband provides for the family. Pek Siew (45) exemplifies this harsh trade-off:

My own husband is a philanderer, but I do not care what he does. So long as he gives me the housekeeping money, whatever he does, I do not care. It is because I can close one eye that we can continue like this. If I cannot, it's gone … what else can you do? The more you quarrel with him, the worse it becomes, isn't that so? It's better to be blind in one eye, to pretend not to know, then it's finished.…

Lai Yin (thirty-nine), who does home-based work and, like Pek Siew, has four children, uses nagging and crying against her husband's gambling. 'If you continue like this,' she threatens, 'I will run away with the children,' or 'I will commit suicide.' However, her threats have no effect as he knows she will never leave because of the children:

How can I bring up four children on my own? If a woman's economic standing is good, and she can support herself and her children, and if her husband is not too good toward her, then divorce can be a way out. But if she is dependent on her husband, she will have to think of her children's future, then she will have to tolerate her husband for the sake of her children.

Yet some women, albeit a minority, do seek divorce or separation to end an intolerable situation. Nine of our respondents have either experienced divorce or separation or are in the process of getting divorced.[18] Though the sample in this study is small, the higher incidence of divorce among the Malay respondents corresponds to national figures. Data for 1990 indicate that the divorce rate for Malays in peninsular Malaysia was over eight times that for Chinese and Indians (Tan and Ng 1995). The national data surely reflect many divorces initiated by husbands rather than wives, in some cases no doubt against the wives' wishes; as well as a greater emphasis on legal proceedings for Muslims. Yet, among our respondents, nearly all the divorced and separated women had sought this action on their own, despite the difficulties for Malay wives under *syriah* law of initiating divorce proceedings.[19] Unlike the Chinese women quoted earlier, Malay women feel they are entitled not only to financial support but to fair and kind treatment by their husbands, even if the marriage is polygamous. If the men neglect their responsibilities or abuse their wives, then these women see divorce as their right. In fact it is only when they talk about divorce that the Malay women in the study use the word 'right', or *hak*, in contrast with other topics such as childbearing or contraception. They are aware that they are entitled to divorce, particularly in cases of violence or neglect by their husbands, and fully understand that they too can make the move to initiate and file for divorce at the office of the *kadi* (the official who presides over the religious court and matters pertaining to Islamic personal law). If divorce is inevitable, these women also stated that they and their children are entitled to *nafkah*, or maintenance. This sense of entitlement seems to reflect a stronger climate of support for divorce in Malay families and communities relative to the other groups.

Faridah, an urban Malay respondent, for a long time tolerated her first husband's infidelity and physical abuse because she was unemployed and had no income. In the end, however, even with eight children and no job, she could no longer stand the physical abuse and filed for divorce. Four rural Malay women (three in their mid-forties and one thirty-three), all forced into marriage by their parents, later used divorce as a means of getting some form of independence. They eventually walked out of their marriages and, by refusing to return to their husbands, created a *fait accompli* that led to divorce. As divorced women they had a lot more freedom than they had had as young single women to choose their own (new) partners. In these cases, the women seem to have used divorce, usually dreaded by women, to their advantage – a manoeuvre made easier by the support they received from their families.

For other women, having their own earnings became the ticket out of an unhappy marriage. Uma and Devi – both Indian, aged thirty-five and employed – left their husbands because they too could no longer tolerate their jealousy, violent tempers and efforts to restrain their mobility. Uma's husband forbade her to communicate with outsiders, particularly men; if she ever ventured out of the house alone, he would beat her. She – like Devi and most of the Malay divorced and separated respondents – had independent means of financial support. The number of children a woman has is another strong factor affecting her decision to seek a separation or divorce. Except for Faridah, who had eight children when she finally divorced, the others had only one or two children. They were also still young and had prospects for another marriage as well as strong parental support when they walked out of their respective marriages.

Whatever her economic circumstances, in order to obtain a divorce – whether civil or religious – a woman must be willing to negotiate her way through a daunting set of bureaucratic and legal hurdles. Che Ton, who runs her own home-based business, found the process of obtaining a divorce so long and difficult that, despite her economic resources, she finally gave up. Having been battered by her husband, she attempted to apply for divorce using her rights under *takliq*. When she went to the *kadi*'s office, she was told to come back again with her *takliq* letter. Since she was in pain from the beating, she also went for medical treatment and was advised by the doctor to report the beating to the police to facilitate her divorce process. By then she thought the process too cumbersome to continue.

In sum, the ability to take action, to walk out of the marriage, to file for divorce, and to actually win it will often depend on a number of practical realities, including a woman's age and number of children; the willingness and ability of her husband to provide maintenance, or alternatively, her own access to financial resources and/or familial support networks; and, finally, her own persistence and stamina. Having a sense of entitlement is one thing, realizing it another.

Childbearing and fertility regulation: 'I am the one to ... decide'

In Malaysia, across all ethnic groups and generations, marriage is inseparable from childbearing, and childbearing is a necessary proof of womanhood. Children are deemed valuable as a source of joy and companionship, to continue the family lineage and to provide support and security in old age. Having more children is a hedge for the future, since there is uncertainty whether all children will survive into adulthood. Conversely, a wife's infertility is considered reasonable grounds for her husband to take a second wife or a mistress or even to divorce her. Speculating on what she would do if she were infertile, Kui Meng, an eighteen-year-old unmarried woman from Sekmai, muses:

> Well, I could be generous. Let him take another wife to have children for him. Since I cannot have children, I should not keep him for myself only. This way, the children will call me 'big mother', at least I will have stepchildren.

Kui Meng's assumption that having stepchildren is preferable to being a childless though exclusive wife indicates the great importance of motherhood in structuring women's lives and identities in Malaysia. If a woman cannot have any children of her own, adoption is commonly seen as a solution, especially among the Chinese. 'I'd adopt, buy!' exclaims sixteen-year-old May (urban Chinese) in contemplating the prospect of infertility.

The respondents in this study do not use language denoting entitlement when they talk about procreation. Rather, they see having children as something natural and view women without children as pitiable. Even single women find themselves encouraged to have children; if marriage eludes them, their family and neighbours will often suggest that they adopt. On the other hand, it is clear that unmarried women are not entitled to bear children. The respondents often reflect society's normative values by treating out-of-wedlock childbearing as sinful, speaking of it in hushed tones. On further discussion, many speak of the social problems that unmarried mothers face rather than imputing to them any wrongdoing. Given the strong cultural sanctions, it is not surprising that women commonly seek to prove their fertility to their husbands, families and in-laws by getting pregnant very soon after marriage. Occasionally, however, our respondents complained about this pressure. Lily, for example (twenty-eight, urban Chinese), who has two children, admits, 'I was pregnant one year after my marriage. If not for the noises that my in-laws made, I would have postponed my pregnancy. To a woman, children are a lot of responsibilities.'

This theme of the burdens and responsibilities of motherhood echoes time and again among our respondents, evoking the tension many women in Malaysia seem to experience between the dominant cultural values regarding fertility and their own realities and aspirations. As in the matter of resolving marital conflicts, the strategies many women use to negotiate this tension involve a strong sense of entitlement to regulate their own fertility, but one that is expressed more through behaviour than through explicit words or confrontations, and more among younger generations (teens, twenties and thirties) than older. When asked about the ideal number of children in a family and who should decide, the older Malay women typically respond, 'It's up to God,' or 'My husband will decide.' Yet the fact that all but a handful of these women have had far fewer children than would be 'natural' over their reproductive lifetimes indicates that they too are exercising some deliberate (and effective) means of limiting their fertility.

In fact, contrary to national trends, in which Chinese women have the lowest levels of fertility of the three ethnic groups (Ganga 1993), our urban Malay and (rural) Indian women have had fewer average births than our Chinese urban and rural women. This probably reflects, in part, the higher employment rates among the women in Kampung Liri and the oil palm estate relative to those in KL Flats, suggesting that local material conditions may influence ethnic fertility differentials. Similar to national trends, however, the younger women in our study can be expected to have fewer children compared to the older women. While ten of the rural respondents have had five or more children, the majority of these were married young and are now in their late forties or fifties. An exception among the older cohorts is Hoi Chiew, fifty-nine years old at the time of the study and with only two children. Yet she is an exception who in some ways proves the rule, given her work history. Although she has had no formal education, Hoi Chiew has been working from a young age – mostly as a tin mine worker – and considers herself a trendsetter in the community, a woman with 'modern' ideas. At the time of her retirement, she held a regular waged job as a municipal garbage collector and now takes care of her grandchildren. Most of the respondents who have only one or two children, however, are still young (in their twenties) or married late. For example, Sutinah (thirty-one), who married at twenty-eight years, now has two children; Che Aza (thirty-five), who married at twenty-nine, has one child. It is also interesting that, while only one ever-married Chinese woman in her thirties has two children (Mei Mei, age thirty-eight), six of the Malay women in their thirties do. In addition to the two who married late (rural), the other four live in the city and are employed full-time as factory or service workers. This suggests that, increasingly, occupation and urbanization may play a stronger role than ethnicity in determining Malaysian women's fertility patterns.

In addition to pregnancy outcomes, the interviews offer plenty of evidence that women in all three ethnic groups assume a sense of entitlement to regulate their own fertility, even if they must enlist the support of family members to get their way. Janaki, for example (twenty-eight, a rural Indian), underwent seven difficult pregnancies, three of which ended in miscarriages, and was advised by the doctor not to have any more children. She wanted a tubal ligation, but this required spousal consent:

[The doctor] asked me if I had enough children; I said 'Enough'. I asked my husband about the operation [tubal ligation]. He disagreed as he wanted another son. I told my parents. They spoke to my husband saying that another pregnancy might kill me. Then my husband signed and the operation was done.

Some of the women hide their contraceptive behaviour from disapproving husbands but persist none the less. Karuthama, for example, started taking the pill after her seventh pregnancy without the knowledge of her husband. He had prohibited her from using contraception on her own, though at one point he came home with a condom (see below), a method he was willing to use presumably because it was controlled by him. However, with the help of the nurse at the clinic, Karuthama managed to use the pill effectively for a period of five years before an accidental conception occurred:

If I tell him that I am taking the pills, he will scold me. He'll ask me why I am taking the pills. We get babies very fast; by the time one child learns to walk properly, there will be another baby. Mrs Selvam [staff nurse at the estate clinic] taught me a lot. She told me to take the pills so that I won't have any more children.... Nobody except she knows that I take the pills.

Similarly Noraini, a 23-year-old rural Malay housewife with two young children, decided to take traditional herbs without telling her husband. Noraini feels she is entitled to decide and to take contraceptives behind her husband's back even if he disagrees because, as she says, 'I'm much more tired than he is. He goes and comes back once in a while. I'm the one who has to fight with the children.' Lai Yin, a 35-year-old rural Chinese woman, expresses a similar sentiment, although she does discuss contraception with her husband, who defers to her. Eloquently, she expresses a sense of entitlement derived from the burdens and responsibilities of mothering:

I am the one to make the decisions where family planning is concerned. After I decide, then I tell him that we should not have so many children or that we should not space them so closely.... because caring for them is difficult. Childrearing is not by him, his responsibility is only to bring the money back. When he comes home, he sees the children are already fed and bathed....He only plays with them, he does not take care of them. Getting up in the middle of the night to give them milk, taking them to the doctor when they are ill – all this is my responsibility. He does not suffer, the suffering is all done by me. So when I tell him that we need to use the contraceptive, he cooperates.

In a cultural and social context that places a high value on children, women must have good reasons for wanting to stop bearing them. This is particularly true in Malay communities, where children are considered gifts from God, not to be spurned. Thus Malay women often use the language of 'spacing' to explain their actions to limit births. In all three ethnic groups, the main reasons women give for limiting the number of children are economic considerations and problems in arranging child care. Financial constraint as a principal motive reflects the women's aspirations for a better quality of life and, in particular, a desire to have their children achieve a higher level of education. Moreover, childrearing and child care require skill and commitment, largely on the woman's part, as well as resources such as money, time and energy. This concern, which was expressed by all the women interviewed, reinforces their strong sense that they, as the ones responsible for household management, must determine family size, not their husbands. Hapsah, for instance – a 34-year-old urban Malay mother-of-three who works as a hotel cleaning woman – says laughingly that she 'never discussed' the issue with her husband: 'The problem is our income is small. We really have got to think if we were to pay a childminder. Too many children will bring us problems.... Whatever the planning is, I plan on my own.'

The problem of finding adequate, affordable child care is particularly difficult for low-income women in the city, like Hapsah, who go out to work. Although she feels the more children the better, 'when I work,' she explains, 'there is a question of who is going to take care of them. Even with only two children it was a problem to find someone to look after them.' Women in the rural sites also express this concern. Siti (twenty-five, rural Malay) worries about children being 'too close' and 'not being able to take care if there are too many'. Sin Fah (29, rural Chinese, with four children) had an abortion when she discovered she was pregnant one year after her third child was born:

> One thing is that conditions were difficult, the other thing is that I am not able to care for them – one year one child, so close, and the others were still so small. Only myself alone, how can I handle taking care of so many children?

This is not to say that the provision of affordable quality child care will encourage women to have more children, although it will certainly improve the quality of women's lives. The responsibility of childrearing goes beyond physical child care, and women do feel constrained by bearing the whole of it. Kum Mooi (thirty-five, rural Chinese), who has four children already and whose youngest is five years old, explains why she too had an abortion recently:

> I myself do not want another child. All my children are so big already. If I give birth to another one, it will be difficult for me. I will not be so free; cannot go anywhere.... Even if I have money, I still think that four children is enough. My husband is the one who wants one more if he has the money. He does not have to take care of them; he does not know how difficult it is.

As Kum Mooi illustrates, women's determination to limit their number of children stems not only from economic calculations and aspirations for a better life for their families, but also from women's personal longing for greater mobility and freedom.

Contraception and abortion

Respondents in our study reflect a similar pattern of contraceptive use to that appearing in statistical data from recent national surveys (Tey 1993, Rashidah 1993, Tey *et al.* 1995): contraceptive use is highest among the Chinese (both urban and rural), high also among the urban Malays and rural Indians, and lower among the rural Malay women, who show a preference for traditional herbal methods. But our qualitative data also reveal ethnic differences in women's strategies to control their fertility, as well as the difficulties they encounter. Many of the married women we interviewed report problems in finding a suitable contraceptive method that they can use with confidence in its safety and efficacy, without suffering unacceptable side effects. While the pill is the most widely used method among Malaysian women nationally, our study shows a more complicated pattern. Nearly half the married respondents in the study (24 out of 50) were either currently using the pill or had used it at some time. However, although the pill was the most widely tried method among the Chinese and urban Malay women, many dropped it after experiencing side effects, ultimately preferring the condom or the rhythm method.

The Indian respondents were even less inclined toward the pill, only three having ever used it, two of whom stopped within four months because of side effects. Like Indian women nationally, those in our study seem to prefer tubal ligation because of the absence of side effects or the need for follow-up. Of the six married Indian women who are currently using contraception, four had reached their desired family size and opted for tubal ligation ('tying the stomach') after learning about it through co-workers. This is in sharp contrast to the Malay women, who, due to Islamic prohibitions, avoid sterilization except in cases of medical necessity. In part, the prevalence of sterilization in the Indian community may be a result of subtle coercion. Prior to 1988, the plantations pushed for sterilization in order to ensure high productivity and profits. A high rate of sterilization would mean lower numbers of women workers going on maternity leave and thus lower costs for the estate in child care and maternity benefits.[20] Conversely, some women who might choose it may be discouraged from getting sterilized because of the required consent of husbands, who, like Janaki's, often disapprove.

Like Sin Fah and Kum Mooi, many of the rural Chinese women rely on a combination of medical or barrier methods and abortion to achieve birth spacing and the number of children they want. In contrast, most of the rural Malay respondents who use contraception choose to take traditional herbs (Tey *et al.* 1995). Although modern contraceptives are available at the government health clinic servicing Kampung Pulau, they are culturally and socially unacceptable to the women who were interviewed. First, the women are unsure whether Islam condones the use of modern contraception.[21] Second, since family planning is viewed as a highly personal matter, the villagers do not talk about it openly, and the women feel compelled to hide their efforts. Third, many of the women interviewed associate modern contraceptives with side effects and ominous reports of friends and neighbours who conceived and gave birth to disabled children while using modern contraceptives.

Latifah, aged forty-five, is the only one among the rural Malay respondents who tried to space her children using modern contraceptives. She discussed this with her husband, who agreed to her use of the pill after her third pregnancy. Nevertheless, wanting to keep it a secret from the other villagers, she travelled to a clinic in another village to obtain the pill. Later, however, she experienced side effects and was advised by her mother-in-law, a *bidan kampung*, to change to traditional herbs. But these never worked for her, and six more pregnancies followed, so Latifah ended up with nine children. After her mother-in-law died, she went back to the government clinic in town and had an intra-uterine device (IUD) inserted.

Although modern contraceptives did not work for Latifah, they seem to work well for other women like Siti (twenty-five) and Che Ton (forty-five), who do not see any need to change to another method. Indeed, Latifah's case epitomizes the intricate ways in which rural Malay women attempt to navigate between local cultural expectations – often conveyed through the influence of older female kin – and their own sense of entitlement to control their fertility. Unlike rural Indian women such as Karuthama, who lives apart from her extended family and whose contraceptive decision-making was guided by the estate's clinic nurse, rural Malay women are influenced by female kin and husbands rather than reproductive health providers.

Although we found numerous instances of cooperative husbands, especially among the younger generations, in general husbands are the most important constraint on women's effective contraceptive use. Usually husbands do not take an active part in family planning, and often they try to forbid their wives from using contraceptives. Uma's husband, for example, was so angry that she used an IUD without his consent (to avoid pregnancy after her third child) that he left home and has not returned since. Far from exerting control over his wife's body and reproductive agency, Uma's husband left precisely because of his inability to exercise control over her (cf. Ong 1994). Many of our respondents manage to challenge or elude their husbands' opposition as well as the state's pronatalist policy. Judging from national fertility declines among all ethnic groups, their tenacity exemplifies the majority of Malaysian women.

Despite their clear commitment to limiting their fertility, however, some respondents also revealed serious misconceptions about particular contraceptive methods, indicating poor information or inadequate counselling as well as cultural barriers against certain methods. Some take the pill only erratically, in an attempt to avoid unpleasant side effects, also believing they do not need to take it if their husband is away from home. A few distrust the

IUD, having heard that women can become pregnant using it or feeling uncomfortable about 'putting something inside'. For older women, the condom is fraught with negative connotations. Karuthama, for example – who, as we saw, ultimately used the pill without consulting her husband – dreaded it:

> When he brought it home, I put my two hands together in prayer and begged him not to show it to me again.... I was afraid that by using it, we might get hurt or injured somewhere.... I might get wounded. I never asked anybody whether I will get hurt or what, but it is just in my mind, that I might get hurt or wounded.

Some of the older Chinese women believe that using condoms is detrimental to men's health: 'It will spoil the eyes of the man', Yit Meng (aged forty-two, rural Chinese) warns. Or, according to Yow Lan (fifty-four, rural Chinese), 'People say that it's bad for the men. The semen cannot come out, it's all blocked up. Men go out to work; if you spoil their health, then it's hard for them to earn a living.' Nevertheless, many of the younger or more assertive Chinese women feel the condom is safe and acceptable. Lai Yin – one of the most self-determined women in the study – finds it very suited to the 'cooperation' she insists on from her husband in transacting 'this family planning business'; they have been using it successfully for twelve years or so:

> It's very safe; when I wanted to have my second child, I stopped using it and immediately I conceived. I have never conceived while using this method. My husband did not object to using it. If my husband is here, then I use it; if he is not here, I don't have to use it. If I take the pill, I have to take it the whole month even if we have intercourse only once, it's too inconvenient. And it's not good for health either.

Whether because of method failure, misuse of a method, or nonuse, many of our respondents have experienced unwanted pregnancies and resorted to legal or semi-legal abortions as a back-up. As discussed earlier, abortion access for women in Malaysia has suffered from the combined impact of patriarchal/religious revivalism and the pronatalist population policy. The result has been that many women, particularly among low-income Malays, resort to traditional methods or continue with their pregnancies even when their health condition indicates the need for safe, low-cost abortion. At the same time, the expanding private sector (nursing homes and clinics) and *bidan kampung* continue to perform induced abortions, and traditional herbal abortifacients are freely available through informal networks and the Chinese medicine shops.

The expressed views of our Malay respondents concerning abortion reflect the prevailing climate of legal and moral ambiguity. Most call it a 'sin', justified only for dire health reasons, and frown on the idea that unmarried women might resort to abortions. Only one out of all the Malay women interviewed admitted ever having tried to obtain an abortion. Noraini, who has resisted in many ways the norms of her community, became pregnant while living with her boyfriend in Kuala Lumpur and tried to get an abortion. But by the time she managed to raise the necessary funds her pregnancy had advanced, the price of the abortion had increased, and she could no longer afford it. She also tried various traditional methods, which were unsuccessful. Clearly Noraini is a victim of the reduction in government abortion services, reflecting its harsh impact on low-income women. Yet, if Noraini is exceptional among the Malay women interviewed, it is only in her candour. Although none of them reported having had an abortion, all the Malay respondents seem to know about the traditional methods, which they claim to have learned from the *bidan kampung* or other women in the community. The knowledge and availability of traditional herbal abortifacients in the Malay community belie the general view that abortion is uncommon among Malay women and confirm the impression that they significantly underreport both attempted and realized abortions.[22]

Attitudes among the Chinese respondents also reflect the impact of the more restrictive political and cultural climate, insofar as many of them have the mistaken belief that abortion is illegal and express moral reservations about it. Yet, in contrast to the Malay women, most of the Chinese speak of their abortions openly and pragmatically as a necessary back-up to be used when contraception fails. The rural Chinese respondents widely practise abortion despite their expressed belief that it is dangerous to women's health. Out of the 12 married women interviewed in Sekmai, four had undergone an abortion once and one had had two abortions; these mostly took place at private nursing homes or clinics. Two of the women had used traditional Chinese herbs taken orally; both ended up in the hospital when they started to bleed uncontrollably. Among the urban Chinese respondents, four of the women interviewed have had abortions, two of them twice.

Yet these practices are in striking contradiction to the same women's expressions of moral disapproval regarding abortion. In fact, two of the rural women who underwent abortions during the period of the research had earlier professed to view abortion as morally reprehensible. Kum Mooi (thirty-five, rural Chinese) initially told the interviewer that she considered abortion 'very wasteful' and would not have one if she experienced another pregnancy. When she subsequently found herself pregnant after neglecting to take her pills, she nevertheless got an abortion (with her husband's approval) at a private nursing home. Having four children already, considering herself 'getting old', and wanting to enjoy the freedom that is possible with children who are no longer small, she abandoned her earlier scruples.

When it comes to abortion, then, our evidence shows a considerable gap between professed values and behaviour among both Malay and Chinese respondents. This gap confirms the earlier observation in regard to fertility control: that the resurgence of patriarchal and pronatalist ideology in Malaysia may be influencing what women say more than what they do. The distinct, if implicit, sense of entitlement revealed in the women's behaviour emerges more sharply among the Chinese than among the Malay respondents: all the rural Chinese women who had abortions say the decision was theirs, with only Kum Mooi having sought her husband's prior approval.

With regard to contraception, among all the groups interviewed, whenever there are disagreements, wives tend to be the ones who want to use contraceptives while husbands tend not to share their wives' feelings of urgency about it. Overall, whatever strategies they use to accommodate, subvert or resist dominant community norms or the wishes of husbands or in-laws, a surprisingly high proportion of the women in our study, across the three ethnic groups, seem to be taking a firm hand in shaping their own reproductive lives.

Conclusion

Our study suggests that Malaysian women are currently in a state of transition in which education, work, and access to independent economic and social resources are beginning to play a greater role than ethnicity and tradition in reproductive and sexual decision-making. Although the women we interviewed did not talk about their economic or reproductive 'rights', significant numbers from both urban and rural Malay and Chinese communities assert entitlement to decide for themselves about whom and when to marry, the number and spacing of children, the use of contraceptives, and whether and where to work. Indian women seem less likely to assert a claim against their husbands' or parents' will, yet they too, through their actions if not their words, manifest a sense of entitlement to make their own decisions about important aspects of marriage, work, and childbearing. This awareness, however, emerges more strongly in some arenas than others and remains difficult to realize for some women because of their lack of economic, social or infrastructural supports.

While most of the women interviewed accept the social norm prescribing marriage and motherhood as their ultimate goal, the majority of women under forty also expect that they, like men, should acquire an education and earn income before and after marriage in order to provide a better quality of life for themselves and their children. The younger women seem to value the economic independence they gain from education and work, which allows them to negotiate their family lives with greater autonomy. This generational change is evident in one of the principal findings of the study: the increasing tendency for younger women to exercise freedom in their choice of marriage partner and to delay marriage in order to pursue education and work. The shift is particularly striking in the case of young Malay women in the study, whose mothers tended to comply with parental arrangements and who consider such arrangements completely out of date for themselves.

We also found that, despite the pressures of Islamic revivalism, the Malay women in our study showed an even greater sense of entitlement than either the Indian or the Chinese women to initiate divorce if their marriage becomes intolerable due to spousal abuse, violence or neglect; indeed, they explicitly view divorce in such cases as their 'right'. This is one of the few instances, along with the traditional notion of women's right to be supported by their husbands, in which the synthesis of religion and tradition seems to work in Malaysian women's favour and to give them a basis for invoking rights. But the practical ability to act on this right may be significantly hampered by lack of access to independent economic resources, child care, or familial support. The Chinese and Indian respondents, on the other hand, were more likely to tolerate abuse, violence or infidelity from husbands so long as they carried out their duties as breadwinner; when pushed to the wall, they would seek separation but not necessarily formal divorce. Here too, however, the will to separate seems to hinge on the presence or absence of material resources and the calculation of one's practical possibilities to survive and raise children without a husband.

Indeed, while our respondents often expressed being pulled by traditional expectations about gender roles or the pressures of husbands or in-laws, the most decisive factor shaping their decisions about whether or not to work outside the home or remain married was the issue of child care and responsibility for children. The data also reveal an interesting contrast between women's public pronouncements of adherence to traditional or religious norms and their private, sometimes resistant words and actions. This discrepancy emerged, for example, among Malay women who ostensibly accommodated husbands' demands that they not work outside the home yet satisfied their children's need for additional income and their own need for independence by doing home-based work or conducting a business on the side. Another, even more striking example is the multiple strategies respondents from all three groups used to evade religious, community or spousal prohibitions against contraception and abortion.

More than in any other domain, we found a strong sense of entitlement among the women in this study in regard to decisions about fertility. While there were clear ethnic and urban–rural differences in patterns of contraceptive use and methods preferred, nearly all the women we interviewed decided to limit their childbearing through contraception, sterilization or abortion. And more often than not, they decided on their own, without the knowledge or consent of husbands. Not all were equally successful in this resolve; many were unable to find a really satisfactory or effective method (as demonstrated by the high rate of disaffection from the pill); sometimes there was evidence that they may have been unduly pressured into selecting a particular method (as in the case of the sterilized Indian women). But the resolve itself cut across ethnicity, especially among younger generations of women.

In part this sense of entitlement may reflect the accessibility of reproductive health and family planning services in Malaysia, albeit with limited choices. But even more it is a reflection of how women themselves are responding to the demands of economic development, education and work, combined with the absence of facilities or shared male responsibility for child care. Especially for younger women, the biggest factor motivating a sense of entitlement to postpone marriage, have fewer children, and use contraception seems to be a 'modern' set of values prioritizing women's education and contribution to family earnings. Married women in all three groups invoked their status as mothers – as the ones primarily responsible for and most burdened by children's upbringing – to justify their entitlement. Lai Yin might be speaking for many others when she says, '... all this is my responsibility; he does not suffer, the suffering is all done by me.' Yet the ability to express openly their right to reproductive and sexual self-determination still eludes a good many women in our research because of the contrary pressures created by the patriarchal/religious resurgence and its traces in recent state policy.

At the same time, several distinct voices resound in this study asserting women's reproductive entitlement, on behalf not only of their maternal duties and needs, but also of their personal aspirations for greater freedom, mobility and independence: Sai Leng, who urges her teenage counterparts to work after marriage so they can 'move out whenever you like'; Kum Mooi, who insisted on getting an abortion after four children so she could be more free and mobile; Lai Yin, who favours condoms because they are better for her health; Uma, Devi and Faridah, who walked out on abusive husbands despite having children to care for and meagre economic resources; Yati, who is convinced that 'women can survive without a man'. While these women do not verbalize a sense of ownership over their bodies, this idea is implicit in both their words and their actions. To the extent that economic development, the education and employment of women, and a growing women's movement overcome the propagation of patriarchal family values by the state and religion, the future Malaysia may hear many more voices like theirs.

Notes

1 The mean monthly household income (1990) for Chinese was RM1,631 (US$652), followed by Indians at RM1,201 (US$480) and Malays at RM928 (US$371).

2 Malays are defined in the constitution as people speaking the national language habitually, practising the Malay *adat* (custom), and being Muslim. In contrast, the Chinese in Malaysia practise a combination of Buddhism, Taoism and Confucianism, 'a syncretic religion embracing the ancient cult as its basis and Buddhist and Taoist elements as secondary features' (Chan Wing-tsit, quoted in Ju 1983:3). The official language in the country is Malay or Bahasa Malaysia, but other languages and dialects are widely spoken, including English, Mandarin, Cantonese, Hokkien and Tamil.

3 The average daily rate for a male transporter is RM21 (US$8), while that of a female transporter is RM14 (US$6) (Malaysia Department of Statistics 1993). The Equal Pay for Equal Work Act (1969) covers only the public sector.

4 In a very illuminating article, Lynn P. Freedman argues that the term 'fundamentalist', while problematic and reductive as a category, none the less is useful in pointing to certain resemblances across cultures and religions. Among others, its characteristics include, according to Freedman's analysis: a view of one's own community as endangered; a confrontational and apocalyptic view of the world; a tendency to reinvent tradition; and above all, a tendency to use women in the project of mapping tradition, particularly through the implementation of laws that regulate women's reproductive and sexual behaviour (Freedman 1996: 56–58).

5 *Syriah* is the common Southeast Asian spelling of *shari'a*, or Islamic holy law.

6 At the date of writing, no Malaysian women's group identified itself explicitly as 'feminist', nor did any organize openly around issues of lesbianism or sexual orientation. The use of the term 'feminist' to refer to such groups as JAG and the National Women's Coalition is based on the emphasis by such groups on a process of collective decision making, a nonhierarchical structure, and an analysis of gender oppression as systemic within the family and society.

7 These Malaysian government figures differ from those estimated by United Nations agencies: for infant mortality, 13 per 1,000 live births in 1993 (UNDP 1996); and for maternal mortality, 80 per 100,000 live births in 1990 (WHO/UNICEF). See Table 9.1.

8 The team consisted of eight members with varying backgrounds and work experiences and reflecting all the country's major ethnic groups. Five are university lecturers in the fields of public health, medical anthropology, education, communications and political science; the other three work with a regional NGO, the Asian-Pacific Resource and Research Centre for Women (ARROW), and have extensive backgrounds in family planning research and evaluation, maternal and child health, development, and advocacy for women's rights. Most of the team's members have been involved in Malaysian NGOs concerned with women's issues, particularly around health and domestic violence.

9 In the case of the Indian respondents, who were all employees of the oil palm estate, the estate manager gave them days off with pay to facilitate their participation in the research.

10 All five sites, as well as the women interviewed, have been given fictitious names to protect their confidentiality.

11 During the 1948–60 Emergency, when the Communist Party of Malaya fought against the British colonial government, the rural Chinese population throughout the country was uprooted and resettled. Sekmai is the centre of one such resettlement

scheme. Rural Chinese villagers throughout the area were regrouped around Sekmai town, forming Sekmai New Village.

12 Kelantan is the only opposition state in Malaysia, and its ruling opposition party – to which Kampung Pulau's headman belongs – maintains an uneasy relationship with the federal government. Partly as a result of this political situation, the area's economic growth rate is one of the lowest in the country.

13 The visiting medical officer (VMO) usually comes only once a week for half an hour in the morning, when the workers are out in the field. Since the VMO and the other general practitioners practising in the nearest town are all men, this causes some communication problems for many women living on the plantations, who feel embarrassed to talk about their reproductive health needs to male doctors.

14 This pattern differed somewhat among the rural Indian respondents, among whom the majority had between five and nine years of schooling, and one (in her forties) had none. However, two of the Indian women had been educated beyond secondary school and were working as teachers.

15 Only among the Chinese women in our study, both urban and rural, does there seem to be no correlation between educational attainment and age at marriage; that is, the majority of the Chinese married respondents of all age groups married in their early to late twenties but only a very few had more than nine years of education.

16 The three respondents from Kampung Liri who reported having had arranged marriages, like the Indians, agreed to the arrangement and did not feel coerced.

17 Close proximity (*khalwat*) laws are more stringently enforced in rural Malaysia, particularly in Kelantan state, than elsewhere in the country. Under these laws, a single man and woman caught together, even walking on a beach, are subject to punishment by fine. Often parents and the community put pressure on the couple to marry.

18 They include five rural and one urban Malay women, one urban Chinese who has filed for divorce, and two rural Indian women who have separated from their husbands.

19 To obtain a divorce under *syriah* law, a Muslim wife with the necessary resources can compensate her husband with a mutually agreed sum of money. Alternatively, through the *takliq*, she must establish a breach of the marriage contract by the husband, on the grounds of either his failure to maintain her and the children during marriage, or separation for a year, or cruelty (including violence). Either strategy is quite difficult unless a woman has her own financial means (Mehrun 1988).

20 Personal communication with the former director of services of the government family planning organization. This official indicated that in the late sixties and seventies he and his staff visited many plantations to set up vasectomy programmes (this was the same period in which vasectomies were being widely and coercively imposed by Indira Gandhi's government in India). Denying that this programme was specifically aimed at the Indian population, the former director (himself an Indian) expressed the view that sterilization was simpler and easier to understand for this population.

21 Their uncertainty about this is misinformed, however, since Islamic teaching has traditionally accepted the use of all forms of contraception except sterilization (Obermeyer 1994; Omran 1992; Ong 1994). The decision of the Fatwa Committee of the National Council of Islamic Affairs in 1982 spells out the circumstances in which family planning is allowed: although sterilization of men and women is forbidden, nonpermanent contraception to limit the number of children is permissible under certain conditions, including health needs of the mother, hereditary illness of either parent, too frequent pregnancies, and to space children for health, education

and family happiness (Askiah 1993). Un-Islamic reasons for family planning include fear of pregnancy and childbirth, concern that it may affect the woman's figure, sex selection, desire for a more comfortable material life, or wanting to be free from the burdens of childrearing.

22 The same may be true of our Indian respondents as well, who admitted knowing about abortion methods though not having used them. Rashidah notes that, according to the 1984–85 Malaysian Population and Family Survey (MPFS), 14 per cent of Chinese married women, 6 per cent of Indian married women, and only 0.8 per cent of Malay married women reported ever having had an abortion. But, she adds, the survey itself 'cautioned against accepting these findings at face value ... as underreporting was very likely,' due to the restricted legality of abortion in Malaysia (1993:71).

5 'Because They Were Born From Me'
Negotiating Women's Rights in Mexico

ADRIANA ORTIZ ORTEGA, ANA AMUCHÁSTEGUI AND MARTA RIVAS*

Grassroots women in Mexico are in the process of constituting themselves as subjects of rights. Research conducted in three localities indicates that they realize a sense of entitlement through their experience at three levels: family, community, and state policy. Few of the women in the study spoke of rights as such; rather, they demonstrated an awareness of the social spaces that enable them to gain autonomy regarding reproduction. Thus, within the family they validate their sense of bodily integrity and selfhood by establishing themselves as mothers with rights to self-determination, in a society where motherhood is a powerful symbol. Within the community, they participate in the growing number of neighbourhood groups, enabling them to share strategies about how to negotiate their personal notions of entitlement. And within the limited framework of national family planning policy, codified in 1974, they make decisions about their fertility, albeit in ways that do not always serve their reproductive needs or rights.

Our research indicates that women's awareness of entitlement at these three levels facilitates their ability to engage in collective discussions and validates their right to make decisions regarding their fertility. All the participants, for example, perceive that bearing and raising children entails social, emotional, and economic labour that imposes hardships on women. Yet they also recognize that that role grants them decision-making power, since motherhood and caring for the elderly remain primarily female activities that carry great symbolic status in Mexico. By participating in community groups, most of which are organized to fight for economic rights, they develop a general awareness of rights and at the same time

* This chapter was written in collaboration with Irma Henze and the late Guadalupe Musalem who, with Ana Amuchástegui and Marta Rivas, conducted field research under the overall coordination of Adriana Ortiz Ortega. We would also like to acknowledge Teresita de Barbieri, Juan Guillermo Figueroa, Lucero González, Sylvia Marcos, and Alicia Elena Pérez Duarte, who contributed background papers; Joanna Gould Stuart and Iris Lopez, research consultants; and Rosamaria Roffiel, who administered the project and assisted with translation.

exchange information about sexuality and contraception or how to resist domestic violence. Finally, they acknowledge reliance, although in more problematic and unmediated ways, on state family planning clinics to practise their right to regulate their fertility *vis-à-vis* their husbands, in-laws, and families of origin.

In recent years, grassroots women's interventions in the public sphere have been interpreted by both movement activists and social scientists as an extension of their roles as wives and mothers in the context of decreased living standards and economic crisis (Logan 1990; Kaplan 1990). Women's inability to carry out the private roles expected of them, it is argued, forces them to act, expanding their role as mothers to encompass a public image, presenting their demands in the form of endorsing the needs of others (Safa and Butler 1992). By contrast, our research found that grassroots women use community group meetings to discuss their own private-sphere concerns, such as domestic violence and strategies to deal with it, or how to obtain reliable birth control, as well as the constraints imposed on these strategies and efforts by public-sphere reality, namely the unreliability of state institutions or the imperiousness of health officials.[1]

Grassroots women's ability to translate their emerging sense of entitlement into rights must be understood in a particular context: a culture in which women's rights to selfhood and control over reproduction do not derive from citizenship but must be earned or bestowed by others, mainly through suffering, work, or mistreatment; a legacy of official corruption that results in great distrust, especially among poor, rural women, in legal and judicial institutions and even the medical community; and limited social and geographical mobility, especially for rural women, which constrains their sense of citizenship beyond the community. For all the women in this study, democracy and civil participation are still foreign experiences, and legal institutions and government affairs are regarded as the privileges of elite groups.

Somewhat moderating these constraints on civil and democratic participation, however, is the visibility and success of grassroots agitation in Mexico since the early 1980s. Following the economic crisis of 1981, the Mexico City earthquake of 1985, the decline in the ability of the ruling party to control all aspects of political life, and the rise of civil and political participation outside political parties, community group activism became a means by which poor women were able to obtain housing, basic services, or food for the entire family (Logan 1990; Hellman 1995).[2] As this research confirms, grassroots women's success as both collectors and distributors of scarce resources has served not only to politicize their demands for social services but also to help reconnect the public and the private dimensions of their reproductive activities. This is true throughout the different research sites, both urban and rural, suggesting that women's community participation is neither isolated nor limited to urban centres.

Although group participation has allowed women to enhance their sense of entitlement, in both the personal and public spheres, it has not yet changed their perception of the Mexican political and economic structure. This suggests that so long as justice is implemented both arbitrarily and preferentially, and so long as human, social, economic, sexual and reproductive rights receive only limited respect, grassroots women might be able to enhance their personal sense of entitlement but will not be able to translate this into demands for legal rights and their effective enforcement through public agencies.

The voices presented here are neither those of the poorest and most dispossessed nor those of exceptional social agitators. Rather they are representative of a growing movement of grassroots women's political activism in Mexico, one that builds on a strong tradition of women's communal participation as both consumers and distributors of services (Tarrés 1992). Such participation by women in informal social support networks grows out of a long history dating from the revolution of 1910 and the process of nation building that followed (Logan 1990, Hellman 1994, Macías 1982).[3] Yet the last twenty years have seen an enormous increase in women's social visibility and political activism. Whereas in the 1970s a few hundred women were engaged in social movements, today they number in the thousands; once locally based only, women's groups have allied into several networks, among them La Red Contra la Violencia Hacía la Mujer (Network Against Violence Toward Women), La Red Campesina Nacional (the Feminist Peasant Network), and La Red Nacional de Educadores Populares (Network of Popular Educators).[4] In an effort to reconcile their traditional roles with demands for change, grassroots women have both drawn on their tradition of communal activism and developed new strengths – joining the democratization movement, agitating for land reform, defending human rights, and organizing for workers' rights (Logan 1990; Lamas *et al.* 1995; Stephen 1995; Massolo 1989; Tuñón Pablos 1987).

More recently, the Zapatista movement, which burst upon the political scene in 1994 and in which peasant women have played an important part, has endeavoured to connect women's demands for radical social transformation with reproductive health issues, including access to information, nutrition, health services, and control over their own fertility (Marcos 1994). These movements suggest a process by which the collective construction of grassroots women's voices around human and social rights can lead to an insistence that issues of sexuality and reproduction be included on the agenda for large-scale social and political change.

An Action-oriented Project

Recognition of women's growing involvement in political life was considered particularly important for the IRRRAG project in Mexico, since it sought to explore grassroots women's decision-making regarding sexuality, contraception and childbearing in the context of their efforts to promote social change as well as their limited access to material and social resources. Members of the Mexican research team, including academics and activists, lawyers and health professionals, shared the belief that women's empowerment could arise only in the context of the broader society, and that concerns specific to women are always grounded in issues of poverty alleviation, equality, and the extension of democracy to large numbers of people. As a result, the team decided to adopt an action-oriented approach focused on grassroots women, including indigenous women, in both rural and urban areas, who were active and regular participants in community organizations. We wanted to test the hypothesis that women who had participated in the public arena through their community involvement could reconnect the public and private dimensions of reproduction in the way in which they constructed entitlements.

The women interviewed were neither members of privileged economic or educational groups nor leaders of their groups. Of the fifteen organizations covered in the study, twelve were grassroots popular organizations, including (1) neighbourhood or community groups involved in organizing citizens' demands around housing, health, and public services; (2) independent cooperatives formed by women to produce agricultural products, manufactured goods, or handicrafts; and (3) religious groups.[5] The remaining three organizations were trade unions, the traditional means through which grassroots women who enter the formal labour market organize.

Table 5.1 Mexican Women's Status in Three Regions[6]

INDICATOR	NATIONWIDE	MEXICO CITY	OAXACA	SONORA
Women with schooling (%), 1992	91.5	97.2	78.8	97.2
Women as % of workforce, 1992	33.4	44.0	45.8	30.3
Total fertility rate, 1990	2.5	2.0	2.8	2.5
Maternal mortality ratio, 1992–4	1,399	115	100	24

Sources: INEGI, 1990, 1992, 1993

Research was carried out in three different localities: Mexico City, Oaxaca, and Sonora. In Mexico City, the federal capital, where economic services and political resources have historically been concentrated, women's schooling and employment rank above the national average and both fertility and maternal mortality rates are below the national average. Oaxaca, a southern state with a large Indian population, limited formal-sector employment, and high out-migration rates, has among the highest fertility and mortality rates in the country. Sonora, on the US border, has the country's highest per capita income. Although women's literacy in Sonora is higher than the national average and their fertility rate is approximately that of the nation as a whole, their labour force participation is somewhat below the national average, as indicated in Table 5.1.

Data on education, occupation, marital status, and fertility were collected for each of the women quoted in this chapter (see Table 5.2 on pages 176–7). Since the goal was to get qualitative rather than comprehensive survey data, open-ended individual interviews were designed to allow the women to articulate their own views of reproduction and motherhood, group participation and decision making. Group interviews, which involved a total of 141 women, served to re-create the context of each organization and provided a source of additional observations.[7] Men or other authority figures were not present. In Mexico City and Oaxaca, dramatization allowed the women to voice their concerns and explore their feelings and emotions without fearing that their individual lives were being exposed or their identity and privacy endangered.

After group interviews, two to three women were invited to participate in in-depth interviews, which were carried out in at least two and sometimes three separate sessions. Individual interviews were conducted with twenty-nine women, plus there were an average of two group interviews for each organization. In Sonora, ten individual interviews were conducted, along with two group interviews in Nogales, a border city with a flourishing *maquiladora* (assembly) industry; one with Yaqui women; and five in Hermosillo, the state capital. In Mexico City, nine individual interviews were conducted and six group interviews. In Oaxaca, ten individual interviews were conducted plus five group interviews, involving women from the city of Oaxaca as well as from the various indigenous communities of the region.

Through its research, the Mexican team came to recognize that reproduction is not simply a biological activity that takes place in women's bodies during their fertile years. Instead, it is a social realm that connects female biological reproduction to women's care of children and the elderly, together with their traditional roles as family makers and community caretakers. Thus we shared the Brazil team's perception that a woman's so-called reproductive career, including child care and household tasks, stretches throughout her life (see Chapter 2). We believed that among grassroots women, those who participate in groups would be best able to articulate the gaps between women's position in the sphere of reproduction and their ability to exercise reproductive rights.

This chapter examines the process by which grassroots women in three communities in Mexico are carving out a sense of entitlement as increasingly vocal participants in the current period of growing political activism and efforts to revitalize Mexican democracy. It presents their voices in an effort to capture the possibilities and limits of their daily negotiations around reproductive rights and concludes with a discussion of the structural and personal changes necessary to allow grassroots women's reproductive rights to become a reality. As in all such studies, the results are conditioned by what Rosaldo (1991) calls the 'situatedness' of the researchers: attitudes and conceptions that influence their interaction with participants and the kinds of knowledge constructed. Age, race, gender, class, sexual orientation and educational background all influence the kind of bonds established with participants and the information produced. In our case, one of the main lessons learned during this process was the difficulty, for both participants and researchers, of talking about sexual practice and feelings in ways that allow room for the expression of difference. This was made clear by the fact that during the interviews there were no expressions of sexual activities other than the dominant model of heterosexuality within stable relationships. Along with other IRRRAG teams, members of the Mexican team had to reconcile our belief in the nature of individual empowerment and choice with our concern to listen to the priorities of our respondents.

The Political Economy of Women's Lives

Despite the emergence of non-state-controlled forms of political participation since the 1980s, the Mexican state is still dominated by the Institutional Revolutionary Party (PRI), which has been in power since its founding in 1929. It remains overwhelmingly clientelist, deriving its legitimacy from interlocking chains of patron–client relationships (Cosío 1974).[8] Prior to the 1960s, the state actively directed the expression of political pluralism, mass mobilization, and political demands. Since then, while social movements, especially the 1968 student movement as well as women's movements, have opened spaces for greater democratic participation within civil society, their attempts to mainstream their demands in the institutional arena continually confront the power of the system to coopt and redirect these efforts (Hellman 1995).[9]

Women's participation in growing efforts to bring about political change reflect their increasing involvement with a dependent economy based on foreign capital accumulation, one that relies heavily on foreign investment in areas of high short-term returns, such as assembly plants, the tourist industry, or the stock market. This pattern of capital accumulation has been accompanied by a sustained transfer of resources to the countries of the global North, in particular to the United States – especially after the economic crisis of December 1994.[10] To satisfy international lending institutions, the Mexican government has adopted harsh structural adjustment policies, including cuts in social spending and the prioritization of debt repayment. During the first three months of 1995 the amount of resources used to pay interest on the foreign debt equalled the foreign investment that entered the country between 1993 and 1994 (Fernández 1995).

Structural adjustment has resulted in increased unemployment among skilled workers along with increased demand for cheap, unorganized labour. Unemployment jumped from 3.4 per cent in 1981 to 22.9 per cent in 1987 (Parés 1990). Women's participation in the labour market has risen steadily from the 1950s, when it stood at 13 per cent; by the early 1990s, women were fully one-third of the labour market (Hernández and Hernández 1995). Despite this, family standards of living have decreased since 1980, along with individual purchasing power. Per capita income dropped 15 per cent from 1980 to 1989 (Benítez 1990). In the 1990s, almost half the Mexican population, 40 million people, live below the poverty line, and it is estimated that some 17 million of these live in absolute poverty (Pamplona *et al.* 1993). Nor has women's participation in the labour force improved their own conditions, since women, along with children and the elderly, are those most severely hurt by the effects of structural adjustment policies on wages as well as on family income and standard of living.

Poor women in particular lack the support system that permits them to join the formal labour market and must take jobs that allow them to combine work and domestic responsibilities. Women's employment is concentrated in the lowest-paying positions in the informal sector, such as domestic service and food vending; 70 per cent of employed women work in the informal sector, and women made up 96.6 per cent of domestic employees in 1990 (Suárez 1992). The average age of employed women ranges from twenty-five to thirty-four years, compared to the 1960s, when the working female population consisted of single women ranging in age from twenty to twenty-four years. The increased entry of women of childbearing age into the labour market testifies to the fact that one income is no longer sufficient to cover the needs of the family (García 1993). It has also made it more difficult for younger women to find employment.

Women's job opportunities are also constrained by the extremely uneven allocation of educational opportunities in Mexico, where 6 million people, 62 per cent of them women, are illiterate. Illiteracy is concentrated in the southern states, which also have the highest Indian and rural populations. The number of high schools and technical schools has increased three and a half times while the number of elementary schools has increased only one and a half times over the last twenty years (Gutiérrez 1992). Moreover, educational resources are concentrated in a few urban centres, in order to produce the professional and technical workers needed by foreign firms. As the state finds it impossible to satisfy the elementary educational needs of 20 per cent of the people, it simply disregards the needs of the rural poor.[11] As a result, more and more women have moved to the cities in search of jobs, while men stay in the country to work the land. Since the 1950s, women's interstate migration has surpassed that of men by a ratio of 100 to 88. Today women are also increasingly migrating to the United States (Cantú Gutiérrez and Moreno Neira 1990). Young women especially seek to augment declining rural family incomes by finding waged work in the city and sending at least part of their earnings back home.

Urban migration, housing shortages, and increased entry of women into the labour force at low wages have combined with women's greater life expectancy and the continuation of their traditional roles to create a revival of the extended family. Extended families (which may include an array of relatives in addition to parents and children) represented 22.7 per cent of all families by 1970 and 25.1 per cent by 1985 (De Oliveira 1988). Moreover, by 1984 the number of female-headed households had grown to 58 per cent of all families from 27 per cent in 1970, justifying the use of the term 'feminization of poverty' (Acosta 1992).

Women's Health

While women's tasks in both production and reproduction have grown significantly, this reality is not acknowledged by social institutions. The deterioration of living conditions and women's increased care-giving responsibilities take the most dramatic toll in the arena of health: trends in relative life expectancy bear a direct relation to declining living standards (Jiménez 1993). Since the mid-1980s, life expectancy for women has increased at a slower rate than that of men, although in 1990 women's life expectancy was still six years greater. The diminishing gap reflects women's changing labour, family, and political activities.[12]

Among the causes of female mortality, reproductive-related contingencies are at the top of the list. The four most common reproductive-related deaths, which accounted for almost 80 per cent of all maternal deaths in 1984–86, were toxaemia, haemorrhage during pregnancy, sepsis and abortion complications (Comité Promotor para la Maternidad sin Riesgos en México 1993). It is important to note that most of these deaths could have been prevented had medical attention been provided on time. Their mere existence reflects social inequality, because it is poor women who live in remote areas and who therefore die more often of these causes. Abortion remains the exception: a high estimated abortion-related mortality rate exists across the country, since abortion remains illegal in Mexico (except under certain restricted conditions) and services are difficult to access.[13] None the less, access to treatment of abortion complications by public clinics is worse in areas inhabited by poor women; thus the incidence of abortion-related mortality and morbidity is also likely to be higher among them.

The gap between maternal mortality in Mexico and the United States has widened during the period 1940–85, for which we have comparable data. In 1940 the risk of dying from a pregnancy-related cause in Mexico was 1.4 times that in the United States; in 1985 it was 7.5 times greater (Langer *et al.* 1993). In 1990, the estimated maternal mortality ratio was 110 deaths for every 100,000 live births, compared to 12 deaths for the same number of births in the United States and Canada (WHO/UNICEF 1996).

AIDS now ranks seventeenth in causes of female mortality in the country, with a rate of 3.6 deaths for each 100,000 inhabitants (Secretaría de Salud 1994). The prevalence of AIDS has increased more than tenfold in less than three years, and in 1996 Mexico ranked eleventh in the world and third in Latin America. HIV/AIDS is no longer limited to male homosexuals and women infected through blood transfusions but has become a heterosexual disease. Thus, while in 1987 there were 23.6 men for every woman with AIDS, by 1988 the ratio was 14 to 1 and by 1990 it was down to 6.6 to 1 (Bronfman 1990). In the first three months of 1995, of the 3,095 adult women AIDS cases, 50.2 per cent were heterosexually transmitted (SIDA/ ETS 1995). While the greatest incidence of the disease is still among homosexuals and bisexual men, the number of seropositive men who engage in heterosexual relations increased from 85 per cent in 1990 to 94 per cent in 1995 (SIDA/ETS 1996).

In fact, the fastest-growing group of HIV-infected people is women who acquire the disease through sexual intercourse with their husbands, most of whom become infected through sex with other men.[14] Yet health officials refuse to acknowledge male bisexuality and the vulnerable position of women within married or consensual unions or that of young women who have initiated a sexual life. As this study testifies, sexuality is territory women feel less entitled to negotiate, making them particularly vulnerable to infection within stable relationships.

Culture, Gender, and Fertility

Attitudes towards women's health, especially reproductive health, reflect perhaps as much as anything the contradictions of a mestiza (mixed ancestry) society, the product of the struggle of indigenous nations and peoples to preserve their cultures under colonial rule. During the period of Spanish colonization, which lasted from 1594 to 1834, new meanings were assigned to sexuality and the body, elements of which continue to define forms of resistance and accommodation in Mexico today. While the indigenous population incorporated values and practices that most resembled their own traditions, such as the worship of certain deities,[15] the colonizers were unable fully to replace existing ideas about sexuality and reproduction. They were never able to impose the idea of the separation between body and mind, for example, which in Western culture served to control sexuality by relegating it to a 'sin of the flesh'. Indigenous peoples believed that different emotions were centred in different parts of the body, and that this determined the way in which energy circulates and how the individual relates to the divine. Moreover, because these cultures assumed an integration of the masculine and feminine in their cosmology, the Indian body, both male and female – albeit in different ways – occupied a symbolic place of resistance

(López Austin 1984; Marcos 1991 and 1992; Viqueira 1984).

Yet the realm of the symbolic coexisted with violence in the realm of practice, and women's bodies were most vulnerable to impositions resulting from colonization. Mestizo society itself resulted to a large extent from the rape of Indian women by Spanish men at the same time as virginity was sanctified as a measure of women's worth. Local populations continued to use abortive herbs even as abortion was met by capital punishment by the Holy Inquisition. Children born out of wedlock were incorporated into society, resulting in the phenomenon known as *mestizaje*. Local resistance practices resulted in attempts by the Catholic Church to regulate sexuality throughout the colonial and postcolonial period. Although after independence the Mexican state declared itself independent of the Church, it supported the Catholic ideal of women's fertility as subordinate to the rule of the family and its prescribed needs, including numerous children (Ortiz-Ortega 1996). Thus, while divorce was legalized in the early 1920s, contraception remained illegal until 1973. Starting in 1920 and throughout subsequent decades, women were encouraged to show their loyalty to the state by becoming mothers and workers.

By the mid-1970s, however, Mexico's population was growing rapidly, causing increasing concern among national as well as international development agencies. The government response was mixed: on the one hand it promoted population control, while on the other it advocated the individual's right to family planning as a form of self-determination. In so doing it contrived to maintain a degree of autonomy from Western-led population control institutions, from the Catholic Church, and from feminist groups, who were demanding the right to sexual autonomy and equality before the law. Thus in 1973 the government amended the constitution: contraception was legalized, individuals were given the right to decide 'in a free, informed, and responsible manner about the number and spacing of their children', and women were made equal before the law. The state's objective in granting women's equality was to facilitate their direct access to officially distributed contraceptive methods, eliminating the need to get approval from husband or partner. To avoid charges that it had given in to imperialist demands, the government advocated an informed family planning model which sought to limit and space births. To avoid straining its relationship with the Catholic Church, abortion was left outside the scope of the new population policy, which was characterized as a campaign for 'planned parenthood'.

The national population policy, introduced in 1974, focuses on public education as well as on the dispensation of oral contraceptives, the insertion of intrauterine devices (IUDs), and the promotion of sterilization. Its timing apparently coincided with a demographic transition already under way. Surveys in urban areas showed that women wanted to have three instead of four children (Elu 1970). Over the two decades that the population policy has been in place, Mexico has reduced the national fertility rate from 3.1 to 2.5 (see Table 4.1), but how much this decline reflects women's desires and will is currently being debated. Overzealous efforts to get women to accept permanent or semipermanent contraception have been widely criticized by women's groups, who charge that doctors, urged by the health ministry, regularly pressure women to accept IUDs or undergo sterilization, especially at government clinics, which serve about 80 per cent of the population (Katz 1995). Medical personnel fail to inform women about other methods of contraception and often insert IUDs or perform sterilization operations without the woman's consent. Although difficult to obtain legally, abortion is still widely used. Currently, over half a million induced abortions are performed each year in Mexico, and women's rights groups estimate the number to be considerably higher (Langer *et al.* 1997; Katz 1995). According to a 1992 national poll, at least 69 per cent of the population believe that the decision to have an abortion does not belong to the state or the Church but should be left to women (Cohen 1995).

Mexico signed the Convention on the Elimination of all Forms of Discrimination Against Women in 1981 and more recently endorsed the ICPD Programme of Action in Cairo in 1994, which specifically condemns family planning coercion, and the Platform for Action of the Fourth World Conference on Women in Beijing in 1995, which further recognized women's reproductive and sexual rights. Yet efforts to legalize abortion have faltered, and programmes to enable women to make informed choices among a range of family planning methods and to achieve full reproductive health have not materialized, as a result of the failure to translate constitutional provisions into appropriate enabling legislation and to allocate state resources for implementation.

Constructing Entitlement: Women's Voices

Notwithstanding the national population policy, our study suggests that popular traditions of resistance combine with newer forms of group activity and shared consciousness in grassroots women's decision-making about fertility. The concept of entitlement as the IRRRAG teams came to understand it embraces what women consider theirs, including notions of identity, bodily integrity, self-ownership, and motherhood. The word 'entitlement' has no exact Spanish translation, which points out the difficulty of considering women (or men) as subjects of rights across diverse cultural and national boundaries. Nevertheless, the concept enabled us to evaluate the conditions that shape women's choices in personal, family, and health spheres and the terms and strategies whereby they envision and strive for self-determination.

Group Participation: 'Nothing will stop me ...'

Interviews at nearly all the sites confirmed the hypothesis that group participation provides a sense of belonging that enables women to recognize themselves as subjects of rights in certain areas of their lives.[16] In most locations studied we found that participation in a group is a vital pre-condition for women to voice their rights publicly. Even in groups created by priests or nuns, government authorities, or male grassroots leaders, it was found that as long as the women meet regularly, they appropriate the space provided for the group as their own. A woman from Sonora explained that because she went to group meetings, her husband claimed she had another man. 'I told him: I am already there, and nothing, not even you or my children, will stop me from going to the group.'

Group participation is an activity that bridges the private, the public, and the communal realms; it is women's entry point into the public arena. Most of the women interviewed join groups in order to fight for better housing, public services, health benefits, or simply to increase the well-being of their communities. Those who joined religious groups did so for the relief that faith brings to their lives but stayed for the knowledge they gain. As a member of the Whole Women's Health Collective in Mexico City explained: 'Last year Leti [the community health worker] gave us some information about how we can help advise our families, how we can prevent sexual abuse; we learned more about nutrition, pregnancy and childcare.'

Once active, women found they were able to provide each other with the support that builds their sense of personhood. After a few years, some felt entitled to work outside the home, for example, or to decide more openly on the number of children they will bear. A woman from an Oaxaca trade union explained:

> To me, to have rights means that you can carry out an activity, you can work and cooperate in the house with money; I mean, not just because your partner is working should you expect him to be the only one taking decisions, or giving you pocket money. We also have the right to cooperate and to make choices. There are still many people who think, even today, that women don't have the right to work and that men should give them everything. Well, it's not like that.

Interestingly, the only two groups in which women did not gain this sense of support were those directly related to their work. In a *maquiladora* child-care centre in Nogales (Sonora), women explained that meetings are chaired by childcare personnel and only daily activities relating to the centre are raised. Similarly, in the Metropolitan University Union (SITUAM) in Mexico City, respondents said that because of political rivalries in the union and the university, it was not appropriate to discuss personal matters during their gatherings.

One of the reasons the group plays such an important role in these women's lives is that the family, whether extended or nuclear, does not allow them the space to express their concerns easily. Thus attending groups becomes a right they conquer only after resisting partner or family opposition. Not surprisingly, group participation creates a tension in male–female relations, which often goes unresolved. Sara, a member of a religious group in Oaxaca, explained:

> What I would like is to have more freedom, that's what I want. I'd like to make him understand that I'm not going out to waste my time in the streets. I never go out feeling relaxed because the minute I go out I start feeling nervous and thinking that I have to go back home immediately. I want to go back because he gets really mad, and I live with that concern all the time.

Since the struggle to participate in a group can often last for years, groups formed to deal with diverse social needs easily become consciousness-raising platforms. For respondents in all three communities, 'el grupo' represents the only space in which they can share experience about such secret subjects as sexuality and reproduction.[17] It is in sharing this experience, we believe, that they develop a sense of entitlement. A woman in an Oaxaca trade union explains:

> If I'm worried about something I cannot solve, and I don't have a clue and I share it with the group, new ideas come up and each of us gives something and tells you 'I did this or that.' So I think that it's very important to have a group. Besides, in your spare time, which is reduced every day, you can always call on the group. Perhaps we come to the meetings to get rid of all the little nuisances of the day, right? and, above all, one learns more everyday. Like this minute, for instance, this is a good opportunity to share our ideas and any experience that we've gone through, right?

Because of this support, some respondents stated that group participation enabled them to manage violence from their husbands or partners. A participant in the Indian group Xande in Oaxaca stated:

> When the husbands go out to work you don't have any problems of them repressing you about where you are and why you come in late and all that. For me, when I started, it was a deep problem, but I saw that what we do is good for the community and I said to myself, 'I don't care what he says, I'm doing good, I'm not pursuing bad' … only when he drinks, when he's drunk I have more problems.

Group participation can help these women to realize that violence and economic deprivation are conditions that not only affect them but are problems for vast numbers of women. Similarly, by breaking their isolation, group participation was especially important for those who live in remote communities and have become outcasts – primarily single mothers and in some cases single or widowed women who refuse to conform to dominant sexual values. In the cases where respondents had become health promoters or achieved self-sufficiency through group participation, they explained that they sometimes gained respect from their communities later. Natalia, a single mother and participant in a Zapotec health education group in rural Oaxaca, described such a change:

> Joining the group has been very important for me because now the people in town see me differently. It's not like before. Before, I was nobody, so to speak. Not now. Nowadays, everybody says 'let's go to her, she knows'... or they come and consult me about their problems and ask 'what do you recommend about contraceptives?', or 'what shall I do about this little problem?', and so on.

But Laura, also from Oaxaca, shows that this is still quite complicated:

> Only now do I have more freedom, but I am not really free even now, they still watch me. When I was fifteen I couldn't go by myself, not even to the store, my mother wouldn't allow me. Neither could I go with friends, only with her or with other grown-ups. That still happens today; it is not accepted for women to be on the streets by themselves. I have a friend that won't leave home. She's single, she's twenty-seven, but since she goes by the rule, she can't go out.

The testimonies suggest that although family members may support women, especially single women, in caring for children, they still perceive them as lacking authority to make decisions. This is particularly true for single mothers, who are often seen as irresponsible and therefore required to do endless domestic chores or work outside the house in order to support the family while the grandmother takes care of the grandchild. This pattern provides a cushion against the impoverishment of single motherhood, but it makes opportunities for autonomy even scarcer.

By participating in groups, especially those concerned with education or health, women appear better able to recognize rights they should have in their daily interactions with their husbands. A woman from CODIC in Mexico City said:

> We are married by the church and the law, and our man is unfaithful to us ... they think they have the right to go on and do as they wish, and that we have to accept? Not me ... I don't know what kind of sicknesses he will bring to me from outside, and why do I have to be there for him? It's my right and my decision to say no.

Some shared strategies for negotiating these rights. A woman in Oaxaca gave the following advice in a group interview: 'To prevent your husband getting angry you need to take care of housework, so that as you are about to leave the house you can tell him: look, I am going to go there, you know what I am going to do.' Such comments illustrate the trade-offs grassroots women make in order to realize some degree of personal autonomy, a kind of personal accounting that recognizes that nothing is won without a price (Behar 1993). They also show the hesitancy respondents feel in confronting their partners directly; for them, the group is just a first step in attaining self-authorization.

Motherhood: 'because they were born from me'
For most of the women in this study, the socially sanctioned status of motherhood, far from being uniformly viewed as oppressive, was described

as the crucial experience that allowed them to feel entitled. Motherhood serves not only as a validating experience, the primary basis for claiming personal entitlement, but also as the framework in which these women organize all their activities, whether those in the community or the various economic activities by which they earn income and provide for their families. In all three regions, women interviewed stated that before becoming mothers, they rarely made decisions or took any deliberate action concerning their reproductive health. For many of the women interviewed, only after having at least two children did they begin to make claims on behalf of their bodily integrity.

In all the interviews, the discussion of motherhood evoked memories of suffering and risks. Yet at the same time it represented the means by which women authorize themselves to fight for the satisfaction of needs that are otherwise not acknowledged. The similarities across sites in this respect were especially apparent regarding violence. Most of the women interviewed said they had experienced violence in their family of origin or from their partners and husbands. For most, while group participation may allow them to share strategies for becoming less dependent on violent husbands, it has not yet prevented them from submitting to male subjugation and violence. However, women who had been mothers for some years stressed their belief that they should not let the husband inflict domestic violence on them or their children. For example, Hortensia, who is forty-three, says of her partner: 'I don't allow him to hit me any more. If he hits me, I hit back. And, God forgive me, I've even taken a knife and almost stabbed him. Above all, there is the courage my children give to me.... Before, I felt so alone without my parents' support that I would put up with almost anything.'

The importance of motherhood as a shield against physical abuse was articulated at all three sites. Thus Marta, a forty-year-old Yaqui widow, asserted:

My husband was violent and he would sometimes cry and ask: 'why? why is it that you defend your children and my mother never defended me? why do they go under your skirt when I'm about to hit them and you impose yourself on me?' 'Because it hurts, because I paid the price for them, because they were born from me, from me they were born and it hurts if someone hits them. Look at you, you can leave this house anytime and who is going to stay suffering with this child? Isn't it going to be me?'

Many respondents were engaged in reassessing the ways in which their mothers dealt with domestic violence. Alicia, a single woman in Mexico City, stated:

I used to tell my mother, 'How can you allow him to hit you? Throw the pan back, or whatever you can', and she would answer: 'No, because he will beat me harder and you are going to get involved....' Once he started beating her up and I told him: 'Don't do that in front of me, because even though I'm a small girl I won't consent to this'. When I saw those things, I said to myself: This won't happen to me, ever.

Angeles, forty-one, now living with a second partner in Mexico City, said of her mother: 'Her life was difficult, my father would beat her up and didn't give her any money at all, so she used to sell food. He had a good salary, but he would spend all the money on other women.'

In viewing motherhood as a validating experience respondents are carving a space for themselves against two forms of pressure – pressure from families and partners to become submissive mothers, and pressure from the authorities to have fewer children, without access to appropriate information. These contradictory pressures create a situation in which the women's wishes are difficult to assert. In this context, motherhood appears as a way out of the contradiction: the more the women felt they had fulfilled the ideal of motherhood within their community, the more they entitled themselves to control their reproduction.

Respondents' decisions around the number of children to have varied across regions. In rural areas of Oaxaca and Sonora, older women who had two children or more felt they had accomplished what was expected of them and thus felt more entitled; for the most part, though not in all cases, these were the women who had been sterilized. In Mexico City and Sonora, by contrast, urban and better-educated women said that ageing was not necessary to enhance their social status, though these women also had either been sterilized or had IUDs inserted. In all three regions, however, respondents stated that women needed to have at least two children to establish themselves as 'mothers with rights.'

The findings suggest that so long as motherhood remains an emblem of womanhood in Mexico, women will find it difficult to define themselves primarily as citizens with rights in the public arena. Yet at least some of the women interviewed are able to draw on their role as mothers to carve a notion of rights that emanates from their practices. While the group allows participants to engage in the collective articulation of the factors that shape their experiences, motherhood gives them a reason to resist and struggle in life.

Birth control: an emergency strategy

Despite the overall sense of entitlement conveyed by motherhood, its strength varied depending on the specific arena of reproduction. Thus it was particularly strong regarding birth control decisions and weakest regarding sexuality. Many of the women interviewed found it difficult to use contraception before they became mothers, because sexual practice without reproduction is seen as sinful or wrong. Once they had had at least two children, however, fertility control was the aspect that respondents identified most clearly as a subject of their rights. This realization of their right to control their fertility was hard-won, coming only after an early beginning of sexual/reproductive life, mainly at the request of a partner, and a common experience of hardship, mistreatment, and limited care during pregnancy and childbirth. Even then, the women's patterns of contraceptive use reflect their extremely limited knowledge about sexuality and birth control (see Table 5.2).

Respondents' descriptions of the conditions necessary to make family planning decisions vary depending on age. Older women stated that when they were in their childbearing years nothing permitted them to decide on the number of children they would have. Most expressed regret at this. In contrast, younger women in both rural and urban areas, independent of their level of education, agreed that birth control is a woman's decision. None the less, the younger women had only reached this position after much distress and pain. In all cases such entitlement was constructed in retrospect. Thus a group participant from Oaxaca said:

> I had five children. The first four were boys and my husband would say: 'We'll go on until you have the girl.' It was good that the fifth child was a girl, but the truth is that I think that it must be left to the woman to decide how many children to have, right, because she's the one who suffers from childbirth?

Other factors affecting women's attitudes toward their right to make such decisions included access to the labour market and childcare support from the extended family. Child care is still regarded as exclusively the woman's responsibility. Indeed, some respondents were glad of this; rather than risk men becoming more involved in decisions about children, they have set up networks of support that extend across generations.[18] However, few participants had any sense of entitlement to (public) institutional support in child care, and only those who belonged to trade unions believed that child care was a right that employers should provide. Yet most working women in this study indicated that considerations of childcare options influenced their reproductive decisions. In Nogales, for instance, a border city where the *maquila* industry is flourishing, respondents showed a greater possibility of making reproductive choices, such as using contraception early on in their sexual activity and demanding support in childrearing. Among the determinant factors here are that these women have long been part of the formal labour market and have finished their elementary education. Also, since they have migrated to the area, they have few family members to draw on for support (see Table 5.2).

In southern Sonora, on the other hand, where 60 per cent of the population are Indian and speak only Yaqui, women interviewed started to use contraception only after several children. Two of these women had the highest fertility of all women in the region: one had eight and the other seven children, although both had begun using the IUD after six and four pregnancies respectively. Yaqui women, however, enjoy sharing childraising activities with other families and the community at large, and derive some status from this activity.

However, there is a difference between awareness of the existence of contraceptive methods, which is widespread due to media campaigns, and knowledge about how to use them. Most respondents experienced difficulty as a result of unfamiliarity with how the methods work. Hortensia, who lives in Mexico City with ten children, illustrates this point:

> There are shots, a lot of dirty things like that: foams, all these dirty stuff that I feel sick about. How am I to put all these dirty things in there?... To be honest, I feel sick to touch myself, very bad ... and if you have your period ... it looks awful and all that. I mean, it's very dirty to put those things inside you with your own hands. These things are ugly. Especially that thing that gets entangled, the IUD. It's uncomfortable; they say when they have sex it bothers them.

Some studies have shown that even when women do know about contraception before they have sexual relations, many refrain from using this information for fear of being perceived by others and themselves as 'loose' (Rivas and Amuchástegui, 1996). Showing knowledge of contraception would violate the expectation that women should at least pretend to be ignorant of anything regarding sexual practice. In Mexico City, Hortensia, forty-three, said: 'When you go to the clinic they come up to you with their material and sometimes it's even boring. There are lots of information talks, but sometimes you just don't want to go. Women don't want them because they are afraid to harm their bodies.' Emilia, thirty-one, a single mother, agreed: 'To have sex wasn't important for me. Neither was it to control myself [to use contraception]. Even my boyfriend would say "control yourself." Well ... I didn't know what to use because I didn't want to get any information about that.'

In most cases, therefore, respondents' decision to use contraception represented an 'emergency strategy', one taken in order to stop having children rather than to space and limit their children. This was true across all three regions. In southern Sonora and Mexico City none of the women used contraception during their first sexual encounter, while in Oaxaca most respondents began to use contraception only after the second pregnancy. In this context, respondents' eventual recognition of the need for contraception cannot be underestimated. First, it represents the first deliberate action they take to separate sexuality from reproduction. Second, it is a step toward acknowledging their reproductive rights as stated by national and international official documents (although they never refer to them and probably do not know they exist). In this sense, the conviction that fertility control is a domain that belongs to them helps them confront the limited contraceptive options available to them and supports them against the opposition of partners.

Constrained choices: sterilization and abortion

That respondents considered the regulation of their own fertility as a subject of self-determination reflects the contradictory influence that population policies have had on women. In one respect, the very existence of family planning services helps to create an expectation among women that they are entitled to those services and even to decent treatment and respect from health providers. However, in Mexico as in many other countries, women's contraceptive options are determined by demographic goals rather than by the needs and desires of the women themselves. Government-sponsored family planning programmes and their personnel share a perception of women as ignorant about their own needs and a bias in favour of medically controlled methods, such as female sterilization and the IUD. In Mexico, female sterilization is the fastest-growing method of birth control, followed by the IUD and the pill (De Barbieri 1998, Figueroa 1990).

Yet the decision to be sterilized is highly problematic in Mexico, where 'informed consent' is limited at best. A 1987 survey of 9,310 women aged 15–49 revealed that of those who had undergone sterilization, 10 per cent had not participated in the decision; 40 per cent had not signed a consent form; and 25 per cent had received no information about other options (Figueroa 1993, 1994). A 1988 health ministry survey of three states found that 24 per cent of women who 'chose' sterilization did so because it was the only method they knew about (Figueroa *et al.* 1993). The same survey found that 18 per cent of women using an IUD had had the device inserted without their knowledge. And a recent study of service delivery in four states found that the government 'heavily promoted' the IUD, emphasizing its convenience for women while concentrating on the difficulties and side effects of the pill (UNFPA n.d.).

Our respondents confirmed this pattern. Many explained how their choice of contraceptive method was taken mainly on the advice of personnel at the public clinic they attended. Isabel, who is married with four children in Sonora, said, 'When we lived on the ranch, after I had the third [child] a lady started to bring [contraceptives] … she was a nurse from the Health Centre, and she … knocked on every door and invited us to go if we wanted pills to stop having children.' Angeles, who has three children, indicated it was the same in Mexico City: 'I didn't have any counselling about whether or not I should get sterilized, I did not realize the pros and cons of it. I was ignorant. Now, after what I've been through, I feel I have gained in experience, but then I didn't [know]. If I had had information about the operation I would have done something else.'

After three years of attempting to get pregnant again without success, Sofia, her husband and their Mexico City physician had the following conversation:

'You're fine, you could give 30 children to your husband' [says the doctor]. 'Then why can't she get pregnant?', asked my husband. And the doctor said: 'You had a caesarean, right? And you didn't give your authorization to be sterilized, right?' 'No, I didn't', and I asked my husband, 'did you?' 'No, I didn't'. And the doctor said, 'you know what? I think they sterilized you, even if you didn't give your consent.'

Younger women confront a different medical bias but the same lack of control. A university worker explained what happened at her Mexico City clinic: 'The last time I was pregnant I had the girl. I was using an IUD, and I got really mad because it didn't work. They haven't agreed to sterilize me because I am still very young. They say that maybe, in the future, I would want to have more children.'

Other respondents said that, to have the operation performed in a public clinic, they were asked for their husband's authorization, even though this is not required. A member of SITUAM, the University Union in Mexico City recalled:

> At the hospital they put an IUD in me two days after my son was born. Someone had told me, 'don't use it because it can pierce your womb.' They [doctors] say that they don't force you, but it's almost like … if you don't agree, they won't let you go. At the hospital I put it in because it was a condition to go out. They would come to see me once or twice a day and they would say, 'I'll talk to your husband.'

By contrast, abortion was never presented as an option in the institutional context. Abortion, although legal under certain circumstances, is condemned as a crime by the state and as a sin by the Catholic Church. In this context, women struggle to construct their right to interrupt a pregnancy, even in life-threatening situations. In all localities, almost all respondents agreed, especially during group interviews, that abortion was both a 'sin' and a crime'. Yet in individual interviews many justified the interruption of pregnancy, although few said they had actually practised it. They saw abortion as appropriate both for the mother and the foetus in cases of extreme adverse economic conditions but not in cases where the pregnancy interferes with personal plans and desires. Respondents saw abortion as a desperate measure to avoid more damage for the whole family rather than a personal entitlement. Thus Pilar, who lives in Mexico City, expressed her desire not to have a third child, but was persuaded by her relatives:

> I told my husband that I didn't want to have the baby and that a friend had offered me some shots to have a miscarriage. He said it was a sin, that God sends children to us. To be honest, I wanted to rebel against that. I said, 'why do you say God sends children? They come because we had sex, not because God came to me and touched my stomach!' But then he called my in-laws and they said that what I wanted to do was against nature.

In a heavily male-dominated society, where the Catholic Church retains a strong influence over policy, a woman's most basic rights must be endlessly negotiated, even in cases of risk to her life or health. A woman who got pregnant while using the IUD challenged the doctor who wished her to continue with her pregnancy:

> The doctor said, 'You cannot remove the IUD because you run the risk of having an abortion,' and I said, 'Please, remove it, it's my last hope!' But the doctor

insisted, 'It is at your own risk, are you married, anyway?' I answered that I wasn't, that I was a single mother of two, because I feared that he would call my husband and he would refuse to take out the IUD and they would leave me with the baby.

Given all these constraints, many women in this study have more children than they want. Thus, some of the women interviewed described sterilization as a welcome option. Ofelia, a Oaxacan woman, stated: 'I told my husband that I was going to have the operation. He said no, women who do that do so because they have another man. I told him he could think whatever he wanted but that I was going to have the operation.' Eulalia, a *maquiladora* worker in Sonora, said:

> I wanted to have the operation. I did not want to have more children, but the doctor said 'no, you are very young, you don't know, and what if you find another *compañero* [boyfriend] who will ask you to have children with him?' After my second daughter was born I requested to have the operation again, saying that it was my decision and that I had decided and wanted to have it.

In fact, she did not have the operation; the doctor who performed the caesarean delivery said he had never received the papers: 'He said to me, "If you want I can open you again." I felt very bad.'

Sexuality: a burden or a right?

Respondents' ambivalence about birth control reflects their lack of any sense of entitlement regarding their sexuality. Most of them do not consider themselves subjects of their own sexuality and therefore do not take action to initiate intercourse. Rather, they respond to their partners' requests. Amelia, a health promoter in rural Oaxaca, stated: 'I was working in Mexico City when I met him. He was always very insistent, so what shouldn't have happened finally did, and from that I became pregnant. Afterwards, I found out that he was married, so I left him. I didn't want to play the second woman role.'

While a few respondents, especially educated and urban younger women, accept their sexual desires and carry out strategies to satisfy them, their expressions of desire were mostly made apologetically. Thus Alejandra, who lives in a free union in Sonora, said: 'I had the devil inside of me and, Holy Mother of God!, I didn't care about anything and I didn't think about being caught, I just left with him and that's all.' For the most part, respondents do not consider sexuality as a realm of pleasure, and personal satisfaction is very far from their experience. Rather, sex is considered a 'necessary burden' of marriage in order to fulfil the task of reproduction. The overwhelming number of respondents regard sexual activity as a prerogative of masculinity, alien to femininity, and identified mainly with reproduction. Most tend to obey the Catholic doctrine of 'marriage debit' that makes sexual relations an obligation between spouses. As Juana, a sixty-year-old widow in Mexico

City, recalled: 'I would tell him that I didn't want to, but he'd say yes.... No, I wasn't forced, but it had to be like that, [as in] all marriages ... and that's how it was.'

Occasionally respondents voiced their unhappiness with this inequality. Gabriela, a bakery worker in Sonora, expressed this view:

I'm told by my girlfriends, I guess he is like all men, they only care for their own satisfaction, and they want it all the time, every night, and you ... you get fed up, I am fed up because I'm fed up. And with that kind of thing they don't give you the opportunity to feel like it, to want it.... Sometimes he says, 'we'll wait until you're finished,' and I say, 'No! All I want is that you go, I want you to finish and then go,' because they harass you so much with sex that you don't have the chance to like it.

Male authority over female sexual activity is reflected in the importance of women being virgins when starting a relationship. Several women talked about men refusing to marry their partners or accusing them of loss of virginity. Ofelia, who works as a secretary in Oaxaca, said:

I don't know what really happened because when I got married I wasn't a virgin. When we got married, he had this idea that I should bleed, and I didn't, so we had a lot of problems. He said 'if the baby is a boy you can stay, and if it's a girl, you leave'. I agreed, right? During the whole pregnancy I thought that all this happened because I hadn't been a *señorita*. In the end, I had a boy and I could stay with him.

That women remain so alienated from their sexuality reflects in part the silencing of any discussion of sexuality within the family, the neighbourhood, the school, or any other institutions. At least until recently, silence in the family consisted of mothers not feeling entitled to provide their daughters with the most basic sex education. Remarks by Virginia, a married woman in Oaxaca, testify to this:

Before, everything about the period was really secret. Our mothers didn't advise us in any way; on the contrary, when one would approach them to let them know what was happening, they would reply: that's because you're doing bad things.

A dramatic example of how lack of knowledge framed a participant's sense of her body and her sexuality is provided by Pilar, aged twenty-eight:

Once, I saw that a young woman had blood on her feet, and they said she'd been raped, that a man had abused her. I didn't know how that could happen, I mean, I didn't even think they would put their thing inside you. Then, when I got my period, I started to cry. My sister asked me what happened and I said I'd been raped. So they started beating me up and asking, 'Who was it?' and I said 'Nobody'. 'Then,' they said, 'how were you raped?' 'I don't know, blood is coming out of me', but they didn't say I could get pregnant, they didn't say anything.

Thus marriage or establishing a union with a man is rarely framed as a conscious act. Juana tells the story of her marriage, which started by her running away at fifteen:

> He talked to me and I asked him to talk to my parents but he didn't go. One day I just went out and I didn't go to work, I left with him [giggles]. I was foolish, because I didn't have a capacity or a mentality that I could say no. I was foolish. My parents were very angry at me. I just left.'

Likewise, most respondents' first pregnancy was not planned or decided. Some of them did not even know about conception. Sofia, twenty-seven, explained:

> I didn't know much. I didn't imagine anything. For instance, when my period stopped, I asked myself, why? Finally I told him about it and he said, 'it means you're pregnant.' So, I said, 'Am I going to have a baby? This is not possible!'

Some participants had greater information about sexuality and thus felt more prepared to make decisions. Gabriela said of her marriage twenty years ago:

> I was already twenty-seven years old. I already knew [about sex] through my friends' experiences, or by ear, or because I read about it. So you knew what you were up to, you were not naïve any more. I think that I got married at a good age. By then, I had had a great time, with many boyfriends, good ones and bad ones. I already wanted to have children.

Even so, most of the women put their reproductive decisions in the hands of their partner. Eulalia, a young *maquiladora* worker, said, 'I know I agreed … but only with the condition that he was going to take care of me.'

Whether starting their sexual life, responding to the needs of the other, or having their first child, many respondents seemed to be seeking compensation for emotional deprivation and loss. Ofelia ran away with a man who later became her husband: 'I wasn't what you could call in love,' she explained. 'I thought my husband would be my salvation, because of the situation I had at home … but it didn't change, it was even worse.' Pilar, now separated, said of her husband:

> He wasn't rude … he was nice, he would pull the chair so I could sit. He never said, 'I want you', as all men do. He was different. He treated me like a human being, an equal. He told me that his mother used to embrace him and sing songs to him, things that I never had. I remember telling him, 'I would like to have a family like yours.'

It is possible to argue that even in such a context women are exercising individual choices, albeit in ways that contradict the model of rational choice. This model, which has informed population policies for at least twenty years, assumes people choose freely among unlimited options; it does not take into account that all decisions, including those about reproduction, are socially constrained. As numerous studies of reproductive decision-making have pointed out, however, both in the global South and within poor or marginal populations in the North, even though women actively engage in improving their life conditions, they do so within the constraints of a socially, economically and culturally oppressive reality (see López 1993; Petchesky 1990). The Mexican women in this study are no exception.

Most respondents – especially members of trade unions and reproductive health activists in Mexico City – asserted that it is not their obligation to be sexually responsive every time their partner requests it. Yet during individual interviews many revealed that they accommodated their husband's desire to have intercourse, even against their will. Occasionally they tried to resist, however ineffectually. Hortensia, a Mexico City woman with ten children, stated:

> Sometimes when the baby was little he would bother me and I would say 'no, I'll get pregnant again.' One day he hit me very hard because I said no ... he hit me with a shoe because I didn't want to. It was always forced, even now ... I have to run away to the street, I have to leave.

Negotiating entitlements: accommodation and resistance

As this discussion illustrates, grassroots women in Mexico negotiate entitlements to sexuality and reproduction through sometimes contradictory strategies of accommodation and resistance. While the strategy of accommodation implies a trade-off to prevent perceived harm, such as domestic violence or deterioration of their living standards, the strategy of resistance refers to the nexus of practices and perceptions used to transgress dominant gender norms or to manoeuvre in different ways to enhance their entitlements and rights. In general, respondents adopt accommodation for areas in which they experience little control, such as initiating or refusing sexual activity or dealing with health providers. They employ resistance in areas in which they have gained a strong sense of entitlement – specifically, to sustain group participation, fight off domestic violence, and exercise fertility control after having had children.

In employing these strategies, the women we interviewed have not succeeded in subverting gender roles because both strategies are most often aimed at survival rather than at transforming existing conditions. This can be seen especially with regard to coercive sex. Consistently, both in group and individual interviews, respondents revealed a connection between physical violence, marital rape and male alcohol consumption, especially in Mexico City and Oaxaca. In order to survive, a single mother in Mexico City accommodates her partner: 'Since he drank a lot, there were times in which he wanted to have sex, to me it was very uncomfortable but he was so stubborn that I accepted ... and he would insist again.' An Indian woman in Oaxaca, on the other hand, resists: 'My husband gets really mad when I come back from the group, he's almost always drunk, but I just ignore him and that's why I'm much better here, learning new things instead of listening to his drunken babble, and I'm going to keep coming.'

Some of the women began to perceive rape in marriage only after they had been exposed to the information provided in groups. A member of the UNPNT (women's grassroots group) in Mexico City explained: 'Now I have learned what sexual abuse is, it is when you don't want to do it and they force you. Before, they would force you and you didn't protest, or say anything, you thought that it was your duty as a wife.' Most of the women interviewed start adulthood and married life as invisible women, only suitable to fulfil the needs of others. It is only after repeatedly resisting continuous childbearing and after years of group participation that this process begins to be reversed.

The common use of accommodation to deal with sexuality may also reflect the fact that most of the participants did not define sexual activity as pleasurable. Rather, most of the women described sex as a requirement to achieve motherhood, so precious to most of them, or to satisfy the demands of the husband. Some said they discovered later, primarily during group participation, that they were entitled to refuse having intercourse whenever their partner demanded it.

In relating to health providers, the women interviewed similarly employed accommodation in order to experience as little harm as possible. A group participant from the University Union in Mexico City described 'the doctor with his face of physician and his attitude of "weepy woman" ... What can you do? ... just bear!' Women do not complain, she added, 'because, what if you get the same one next time? He will treat you even worse! It's like with the teachers, you complain and then they take it out on the kid.' Pilar's experience with health providers is even more vivid:

> The pain was so strong that I was about to scream ... then I heard what they were saying to the woman who was next to me: 'You should have screamed like this when he was fucking you,' and I said to myself, 'Oh, my God!' It was one of the practitioners, because, unfortunately, the ones who take care of you are the practitioners not the doctors themselves.

Most respondents showed some awareness about state coercion and abuse in family planning programmes, and most were opposed to any form of involuntary contraception. Yet sterilization without consent, though illegal, was usually not contested, especially in poorer neighbourhoods. Alejandra, who lives in a marginal neighbourhood of urban Sonora, stated:

> [After delivery] the doctor saw me and said that he had tied me up [sterilized me], and I wanted to know because I had suffered a lot; after all I'd been through I didn't want to go to the hospital again. The doctor did some tests, and he said, laughing, 'Look, dear, for now you have no problem, you can forget because you'll not get pregnant again. We tied you up, it isn't permanent because you are too young.'

By contrast, respondents used strategies of resistance to gain something positive, as shown by Sofia, whose husband asked her to have an abortion in her first pregnancy:

'Why should I have an abortion?' [I asked]. So my husband replied, 'Because that child is not mine,' and I answered back, 'Well, so what?' and he said, 'I won't support a child that is not mine.' But I wanted something really mine, so I decided I was going to have the baby, to cuddle it, I wouldn't have an abortion.

The diffuse meanings of sexuality and reproduction are such that actions to conceive or not to conceive children can both be interpreted as resistance. In particular, since reproduction takes place within the body of the woman, respondents interpret it as their possession and, therefore, as their right to decide upon. A member of a group interview in Mexico City described her determinaton to be sterilized:

I think this decision should always be made by women. In my case, I was the one who decided. When I had the second child I went to the Family Planning Department and asked for contraceptives. My husband got mad, but I told him I didn't care because I didn't want to get pregnant. Afterwards, I asked them to remove the IUD and had a third child and decided that was enough. I went and asked to be sterilized.

The fact that women can resist partners and families in such cases reflects a social context in which they feel sufficiently confident about gender identity and their ability to survive to challenge dominant cultural norms. But since most respondents consider family and belonging to a community as central to their lives, many times their resistance was not vocal or open. Often it was quiet and covert, reflecting the power that family, social and cultural norms represent in the life of every woman. Regarding forced sex, for example, a woman in an indigenous group in Oaxaca talked about negotiation:

... this is how we are raised here; the man is the boss and we have to obey, right? And sometimes because of illness, or because we don't feel like it, or because of the children or because we don't want to have any more children.... But the man doesn't accept it, he doesn't understand, and he says, 'I'm the boss, not you.'... It's very hard, but we try and little by little we get them to understand a bit.

Regarding medical care, a few respondents were able to resist the medical institution in order to demand more attention to their needs during childbirth. This was especially true among urban, more educated participants. Emilia, a mother of two in Mexico City, said:

I was going to have a caesarean and, supposedly, everyone at the hospital knew about my problem. Then a doctor came to me and said, '*madrecita* [little mother], I'm going to give you this little shot so your delivery goes well.' I replied that I was going to have a caesarean, not a normal delivery, but he answered that he was the doctor, that he was to give orders. But I didn't accept that, so I called another doctor and this doctor called another one. Finally, the head of that floor came and scolded the first doctor, 'How can it be that you didn't pay attention to what this woman was saying? That's what records exist for!'

However, even in cases where women are able to articulate a protest, rarely do they see beyond the immediate aggressor or connect the abuse that the doctor, father, husband or partner infringes on them to the macrosocial context of authoritarianism, poverty and abuse. In this sense, a collective strategy of resistance has yet to be constructed.

From entitlement to action

Across all regions and groups, many respondents expressed great uneasiness with the intervention of government agencies, whether medical, legal, or judicial. Reinforcing this endemic distrust, health and family planning agencies show particular disregard toward women's reproductive rights, emphasizing demographic goals over the provision of information to empower women to make informed choices. This disregard confirms women's belief that they are not viewed as persons with rights or even shown minimal dignity. In Mexico City especially, respondents described abusive treatment by public health personnel, illustrated in the experience of Rosa (who is thirty-five):

> I went to the hospital at six and I was there all night … they left me all alone in the position for having a child. I talked to the doctor, but he said that it wasn't my turn, that I had to wait.… I didn't know, and they hadn't told me how my child was going to be born.… They just left me there with my legs spread apart. If they did that to me now I would protest, but then I didn't … say anything.

Respondents in every location cited such examples, yet the expression of complaints within family or group settings rarely developed into a formal claim for restitution. While all respondents agreed that the insertion of an IUD without a woman's consent was a clear violation of human rights, none of them considered pressing charges. Mostly respondents felt that removal of the IUD was enough and legal action should be undertaken only in the case of involuntary sterilization. Some believed that prosecution should be undertaken only in extreme cases, such as mutilation or the loss of a child. When invited to reflect on actual facts, some respondents were even reluctant to find out about their own situation. Sofia explained:

> I had thought of getting some tests to see if they really sterilized me and, if they did, why did they do it? What gives them the right to take something that doesn't belong to me? But, I don't know, I think that I would be very disappointed. They treated me so well at the hospital!

The reluctance among our respondents to take action against medical abuse must be placed in the context of corrupt and inefficient law enforcement institutions that generate not only fear of retaliation but a sense of futility about claiming reproductive rights. The fact that so many women invest the medical profession with authority over their lives derives in large part from a lack of trust and knowledge about how to access the justice system in Mexico. None of the respondents thought their case would be properly looked at by legal authorities. Patricia, who lives in Mexico City, asserted:

You cannot sue. Things don't proceed. Recently a friend died, she had an ovarian cyst. She went to social security and was operated on there. She had an infection because they left something inside her. They opened her up again and the anaesthetist overdid it. The husband sued but it didn't proceed. From the first time he went to the agency they said, 'Is it against social security? Uhf! You're wasting your time.'

In Oaxaca, many Indian respondents said that they would prefer to call on local leaders – usually men but occasionally women – to resolve such situations. Interestingly, the one woman who had challenged a medical authority was from rural Oaxaca: 'I didn't let them sterilize me, and they said, "In a little while you're going to come back pregnant again." And I said, "that's what you're here for, right? You are here to give us medical attention."' But this attitude was rare. Thus, at a time when women's role in the sphere of reproduction entails both traditional and new responsibilities, including working to preserve their families, the term 'rights' still elicits ambiguous meanings. Most respondents had acquired a sense of rights only through hardship and confrontation and had experienced the conferral of 'rights' by the state as fraught with new obligations. Virginia, also from rural Oaxaca, explained why she objected to such rights:

I think that rights must be personal and not because someone comes and tells you, 'These are your rights'; that's like he is ordering something, right? We women have to say: 'This is my right and this I have to do, I'm not going to wait for someone to tell me,' because it's as if my husband said, 'Do this or don't do this.' According to your life you should choose your rights, I think.

In fact, respondents indicated that group participation has encouraged them to approach the subject of rights from a different perspective. During a dramatization in which women voiced what the term meant for them, ideas like 'freedom', 'movement', 'the right to speak one's mind', 'right to life, education, work, health, food, rest, respect', or to ownership, began to emerge. According to Juana,

A right is when I have something and someone tries to take it away from me, and I say no, because it's my property. If there's an aggression against my children I can yell at the aggressors or avoid the harm because my children are mine, like a cloth that is mine and no one can take it away from me. Only when a daughter gets married and leaves, then I don't have any right anymore.

Respondents' elaboration of the term 'rights' varies according to the type of group they participate in. Those involved in unions and neighbourhood organizations that incorporate political and legislative terms in their educational programmes were more prepared to address how they would use the law to enforce respect for their rights than were those participating in health or education groups. Ironically, however, these same women found it more difficult to articulate how they constitute themselves as subjects of rights in their close relationships and their daily lives than did the women in health and education groups quoted above.

In sum, it appears that women in the groups we studied have appropriated elements that derive from two discourses, human rights and feminism, but without having a fully developed notion of either. At present, a somewhat magical notion of the group's transformative power prevails. As a woman in a Mexico City neighbourhood group put it: 'From the very first time you go to the meetings you are already changed, you become more independent and they [the husbands] don't repress you as much as before.' But, lacking a critical gender perspective, the women have so far not been able to transform this personally validating experience of group participation into a collective exercise of entitlement.

Thus, although respondents rely on strategies discovered in the group to try to improve their power position at home, most of them indicate that they are more willing to engage in collective action around community issues than to change gender arrangements. While stronger connections between feminists and grassroots women's organizations might facilitate the articulation of a critical gender perspective that could enable grassroots women to advance their entitlements, such connections have only recently begun to materialize and remain for the most part tentative.

Conclusion: Women's Rights as Human Rights

This study indicates that notions of reproductive rights among grassroots women in Mexico are not limited to formal legal definitions but include a wider field in which they are constructing a voice of their own. In fact, respondents' knowledge of official laws and dispositions regarding reproductive rights is quite limited. Social and informal formulations of entitlement coexist with legal and formal discourses in varying degrees of appropriation. A crucial issue is that entitlement and rights are not a part of these women's process of socialization. Rights are not defined as something individuals have just because they are human beings but as something to be earned or granted by others, mainly through suffering, work or misconduct of the partner. Thus, among our respondents entitlement takes the form of recalling their needs after the fact. Moreover, violence and coercion within families and within government services make the construction of a female subject of rights very difficult, although this study suggests that participation in groups, by allowing women to meet with each other and thus acknowledge their own needs and aspirations, may eventually change this.

The possibilities of action to claim or assert rights are based on a process of constitution of the subject, that is, on the recognition of her existence by herself as well as others. The main elements of this process are the appropriation of the body as a domain of individual sovereignty and the construction of a voice as the expression of self-agency. If some of these women have been stripped of and, to a certain extent, given up the management of their will, thought and body to others, they do not arrive at a point of authorizing themselves as subjects in certain areas of their lives. In this context, the informal notion of rights that respondents hold has been constructed more as a reactive and defensive strategy against violence and abuse than as entitlement derived from wishes, aspirations, or life projects. For most, we found the statement 'I want' has to be mediated by the needs of others, mainly their children, or replaced by its opposite, 'I do not want', generally as a response to aggression.

The finding that women involved in urban movements fighting for better workplace or community conditions show greater knowledge and appropriation of the law than those participants who belong to education or health organizations raises a question: can an approach to rights from the economic and political spheres be extended to those areas traditionally considered 'private', such as sexuality and reproduction? Our study suggests the process is problematic. Even though respondents in union and neighbourhood groups seem to be more able to use strategies of resistance and have more possibilities to accomplish their goals, there is a gap between these abilities and acquiring the resources to solve problems related to their sexuality and reproduction. They are less likely to engage in daily and personal exercise of their rights as women in personal relations than, for example, in a legal defence against a real-estate fraud. When the struggle for better material conditions is carried out collectively it seems to help women to feel supported in voicing their rights in a way that they are unable to feel when defending rights by themselves, without the presence of the group. In other organizations, less politicized but more focused on family and health issues, the participants showed a deeper capacity to reflect on their bodies, their sexuality, and their rights to decide about them, but showed an even larger gap between such utterances and their practical defence.

Such findings indicate that, regardless of how entitlements are constructed, the risks of acting on them pose practical difficulties. This is not only because of cultural meanings about gender, reproduction, and sexuality that disregard women as subjects of rights, but also because of the social and political marginality of grassroots women which puts institutional remedies out of reach. While the self-appropriation of the body and the notion of entitlement are necessary conditions for the construction of a concept of rights and citizenship, this cannot be accomplished without the active intervention of the social institutions that should legitimize and enforce rights. That is, even given individuals' subjective ability to consider themselves subjects of rights, without the political, social and cultural conditions to protect them, it is impossible to exercise such citizenship, particularly in Mexico.

Today in Mexico the construction of reproductive rights as women's entitlement is tainted by a political culture in which political and social institutions are distrusted and citizenship has little value, because of the authoritarian and antidemocratic context we live in. It is precisely for this reason that legal and formal definitions of rights are alien to most respondents. At the same time, it is this context that is propelling grassroots women's group participation at all levels, resulting in an uneven awareness and collective mobilization around issues of social participation and entitlement in the family and society. This is why the informal notions of rights expressed by women in this study are important: they reveal the means by which respondents are constructing a sense of entitlement, regardless of formal definitions or whether entitlements are named as 'rights'.

Indeed, recent events suggest that grassroots women in Mexico are also making more formal and public claims. The basic proposition of this chapter, that women in Mexico are in the process of constituting themselves as subjects of rights, seemed confirmed in the national and local elections of 1997, which ended the sixty-eight year monopoly of the PRI, and brought to power conservative candidates in several states as well as a progressive left-to-centre party, the PRD (Partído de la Revolución Democrática). Most notably, women voters made up an unprecedented 51 per cent of the electorate, according to federal election officials (Jusidisman 1997). Moreover, indigenous women, especially in the states of Chiapas and Oaxaca, have begun organizing national campaigns to demand better social conditions, greater access to education, and reproductive freedom for women.

Thus, as social contradictions deepen in Mexico, propelling women into the political sphere, new meanings of the term 'rights' are being generated. As grassroots women come together in groups – whether groups focused on workplace needs or groups focused on health – they begin to expand their sense of entitlement in areas connected to reproduction. The collective awareness women are developing is helping them to challenge the state's appropriation of the constitutional right to make decisions governing reproductive health. Although these women have not yet translated their new awareness into forms of collective resistance, the process of group identity itself, by expanding personal expectations and creating awareness, opens up the possibility of rearticulating formal and community usages of the term 'rights' in ways that bring together its personal and social dimensions.

Finally, in recognizing grassroots women as active agents rather than victims of repressive norms and conditions, the Mexican team also recognized that the issue of reproduction was not the main problem with which they were concerned. To understand their priorities more fully, we would need to probe more deeply into women's conceptions about sexuality and pleasure. Such intimate concerns, while a latent part of their emerging sense of entitlement, are likely to remain unexpressed until grassroots women are able to control more of the economic and social conditions that determine their lives.

Table 5.2 Women Interviewed

Mexico City

NAME	AGE	EDUCATION	MARITAL STATUS	WORK	NO. OF CHILDREN	BIRTH CONTROL METHOD
Alicia	43	Technical	Single	None	0	Yes; Not specified
Emilia	31	High school	Single	None	1	IUD (after 1st child)
Pilar	28	Jr high school	Separated	Informal sector	3	IUD (after 3rd child)
Angeles	41	Elementary	2nd partner	Employee	3	Sterilization
Juana	60	None	Widow	None	9	No
Patricia	26	High school	Free union	None	2	Sterilization
Hortensia	43	None	Free union	None	10	Sterilization
Rosa	35	Jr high school	Married	None	2	Withdrawal
Sofia	27	Elementary	Free union	Paid domestic	2	Suspected sterilization

Oaxaca

NAME	AGE	EDUCATION	MARITAL STATUS	WORK	NO. OF CHILDREN	BIRTH CONTROL METHOD
Dolores	30	High school	Married	Secretary	2	Rhythm
Natalia	44	Elementary	Single	Agricultural	3	None
Teresa	46	Elementary	Married	None	8	IUD after all pregnancies
Virginia	27	Elementary	Married	None	2	IUD
Amelia	39	Nursing	Married	Volunteer	2	None
Laura	33	None	Single	Weaver	0	None
Vicenta	21	Elementary	Single	Weaver	0	None
Sara	30	Elementary	Married	Agricultural	3	None
Rocio	40	Elementary	Married	None	3	Sterilization
Ofelia	40	Technical	Married	Secretary	3	Sterilization

Sonora

NAME	AGE	EDUCATION	MARITAL STATUS	WORK	NO. OF CHILDREN	BIRTH CONTROL METHOD
Gabriela	47	Elementary	Married	Bakery worker	3	Sterilization
Alejandra	38	Elementary	Married	Paid domestic	5	Sterilization
Eulalia	28	Jr high school	Single	Maquila worker	2	Pill
Mariana	42	Elementary	Married	Paid domestic	2	Sterilization
Ernestina	40	Jr high school	Divorced	Paid domestic	7	IUD
Isabel	36	Elementary	Married	Paid domestic	4	Pill after 3rd child
Lucia	48	Elementary	Single	Vendor	6	No
Marta	40	Elementary	Widow	Paid domestic	7	Sterilization
Petra	38	None	Widow/ free union	None	8	IUD
Herlinda	27	Elementary	Married	Maquila worker	2	IUD

Notes

1 In this respect our research conforms to more recent work that argues that women's grassroots organizations often combine demands for empowerment with agitation for community needs (see Stephen 1995).

2 Following the 1985 earthquake, several grassroots women's groups took leadership in assisting neighbourhoods with emergency food and water supplies and helping people cope with the disaster (Lamas *et al.*1995).

3 Such participation was made possible, in part, from improvements in health and education for the masses of people which occurred in that period (Massolo 1989).

4 During the UN Decade for Women (1975–85), Latin American women endeavoured to form cross-class linkages between middle-class and poor women, integrating movements against class and gender inequality (Lamas *et al.* 1995; Sternbach *et al.* 1992).

5 Groups participating in the study included: **Mexico City:** Servicios de Desarrollo, Amor y Paz (SEDEPAC), a Catholic community organization; Comunidad de Desarrollo Integral Copilco (CODIC), a philanthropic Catholic organization; Unión Popular Nueva Tenochtitlán (UNPNT), a women's neighbourhood group; Sindicato de la Universidad Autónoma Metropolitana (SITUAM), the university trade union of clerical and administrative workers; and Servicio Integral para la

Atención de la Mujer (SIPAM), a women's health collective. **Oaxaca:** Sindicato de Trabajadores de la Universidad Autónoma 'Benito Juárez' de Oaxaca, the workers' union of the university; Grupo Xande, a group of Tlahuitoltepeca women; Grupo de Promotoras de Salud Voluntarias de los Valles Centrales de Oaxaca, a collaborative women's health project working in several Zapotec communities; DGNAA Ruyin Chee Lahady (Women Who Weave Blankets), a Zapotec group in Teotitlán; and Grupo de Mujeres del Comité del Templo de Ejutla de Crespo, a religious group in rural Oaxaca. **Sonora:** Comunidad de la Y, a communal Catholic organization in Hermosillo; Mujeres Maquiladoras de la Guardería Wilson Jones, nonunionized migrant workers in Nogales organized through the Wilson Jones childcare centre; Sindicato de Trabajadores y Empleados de la Universidad de Sonora (STEUS), a union of about 1,200 university workers; Mujeres Unidas de la Comunidad de la Colonia Marte R. Gómez, a grassroots women's housing and land reclamation group near Ciudad Obregón; and Tribu Yaqui, a Yaqui ethnic group.

6 Redefinitions in 1994 have made these figures difficult to use in comparisons, either with the past or with other countries. For example, 'women who have had some schooling' has replaced the category of women's literacy; women's labour force participation has been redefined to include all sorts of activities in the informal sector.

7 We use the term 'group interview' instead of 'focus group' since the process involved an open-ended exploration of norms and values rather than a guided evaluation of particular themes.

8 'Patrons' are persons with high political status. They provide protection, support in political struggles, and chances for upward political or economic mobility to their 'clients', persons with lesser political status. In exchange, the 'clients' provide loyalty, deference, and such services as voter mobilization to their patrons within the party or bureaucracy.

9 The state's success in this regard has led some to argue that the process of making demands on the system may not in fact further social change but increase the centralization of power and reinforce mechanisms of control, at least in the short term (Hellman 1995).

10 The emergency infusion of funds from the US government, repayment of which was guaranteed (and carried out) on very harsh terms, has accelerated the transfer of capital, making it difficult for Mexico to realize any of the promised benefits of joining NAFTA, the free trade zone with the United States and Canada, in January 1994. While some regions such as Sonora have seen a rise in employment, increased privatization and reduction of protections on local industry have made US firms the major beneficiaries of NAFTA.

11 However, a university education does not automatically open greater employment opportunities for women. Instead, as certain fields become more feminized, they become socially devalued. Educated women find themselves overqualified, unemployed or superexploited as they join the labour market (Muñoz and Suárez 1990).

12 For example, women are now dying more frequently in urban transportation accidents (Hernández 1990).

13 After a bitterly fought campaign for abortion rights in 1981, defeated by an alliance of the Catholic Church and rightwing parties, both politicians and feminists distanced themselves from the issue during the 1980s, concentrating on issues such as support for battered women and rape victims (Brito 1995; Lamas *et al.* 1995). Unwilling to concede entirely to the Catholic Church, however, the state has liberalized the law to allow abortion in some cases, such as endangerment to the woman's life, proven rape or foetal anomalies incompatible with life (Paxman *et al.* 1993; Langer *et al.*

1997). However, these reforms have not been publicized and services to enable women to take advantage of them have not been provided.

14 In Mexico the number of prostitutes infected with the virus is growing more slowly than for any other group, suggesting that sex with other men rather than with prostitutes is the cause of infection for married men.

15 For example, the Virgin of Guadalupe, who resembled the Aztec deity Tonatzin, inspired a cult that is now the most powerful element in Mexican Catholicism (López Austin 1984).

16 In this sense, the experience related by these women conforms to a transformation known in the literature as women's empowerment (Craske 1993; Hellman 1995; Batliwala 1994).

17 Taboos on sexuality are such that this fact itself was only revealed to researchers within the context of the relatively safer individual interviews, rather than in group interviews.

18 For example, in some families in Sonora a tacit agreement exists between mothers and daughters: if the grandmother does not have any more children to raise, the daughters send their eldest children to her.

6 Women's Sexuality and Fertility in Nigeria
Breaking the Culture of Silence

GRACE OSAKUE AND ADRIANE MARTIN-HILBER*

Women in Nigeria today live under an authoritarian military regime that both reinforces and is supported by traditional patriarchal norms. These norms, revolving around age-old myths and rituals meant to perpetuate women's inferior status in society, are particularly rigid in regard to the reproductive and sexual lives of women and girls (Renne 1993). Yet, while many Nigerian women still defend indigenous practices that endanger their health and wellbeing, the reproductive decisions they actually make in everyday life may contravene conventional norms. We sought to learn how Nigerian women negotiate, accommodate or occasionally reject male control over their fertility and sexuality, and how these patterns change over the course of their life cycle. In so doing, we found that the women we interviewed straddle the gap between patriarchal tradition and economic necessity when it comes to reproductive and sexual decision-making. While accommodating traditional gender norms and belief systems, they also attempt to secure certain areas of control for themselves and express a desire for change on particular issues. But this happens more forcefully in the earlier and later stages of life; early marriage and motherhood is the time of greatest accommodation to tradition. To understand this complexity, it is useful to situate it in the context of existing political, economic, and cultural conditions in Nigeria and how they circumscribe women's social activities and reproductive health.

Political Context

The Nigerian state was an artificial creation of British colonial rule, which lasted from 1914 to 1960. This fact is central to understanding the country's

* Substantial contributions to the framing of this chapter were made by the three zonal coordinators of the IRRRAG Nigeria team, Bene Madunagu (Southeast), Jane Osagie (Southwest) and Hajara Usman (North), in addition to the two listed authors. We would also like to thank Beth Richie for her help and guidance as our research consultant and Anton Hilber for help in researching secondary and background sources.

government and politics and their construction through many competing diversities: ethnic, linguistic, geopolitical, religious, and class.[1] British colonialism systematically reinforced and exploited existing divisions and rivalries among ethnic groups, which resulted in the country's parcelling into the thirty-six states and three macro regions – North, Southwest and Southeast – that dominate its map today (Hussaina Abdullah 1996). Since independence, Nigeria has experienced numerous failed attempts to implement a lasting democratic system, followed by uninterrupted military rule since 1983. Competition and open hostility among military as well as civilian leaders have produced the instability of numerous coups and counter-coups. In addition, the country has been riddled with conflicts over regional autonomy and control over vital resources, particularly its richest commodity, oil. This and other disputes have compounded the government's failure to harmonize divergent local, ethnic and sectoral interests and to promote national unity and equitable economic development.

Today the many layers of the government's administrative structure influence every sector of Nigerian life and reach far into the rural areas. The repressive military regime of General Abacha continues in power, intolerant of political dissent and permeated by inefficiency, endemic corruption and patronage.[2] Though the current regime remains officially committed to a transition to civilian rule in 1998, this goal appears ever more elusive, given Abacha's history of repression and political deception (the execution of author and political activist Ken Saro-Wiwa and eight other Ogoni activists in 1995 was only the most dramatic example of this repression). Meanwhile, Nigeria's petroleum-centred economy continues in crisis and is unable to achieve sufficient growth to improve the welfare of a fast-growing population.

Economic Crisis and Its Effects on Women

Despite its rich agricultural and mineral resources, Nigeria remains an impoverished country whose economic potential is largely unrealized. By the mid-1970s it had become the dominant economy in sub-Saharan Africa and the continent's major exporter of petroleum. However, economic mismanagement and a series of external factors led to a precipitous decline in gross domestic product (GDP) and real wages in the 1980s, reducing both to levels below those of neighbouring sub-Saharan countries. An estimated 64 per cent of urban and 61 per cent of rural households lived in poverty in 1984 (Federal Research Division 1991), and by 1993 GNP per capita had dropped to US$300 (UNDP 1996).

While petroleum exports generate over 80 per cent of the government's current revenue, agriculture remains by far the largest source of employment, including for women, and accounts for over 35 per cent of Nigeria's GDP (World Bank 1995). Smallholder farmers, using simple bush-fallow cultivation techniques, produce nearly two-thirds of all agricultural output. Rural-to-urban migration, especially by young men, affected the 1980s rural economy by creating marked changes in the gender division of labour. As large numbers of working-age men left the rural areas for the booming cities, women and children struggled to meet the resulting labour shortage. Today the great majority of the women work in agriculture and related activities, providing well over half of all labour in agricultural production and processing (World Bank 1997).

In 1986, the Nigerian government subscribed to a World Bank-administered structural adjustment programme (SAP) to address its budgetary crisis and improve conditions for long-term economic growth. As in other countries, the SAP-prescribed austerity measures included reduction of government subsidies, privatization of state enterprises, currency devaluation, and severe cuts in government spending on education, health and welfare. All this had a steep social cost, including the escalation of poverty in rural areas and the deterioration of existing healthcare facilities. The ongoing decline in the standard of living is felt at all levels of society, but the rising cost of living and the lack of access to health care affect women and children most acutely, as evidenced by worsening levels of malnutrition, infant mortality and disease (Elabor-Idemudia 1994). The burden of managing household budgets when the currency is continually being devalued also falls most heavily on women (Atsenuwa 1995).

Overall, young women's access to education has improved significantly relative to that of older generations, with one-third of women aged 15–24 having achieved secondary or higher education compared with around 5 per cent of those in their thirties and forties (NDHS 1992). None the less, many women, especially in the rural areas and the North, still lack access to secondary education in consequence not only of the traditional bias against educating girls but also of the economic crisis.[3] With the decline in government funding of education and the rise in school fees, the squeeze on household budgets reinforces the tendency to keep daughters out of school, on the premise that they are destined only to marry. Such gender-biased views of girls are not addressed by public policy, despite clear evidence that women's educational level is inversely related to their fertility and positively related to improved maternal health (Olusanya 1989).[4]

Women's earnings are increasingly essential for the wellbeing of lower and middle-class households in Nigeria. But instead of improving their social status, this economic activity has heightened gender tensions (especially among conservative Muslim groups in the North), contributing to a public backlash in the name of traditional values and women's 'proper place' within society. Despite their vital income-generating activities, women are still expected to perform all the labour of household maintenance and childrearing. As the economic crisis continues, however, women may begin to resist these disproportionate burdens.

Tradition, Law, and the Status of Women

Oko ni olori aya. (The husband is the head of the wife.) – Yoruba proverb

Male dominance has deep sociocultural and religious roots in Nigerian society. Despite growing awareness and activism among middle-class women, the majority of Nigeria's women still appear to accept their secondary status in home and community (Hussaina Abdullah 1996). Valuing their roles as mothers and caretakers, these women defer to their husbands as the decision makers in the family, even in matters that directly affect them such as family size and contraceptive use (Bankole 1995; Adamchak and Adebayo 1987). Such deference is perpetuated by kin groups, traditional healers, and religious leaders, who invoke a male-centred interpretation of the Bible, the Qu'ran and traditional culture to support male dominance in marital and family life (Renne 1993).

Patriarchal power over women and children is partly derived from men's control over the construction and ownership of family dwellings. Sons' inheritance of houses from their fathers and, in some areas, exclusive male ownership of land are regarded as the primary basis for continuing the family legacy (Renne 1995). In this patrilineal system children belong to the father, whose status in the community is largely determined by the size of his family (Isiugo-Abanihe 1994). Nigerians typically define a woman as someone's daughter, wife, mother, or widow. Despite the reality that women perform as much as 70 per cent of agricultural labour (Elabor-Idemudia 1994), in popular discourse and metaphors they are still assimilated to male property and their reproductive capacity is analogized to that of the land men own.

Although law is often thought to be a tool for modernization, in Nigeria it frequently becomes a means of perpetuating patriarchal tradition. The low status of women in Nigerian society is reflected in its legal system, an amalgam of civil law, local custom and Islamic (*shari'a*) law. While Nigeria is a signatory to the Convention to Eliminate All Forms of Discrimination against Women (the Women's Convention), and the 1979 constitution forbids discrimination based on sex, many legal texts still contain references to women as the property of their husbands, and wives are given few rights *vis-à-vis* their husbands. In addition, uncodified customary laws and practices generally override criminal codes in gender disputes.[5] Local customs and *shari'a* law, unlike the civil law, support arranged and polygamous unions and, in the case of *shari'a* law, permit a husband to divorce his wife unilaterally.

To get married, men must pay a substantive or symbolic amount as bride price (or dower under Islamic law), a practice that secures rights over the reproductive and physical labour of wives. Marriage among most rural ethnic groups is only considered complete, and the wife fully accepted into the community, after bride price is paid in full. Among the predominantly

Muslim Hausa and Fulani of northern Nigeria, especially in rural areas, girls still receive less formal education, while early teenage marriages are frequent, followed by seclusion within the household under *purdah*.[6] In recent years, economic pressures have contributed to a decline in new polygamous unions. However, an estimated 41 per cent of Nigerian women, both Christian and Muslim, still live in such unions (Westoff *et al*. 1994). In the polygamous households in the North, female employment outside the home requires the permission of a woman's husband or family.

Patriarchal dominance of women is also based in part on the culturally sanctioned control of women's sexuality and fertility. According to a widely held belief, women possess sexual powers or are sometimes possessed by evil spirits that, if unleashed, can overcome men and enslave women to their own desires. Many traditional practices, some performed by women on women, are therefore aimed at harnessing these powers while reinforcing women's sexual and social subordination. Yet such practices – above all, female genital mutilation (FGM), performed on girls some time between infancy and age eighteen – also create severe risks to women's reproductive health. Although several types of FGM are practised in Nigeria, the most common is clitoridectomy (excision), which is practised widely by Muslims, Christians and African traditionalists alike.[7] While the overall prevalence rate of FGM in the country is 50 per cent, in areas of the Southwest there have been reported rates as high as 89 per cent (Adebanjo 1992; Toubia 1995). Currently no law prohibits FGM, but the National Association of Nurses and Midwives has launched a ten-year campaign to reduce its prevalence, and women's health groups have persuaded some state governments to support efforts to eradicate it. Moreover, the secretary general of the Supreme Council for Islamic Affairs in Nigeria has declared that the Qu'ran provides no religious basis either for prohibitions on birth control or for FGM, thus signalling progress toward the desanctification of this harmful practice (IPPF Open File 1993; Africa Leadership Forum 1992).

Women's Reproductive Health and Health/Population Policies

Lack of information or misinformation, adverse traditional practices, inaccessible and costly maternal care services, and high fertility are the most important determinants of women's reproductive health in Nigeria (Esu-Williams 1991). The total fertility rate has declined since 1980, but only from an average of 7.1 children to an estimated 6.0 in 1990, the latest date for which reasonably reliable figures are available (NDHS 1992; UN 1995). Recent trends indicate that, despite men's traditional desire for numerous children and wives, the economic costs to families of high fertility and polygamy are becoming unsustainable in urban areas (Isiugo-Abanihe 1994). However, high fertility persists among rural women, especially those who are uneducated and poor, and many begin their childbearing as teenagers.

Nearly one million infants every year, or 16 per cent of all births, are born to adolescent women; and infant mortality from such births (121:1000) significantly exceeds the national rate (87:1000) (NDHS 1992).

The tendency for Nigerian women to begin childbearing before age nineteen is the result partly of a tradition of early marriage but also of religious and customary views discouraging contraception and abortion. Only 14 per cent of married women and 13 per cent of all women aged fifteen to twenty-four had ever used any form of birth control in 1990, and some 43 per cent of these were using traditional rather than modern contraceptive methods; moreover, only 6 per cent of married women were currently using modern contraceptives (NDHS 1992). Studies have demonstrated a widespread lack of adequate information about pregnancy, contraception, and sexually transmitted diseases (STDs) among young women, attributed to the prevalent culture of silence in matters of sexuality. As a result, many young women resort to illegal or self-induced methods of abortion because of lack of knowledge, sound advice or accessible family planning and health services (Brabin *et al.* 1995; Feyisetan and Pebly 1989; Makinwa-Adebusoye 1992).

Where contraception is accepted, it is considered the concern of married women only, since premarital sex for women is frowned upon by society, and men, despite their well-known promiscuity, are not expected to negotiate contraception for themselves or their partners. But even for married women who have their desired number of children, few reliable contraceptive options are culturally acceptable. According to the widely held belief in reincarnation, anyone, male or female, who undergoes sterilization will be childless in the next life. Moreover, under customary laws observed not only by adherents of African traditional religion but also by Christians and Muslims, the surgical removal of any body part for the purpose of birth control is taboo. As a result, both vasectomies and female sterilization are virtually nonexistent in Nigeria (NDHS 1992). Denunciation of most medical contraceptive methods by community leaders, elders, traditional healers and extended family members presents a further constraint to contraceptive use that may contribute to the widespread use of abortion.

Maternal mortality is excessively high in Nigeria, at 1,000 per 100,000 live births (see Table 9.1). An estimated 30–40 per cent of these deaths are caused by complications from unsafe induced abortions, directly attributable to use of faulty techniques by unskilled abortion providers (Population Council 1993; Unuigbe *et al.* 1988; Okagbue 1990). Abortion, despite its prevalence, continues to be illegal in the criminal codes of both North and South except where necessary to save the pregnant woman's life. As a result, an estimated 20,000 Nigerian women die every year from the complications of ineptly performed illegal abortions. Poor, illiterate and uneducated women bear a disproportionate maternal mortality risk (Briggs 1993; Population Council 1993). Many rural women receive no biomedical obstetric care at all, while those who receive it tend to present late so that medical intervention can do little or nothing to improve the outcome (Chiwuzie 1995; PMMN 1992).

Additional factors contributing to high maternal mortality are food taboos, malnutrition, and delayed referral during complications (PMMN 1992; Aromasodu 1982). Complications such as vaginal bleeding, protracted labour, and malpresentation of the foetus are treated by many traditional birth attendants (TBAs) with herbal remedies or incantations that delay adequate intervention and often worsen a woman's medical condition (Oyebola 1980). In addition, widespread FGM, the *gishiri* cut,[8] prolonged obstructed labour, and coital laceration due to pre-pubescent intercourse have led to a high incidence of vesico- and/or recto-vaginal fistulae, VVF/RVF – a very painful, and life-threatening ailment (Emembolu 1990; Tahzib 1983). All these conditions create lesions that make women more vulnerable to HIV and other sexually transmitted infections and partly account for the fact that women are one-third of Nigerians testing positive for HIV (CRLP/IFWL 1997; Orubuloye 1996; Adekumle and Ladipo 1992).

Despite these problems, only about 30 per cent of Nigerian women, mostly in urban areas, deliver their children in clinics or hospitals; the vast majority rely on TBAs for delivery and postnatal care (Okafor and Rizzuto 1994). Most women prefer to deliver at home with the assistance of TBAs, not only because of their accessibility and lower fees but also because this allows mothers to observe customary birth practices. Unfortunately, TBAs are reluctant to refer problem pregnancies to biomedical providers, due partly to their lack of skill in recognizing problems but also to their deep mistrust of hospitals and trained nurse midwives (PMMN 1992).[9]

But poor reproductive health outcomes for Nigerian women are due at least as much to structural as to cultural factors. As a result of SAPs and budget cuts, the public health care system – administered by local governments – is in a chronic state of neglect and suffers from shortages of drugs, personnel and equipment. Furthermore, an urban bias and discriminatory practices produce sharp disparities in the availability and quality of medical services. Thus many pregnant women stay away from 'modern' clinics and hospitals, even when they or the TBA are aware of dangers, because they realistically expect to encounter class and ethnic discrimination, prohibitive costs, and facilities that are all but nonfunctional. It is not unusual for women in labour to arrive at a hospital and be refused admittance until they are able themselves to furnish the medications, supplies, and food required for the duration of their stay. Such economic barriers are insurmountable for poor women and their families (IAC 1993).

The nation's first family planning programme was implemented in 1983, and in 1989 the Babangida government formally adopted a national population policy, after a four-year process of 'consensus-building' (Dixon-

Mueller 1993). Although this process failed to consult women's groups, it resulted in some goals that could improve women's health and status if implemented seriously: to make voluntary family planning services universally accessible, to reduce maternal and child mortality, to raise the minimum age of marriage for women to eighteen, and to initiate programmes to realize the government's commitments under the Convention on the Elimination of All Forms of Discrimination against Women (Women's Convention). However, the policy focuses its fertility reduction target (a reduction to four children per woman by the year 2000) exclusively on women, merely 'encouraging' men to limit their wives and children to a number 'they can foster within their resources'. Not only does it thus place all the burden on women and implicitly endorse polygamy; it also promotes traditional patriarchal values, stating:

> In our society, men are considered the head of the family, and they make far-reaching decisions including the family size, subsistence and social relations.... The patriarchal family system in the country shall be recognized for stability of the home. (Federal Republic of Nigeria 1988: 19)

Nigeria's endorsement of the International Conference on Population and Development (ICPD) Programme of Action and the Platform for Action of the Fourth World Conference on Women (FWCW) stirred hope that the Ministry of Women's Affairs, established in 1995, will uphold these international commitments and help to implement the new government healthcare policies. But to date few resources have been allocated by the government to realize its commitments, leaving women's groups with an enormous task of maintaining pressure on the state.

The Women's Movement

Both despite and because of its economic and political problems, Nigeria harbours a vibrant civil society, a broad intelligentsia and outspoken media, and a courageous human rights and pro-democracy movement. Independent women's health and rights organizations are a dynamic part of this movement and continue to pursue an agenda for change, despite persistent government efforts to coopt and contain them.

In 1959, just prior to independence, the National Council of Women's Societies (NCWS) was created. This marked the beginning of state involvement in the women's movement through domination of its leadership by wives of ruling politicians and bureaucrats – a phenomenon Hussaina Abdullah has called 'wifeism', or 'state-sponsored pseudo-feminism'. The NCWS redirected a previous focus on grassroots activism and protest demonstrations towards collaboration with the government. Today it is the only umbrella organization representing the women's movement that is recognized by the government, and all organizations wishing to be accredited by the state have to affiliate with it. With control over all government financing of women's NGOs and the president's wife as its 'patron', the NCWS in effect serves to neutralize women's autonomous actions and reinforce patriarchal domination (Hussaina Abdullah 1996).

In the wake of the UN Decade for Women (1975–85), the Nigerian government established the National Committee on Women and Development (NCWD) as a liaison between women's NGOs and government-sponsored activities related to women. NCWD programmes have included training in traditional areas such as home economics, arts and crafts, literacy and income-generating activities. When the 1980s decline in rural living standards required women to increase their contribution to household earnings, the government initiated the Better Life for Rural Women Programme (BLP), under the direction of Mrs Maryam Babangida, wife of the then military ruler. With rhetoric dedicated to creating a 'new rural woman', the BLP attempted to coopt the feminist agenda through government-provided funds and supports. In practice, however, its rigid hierarchical structure reinforced gender subordination in the guise of women's activism and was completely controlled by Mrs Babangida. The pattern of 'wifeism' continued under the new regime when Mrs Mariam Abacha's Family Support Programme, launched in 1994, again used state power to promote conservative images of women as primarily wives and mothers (Hussaina Abdullah 1996; Kisekka 1992).

Yet state policies of containment did not prevent numerous activist groups emerging during the 1980s that were highly critical of military rule and the government's economic policies, as well as opposing women's low status in state and society. Women in Nigeria (WIN), founded in 1983, pushed to change social norms and government policies that reinforce gender inequality. In the late 1980s and early 1990s, its members initiated programmes on women's reproductive health and rights, sexual harassment and violence, and awareness about harmful traditional practices such as FGM and widowhood rites. Since WIN steadfastly refused to affiliate with the NCWS, it never acquired legal status as an NGO, and its increased alliance with progressive organizations led to strained relations with the state. Unfortunately, WIN has undergone recent internal divisions and a takeover by a male-dominated faction, resulting in the disaffection from its ranks of many feminist activists and former leaders.[10]

Also important among independent women's groups is the Country Women's Association of Nigeria (COWAN), a rural-based grassroots organization dedicated to addressing the needs of rural women through participatory means – for example, by incorporating women's health initiatives into local income-generating programmes (Ikeji 1996). Other progressive, non-traditional women's organizations include EMPARC (Empowerment and Action Research Centre), Girl's Power Initiative, the Women's Health Organization of Nigeria (WHON), and the Nigerian chapters of Women in Law and Development–Africa (WILDAF) and Women Living Under Muslim Laws. These organizations and their initiatives often ally with more mainstream civil rights groups to promote women's empowerment, education and democracy.

Despite oppressive state control and many debilitating financial and organizational difficulties, women's health groups in Nigeria have had a real impact; their achievements have included the formation of the Nigerian Safe Motherhood Movement and a National Task Force on VVF (National Taskforce on VVF 1994). Taking advantage of Nigerian participation in international forums such as the ICPD in Cairo and the FWCW in Beijing, leaders of the women's movement have begun to hold the government accountable for its public pledges and declarations (Ikeji 1996). They are demanding not only greater access of women to economic and political resources but also reproductive and sexual justice for women in all sectors of the society. IRRRAG's research, undertaken under conditions of austerity and repression, is intended to provide data that will further fuel this broad challenge to the patriarchal status quo.

Methodology and Process

IRRRAG Nigeria emerged out of the feminist movement with a commitment to the investigation of grassroots women's beliefs and decisions about sexuality and reproduction, in the face of taboos surrounding these subjects.[11] Unlike previous studies, we wanted to focus on ethnic minority groups and to explore how women themselves view and act on their sexual and reproductive options, often without the cooperation or consent of men. (Compare Adetunji 1997; Bankole 1995; Isiugo-Abanihe 1994; Makinwa-Adebusoye 1992; Mothercare 1993; Oni and McCarthy 1990; and Pearce 1995.) Words exist in all local Nigerian languages for the term 'right', and frequently these words may be translated literally to 'entitlement'. Thus we were able to explore these concepts among women from minority ethnic groups who have been underrepresented in earlier studies. Although the women we interviewed are only a small segment of Nigeria's women, they are sufficiently varied to provide a larger picture of reproductive and sexual rights in Nigeria than any one community or ethnic group could provide.

Research was conducted in the three main zones – the North, the Southwest and the Southeast – each under the supervision of a zonal coordinator. All researchers and assistants who conducted fieldwork in the local areas spoke at least one of the relevant ethnic minority languages and were responsible for translating tapes and field notes into English. The team adopted a strategy for sample selection intended to capture both diversity and comparability across diverse groups. In each zone, data were collected within one state: Kaduna (North), Cross River (Southeast), and Edo (Southwest); in each state, specific sites were selected in urban, rural and peri-urban areas.[12] Emphasis was given to documenting the views of women from less-researched ethnic groups, such as the Kataf and Igala in the North, the Efik and Ibibio in the Southeast, and the Bini and Edo in the Southwest. Only 19 per cent of our in-depth interviews were from one of the major ethnic groups, mainly Hausa from the North.[13] To enhance diversity further, we used personal contacts to locate women in a variety of organizations, such as professional and trade associations, religious groups, economic cooperatives, and self-help groups – a method that facilitated access to and the confidence of respondents. Most important, in terms of the team's strong emphasis on follow-up interventions, these contacts provided avenues for 'giving back' to the communities during the action phase of the project.

All data collection was done through face-to-face interviews (in focus groups, guided individual interviews, and 'case studies') to accommodate the prevalence of both oral modes of communication and female illiteracy in most Nigerian communities. A total of 354 women, spread among nine rural, twelve urban and twelve peri-urban locations, participated in 36 focus group discussions held in the three zones. A sub-sample of 72 women drawn from the focus groups participated in the individual interviews, 9 of whom were selected for more detailed case studies.[14]

Although the Nigeria team did not interview men directly, the views of men may have influenced responses in some locations where male elders were situated near the focus group discussions.[15] Similarly, where women of different age cohorts formed discussion groups, traditional views favoured by older women tended to prevail. Both these conditions confirmed our expectation that group interviews would be a source of information about dominant values rather than actual behaviour or views deviating from the norm – especially with regard to traditional practices and the use of birth control.

Gender Socialization, Education and Work

Research participants reported marked differences in the way females and males are treated, reflecting the gender norms of a patriarchal society. Females are generally considered inferior to males, and in many communities girls are taught traditional values and skills related to domestic tasks, while boys are educated to be strong heads of households and given more freedom of movement. Osaro, a 35-year-old Bini Christian trader and mother-of-four in the urban Southwest, recalls her upbringing relative to that of her brothers:

> I was only taught how to trade, cook and be a good housewife, while my brothers were given a very sound (formal) education because my father felt that it is the men who will bear his name throughout life.... He felt that when women are trained in school, they will later carry the wealth to their husband's family.

Such strict gender division transcends generations. Eki, a 15-year-old Edo student from the rural Southwest, similarly describes the gender norms she learned growing up: 'Boys take care of girls and discipline them when needed. Boys behave like the owners of the house while girls are not to discuss or decide matters related to the home.'

Early in their lives, young girls are socialized by their mothers and other adult women to be modest and obedient to their fathers and husbands and to act with shyness, or *kunya*, as it is called among the Hausa. They are also instructed how to sit, stand, walk, and talk in a 'dignifying' and feminine manner, not to raise their voices, to cry when necessary, and to be gratified by male attention. They are not allowed to discuss sexuality or basic reproductive functions such as menstruation, childbearing and menopause. As a result, women often approach sexuality, pregnancy and childbearing uninformed and fearful of what is happening to them.[16] While their socialization process contributes to the subordination of women at all stages of life, its repercussions fall harder on married women and mothers than on their unmarried daughters. In Hausa communities, unmarried daughters hawk foodstuffs for their mothers who are in *purdah*; these daughters exercise more mobility and freedom as girls than they will enjoy as mothers and wives. According to a Bini custom in the Southwest, when a girl becomes a young woman she is exempt from beatings by her father or brother; mothers and wives, however, can still be beaten by fathers or husbands for 'correctional purposes'. In Bini culture, married women possess no distinct identity apart from wife and mother, even when they earn their own income.

Confirming national patterns, all study zones reported that boys get preferential treatment when it comes to education, particularly in the North (DHS 1990; WIN 1991). Girls often do not receive a formal education and are instead expected to focus on skills such as sewing or trading in preparation for marriage. Many rural respondents reported that girls were kept from schooling not only because parents saw no need to educate them but also to protect their morality. As Maryam, a 57-year-old Hausa, Muslim housewife from the North, recalled:

> I wasn't sent to school because in our time, as far as school was concerned, it was only for boys ... sending female children to school was sending them to have their eyes opened. It was believed that a girl who went to school would be morally spoiled and would therefore spoil the family name.

Such gender discrimination in education and upbringing is a matter most respondents, regardless of age, resented. A majority expressed dissatisfaction with the way they had been brought up and were determined to educate girls and boys equally. Thus Monat, a 35-year-old teacher and mother of five from the rural North, declared:

> This type of double standard will have to be changed. I have a son and a daughter

and I am bringing them up the same way now. I know how I felt when I was growing up, and I am not going to allow my daughter to go through that.

The level of education among our respondents varied considerably by age: younger cohorts had received more education than their mothers and grandmothers. Eighty-five per cent of respondents under nineteen years of age had pursued secondary school or post-secondary study, compared with 65 per cent of those aged twenty to forty-five and only 30 per cent of those over forty-five. In the older age group (over forty-five), both urban and rural, half had received no formal education at all. This trend towards greater educational attainment by younger women corresponds to national statistics indicating an increase in education for girls, particularly in urban areas (UN 1995, Table 7).[17] Even when girls receive a formal education, however, it is usually in preparation for traditionally female occupations. While the majority of our personal interview respondents were working outside the home or in school, nearly all those employed, including those with secondary or higher education, were engaged in such traditional occupations. The largest number (32 out of 72, or 42 per cent) were employed in the informal sector (farmers and self-employed traders, seamstresses, caterers, etcetera); while others were teachers (mainly in primary schools), clerks or civil servants, and nurses or TBAs. Two worked as security guards, and fourteen were students at the time of the interviews.[18]

Yet, if their economic tasks are mostly gender-segregated, the women in our study – whether married, single or divorced – are clearly contributing significantly to their families' livelihood. At least 70 per cent (including some students) are performing productive, income-generating work outside the home, and many are working two jobs – most typically, farming and trading – in addition to the unpaid reproductive and household labour they are expected to perform as women. For our respondents, the issue of empowerment revolved around improving income levels through skills, training, equipment and loans, especially as independent producers, traders and craftswomen.[19] Unstated but clearly implicit in this strategy were the assumptions that (a) they ought to contribute more cash to meet the family's economic needs; (b) such contributions would increase their power and respect in the family and community; and (c) thereby their decision-making power in the 'private' sphere of sexuality and reproduction would be enhanced.

Sexuality Through the Life Cycle

The general belief in a double standard of sexuality – that men require unlimited sexual freedom while women should be restricted to only one partner – permeated the focus group discussions. This notion that a man cannot be satisfied by only one woman forms the basis for polygamy, still widely practised in Nigeria, particularly in the North. Moreover, many ethnic groups also believe that wives have no right to know or discuss their husbands' sexual activities (Orubuloye 1996). Reinforcing the culture of silence among women, the socially accepted behavioural constraint of *kunya* dictates women's reserve, modesty and discretion in sexual matters. Any discussion of sex, even among women, is taboo throughout the society, based on the belief – expressed most emphatically by respondents from the North – that open discussions of sexuality would encourage girls to be 'promiscuous'. The most severe form of control over women's sexuality and sexual expression is the practice of FGM, intended to curtail women's sexual pleasure and thereby inhibit their sexual activity outside the bounds of marriage. Both the culture of silence and FGM contribute to the escalating risks for women of HIV and other sexually transmitted infections, in the first instance by depriving women of the information necessary to protect themselves and in the second by creating lesions that, like the *gishiri* cut (see above), aggravate susceptibility to infection. They thus further violate women's right to sexual health and freedom and exacerbate the vicious cycle of risks and restraints (Adekunle and Ladipo 1992; Elias 1991; Orubuloye 1995, 1996; Wasserheit and Holmes 1992).

Women's experience of menstruation illustrates the widespread lack of information and misinformation about their bodies. Most respondents did not learn about menstruation until it 'happened' to them; their mothers or guardians taught them accepted methods of personal hygiene, above all how to conceal the menstrual blood. Respondents from all three zones described the shameful aura that surrounds the onset of menstruation: 'I felt anxious, I felt it was bad because I had not been told' (Southeast); 'I did not like it, I wept; it was a terrible experience, I even cried and thought I was sick' (North); 'I had no knowledge of it when I saw it for the first time; I felt afraid, embarrassed, sad, ashamed, weak, uncomfortable and I wept' (Southwest). But the strongest message mothers or guardians convey to their daughters at this time is to beware of men and the dangers of premarital sex. As Monat related:

> I didn't know anything about menstruation before I saw it.... I ran to my aunt who told me how to use rags and keep the rags clean. She ... added that I was now mature and that if a man should touch me, I would be pregnant. When I was menstruating one day in school, a boy touched me and I started crying, thinking I was pregnant. It was a female teacher who saw me and called me to explain that one has to sleep with a man before one could get pregnant.

Monat's experience, like that of nearly all the women we interviewed, corresponds to recent data from a survey of urban youth showing that the largest proportion received whatever meagre information they had about reproduction and sexuality from friends or schoolmates, or secondarily the mass media; 'the least common sources of information were aunts, mothers and other relatives' (Makinwa-Adebusoye 1992: 68). Some of our urban and peri-urban respondents had made efforts to improve their deficient sex education by reading books in school, while their rural counterparts claimed to have learned the basics only through marriage.

The silence and shame surrounding menstruation thus lead to emotional suffering for girls which is intensified by their isolation. In all three zones of our study we encountered old pollution taboos associating menstruation with uncleanness and justifying the isolation of menstruating women from the family. The rationale for these restrictions lies in the traditional belief that contact with menstruating women can contaminate, reduce or destroy a man's sexual powers. Thus during menstruation women are encouraged not to engage in sexual intercourse, nor to cook for husbands or enter religious places. In more traditional households, women are also required to go into seclusion in a separate *owa ehe* (menstruation hut). Only married women are subject to this and other menstrual restrictions, confirming that wives generally have a lower status than daughters. Urban respondents in all three zones expressed unhappiness about being isolated from family members and treated as pariahs during menstruation. Abude, a 47-year-old teacher and widow said: 'I didn't like the disparity between daughters and wives, because we are all human and it is a natural phenomenon that a woman should menstruate. So why all that restriction?'

Yet some women, while unable to escape menstrual restrictions, are apparently able to use them to their advantage. Some saw menstruation as a time when women have the right to rest from household work, others saw it as a convenient pretext for avoiding unwanted sex with husbands. Urban women traders belonging to a self-help group in Benin city – Eubayoboru (Labour of Our Hands) – for example, expressed a preference for the 'old days' when women were forbidden to sleep with their husbands during menstruation. These examples illustrate a phenomenon we observed many times in which women turned accepted cultural or religiously based practices to their own uses. In the case of menstrual taboos, such strategic accommodation may be about not only avoiding sex or household chores, but also perhaps recapturing an older sense of gender *complementarity* (if not equality) that came from menstrual blood as a perceived source of female power (Sanday 1981).

Statements strongly affirming the high value placed on virginity before marriage were expressed in all zones, particularly in rural areas, where respondents associated virginity with 'good girls' and 'respect for the girl's family'. Older women in urban and peri-urban areas also affirmed the preservation of virginity for girls as a means to prevent premarital pregnancy and sexually transmitted diseases. Various customary practices are intended to enforce the virginity code, including restrictions on the freedom of movement of unmarried women, withholding of information about sexuality and reproduction from young girls, FGM, early marriage, and the shaming of non-virgin brides. Most often the gatekeepers who enforce these practices are mothers or older female kin, who anticipate the honour and gifts bestowed by in-laws when a virgin daughter is married. Yet the practices involve certain contradictions, since early marriage as an antidote to premarital sex is also a principal cause of adolescent pregnancy in Nigeria; moreover, prospective brides are often expected by a man or his family to prove their fertility through pregnancy *before* marriage.

Younger women, especially the under-nineteen age group in urban areas, were more open about rejecting traditional taboos and embracing the changing sexual attitudes found by researchers among today's urban young women in Nigeria. These include more open engagement in premarital sex and a tendency to delay marriage and childbearing (Feyisetan and Pebly 1989; Makinwa-Adebusoye 1992). Unmarried urban respondents in both the Southwest and the North voiced disapproval of cultural traditions that seem to them outdated and discriminatory, particularly the double standard dictating that boys should have many sex partners before marriage while girls should remain virgins. Ayesha, a Hausa Muslim student in her teens, objected, 'I don't agree with this rigid rule on virginity, because both males and females have equal feelings about sex'; and a young unmarried focus group participant in the North asserted boldly, 'Whenever I feel like sleeping with my boyfriend I go to him.' Yet, despite this openness, our adolescent respondents did not appear to know about or use contraception. Again this confirms other studies, which have found that most sex among urban young women is unprotected against either pregnancy or disease.[20]

Even among older respondents, there remained a large gap between the ideals of social behaviour as described in the focus groups, and actual behaviour as revealed in individual interviews. Regardless of ethnicity, religion, education or age, 39 per cent of all in-depth interviewees either had children prior to marriage or were pregnant at the time of their marriage. The rate of premarital pregnancy was especially high among our married respondents in the Southeast sample, nearly all of whom were over thirty-five and had become pregnant or given birth prior to marriage. Some of this pattern of premarital pregnancy no doubt was driven by the need to prove fertility prior to marriage.

Existing taboos regarding women's sexuality perpetuate the myth that sexual initiation and pleasure are a terrain belonging strictly to men. Aghatise, a 45-year-old teacher from the Southwest, now in her second marriage, confirms this attitude, though not necessarily with approval, when she remarks, 'We have been made to believe that women who initiate sex are prostitutes and flirts.' Confirming it in a tacit way, most Southeastern respondents without formal education provided no response at all to the question of whether they enjoyed sex. For many Nigerian women, especially in the North, the very idea of sexuality as a source of pleasure remains beyond imagination. Zenaib is a rural Muslim housewife aged thirty-eight but married at age thirteen, now the mother of four children. Her story is not untypical:

I got married before I realized what [sex] was all about ... at the age of thirteen to a man of about thirty years. My husband made sexual demands right away. I used to shout and run away from him because I found it a painful experience. There was a day I slept in the goat's shed rather than share the bed with him. After some time, he reported my behaviour to my father who came and gave me a thorough beating. He also threatened me with all sorts of unpleasant things, so I stopped running away. As far as I am concerned, a woman does not have to enjoy sex. If she is able to give her husband pleasure and get children out of the act, I feel that is enough reward. Hausa women usually do not show any signs of enjoyment during sex because their husbands will think they are wayward.

Others, however, voiced less traditional attitudes toward sexual enjoyment for women. This was especially true of urban educated and divorced women, as well as women in the older age cohorts, beyond childbearing and early motherhood. For example Amina, a 45-year-old Hausa Muslim university administrator from the North, remarked, 'I do enjoy sex. I started having sex at fourteen when I got married to my present husband'. And 35-year-old Orobosa, a trader and mother-of-four from the urban Southwest, told us candidly, 'I enjoy sex to satisfy my urge; it is natural.' Some respondents openly expressed a desire to have more fulfilling sexual relationships, including the freedom to initiate the sexual act. Oghogho, a 38-year-old divorced woman with six living children from a rural site in the Southwest, was most forthright: 'It is bad for only the man to ask for sex always, because love should not be one-sided. It is her body, she should be free to have control over it.'

Most of our respondents, however, probably fall somewhere in between Zenaib's stoic resignation and Oghogho's assertive feminism. More typical perhaps are the tensions and ambiguities present in the remarks of Huseina, a 57-year-old Kataf farmer from the North who has been married monogamously for forty-two years. On the one hand, she echoes the rural analogy of the wife's body to landed property: 'Sometimes when I don't want to, I just bear it, because the farmer cannot go to his farm and be prevented from working on it.'[21] Yet she also finds space to act on her own desire:

With time I even began to enjoy relating with my husband sexually. I have never in all my years of marriage blatantly or obviously initiated sex, but what do I have my feminine wiles for? When I desire my husband, I take my bath, wear some sweet-smelling perfume and make myself attractive. He always understands.

As with menstruation and sexuality, our respondents also exhibited very limited knowledge about STDs and HIV/AIDS. Both were described by those in the Southeast as 'diseases of wayward people', and everywhere respondents echoed the prevalent view among both men and women in Nigeria that STDs are a 'women's disease' and those afflicted by it 'promiscuous, loose and irresponsible' (see Gogna and Ramos 1996). Edem, a middle-aged trader with primary school education who has given birth to nine children (four still living), conveys the extent to which the onus for

STD infection is borne by women within marriage: 'A man won't even come near you and will divorce you if he can be sure it is not from him.' Yet Zenaib implies that the label 'women's disease' may have a converse meaning, one involving women's right to avoid risk. She asserts: 'If a man is infected with AIDS or any other STD his wife should be free to refuse to sleep with him in order to protect herself.'

In the light of prevailing gender stereotypes and stigma, it is not surprising that women who find themselves infected with STDs seek clandestine treatment. In Monat's words, 'If I have an STD I will go to a private doctor or chemist who will keep my secret.' Both traditional and modern treatments exist for STDs, but for anonymity as well as to avoid the prohibitive costs of modern clinics, most women prefer simply to purchase medication from the local chemist or to go to traditional healing homes. Some respondents reported that men are more likely than women to seek treatment for STDs and that it is not uncommon for a man to bring home medications for his wife to take without a full explanation of what the drugs are for. While this behaviour shows more responsibility than is shown by husbands who ignore their wives' risk of infection, such secrecy serves to perpetuate the myth of women's primary responsibility for the spread of sexual disease. And it signifies the inequities built into marital relationships.

Contradictions of Ageing

The entry of Nigerian women into their post-childbearing years is freighted with contradictory meanings. Like menstruation, the topic of menopause tends to be veiled in secrecy and silence, resulting in widespread mis-information and fear among women. As menopause approaches, many women attempt to hide the fact for as long as possible, especially if they are childless. Yet clearly post-menopausal women recognize the new respect and freedom they gain; compared to the years when they were bearing and rearing children, their social status improves, and younger women are expected to show them deference. The post-menopausal status generally enhances women's liberties and power within the home and the community. Older women are believed to be more mature and experienced and are expected to take on the task of socializing girls and young women in the home, including not only daughters and granddaughters but co-wives and co-wives' children. Sometimes the end of menstruation frees women from religious taboos and bestows decision-making powers normally associated with men only. In the Southeast, post-menopausal women gain the right to be initiated into otherwise strictly male associations and societies, while in the North they secure admission to the mosque, though remaining segregated.

In addition to these new advantages in the public sphere, the post-menopausal woman can also improve her position within the household by trading her 'right to the husband's bed' for increased respect and some rest from household chores (Pearce 1995). On the other hand, some post-menopausal women in the North apparently parlay their higher status as older women into an expanded sense of entitlement with regard to sexual activity. Respondents from polygamous marriages insisted that, unless a menopausal woman gives her husband the right to sleep with another wife when it would be her turn, he has no right to do so. And one member of a rural focus group invoked a clear sense of her own right to sexual pleasure as a woman when she asserted, on behalf of post-menopausal women: 'We are not too old to have sex, and why should we give up anything? Menopause is not an illness; after all, the older men still have sex.' In the Southeast as well, all post-menopausal respondents indicated they they had remained sexually active. Those from the Southwest were divided on this question, with a few expressing the belief that they would be more susceptible to illnesses if they abstained from sex. A majority of Southwest respondents, however – including both urban and rural women and across the age groups – held that women should not continue to engage in sexual intercourse after menopause because now they had 'become men'; or, as one respondent put it, 'a man cannot make love to a man'. A few said that post-menopausal women who no longer engage in sexual activity are stronger than those who do and claimed that this principle also applied to men.

While there is disagreement among our respondents as to whether becoming more male-like means that older women finally achieve some right to sexual pleasure, and while no one thinks being 'like' men means being equal, post-menopausal women clearly have more power both within the home and outside it than at any previous life stage. Freed from the confines of childbearing and motherhood, they are finally able to assert some authority, though this is most often over younger women and within a recognizable gender-divided sphere. Yet some respondents claimed a larger space on behalf of older women. According to members of the Labour of Our Hands self-help group in Benin City, not only is menopause 'natural' but after menopause a woman can 'do what she wants' and mix freely with men without fear of polluting; indeed, freed from the taint of menstruation, she can now even become a chief.

Marriage and Women-only Monogamy

Among our respondents, the assumption that marriage is the 'natural' destiny of women was virtually universal; young single women expect to marry when of age, and those who are divorced or widowed would prefer to remarry given the opportunity. Focus group discussions in all three zones and across urban and rural areas pointed to the fact that women derive their respect and status in society through marriage and childbearing: 'single women are not respected in society'; 'a woman is not considered truly a woman, nor does she feel fulfilled, until she is married'. Indicative of the tremendous social pressure for women to marry are the belief that it is an abomination for a woman to die unmarried (North), as well as the many taboos about bearing children out of wedlock. Unmarried women are considered socially and professionally incompetent, regardless of their educational level or qualifications, and are often denied jobs, promotions and political appointments.

Under prevailing local customary and Islamic laws, marital relations are normally defined according to patriarchal norms that are severely disempowering for women. Even so, most women tend to revere marriage customs and rituals, and as young women they enter into marriage with high expectations of achieving greater respect and status. In reality, however, as 'good wives' they must be subservient to their husbands, forfeiting their decision-making power and, in the North, even their freedom of movement, as mandated by the rules of *purdah*. We found ample evidence that the power and life force associated with motherhood is attainable only through marriage. All ethnic groups concur that a woman's value and respectability are largely determined by her childbearing ability and the extent to which she measures up as a 'good wife', in the sense of being able to bear children, maintain the household, and satisfy her husband sexually.

Focus group respondents accepted the custom of payment of bride price by their husband's family as a signifier of the bride's value to her new husband. In some areas bride price increases if the bride-to-be can offer proof of her virginity; this reinforces women's acceptance of such practices as FGM and the 'protection' of young girls as insurance of marriageability. After marriage, women also generally adhere to the expectation of wifely obedience, remaining faithful in the face of a husband's infidelity and polygamy. Marriages are rarely ended by women, even by those who suffer continuing violence and abuse, because divorced women incur societal disrespect in addition to financial hardship and the risk of being an outcast from the family.

Table 6.1 Number and Percentage of Respondents Who Married as Adolescents

	SOUTHEAST	SOUTHWEST	NORTH	TOTAL
Under 19	0	0	2	2
20–35	1	1	2	4
36–45	2	0	5	7
Over 45	6	3	2	11
TOTAL	9 (38%)	4 (17%)	11 (46%)	24 (33%)

Other traditions that are disempowering for women but nevertheless condoned by most are child marriage and polygamy. Despite the increased risk of infertility, VVF and infant and maternal death, child marriage is practised in all zones, but most commonly in the North and in rural areas.[22] As Table 6.1 indicates, one-third of all our individual respondents were married as adolescents, with the highest rate in the North. Most of these women lived in rural or peri-urban areas, but even more important is age: in all three zones, and across rural–urban and ethnic differences, the trend seems to be shifting away from early marriage: none of the under-nineteen age cohort in either the Southwest or the Southeast had married at the time of the interviews. This pattern undoubtedly reflects both economic constraints and the fact, cited earlier, that younger women stay in school longer than their mothers and grandmothers. The great majority of the under-nineteen women we interviewed, both rural and urban, were currently students.

Regarding choice of marriage partner, participants from rural and peri-urban areas in the North reported that their parents or guardians had made or would make this decision for them. In contrast, participants from urban areas in all zones, as well as some from rural and peri-urban areas in the Southwest and Southeast, observed that 'there is a choice these days'. Marietu, a 47-year-old farmer/trader from the Southwest, told the story of her arranged marriage as an example of earlier ways:

> When I was of age [17], without my consent and probably without my mother's, I was forcibly given out in marriage to a man I never knew until I was taken to him by some unknown men. On the day of the marriage I saw some strange men with my father who after a few minutes of discussion suddenly seized my hand and whisked me off into a waiting car. I struggled with the men, kicked and cried, but no help came. My mother wept helplessly while my father showed no sign of sympathy nor concern. For almost two weeks I refused food and drink. I was not given freedom of movement in the new home I now found myself in. I had constant escorts to the toilet and bathroom and any attempts to run away were foiled.

Except for the rural North, Marietu's experience is becoming a thing of the past. Though parents usually insist that prospective husbands be presented to them at home, the choice of a marriage partner is more frequently made by the young woman herself. Some rural respondents attributed this change to socioeconomic conditions and the migration of young girls to towns to seek work, thus weakening the control of parents in choosing husbands for their daughters.

Overall, 33 per cent of married respondents indicated that they were in polygamous unions, a rate below the estimated national average of 41 per cent. Of those in polygamous unions, 17 per cent were Christian, 50 per cent Muslim and 33 per cent adhered to African traditional religion. In the

Southwest, polygamous unions represented nearly half of all marriages among respondents, while in the North they represented 28 per cent and in the Southeast (where a greater number of individual respondents were single) only 11 per cent.[23]

Many of our respondents indicated their acceptance of polygamy as part of tradition, but nearly all the respondents in the under-nineteen age group from the Southeast and Southwest, who were all single, strongly rejected it. Many Christian respondents did as well, saying 'polygamy is not right because it is forbidden in the Bible', despite the proclivity of Christian men to take multiple wives or mistresses. Moreover, both Muslim and Christian respondents from the North, including some of the older women, agreed with this exceptionally candid statement by a focus group participant: 'Polygamy breeds jealousy, suspicion, hostility and quarrelling among co-wives, and it is always a source of disappointment for the wife who gets a mate. These things occur no matter how prepared a woman may think she is.' Indeed, one monogamously married respondent in the Southwest threatened to pack up and leave if her husband took another wife. A discussion among a group of women in a peri-urban farming community in the Southeast revealed a consensus among speakers (who were mainly over thirty-five) that most young people today would not accept polygamy because it causes too much quarrelling in the household.

Given these views, it remains unclear why polygamy was supported by so many, even those who expressed strong reservations or clear dissatisfaction with their own polygamous marriages. Undoubtedly, the prevalent cultural view of marriage as a woman's natural destiny, along with the popular assumption that 'the Nigerian man is born polygamous', makes polygamy seem a more acceptable condition for a woman than being without a husband. More important, acceptance of polygamy for some women may be simply pragmatic, as suggested by this remark of a Christian focus group participant from the Southeast: 'Polygamy is good. It reduces the household chores for individual women, since the work becomes shared by more than one wife'.

Polygamy is only one expression of the sexual double standard in Nigeria regarding extramarital sex. Older focus group participants from all three zones reflected their accommodation to the prevailing double standard with such remarks as: 'Husbands must look after wives, and wives in turn must be faithful'; 'Women must accept male infidelity, there is nothing they can do about it'; and 'My husband can do what he likes, provided he does not bring it to my notice.' Again, young single women expressed more idealistic views. Christian respondents in the under-nineteen age group from the Southeast and Southwest objected to extramarital liaisons for both males and females, arguing on behalf of a biblical standard of mutual fidelity and love in marriage. Among most of the married respondents, however, husbands' extramarital affairs – and, for some, polygamy – appear to be a price they are willing to pay to ensure the preservation of their marital status, their connection to their children and their place in the community.

Divorce, Widowhood and Inheritance

Divorce is not uncommon in Nigeria, particularly in urban areas, but most instances of divorce are governed by local custom or *shari'a* courts rather than the formal mechanisms of the state and civil law. Not only is divorce permitted under Islamic law, but both the ease and the incidence of divorce and remarriage appear to be greater in the North, where *shari'a* law holds sway. In the North divorced women are encouraged to remarry, since unmarried women are an object of repudiation, and it is considered an abomination to die unmarried. None the less, divorce is viewed as an extreme measure, contrary to the norm by which marriage is meant to be 'for life'.

To protect the institution of marriage, there are many social sanctions against divorce, affecting women almost exclusively. No matter what has occurred within the marriage, even physical abuse, the wife is supposed to be patient and try to 'tame' her husband instead of resorting to divorce. Focus group participants from all three zones noted that society treats divorced women harshly, stigmatizing them as 'flirts', 'troublesome' and 'bad women', whereas divorced men are more an object of pity. Above all, divorced women in all the zones risk forfeiting custody of their children. At best they are granted visiting rights or, at the discretion of the husband and his family, the right to continue raising any small children not yet of school age.

We did find evidence that divorce is becoming more accepted for women. Many respondents among the under-nineteen age group from all three zones agreed that, although marriage is considered a lifelong contract and divorce undesirable, there may be circumstances such as abuse and infertility under which it becomes necessary. Urban women in the North were particularly vocal in expressing a sense of entitlement for a woman to divorce her husband if he systematically beats or fails to satisfy her, for example because of impotence. And members of the Labour of Our Hands group in the Southwest asserted that, if a woman is unhappy in her marriage, she should 'just take her things and go away'. These justifications for divorce imply a view among respondents that women after all have certain basic rights in marriage: the right to be provided for (a home and food for the wife and children), the right to life and bodily integrity (not to suffer physical threats to her life and safety from the husband), and the right to gain honour and respect in marriage (not to be humiliated by public display of extra-marital affairs).

On the other hand, fewer than 10 per cent of our married respondents had previously divorced or were seeking to divorce. Perhaps this is because most are satisfied that their marital needs are being fulfilled. More likely, however, it indicates that fears of social repudiation and losing support for themselves and custody of their children act as deterrents that outweigh the personal suffering some undoubtedly endure.[24] This seems clearly to have been the case with Marietu, whose forced marriage remained a bitter trial:

> All these years of marriage I have never enjoyed sex, never was happy seeing him, never able to forgive him even though he tried to be nice. I have always seen him as the father of my children and not my husband. For the past ten years now, I took a decision to live life under my husband for the sake of my children.

The social meanings and stigmatizing effects of widowhood for women are considerably different from those of divorce. Widows in all regions are subjected to traditional practices that are humiliating and degrading. Many ethnic groups attribute a husband's death in some manner to his wife's evil deeds or supernatural spells. It is believed she must have committed adultery or procured evil charms capable of killing her husband or her children, especially her sons. To cast off suspicion, widows are expected to go through rigorous mourning rites that may include sitting on the floor, remaining unwashed, wearing the same clothes for three to seven days and/or wearing black, not cutting their hair or shaving their heads, and remaining confined indoors for one to three months.[25] In general, the relationship between a woman and her late husband's family determines the nature and severity of the rites and ordeals to which she is subjected. If a widow manages to go through all the rites without falling ill or dying, she is exonerated of any guilt in connection with her husband's death. Failure or refusal to submit to the rites, on the other hand, results in the presumption of culpability, loss of her children, and their neglect by his relatives. In contrast, men whose wives die are expected to observe much milder and briefer mourning rites or none at all.

In focus group discussions and personal interviews, a consensus emerged that mourning rites for widows should be reformed and the same rites and obligations should be applied to widowers. Christian widows, supported by their churches, are increasingly refusing the rites, seeing them as 'unchristian'. Women in the Southwest wished merely to wear black clothing for a time, while those in the Southeast felt strongly that they should not be required to shave their heads. Muslim women from the North found it demeaning to have widows secluded until it could be determined whether or not they were pregnant. Above all, urban, peri-urban, younger women and nearly all women in the North strongly objected to the loss of property rights a widow suffers, especially if she had contributed to household income during the marriage. Abude, a 47-year-old Bini schoolteacher from the urban Southwest, laments:

> My suffering was compounded because dowry [bride price] was paid on me and there was no issue [child] by the marriage. Everything, apart from a few personal effects, was taken from me. I had to start life all over again.

Abude's experience is like that of many other widows, since women are only able to inherit as custodians of their children. In the Southeast, if a widow decides to remarry outside her husband's family, she forfeits the right to inherit any property. Redress in an inheritance dispute is rare, especially for women married under customary law. It thus seems clear that our respondents accommodate to existing traditions governing divorce and widowhood largely because of the economic and social constraints pressuring them. The issue here is really one of *reproductive* rights – both for widows like Abude who, being childless, 'lose everything' and for married women like Marietu, who must trade away their right to divorce or to escape an abusive or unloved husband in order to prevent losing their children.

Childbearing and Fertility Regulation

In all the research sites, it was assumed that childbearing is the most important reason for marriage; voluntary childlessness among Nigerian couples appears to be unknown. Wives endure the brunt of the intense family pressure to beget. As in Abude's case, the man is often urged to take another wife or try other partners, while the woman is typically blamed for the condition and accused of promiscuity, witchcraft, or offences towards deities or ancestors; she also becomes highly vulnerable to divorce. Childless women must pay repeated visits to herbal healers to demonstrate their intent to get pregnant, while tolerating a husband's extramarital affairs or decision to take another wife.[26]

Respondents everywhere, but especially in rural areas, pointed out the prevailing cultural preference for male children, illustrated in such remarks as 'a woman without a male child is looked down upon' (North) and 'male children will perpetuate the family name, while girls will be married out to other families' (Southeast). The burden of son preference borne by women, in terms of both social stigma and high fertility, was conveyed graphically by Marietu, who found herself a co-wife after only two years of marriage:

> Another woman was betrothed to him as a wife because I failed to have children early in marriage. This second wife had a female child. She later divorced him and left the child behind under my care. After the second wife left, my first three children were born one after the other, and all were girls. This trend angered my husband's family, who felt that their son and brother should have a son [and heir]; so they wanted him to have a third wife who would bear him the much-desired son. But my husband refused to accept the family's suggestion.... After this, I had three boys and a set of twins, bringing the number of my children to eight, among them four boys.

Fifty-seven-year-old Maryam (Muslim, rural North) was married at fifteen to a man she had been betrothed to at birth. She had her first baby within the first year of marriage (at age sixteen):

When I had the first four girls, my problems didn't come from my husband but from his family. They called me names, mistreated me, ignored me at family gatherings. It was as if I was childless. This was very sad and I was not happy, because it is God, not me, who gives children ... the only good thing was that my husband didn't listen to his family, and in God's time I had three boys. Their attitude towards me changed.

In total, Maryam bore thirteen children, the highest number of any of the seventy-two in-depth respondents. She expresses a clear sense of injustice about the travail of childbearing she was put through to perpetuate the preference for males; and her remark that 'it is God, not me, who gives children' was echoed by others. As one focus group participant from the rural Southwest put it, 'a child is a child whether male or female'. Such sentiments suggest a feeling of resentment, particularly among older women who are looking back on their reproductive lives, about not only the pressure to continue childbearing until sons are produced but the gender bias it signifies.

We found that respondents conformed to the national pattern of early onset of childbearing, usually (but not always) associated with early marriage. Older women (>45) began having children at an earlier age than younger ones, with a median age of 17.9 years, as opposed to 21 years for the 36–45 group and 21.4 years for the 20–35 group. Only Maryam had given birth as young as age 16. Respondents reported having had very little information about pregnancy and childbirth before a pregnancy occurred. Once pregnant, young women are taught the customary rituals and restrictions of their ethnic group, religion and community. They also learn what to expect during labour, how to nurse and nurture the baby and how to delay the next pregnancy through such means as prolonged breastfeeding or sexual abstinence.[27] Such advice is given by mothers, friends, mothers-in-law, co-wives, TBAs and, less frequently, medical personnel.

Customary restrictions on the movement of pregnant women prevail in all the research sites. Some are meant to ensure that the unborn child is not possessed by evil spirits – for example, being forbidden to walk in the hot sun (North) or to sit in the doorway or walk and eat at night (Southwest). Pregnant women are also prohibited from performing heavy work in order to avoid miscarriage or difficult labour. Dietary restrictions vary in kind and severity according to region, ethnic group and religion. The main rationale behind them is to protect the foetus from harm; the pregnant woman's health is a secondary or minor concern. In the North, women in seclusion who wish to seek any medical care must secure permission from their husbands, for whom the thought of male doctors treating their wives is unacceptable. Even in the case of an emergency or complications, no one will dare take a secluded woman to a hospital without getting her husband's permission. Such restrictions increase the risk of VVF/RVF, haemorrhage and even death arising from prolonged, unmanaged labour (PMMN 1992).

Our respondents resembled other Nigerian women in using a combination of traditional, faith-based and modern forms of reproductive health care, which are seen as complementary (Adetunji 1997). Delivery at home with the assistance of TBAs is common in all zones, though more prevalent in the Southeast and North, where women pride themselves on their stoicism during labour. Women from these regions reported that they go into a room by themselves when labour begins and do not call anyone until after the baby is born. For delivery, the labouring woman gets on her knees and pulls on a rope for added support. In Zaria in the North, a TBA is called only to cut the umbilical cord. In contrast to the prenatal focus on the foetus, postnatal care of the mother is extensive, lasting for as long as forty days after delivery. Besides limiting her exertions, it includes regular massage of her abdomen with hot herbal water and having her sit over a pot of hot water infused with herbs to help the uterus to contract.

Typically, urban women and most peri-urban women go for pre- and post-natal care to government health facilities, which are less expensive than private ones, and, to a lesser extent, to the homes of spiritualists. Rural women and some peri-urban women tend to rely for such services on TBAs, who can almost always be found in a neighbouring house. Although ritual and custom have some influence on the decision of most women to deliver at home, social and economic factors also contribute. Respondents specifically cited the cost of modern healthcare services in terms of money, time and travel distance, as well as the disrespectful attitude of medical personnel and the fact that doctors are predominantly male. Respondents from a focus group in the North complained bluntly that 'the doctors arrive late and the nurses are harsh'. Because of such barriers, women go to the hospital only as a last resort, preferring self-medication and traditional healers. Urban and peri-urban respondents urged the need for a reduction in hospital fees, free services for pregnant women, the availability of drugs at subsidized rates, and an improvement in the attitude of hospital staff toward patients.[28]

Many recent studies document the patriarchal tradition among Nigerians of communal rather than individual decision making with regard to family matters, including those related to family size and fertility. Husband, parents-in-law, parents, community elders, and the woman herself all have a say, but the decision of the husband weighs most heavily, followed by the views of his parents and then of the woman's parents (Isiugo-Abanihe 1994; Mothercare 1993). In addition, survey data show over 60 per cent of Nigerian women expressing the belief that their fertility or family size is ultimately up to God (Feyisetan and Ainsworth 1995). In focus-group discussions, most respondents in our study echoed these traditional views, including the tensions within them. Thus a majority of respondents from the North declared the power to decide when to have a child was the man's, as head of the household, otherwise 'a woman could be accused of promiscuity'. On the other hand, a minority of Christian and Muslim respondents held that 'children are from God, so God decides'. And a few respondents in the North expressed a more egalitarian view, insisting that childbearing decisions must be made jointly by the couple 'because they are partners in the relationship'.

Yet data derived from individual interviews and case studies suggest that, in practice, our respondents may be exercising more initiative with regard to childbearing decisions and the use of contraception than these conventional statements imply. This is particularly true among more educated women and older women who have already had several children.[29] Our interviews, both urban and rural, confirm an increasing use of contraception or, failing that, abortion, in response to economic pressures – sometimes kept secret from husbands (compare Isiugo-Abanihe 1994). Monat, a Muslim schoolteacher in the rural North who had had five children in fifteen years of marriage, remarks:

> For married women, contraceptives are often used for spacing and to prevent having too many children. The economy is very bad now, and no one can afford to have many children like in the old days. I got my contraceptives from a family planning clinic attached to a public hospital. The doctor explained all the methods to me and I chose the pill, but when I was having trouble with it, I went back to him and changed it to an IUD.... Abortion is not a method of contraception. It is better to use a family planning method to prevent pregnancy, but if it fails one will have no choice but to abort. It is better to abort than to keep an unwanted baby.

Unlike Monat, who has more education than most of our rural respondents, others from the rural areas seemed to know little if anything about modern contraceptives, but their knowledge of traditional methods is extensive. A woman from the Southwest identified sixteen traditional methods of contraception and indicated that many rural women in Nigeria are aware of and use them. The most common of such methods used by our respondents were abstinence during breastfeeding; withdrawal; herbs, roots and talismans; and douching. The taboo on sex during breastfeeding is an accepted way for rural women to avoid unwanted pregnancy and achieve desired birth intervals.

All respondents concurred that the responsibility for using contraception was the woman's, and many seemed reluctant to consult husbands. This is consistent with data from the 1990 Nigeria DHS, where only a little over one-third of currently married women aged fifteen to twenty-four reported ever discussing family planning with their husband (DHS/Macro International 1996). Women from the North reported that they discussed fertility control with their husbands to get permission to obtain contraceptives, because some family planning clinics require a husband's written consent. Some respondents used the well-known device of presenting another man to the clinic as her husband, thus protecting their right to confidentiality and control in contraception in the face of cultural and institutional barriers.

Most respondents from the North and Southeast, however, did not admit to using contraceptives at all. We infer that they must have been using something that worked – including abstinence or abortion – from the fact that hardly any of the women 35 and over in those zones had borne more than six children. The mean number of children among 35-and-older respondents in the North was 5.8 and in the Southeast, 4.7, while that of older women in the Southwest was 6.3.[30]

Married or previously married respondents differed markedly by region in their openness about using contraception (generally, use of contraception among unmarried women in Nigeria is neither condoned nor acknowledged). Almost all those from the Southwest, both urban and rural, stated that they currently use or have used a form of contraceptive, while only around half of those from the North and a little over one-third of those from the Southeast did so. In part the greater willingness of women in the Southwest to admit using contraception may be because of the more widespread acceptance of traditional methods in that region. Women in the North who identified as contraceptors, on the other hand, were more likely to be urban and/or educated and to associate contraception with the pill or the IUD; one had even had a tubal ligation, extremely rare in Nigeria. Generally, economic hardship was the most frequent reason respondents in all locations gave for using contraceptives. Vivian, however, an urban nurse and mother-of-three from the Southwest, acknowledged that 'one can have sex freely without fear of becoming pregnant'. And fifteen-year-old Eki, a rural Southwest student, asserted that contraception is good because it 'helps girls to continue with education' – suggesting that young unmarried women too have a right to sexual expression free of fear. But Vivian and Eki were atypical in the clear link they drew between contraception and sexual freedom for women.

The most common objections our respondents made to using contraceptives had to do not with traditional or religious taboos, but rather with perceived side effects. These included the 'malfunction' of the baby, infertility and even death (North); the belief that some women get pregnant even when using contraceptives; and the fear of suffering heavy bleeding, menstrual irregularity, weight gain, or cramps (Southwest). At least some of these side effects are known to be associated with the most common medical methods used in Nigeria – the pill, the IUD, and injectables (NDHS 1992). It would seem from this evidence that only 6 per cent of Nigerian married women are using modern methods of contraception because of the methods themselves – their perceived effects as well as their cost and the poor quality and lack of services (compare Feyisetan and Ainsworth 1995; and Okafor and Rizzuto 1994). None the less, out of economic necessity both rural and urban women do seek to regulate their fertility through spacing births and ending childbearing after four or five children. They do so through a variety of resourceful but sometimes ineffective means, including mainly traditional methods and, to a large but undeterminable extent, the clandestine use of abortion.

For most respondents, abortion means the termination of a pregnancy and is not considered a contraceptive method. But attitudes toward it vary greatly. Most nonurban respondents as well as a majority of the over-45 urban participants in all three zones stated that, if a woman finds herself with an unwanted pregnancy, she has no option but to carry the foetus to term unless the pregnancy will endanger her life. Rural and older respondents who expressed objections to abortion tended to do so in terms of Christian or Muslim teachings, associating the practice with 'sin', 'murder' and moral taboos as well as social stigma. On the other hand, urban and peri-urban respondents who voiced negative attitudes towards abortion did so primarily in terms of perceived health and safety risks – of haemorrhaging, damage to the womb, infertility, and death. Aware that these risks result from conditions of illegality and secrecy, some focus group participants felt that a more liberal abortion law may be needed in order to provide safer, more efficient and cheaper abortion services for women.

Our data confirm what scant information exists about abortion in Nigeria. For instance, in one 1984 study of hospitals in eight states, around 85 per cent of reported abortions occurred among young unmarried women. The study also found that both hospital records and 'patients themselves usually deny' that the procedure had occurred, even in the face of 'clear clinical evidence'. None the less, practitioners informally concede that illegal abortion in Nigeria 'is much wider than any recorded data available can indicate' (Okagbue 1990: 200–201).

Such findings support our suspicions about the covert practice of abortion amid pervasive silence, including among our respondents. Cultural restrictions and social taboos contribute to a common perception that abortion is only justified for and practised by unmarried women. However, statistics based on hospital records show that both married and unmarried women resort to abortion (Okagbue 1990; Oni and McCarthy 1990). Confirming these reports, some of our older respondents indicated that they would not hesitate to get an abortion without their husbands' knowledge or consent. Efe, a 43-year-old security guard from the rural Southwest who had borne seven children (five living), told us, 'I will not discuss with my husband before doing it.' And Eghe, a 50-year-old farmer with eight children from the same region, said she would 'go ahead and do it' if her husband objected. More significantly, urban respondents in all three zones, particularly those under nineteen, consider abortion an acceptable option for women in a wide range of conditions: if (1) the pregnancy was unplanned; (2) the woman's health is at risk; (3) there are financial constraints; (4) the baby is unwanted; (5) the woman has too many children; or (6) the father is irresponsible or unknown. Some also stated that women who did not decide to have an abortion under such circumstances might end up 'hating the baby'.

That young urban women, across religious and ethnic divides, are openly rejecting the dominant cultural views against abortion suggests important changes in attitude between generations. As the economic situation deteriorates, women are saddled with increasing financial responsibilities. Many are now determined to control their own fertility, even if it means violating religious and social norms or circumventing husband and family. This shows two levels of awareness: first, that economic hardship hands this responsibility to them, as childbearers; and second, that they can and must make their own decisions about childbearing, behind the cover of deference to husbands or God. Since the great majority of respondents are working to support their families, they are quite aware of the economic conditions that necessitate such determination. But how well they are able to carry it out in practice depends on conditions outside most Nigerian women's control: their place in the life cycle and their access to reliable methods, education, and economic resources.

Conclusions

1. Respondents' ability to express a sense of entitlement in reproductive and sexual decision-making varied significantly across the life cycle, being highest during late childbearing and menopausal years and lowest during early marriage and motherhood. It would seem that the function of childbearer actually lowers women's position in Nigerian society; only when they have passed that life stage are they accorded a degree of respect.

Nigerian women's expectation that they will achieve greater status and honour through marriage and childbearing appears in many ways to be contradicted by the reality of our respondents' married lives. Young women under nineteen are afforded an even higher status than their mothers within their father's home, for example, being exempted from domestic violence. This status declines with marriage and childbearing, when women are expected to defer to the authority of husbands and in-laws in matters of work, fertility, and reproductive health care. While the responsibility for limiting or spacing children is seen as theirs, this responsibility is not accompanied by any recognized rights.

As women grow older and have proven their ability to bear and care for children, they become more willing to transgress dominant social values and traditions affecting their reproductive health, through their actions if not their words. Respondents over thirty-five indicated various ways in which they manoeuvre within the prevailing patriarchal norms to achieve certain goals they clearly see as both personal entitlements and economic necessities, for example, using traditional taboos against sex during breastfeeding or exertion after childbirth in order to secure their desired number of children or a respite from domestic burdens. By the time they reach menopause, these women gain a stronger sense of their entitlements owing to the increased stature and negotiating power the society accords older women (with the exception of childless widows) relative to men.

Urban young women in the under-nineteen group expressed a greater sense of entitlement to explore their sexuality, even before marriage, than their mothers. These younger women rejected the double standard in which unmarried boys are encouraged to gain sexual experience while girls are expected to remain virgins. There was also a strong consensus within this group against arranged marriages and polygamy and in favour of choice of marriage partner. The majority endorsed the freedom to protect themselves from unwanted pregnancy by using contraception and a wide range of circumstances in which they should be entitled to a legal abortion. This sense of sexual entitlement often wanes during the years of childbearing and maternal duties, but with menopause some women claim an entitlement at last to enjoy sexual pleasure without shame.

2. Despite their verbal acceptance of traditional gender norms, we found instances of subversion among women of all ages and across diverse groups in deciding about contraception and abortion and, to a lesser extent, sexuality. But usually such transgressive behaviour took the form of strategic accommodations or secrecy rather than outright resistance.

For example, although most married respondents claimed to defer family size decisions to their husbands or God, we found that many regulated their fertility through some methods (usually non-medical) that could be used without their husbands' knowledge. And while few admitted to having had abortions, evidence suggests that induced abortion is prevalent among them in a continued climate of illegality and danger. In regard to sexuality, contradictory tactics for accommodating but also subverting traditional cultural and religious values highlight the need for further investigation of how Nigerian women negotiate both sexuality and sexual risk; whether they find pleasure and satisfaction in their sexual relationships; and to what degree they find their sexuality constrained by traditional practices and norms.

3. Traditional beliefs and practices have complex, ambiguous meanings in respondents' reproductive and sexual lives – sometimes undermining their health and power; sometimes being wielded by older women to assert their authority over the young; and sometimes helping women to subvert their subordination and expand their margin of control.

The life-cycle transitions analysed above have a contradictory underside from the standpoint of women's empowerment, for they are based on a generational hierarchy that assumes the subordination of younger women and the role of older women as the principal upholders of patriarchal tradition. We saw this during group discussions, as older women were usually the ones privileged to speak for the rest and were seated in positions closest to the interviewers, as well as being the ones who defended premarital chastity for women, FGM, and other customs.

That older women still derive substantial authority from upholding tradition *vis-à-vis* younger women was evident in nearly all our research sites. Nowhere does this generational power exert itself more forcefully than in the withholding of information about sexuality, pregnancy and contraception from young unmarried women. Older women may thus resist the introduction of modern methods of contraception to younger women by outsiders because of how this threatens their gatekeeper position and fragile power within the patriarchal system.[31]

No doubt many of the traditional methods and ways that sustain older women's authority take a heavy toll from all women's reproductive health; they perpetuate conditions that produce adolescent and unwanted pregnancies, clandestine abortions, STDs, VVF/RVF, and women's lack of sexual entitlement. Yet our findings also show that some methods and practices usually defined as traditional can serve to ease women's reproductive burdens and to strengthen intergenerational bonds during pregnancy and childbearing. In contrast to the silence that meets young unmarried women, married and pregnant women receive both advice and care from older female kin and neighbours. While some forms of intergenerational knowledge – for example, food taboos – may be bad for women's health, others, such as weeks of relief from housework and labour in the fields, are probably salutary.

Finally, traditional methods of birth control, in the context of existing cultural and institutional restrictions, may have some real advantages over 'modern' ones. Besides being cheaper and more accessible, they are more within women's control; they carry fewer risks of side effects or social stigma; and they usually do not require a husband's permission. Our respondents' complaints against medical providers in clinics and hospitals point to serious deficiencies in the quality of institutional care, including the priority given to male authority and consent over women's knowledge and empowerment. These deficiencies reinforce women's preference for TBAs and healers.

4. Respondents' expressions of entitlement to reproductive and sexual knowledge and self-determination seem to be growing among younger generations, in part due to increased levels of education among younger women in Nigeria. Whether this trend will be sufficient to break the cycle of women as bearers of tradition will depend on the educational work among girls and young women that women's health activists are able to carry out in years ahead.

Despite the tendency among older women to support traditional ways and to act as gatekeepers of sexual knowledge toward young women, many also expressed approval of more egalitarian educational goals and a desire that their daughters be given knowledge that was withheld from them when they were young. Only rarely, however, (as in the case of Monat and her children) did this desire translate into practical change. Among our informants neither older nor younger women reported that mothers were breaking social taboos against discussion of sexuality with the aim of better informing their daughters. Instead young women were securing sexual knowledge from friends, school and books – resources to which older women had less access.

Although younger women tend to evince more resistant attitudes than older generations to dominant cultural values about sexuality and birth control, it remains to be seen whether these views will endure later in life. Given the life cycle shifts described above, in which more compliant behaviour and values take over in early marriage and motherhood, we have to wonder whether education alone is enough to break the cycle. If the only power available to older women in Nigeria continues to come from acting as guardians of tradition, then change will be very difficult. With increased education and skills, younger women may demand more recognition of their economic and social contributions and their right to make personal choices. Yet breaking the culture of silence around sexuality, contraception and abortion will not happen automatically. So long as most women's sexual and reproductive decisions are veiled in secrecy and accommodation to tradition, it will be impossible to gain public legitimacy for healthier, more gender-equal alternatives.

This sobering reality forced us as researchers and activists to reevaluate our own preconceptions about gender as well as our relationships with grassroots women and the very goals of our work. We became aware that all our actions to achieve women's health and reproductive rights must begin by breaking down the cultural constraints to discussing sexuality. Projects like the Girls' Power Initiative (begun while the IRRRAG research was under way) can create safe spaces for girls and young women to begin to talk more openly about the most intimate pressures and fears they experience about their bodies. None the less, to transform greater openness into power over our reproductive and sexual lives will become possible only when the movement for democracy and shared wealth in Nigeria succeeds in opening the way for real political and social change.

Notes

1 Among the country's approximately 250 ethnic groups and 250–400 distinct languages, the Hausa and Fulani in the North, the Yoruba in the Southwest, and the Igbo in the Southeast are considered the most important. Nearly half the population is Muslim (residing mainly in the North) and about 35 per cent is Christian, with many of these as well as the remaining 15 per cent practising various forms of African traditional religion (Hussaina Abdullah 1996; NDHS 1992).

2 In both the 1996 and the 1997 Corruption Perception Index, Nigeria was ranked as most corrupt nation worldwide (Transparency International 1997).

3 In Nigeria's rural areas, 38 per cent of females between the ages of 15 and 24 have no education, with the rate of female illiteracy for the North three to four times higher than that for the South and Southwest (DHS/Macro International 1996).

4 In one study illiterate women were found to have an overall maternal mortality rate nearly three times higher than that of women with primary education and eleven times higher than that of women with secondary education or above (Briggs 1993).

5 Two distinct sets of criminal law are in force in Nigeria: the Criminal Code in the Southern region and the Penal Code in the North, reflecting the adherence to *shari'a* law among the predominantly Muslim population in the latter. For a discussion of Nigerian criminal and family law, see CRLP/IFWL 1997.

6 *Purdah* is the seclusion of the wife or wives within a walled compound. The wife's movement is restricted by her husband, who has to give permission for her to leave even in the case of a health emergency. Being in *purdah* means that the woman is economically dependent on her husband and extended family (PMMN 1992).

7 This confirms other research documenting that in West Africa FGM is as or even more prevalent among Christian and African traditionalist groups than among Muslims. See *Population Briefs* (Spring 1997), reporting on research conducted in Burkina Faso, Côte d'Ivoire and Senegal. Our research shows that the age at which the procedure is performed varies widely in Nigeria, depending on the ethnic group.

8 The *gishiri* cut is a surgical incision in the labia minora traditionally applied to treat a number of ailments, ranging from prolonged labour to coital difficulties and infertility (Ityavyar 1984).

9 Numerous recent studies have documented the positive and adverse roles TBAs can play in childbearing and the proven health benefits of providing them with further training. See PMMN 1992 and Mothercare 1993. The health system in Nigeria includes traditional medicine, commercial pharmaceutical outlets, government hospitals and clinics, and both non-profit and for-profit private facilities.

10 From the start WIN defined itself as an organisation 'for' rather than 'of women', which meant that men were included in its membership. See Madunagu 1997. Originally the IRRRAG Nigeria team was affiliated with national and local branches of WIN, but eventually it became an independent entity.

11 The IRRRAG team was composed of eighteen women and two men with professional experience in reproductive health, community organizing, community-based development, and social and feminist research. The three zonal coordinators and the country coordinator are activists in national and/or international women's health NGOs.

12 Based on local usage, the team defined 'urban' as state capitals characterized by large populations of non-indigenous inhabitants (migrants), the presence of industries and increased commercial activity, and comparatively well-developed public services and infrastructure (public transport, safe drinking water, electricity); 'rural' as areas that are largely agrarian-based, lack government presence and public services, and have few or no non-indigenous inhabitants; and 'peri-urban' (or rural/urban) as areas with mixed rural and urban characteristics, including small rural towns and communities on the periphery of major urban centres as well as small agricultural enclaves within predominantly urban areas. The selected urban sites were Zaria (North), Calabar (Southeast) and Benin (Southwest); the rural sites were Koraye (North), Awi (Southeast), and Ekiadolor, Odighi and Obarenren (Southwest); and the peri-urban sites were Samaru (North), Odukpani (Southeast) and Oliha and Evbiemwen quarters (Southwest).

13 Although Muslims constitute around 50 per cent of the Nigerian population and the vast majority of those in the Northern states, they were only around 10 per cent of our study sample. This was, first, because we chose to concentrate on minority ethnic groups, and second, because of the difficulty of gaining access to Muslim women, who are not frequently organized into groups and are often in seclusion.

14 Respondents selected for individual interviews tended to be those in the group discussions (not necessarily 'leaders') who appeared to have more to say on areas of particular interest to the study. Those selected for case studies were women who drew lessons for others from their experiences and expressed a need to effect change. We divided respondents into four age cohorts: 19 years and below (= 19 per cent), 20–35 years (= 29 per cent), 36–45 years (= 24 per cent), and above 45 years (= 28 per cent).

15 During a visit to the Southeast village of New Netim, the village chief and other senior men were seated nearby throughout a group discussion that touched on such sensitive matters as widowhood rites, contraception, and FGM; the women's responses on these topics notably conformed to traditional norms.

16 The culture of silence is an issue complicated by the history of colonialism, since in many areas Westernization and Christianity supplanted indigenous practices, such as initiation rites, that taught young girls about sexuality.

17 Acquiring post-secondary education in Nigeria does not necessarily signify high earnings; teachers, nurses and civil servants generally have low pay and modest class status.

18 Some respondents were holding two jobs. Many of those involved in petty trading, for example, were also employed in farming.

19 A visit to Awi, a relatively prosperous rural village in the Southeast where nearly all the women are employed in cultivation and food processing, illustrated this concern with economic needs. When the research team arrived forty-five minutes late, we were told many of the women to be interviewed had left to go to the fields; they could not afford to lose time from work because 'time is money'. Those remaining spent two hours discussing matters of marriage, childbearing and fertility regulation with the researchers. At the end we asked what could most empower them in these areas. Their answer: money for a *gari* pressing machine to squeeze water from the ground cassava root.

20 Makinwa-Adebusoye (1992), in a 1988 study of around 5,600 young men and women ages 12–24 in five large metropolitan areas, found that 44 per cent of the entire sample of women and 25.5 per cent of those aged 15–17 were sexually active, yet only 20 per cent and 6.7 per cent of each group were married. Moreover, only 17 per cent of all the females sampled, and 39 per cent of those who were sexually active, reported using any kind of contraceptive.

21 Huseina's marriage was arranged from birth, but she considers herself 'very lucky' in comparison to her friends ('God has been kind to me') because her husband turned out to be nice.

22 Nationally, the northern Hausa and Fulani girls are married on average three years earlier than their southern Igbo and Yoruba counterparts, and 34 per cent of all females aged fifteen to nineteen among the Northern groups are married (NDHS 1992).

23 The discrepancy between national estimates on polygamy and the ratio of polygamous unions in our sample (especially for the North) may be an artifact of our sample selection strategies, including the prevalence of urban and peri-urban over rural sites, the high proportion of single women among our Southeast respondents, and the decision to interview women who are members of organized groups, who may be less likely to be in the traditional situation of a polygamous union. On the

other hand, it might also be indicative of changing attitudes since the national surveys were done, particularly among younger and urban populations.

24 Although the 1970 Matrimonial Causes Act authorizes civil law courts to determine custody disputes within customary and Islamic as well as civil marriages according to the 'interests of the child', in reality most such disputes never make it to the courts and are decided locally in favour of the husband (CRLP/IFWL 1997).

25 According to one authority, the purpose of such confinement is to ensure that the widow does not posthumously assign paternity to her deceased husband for an illegitimate child (Johnson 1982).

26 In reality high infertility rates among Nigerian women are probably caused by untreated VVF, reproductive tract infections, and early intercourse and childbearing among young girls – all conditions attributable to dominant cultural practices and the lack of good reproductive health care. See Johnson 1982; Adekumle and Ladipo 1992; and Wasserheit and Holmes 1992.

27 According to fieldwork conducted by Adetunji in Ekiti State in Southwestern Nigeria, the reason for sexual abstinence during breastfeeding is primarily to prevent semen from contaminating the mother's milk. Prolonged breastfeeding (up to two years) is considered beneficial for the infant, with boys being breastfed four to five months longer than girls (Adetunji 1997).

28 These demands correspond to findings by the Maternal Mortality Network and the Safe Motherhood Project on women's views of obstetric and maternal practices in Nigeria. See Okafor and Rizzuto 1994 and PMMN 1992.

29 Similarly, a recent study among Yoruba in the Southwest indicates that while, during the early years of marriage, a desire for many children is shared by husband and wife – and the husband's preferences prevail – at a later stage the woman tends to want fewer children and to gain greater influence over reproductive decision-making. See Bankole 1995.

30 We have omitted younger groups of women from these calculations of average fertility on the assumption that many will not have completed their childbearing. Reasons why fertility rates among the Southwestern group of over-35-year-old women were higher than those for their counterparts in the other two zones might include, first, the difference in age distribution, since the Southwest sample had a higher proportion of women in their fifties and sixties; second, the greater likelihood among this group of using traditional, and less effective, methods; and finally, the tendency among Bini women to attempt to bear sons for several men, in order that they may all inherit from their respective fathers.

31 In this way, Nigeria resembles many societies where 'older women are gatekeepers for knowledge surrounding fertility and childbirth' (Ginsburg and Rapp 1995: 5).

7

From *Sanas* to *Dapat*
Negotiating Entitlement in Reproductive Decision-Making in the Philippines

MERCEDES LACTAO FABROS, AILEEN MAY C. PAGUNTALAN,
LOURDES L. ARCHES, AND MARIA TERESA GUIA-PADILLA*

This chapter seeks to depart from traditional discourse around reproductive rights, characterized as it is by a highly individualized, legalistic, and bio-medical orientation, and attend instead to the ways in which grassroots women, as strategizing social persons, construe the notions of 'reproduction' and 'rights'. Based on an ethnographic study of women in three communities, the chapter grounds the issue of reproductive rights in the struggles of these women against the social and cultural forces that govern their everyday lives. It contends that through such struggles grassroots women articulate their claims to control their physical and social bodies – that is, their sexuality, fertility, motherhood, and sense of self in relation to others. In recognizing grassroots women's agency in defining and transforming their own lives, therefore, the chapter seeks to challenge deep-seated assumptions about their decisions concerning reproductive rights, especially in the Third World.

The claims articulated in the women's daily struggles are viewed here as 'negotiated entitlements' – embodying the physical, social and moral dimensions of grassroots women's life histories; the forms of resistance and accommodation they employ to achieve their sense of entitlement; and the structures, both material and ideological, that facilitate or constrain their efforts. In uncovering the process by which grassroots women negotiate entitlements, the study looks at these women's role in biological and social reproduction and the implications of the negotiation process for theory, advocacy, and organizing efforts both locally and nationally.

The Research Process

The IRRRAG Philippines team was comprised of academics and prac-

* This chapter was written in collaboration with Cynthia Rose Bauzon-Bautista, Eufracio C. Abaya and Antoinette Raquiza. Ana Maria Nemenzo wrote the material on the history of the Philippine women's health movement. Field research was carried out by Realidad Santico-Rolda, Rosario Nabong-Cabardo, and Maria Teresa Guia-Padilla under the overall coordination of Mercedes Lactao Fabros.

titioners who are active in different capacities in feminist research and/or rural development. Together we developed a multilayered research process, combining both qualitative and quantitative methods. Recognizing that in the Philippines, and perhaps elsewhere, individuals' sense of self or person-hood (*pagkatao*) and 'rights' are both profoundly influenced by relations with others and changes in the life cycle, the team adopted a life history approach. We maximized this approach by looking intensively at mother–daughter pairs, which enabled us to trace the mechanisms by which society's values and norms are transferred from and through mother to daughter within the fabric of the family and the community. A total of fourteen mother–daughter pairs were selected from three communities, chosen in part because of the presence of local women's organizations who were interested in conducting a follow-up programme designed to influence public policy. Toward this end, a quantitative survey, involving a total of 306 respondents, was later undertaken, in order to validate the findings of the qualitative study across a larger research population.

In order to capture the enormous diversity of the Philippine archipelago, the research locations were chosen to represent three major subsistence patterns: Bagbag, an urban poor *barangay* in the northeastern part of Quezon City, adjacent to the capital city of Manila; Rama, a fishing *barangay* in Western Samar, a depressed province in the central islands of Visayas; and Tabi, a lowland agricultural *barangay* in Sorsogon province, on the island of Luzon.[1] Five mother–daughter pairs were selected in both Bagbag and Tabi, and four in Rama. In each case, the women both lived in the same area, both had children, and both were willing to share their experiences with the team.[2] The validation survey included the original three sites plus four additional ones: Silihan, an area of migrant factory workers in Angono, adjacent to Metro Manila; Bilucao, a rural village in the province of Batangas which is now becoming industrialized; Calapi, an upland agricultural community in Western Samar; and Arena Blanco, an ethnic Muslim *barangay* in Zamboanga City in southwestern Mindanao. Silihan and Bilucao are both part of the Calabarzon, an industrial zone close to Metro Manila which the Philippine government projects as the model for the country's modernization.

Life stories were completed in at least two 'formal' sessions of two to three hours each as well as a number of informal chats, following at least two months' residence in each community; follow-up survey interviews were done in two sessions of ninety minutes to three hours. Additional validation was done through focus groups including all the life story participants along with one additional woman in Rama, three in Bagbag, and seven in Tabi. This three-pronged methodology enabled us to look at women's perceptions and behaviour over the life cycle as well as in different locations, allowing us to make broad social policy recommendations.

Negotiating Entitlements: From *Sana* to *Dapat*

Among grassroots women, reproductive and sexual issues are seldom, if at all, discussed in terms of *karapatan* ('rights'). Instead, grassroots women use the term *sana* ('wishes'). On closer examination, however, it becomes clear that the way in which women articulate the concept of *sana* presupposes the notion of *dapat* ('must' or 'ought'), which is the root word from which *karapatan* is derived. Thus, *sana* contains a personal prescriptive component: that which ought to be, that which I ought to have.

This study asserts that grassroots women's sense of entitlement signifies morally sanctioned privileges and engenders behaviour in pursuit of a 'better life' for themselves and significant others. Since this sense of entitlement is continually negotiated in a field of power relations, the term 'negotiated entitlements' characterizes both the process and the outcome of women's struggles for *sanas*. *Sanas* are products of the dynamics of a woman's assertions of what she wants and needs, what she believes her family and society can grant her, and what she actually does for herself. Obstacles to their realization are rooted in the realities of women's lives – including economic hardship or financial constraints, parental or other senior kin restrictions, social norms, heavy family responsibilities, husbands' disapproval, and personal feelings of inadequacy or lack of control over events.

Thus while family relations are a key site of negotiation and renegotiation, such relations are shaped by social, economic and political processes at various levels (family, neighbourhood, national and global). In analysing these differences, the study also pays attention to the impact of national population policy, the healthcare system, and above all, the Catholic Church, in such issues as fertility regulation, husband–wife relationships, and divorce.

The analysis of mother–daughter pairs illustrates the complex process of negotiating for *sanas*, the context in which negotiation takes place, and the methods these women employ in this process. The choice of mother–daughter pairs within each community limited our research population to those who had returned to the neighbourhood in which they had grown up or those who had never left. As a result, the study highlights the complex interrelationship between the reproduction of norms and values within poor communities and grassroots women's efforts to negotiate change within those norms. In paying attention to the terms in which women speak about their lives we can identify several themes that are common to all localities.

First, the process of negotiation is not always linear. A woman may decide to remain in her present state (accommodation), regress to a former state (retreat), or pursue the process toward transformation (direct assertion) over a period of years. Thus, the process of negotiation and renegotiation has a temporal dimension. Indeed, it may even span generations: a woman may negotiate and renegotiate her entitlements on behalf of and through her daughter(s).

Second, as a result of this nonlinearity, a gap between a woman's sense of entitlement and her actual behaviour always exists, even though some degree of transformation may be taking place. If (re)negotiation reduces this gap, the transformation may become more visible and the process of negotiation more open and direct. Such situations clearly represent movement towards asserting entitlements – from *sana*, 'wishful thinking', to an open declaration of *dapat,* 'should be'.

Third, the nature of the negotiation process and the gap between entitlement and reality vary for different *sanas*. Thus for example, women may be seen in most cases to come closer to *dapat* when articulating claims to work, motherhood, and fending off domestic violence than they do when negotiating in the arena of sexual pleasure and fertility control, which for the most part remain *sanas*.

Fourth, much of grassroots women's behaviour continues to involve submission to existing power relations, including those that undermine women's sense of entitlement. In analysing this finding, the study distinguishes between organized, open, and public display of resistance and forms of resistance that are expressed behind the backs of the powerful in order to avoid direct confrontation (Scott 1990). It looks at the contexts in which women's apparent submission is in fact a form of resistance and at those in which women are pushed to more overt forms of resistance.

The Context of Negotiation: Philippines Economy and Society

The Philippine archipelago consists of three major island clusters – Luzon, Vasayas, and Mindanao – covering a total area of 115,000 square kilometres. Over 50 per cent of its 66 million people are under twenty years old, while less than 5 per cent are over sixty. While men slightly outnumber women in the country as a whole, women are more numerous in the urban areas. And despite the fact that urban areas are highly concentrated, 51 per cent of the population still lives in rural areas.

Philippine culture is a mosaic, reflecting its history. Chinese, Hindu, and Muslim traders regularly visited the islands before 1500, adding their traditions to those of the indigenous Malay people. These traditions proved resilient in the face of colonization by Spain in 1565, and occupation by the United States over three hundred years later (1898) especially regarding kinship systems, food, and the economy. In religion, however, the Spanish succeeded in imposing Catholicism, including its feudal perspectives on women; an estimated 83 per cent of the population is Catholic.[3] The Americans, for their part, institutionalized education and legal systems, with the result that English is an official language as well as Pilipino, the language spoken by the majority, and the courts are conducted in English. They also established a system of liberal democracy – and tolerated its suspension for fourteen years (1972–86) under the dictatorship of Ferdinand Marcos. In 1986, democracy was restored under President Corazon Aquino, who was succeeded by the current president, Fidel Ramos.

Throughout the period following World War Two, the Philippines pursued a policy of rapid industrialization based on import substitution and production for the local market along with export agriculture, based especially on sugar, coconuts, and timber. Light manufactures, primarily garments, leather goods, and more recently electrical and electronic equipment, were successfully developed under a system of protective tariffs and subsidies. By the late 1970s, however, large balance of payments deficits – a result of official corruption, inefficient state-run industries, and price supports and credit subsidies to the monopoly-owned sugar industry – encouraged the Marcos regime to seek balance of payment loans from the International Monetary Fund, and in 1980 the first structural adjustment programme was introduced (Sagrario Floro 1994; Hodgkinson 1995).

Since then, successive governments have embraced a series of structural adjustment policies, characterized by trade and financial liberalization, currency devaluation, and deliberately depressed wages, in a vigorous effort to promote export-led industrialization (Sagrario Floro 1994: 116). Throughout the 1980s, farm price supports and agricultural credit subsidies were greatly reduced, particularly in the food crop sector; regulations on industry were lifted; budgets for health, education, and other social services were cut; and debt payments were made a priority. In 1993 total external debt constituted 64 per cent of GNP, whereas total national expenditure on education the previous year was 2.9 per cent of GDP and that on health was 1 per cent of GDP (UNDP 1996).

Despite its emphasis on privatization, however, structural adjustment failed to address the state's continuing alliance with large landowners, bankers, and industrialists, with the result that sugar continued to receive support while the international market plummeted. Bankruptcies, government bailouts and massive layoffs combined with devaluation-impelled inflation to produce a deep economic crisis in 1983-85 (Sagrario Floro 1994:118), during which the economy contracted more than 10 per cent (US State Department 1994).

In 1986, with the election of Corazon Aquino, the government finally eliminated the sugar and coconut marketing monopolies, paving the way for greater investment. And in 1992, the newly elected Ramos administration launched a plan called Philippines 2000, based on attracting foreign investment to new urban industrial processing zones, where there are virtually no regulations on wages or working conditions. Despite a very low minimum wage – about US$6.30 per day – foreign-owned firms, largely from South Korea, Taiwan and the United States, have devised a host of ways to reduce labour costs, including the use of a web of contractors and subcontractors that continually reduce the amount paid to the producer.

Today, after a decade of stagnation, the economy has turned around – but by no means evenly across classes and sectors. Trade deficits are rising, not falling;[4] debt payment remains high, despite some rescheduling, and public spending has not increased. 'Prosperity stops at the borders of the cities,' as one observer noted, 'while in the countryside there is no change at all' (quoted in Richburg 1995). The new factory jobs are primarily for the young, skilled, and those with at least a high school education. In the countryside, agriculture remains stagnant, a consequence of continuing land monopoly, and inadequate investment and financing. Fishing especially has languished, not only because of lack of funds and absence of government support but also because of pollution resulting from mining activities, population growth, and destructive fishing methods (Hodgkinson 1995). Inflation has hit 12 per cent, and there are shortages of subsistence food crops, especially rice, with the result that the price of rice nearly doubled during 1995 alone (Richburg 1995).

The Status of Women

The majority of Filipino women belong to the more than 60 per cent of the population living in poverty. As such they are engaged in a constant struggle for survival – survival not only of themselves but of their families. Widespread poverty, especially in the rural areas, bred by a highly stratified class society, has been greatly aggravated by the policies of structural adjustment, which have resulted in increased food prices, declining real family incomes, and reductions in government expenditures on education and health services (Sugrario Floro 1994: 119).

As traditional manufacturing declines alongside small-scale agricultural production, so do the jobs that support poor families. Increasingly, it is the women who must seek paid work outside the home, normally at very low wages. In a society where the average household size is six, the women, traditionally the household managers, are particularly hard pressed to bridge the gap between a limited family income and the rising cost of living. Despite a tremendous rise in the number of Filipinas joining the labour force since the early 1980s, the labour force participation rate for women is still far below that for men: 47 per cent for women in 1994 compared to over 80 per cent for men. As a result, two-thirds of the labour force is male. A recent survey indicates that among low-income groups, women's ability to enter the labour force is highly constrained by family and housekeeping responsibilities (NCRFW 1995).

Recent surveys indicate that poor women enter the labour force earlier and work on average longer than their more affluent sisters. In 1990, 48 per cent of those 15–48 years of age were in the labour force compared to an average of 39 per cent for women of all ages. Low-income women take what work they can find, generally arduous and badly paid, and clustered in areas that parallel their traditional reproductive roles; only 1 per cent engage in professional and technical jobs compared to 11 per cent nationwide while 37 per cent are unpaid family workers compared to 23 per cent nationwide. Two-thirds of those engaged in the buy-and-sell activities of the informal economy are women, who also make up 56 per cent of those employed in community services (NCRFW 1995).

Women's labour is also increasingly essential to the export economy, which relies heavily on garment manufacture and electronics; a 1988 census showed that women outnumbered men four to one in the garment industry and three to one in electronics. Because of widespread subcontracting in these industries, much of the work is done by poor women in their homes. While this allows women to combine family and household responsibilities with income-generating activities, it also perpetuates the myth that homeworkers are just housewives earning some extra pocket money.

In the rural areas, home to seven out of ten families in poverty, women's struggle to ensure family survival gets increasingly difficult. Rural women start working in the fields from age fifteen, limiting their opportunities for education. Although their participation in agriculture and fishing is ignored in official statistics, a recent analysis of food production systems in Central Luzon documents that women carry out 75 per cent of the activities involved in rice production (Bautista and Dungo 1987). At the same time, the policy of encouraging cash crop production increasingly removes land from subsistence cropping, thereby causing local food shortages and jeopardizing the nutrition and health of poor families. A 1993 survey by the Food and Nutrition Research Institute found that malnutrition stalks preschoolers and children, pregnant women, seasonal farmers, and fisherfolk. As a result, women increasingly seek work in the urban areas; two out of three migrants to the largest metropolitan areas are women (NCRFW 1995).[5] In the cities most of the women migrants find work as domestic helpers, while others, especially young, single women, find jobs in the export processing zones or enter the so-called entertainment industry. A flourishing new sex industry has accompanied the development of foreign business; women who once raised pigs to buy rice now go to city dance halls, and from there enter the sex industry, fuelling an increasingly rapid spread of HIV/AIDS (Richburg 1995).[6]

Gender typing of employment also limits women in middle-class occupations. In 1992 they predominated in the medical, dental, health and veterinary fields while men predominated in transport, storage and warehousing. Despite gains in clerical and sales jobs, women's earnings were less than half those of men in 1992 (NSO 1992). Leadership positions in all fields are still dominated by men, despite the fact that women's educational achievements have outpaced men's.

In general, Filipinos are fairly well educated compared to their Asian neighbours; most children complete elementary school, while children in urban areas typically finish high school. Adult literacy rates and educational enrolment ratios were almost at a par with developed countries in 1993 (UNDP 1996). Perhaps more surprising, women's education has kept pace with or even surpassed that of men: in 1993 women's literacy was virtually equal to men's, while 59 per cent of college graduates and 60 per cent of postgraduates are female (UNDP 1996; NSO 1989). Within the Muslim and indigenous communities, however, where education and literacy lag behind the rest of the nation, the gender gap is wider (Eviota 1993). Moreover, while primary school enrolment in the Philippines is quite high, more than one-third of elementary students do not go on to high school (Philippines DECS 1995). In poor communities, few boys or girls graduate from high school (UNDP 1996). Older children leave school either to attend to household and childcare duties or to go to work to supplement the family income.

Table 7.1 National Demographic Indicators, 1995

INDICATOR	NATIONAL	URBAN	RURAL
Women's literacy rate (%)	94		
Women as % of nonagricultural workforce	40		
Total fertility rate	4.1	3.5	4.8
Maternal mortality rate (per 100,000 births)	280		
Infant mortality rate (per 1000 births)	43	32	44

Source: *Country Profile: Philippines*, Population Reference Bureau, Washington DC, 1996; UNDP 1996.

Despite increasing employment and education opportunities, women of all classes are still hemmed in by society's traditional family and religious values, reinforced in schools and the media as well as by the Catholic Church. In the main, society continues to regard the home as women's principal domain and motherhood as their reason for being. The woman shoulders sole responsibility for the care and welfare of family members. Not only does she provide reproductive and social services such as caring for the husband, children, and the elderly, she also assumes responsibility for household food security and family planning.

The patriarchal model of the family, consisting of a married man and woman and their children, permeates Philippine society, occupying a central place in women's lives. The family is the place where women first imbibe society's norms and values. As such, it is the framework within which the potential for and limitations on women's self-realization are determined. Even as more and more women enter the workforce, men are still regarded as the principal breadwinners and heads of households. This traditional family model is reinforced by the legal system, which outlaws divorce and does not recognize violence within the family, including marital rape, as a crime. While the newly enacted Family Code allows legal separation, the need for financial and legal resources to pursue it limits this option in practice to the middle class. Moreover, the code's provision protecting women's right to work is of little value to the many poor women who lack access to child care. The current Civil Code, now under review, defines rape as a crime not against the person but against 'chastity'; given this definition, it is inconceivable that rape could be committed between partners in marriage.[7]

Women's Health

Women's increasing responsibility for work both outside and inside the home takes a toll on their health in general and their reproductive health in particular. Poor people cannot afford to get ill; instead they suffer malnutrition and chronic respiratory disease, ranging from persistent cough to pneumonia and tuberculosis. The impact of poverty is reflected in the fact that, in 1993, 44 per cent of pregnant women were anaemic, their condition often aggravated by tuberculosis, malaria or hepatitis, and 70 per cent of children under six suffered from iron deficiency (POPCOM 1994; Aslam 1993). Tuberculosis is now a major health crisis; its incidence rose over 30 per cent from 1993 to 1995, and the Department of Health estimates that as many as one in three Filipinos could be infected (Philippines DOH 1995). Moreover, most tuberculosis victims are women, their susceptibility heightened by overwork, fatigue, frequent childbirth, and lack of nutritious food (Philippines DOH 1991).[8]

Pregnancy and childbirth remain a major cause of death for women. While the National Demographic Survey estimated that 209 women died for every 100,000 births during 1987–93, down only slightly from 213 in 1980–86, some estimates are much higher; the UNDP calculates the maternal mortality ratio in the Philippines as 280 per 100,000 births in 1993 (UNDP 1996). According to one study, five to six women die of pregnancy-related causes every day (NCRFW 1995). Young women are especially vulnerable: among mothers under age fifteen, there were three maternal deaths for every four live births in 1989 (NSO 1994a).

Pregnancy with abortive outcome accounted for 10 per cent of maternal deaths in 1989 (NSO 1991). While it is unclear how many of these resulted from induced abortion, unpublished statistics from the Philippine Obstetrical and Gynaecological Society indicated that 24 per cent of deaths reported by seventy-eight hospitals were due to induced abortion (Aslam 1993). Although abortion is illegal, it is widely practised, usually under insanitary conditions and without proper medical care. It is estimated that some 80,000 women annually are treated in hospitals for complications from induced abortions and that about 400,000 abortions occur each year in the Philippines (Singh *et al.*, 1997). The infant mortality rate, though still somewhat high within the region (only Indonesia has a higher rate among Southeast Asian countries), has improved more rapidly than maternal mortality, declining from 54 per 1,000 births in the period 1985–90 to 43 in 1993 (UNDP 1996). A significant number of these deaths are a consequence of low birth weight and other conditions resulting from maternal malnutrition or disease.

Infant and maternal mortality are also a result of inadequate medical services. While a 1993 Safe Motherhood Survey showed that 84 per cent of pregnant women received prenatal care, visiting a doctor, nurse, or midwife at least once, only 32 per cent had postpartum care (NSO 1994b). Government and private health services are both inadequate: in 1990, there were 12.6 beds per 10,000 people, one doctor per 6,656 and one midwife per 5,184 people (WHO 1995). In 1993, 22 per cent of all births were attended by a doctor, 35 per cent by a medically trained midwife, and 52 per cent by a traditional midwife, or *hilot*, and as many as 70 per cent of them took place at home (NSO 1994b). Care varies by region: in the Metro Manila area, 60 per cent of births were attended by a doctor and only 10 per cent by a *hilot*, whereas in eight of the fourteen other regions over 50 per cent were attended by a *hilot* (Philippines DOH 1991). While women employed in the formal sector are allowed sixty days maternity leave, those in the informal sector as well as those working under various contract arrangements return to work immediately after childbirth.

National Population Policy

The main reason for the continued high incidence of maternal mortality, however, is the large and increasing number of pregnancies among Philippine women (POPCOM 1994). The rate of population growth is still the highest in Southeast Asia. So is the total fertility rate, 4.1, although this has declined from almost 6 in the early 1970s. The decline reflects several factors, including women's increased labour force participation and somewhat later age at marriage, along with a government commitment, beginning in 1969, to make family planning an integral part of development policy. Undertaken primarily under pressure from the International Monetary Fund, and in spite of opposition from the Catholic Church, population policy was initially concerned only with fertility reduction. By the mid-1980s, however, the emphasis began to change, incorporating primary health care as well as maternal and child health. The 1987 National Population Policy specifically looked 'beyond fertility reduction' to such concerns as family formation, the status of women, maternal and child health, urbanization and internal and international migration. The Philippine Family Planning Programme was set up to implement these goals in 1990 (UNICEF 1992; POPCOM 1994).

To date, however, there has been little change in the maternal and child health situation, while a recent study showed that the Philippines lags far behind other countries in the region at comparable levels of development – notably Indonesia and Thailand – in terms of reducing fertility (APPRR 1995). The main reason, the study concluded, is strong opposition from the Catholic Church, resulting in failure by the government to implement its population policy. The number of women who say they want to limit or space births but are not using contraception remains high; wanted births were 29 per cent below actual births in 1988–91 compared to 24 per cent in Indonesia and 17 per cent in Thailand (APPRR 1995). While a National Demographic Survey (Philippines NSO 1994a) showed that 89 per cent of women knew where to obtain at least one type of contraceptive (nearly 90 per cent knew where to obtain the pill, and over 80 per cent knew where to obtain IUDs or condoms), only 40 per cent reported currently using some form of contraception. Moreover, as a result of church pressure, until 1993 the government supported only so-called natural or traditional methods of contraception, such as withdrawal or abstinence.

The 1993 Safe Motherhood Survey found that only 25 per cent of currently married women surveyed were using a modern contraceptive method, with 48 per cent stating they had never used such methods. The most common methods currently being used were female sterilization (11.9 per cent) and the pill (8.5 per cent), followed by withdrawal (7.4 per cent) and abstinence (7.3 per cent). (Nearly 30 per cent of the women surveyed, however, had used the pill at some time.) Only 3 per cent were using IUDs and 1 per cent were using condoms.[9] The main reasons for nonuse of contraception, besides wanting another child or being infertile, were infrequent sex (23.5 per cent) and fear of side effects (19.5 per cent); only 4.5 per cent cited 'religion.' Abortion, which is illegal except to save the woman's life, is not considered a family planning method. However, of the 25 per cent who admitted to having had an unwanted pregnancy, 5 per cent said they had had an abortion; 14 per cent had tried to abort but failed; and 4 per cent tried various ways to bring on their periods.

While the government now supports modern as well as traditional methods of contraception, the Catholic Church has strongly denounced this policy, and it is not clear how much access has improved. A 1995 Family Planning Survey indicated that traditional family planning is still the most popular among all currently married women; 19 per cent used such methods (Perez 1995). As all these surveys indicate, women carry the responsibility for family planning. Due to church pressure, family planning services, like maternal and child care, are available only to married women.[10]

The Philippines Women's Health Movement

The need to improve the health and reproductive health of women, especially poor women, is thus an urgent concern for the women's movement. The contemporary women's movement emerged from the struggle against the dictatorship of the late President Ferdinand Marcos. Although sluggish for most of the 1970s, during which the progressive movement built up a broad base of peasants, workers, urban poor, religious and professional people, by the early 1980s rising feminist consciousness inspired the formation of several women's groups. These included Kilusan ng Kababaihang Pilipina (Pilipina), the Centre for Women's Resources (CWR), and Katipunan ng Kalayaan para sa Kababaihang (KALAYAAN), which concluded that women's problems would never be adequately addressed until women created their own political space.[11]

By 1983, with the assassination of Senator Benigno Aquino, women's organizations burst onto the political scene, organizing the first all-women demonstration against the martial law regime; some 10,000 women participated in the 28 October protest. A national women's conference the following March produced a broad coalition of women's groups, later known as Gabriela, which raised a variety of issues related to national, race, gender and class concerns.

Following the election of Corazon Aquino in 1984, in a show of unity women's groups presented the new constitutional commission with a set of women's rights provisions that avoided controversial issues such as divorce and abortion. Ironically, the proposal of the Catholic Church, supported by Pro-life Philippines, to introduce the 'right to life of the fertilized ovum' into the new constitution forced women to confront the issue of abortion. While women's groups were not yet prepared to take a stand, individual women conducted a petition campaign, asking the commission to eliminate the 'right to life of the unborn' on the grounds that women's voices had been effectively silenced by the hostile cultural and social environment and that such a provision would discriminate against women who lack the education and resources to access safe medical services. Gabriela subsequently organized a campaign to link women's groups with health and family planning NGOs to promote women's health issues and lobby the constitutional commission around women's rights.

While the provision was reformulated to read: 'The State shall provide equal protection to the mother and the unborn from conception,' the victory belonged more to the church than to women. As a result, women adopted a broader concept of reproductive rights, emphasizing women's health as an indicator of women's status. If women suffered from ill health and lack of health services, it was because of their low status and lack of control over their reproduction and sexuality. The fusion of women's and health concerns added a new and exciting dimension to the women's movement; women's reproductive health or, more precisely, women's right to reproductive self-determination, became a strategic area for women's advocacy.

The Catholic Church quickly sought to get President Aquino, a devout Catholic, to issue an Executive Order prohibiting the use of government funds for anything other than natural family planning. Women again mobilized, demanding public hearings. While the order was not issued, the threat impelled women toward more sustained and proactive advocacy for reproductive rights. KALAYAAN sought to expand feminist discourse and advocacy to include sexuality and reproductive self-determination. Progressive women's groups, including the Women's Resource and Research Centre (WRRC), Katipunan ng Bagon Pilipina (KaBaPil), the Women's Media Circle (WMC), the CWR and Pilipina, made reproductive rights an essential component in their own advocacy work. The informal network that emerged during the constitutional debates was formalized with the establishment of WomanHealth Philippines, whose mission focused on the advancement of women's reproductive self-determination.

These groups joined with Gabriela in hosting the Sixth International Women and Health Meeting (IWHM) in Manila in November 1990. Meeting in Asia for the first time, the conference was obliged to bring an Asian perspective to the discussions and accommodate perspectives arising from the specific historical, socioeconomic and political realities of the region. A plenary session was devoted to sexuality, for the first time taking up the issue of lesbian sexuality. The possibility of a feminist population policy was debated, along with the question of how to maintain feminist integrity working in mainstream organizations.

The exposure to debates within the international women's health movement had an incalculable impact on the local women's health movement. There was an 'explosion' of consciousness – a catching up with the world. In 1990, with the adoption of the Philippine Family Planning Programme, women were invited to assist in training government health and family planning personnel, an opportunity to influence the programme's orientation. However, many feared this would absorb them into government concerns, obscuring their primary mission of organizing and strengthening the mass base of the movement.[12] In response, several women's health groups formed the Alliance for Women's Health, which supported the activities of its member organizations in education and training, policy research, women-sensitive healthcare services, and workshops related to women's health and reproductive rights. In addition, members of the alliance attempted, with some frustration, to work on a Department of Health task force to implement a women's health framework in the health services.

Beginning in 1991, women's groups convened the First National Conference on Women and Health, taking up issues of reproductive rights, violence against women, abortion, sexuality, and lesbian sexuality. In 1994, many Philippines women's groups participated in the International Conference on Population and Development (ICPD) in Cairo, both in the official conference and in the NGO Forum. Throughout the Cairo process, women in the Philippines criticized the lack of a strong development context and urged agendas that would be more relevant to the realities of women's lives in countries such as the Philippines. Pursuing these broader agendas, Filipinas hosted a subregional conference, focused on violence against women, reproductive health, and problems of working women. From this emerged a subregional network, the East and Southeast Asian Women and Health Network (ESEA), headquartered in the Philippines.

As women's groups expanded, so did their activities, covering issues from peasant women's right to own land, to women's health and reproductive self-determination, to sustainable development. In addition, Philippines women's groups were involved in the successful campaign to terminate US military bases, joined the coalition against the foreign debt service payments consuming 40 per cent of the national budget, and participated in protest rallies against government neglect of migrant workers, particularly women. But some have begun to question whether funders' priorities are distorting the women's agenda, remoulding the broad transformational vision in favour of narrower projects. In part to deal with this concern, women's groups have begun to take up free trade issues. At the 1996 meeting of the Asian and Pacific Economic Cooperation (APEC), held in the Philippines, women's groups opposed the government's plan to hasten the reduction of trade tariffs and urged alternative strategies. Moreover, they linked issues of reproductive and sexual health and rights to the broader political and economic struggle, noting that women's and children's health and welfare will suffer with casualization of labour and the attendant loss of labour and social security benefits.

Poor Families in Three Communities

The constraints of poverty follow women from the countryside to the city, where they struggle to support their families. Within the *barangay* of Bagbag, with about 56,000 poor occupants, two contingent neighbourhoods, Wings and Abbey Road, are home to 8,000 people, all migrants, mostly from Luzon and the central islands. Families typically live in one-storey structures of wood and scrap iron, many partitioned into rooms and rented out to as many families as there are rooms. Few houses accommodate extended families, so that married children are obliged to move. Many families get electricity by hooking into the lines of relatives; some still go to the well for water, lining up as early as 4 a.m. for this scarce commodity.

Bagbag has one elementary school, where thirty-eight teachers teach 2,000 students; a nearby school can accommodate another 2,000. Among the older generation, few are educated beyond the fourth grade, yet their children have generally finished elementary school; about 20 per cent of the younger population have completed high school. Jobs are low-skilled; many of the men work in nearby factories; others are house painters, drivers, vendors, construction workers, and the like. All of them earn very low wages.

Women in Bagbag sell various commodities, from fried bananas to sweepstake tickets, either from home or in the market; others sew dresses in their homes, cook or wash dishes for restaurants. In addition, some work as casual labourers in a nearby garment factory, while a large number go to an adjacent subdivision to do laundry. Even so, the women all complain that even if they break their backs working, they still end up borrowing from relatives or neighbours.

The villages the women leave behind are falling into depression, like the fishing village of Rama and the agricultural village of Tabi. Rama, with a population of 1,282 in 1990, is 19 kilometres by boat from the town of Catbalogan in the state of West Samar, where the poverty rate was 61 per cent in 1990 (compared to 50 per cent nationwide). Ancient interisland ships, which often take close to three hours, are the only connection to the outside world. Houses are built on a small flat land area between the river and the sea. While residents have had electricity since the early 1990s, water is still supplied by springs, which usually run dry in the dry seasons.

Most families rely on fish for income and subsistence, both of which are now threatened by overfishing. While it is mostly the men who fish, women often accompany their husbands or sons and many fish on their own. Fish are sold to traders in Rama, who transport them to Catbalogan. Average fishing income is about 4,200 Philippine pesos per year (under US$200) – enough just to cover food and basic necessities; when the catch does not earn enough income, families are forced to eat root crops only. Fishing is organized on a kinship system; thus while the traders lend money for emergencies they lend only to relatives.

Many women gather shellfish to sell to traders. Others raise pigs and goats and engage in farming and sewing to earn cash or cook snacks to sell in the village. Many young girls go to work as domestic helpers in town or other urban centres. Children are sent to work in June when the monsoon season starts and they return in January. Up to 1957 there was only one teacher for all of Rama, and a full elementary school has been in place only since 1960. Now most of the teachers commute, arriving on a Monday and leaving on a Friday, and so teaching only three days. The nearest high school is in Catbalogan.

Tabi, located in the Bicol region at the southeastern tail of Luzon Island, is one of thirty-six rural *barangays* of the town of Gubat, which also has six urban *barangays*. Rice and coconut are the major products, farmed by local smallholders and their tenants plus an increasing number of landless agricultural workers. Crops have suffered from increased drought and flooding, perhaps the result of intensified logging in the nearby mountains, and the region was devastated by three hurricanes in 1993–94. As a result, many men also work in Gubat, as cargo lifters, construction labourers, or drivers. Women work doing laundry or taking care of children in town.

Tabi has six neighbourhoods, totalling some 1,505 residents in 1991, but most people live in the Sentro, which is one of the few that has electricity and water. Average family income is below the poverty line, although it is supplemented by home-grown food crops. As agriculture becomes more uncertain, both men and women seek jobs in Metro Manila, where women are caregivers, salesladies, cooks or garment factory workers.

In all three *barangays* studied, it is women who do all the household work: after working at one or more jobs, they still do the laundering, cooking, child care, house cleaning, as well as fetching water and even doing plumbing repairs. Males are still regarded as the breadwinners, even if they are unemployed. Thus they do no housework, nor are they expected to. In Rama it is estimated that men put in 8–9 hours a day in production, compared to 7–8 hours for women. Yet women add 9–10 hours for household work and reproduction, while men add only 3 hours. It is different for children; both boys and girls are expected to do housework and usually start doing such tasks by the time they are ten years old.

Health and family planning services are beyond the reach of poor Filipinas. In urban areas, both low-income and some middle-income families attend ill-equipped and ill-staffed government health facilities. They are responsible for all expenses, such as medicines, laboratory work, and so on. Thus in Bagbag, where many people are unable to afford private care, the parish church operates a free medical and dental clinic four times a year. There is also a health centre, known as Kalinga sa Kalusugan ng Kababihan (Care for Women's Health), at which a doctor, nurse, and five health workers attend to patients at weekends. Women's groups are also active; for example, a programme serving meals to children in Abbey Road, sponsored by a private charity, was implemented by a women's organization, since about 50 per cent of children aged 6–11 are suffering from malnutrition. However, most mothers do not report falling ill, saying they cannot afford health care; only when their condition is quite serious – tuberculosis for example – do they go to a doctor or public health centre. Since women do not consider their health a priority, few avail themselves of family planning services except in emergency. They explain that they do not have time to go to health centres largely because of the demands of housework.

In rural areas, health facilities are generally located in town centres. Rama shares a health station at Catbalogan with three other *barangays*, at which there are a midwife, three nutrition specialists, and ten health workers, all women, who carry out the government's family planning programme. Tabi, by contrast, is itself the site of a health centre serving four *barangays*. However, this is rarely used by women; a local midwife explains that 80 per cent of the cases are children and the remainder are adult males. It is through the midwife that women can obtain birth control pills; however, she is not licensed to insert IUDs and does not support the government's family planning programme because she is a devout Catholic.

Articulating *Sanas*: Women's Voices

Grassroots women's articulation of their entitlements reflects their power-lessness in Philippine society. Weighed down by a poverty that has deprived them of education and constricted their social mobility, born into Catholicism and raised within the traditional sexual division of labour, these women face great odds against asserting what they believe is due to them. Often their sense of entitlement emerges in private conversations among women and, particularly, between mothers and daughters. Often, too, it can only be deduced from women's efforts to carve out a space for themselves and their rights within the community and the household. Yet as women talk about their lives, it is clear that they do have a sense of their entitlements. They express these, however, in terms of the norms learned while growing up, within the context of their social relations. Most often this takes the form of a rights discourse that begins with the word '*sana*' (I wish). In *sana* one finds an assertion of what should be in the hypothetical alternative to women's current situation. In marked contrast to the customarily formal and public assertion of rights, which are normally defined by educated people in public documents, *sana* is a private, often unarticulated, assertion of entitlement.

Education and girlhood

For all respondents, their aspirations as women are shaped by the time they enter *dalaga*. Roughly translated, *dalaga* means 'adolescence', but for poor women it is always bound up in work, and sometimes also early marriage. As shown in Table 7.2, only two of the respondents reached college; none completed it. Over half had only six years or less of formal education. This picture has improved for women in the younger generation: whereas eleven out of fourteen women in their mothers' generation had had six years of school or less and only three had had any high school, nine in the younger group had gone to high school or beyond, while only five had been limited to elementary school. Yet it is hard to measure this improvement. Only four actually finished high school, the minimum educational requirement to get an entry-level job in most factories in the Philippines.

Respondents named lack of money as the reason they could not continue their schooling. In Rama, all the young women were obliged to leave school and work as housemaids as soon as they finished elementary school, and some even before. In Bagbag, Dada and her daughter Jean mentioned that they had to start working because they had many siblings, whom their parents could not adequately provide for. Like her mother, Jean aspired to finish a vocational course, such as tailoring, so that she would not have to work as a domestic helper. But because she had to give her salary to her mother to care for her siblings, she was unable to realize her dream.

Minia had wanted to stay in school beyond grade six. She decided to go to Manila and work as a domestic helper: 'I could depend on my parents. I had so many siblings, and so the income was never enough.' Tasing, who also finished grade six, explains:

> For those who were poor, it was the practice to become a domestic helper as soon as one was old enough. Whenever some people came home from Metro Manila, they would bring news of job openings there. Of course I went with them so that I could buy clothes. If I stayed here I would not be able to buy things that I wanted. After all, when one becomes a young lady one becomes fond of clothes.

Among those who did manage to go on with their schooling, many got sidetracked and dropped out. Sadly, despite their desire that their children should get more schooling, the mothers in many cases precipitated the decision to quit school. Laida, for example, graduated first in her elementary school in Rama and wanted to become a teacher. An aunt offered to send her to school in exchange for household help, but her mother refused; she was afraid the aunt's husband, who had allegedly raped Laida's cousins, would do the same to Laida. Not knowing what else to do, Laida stumbled into marriage when she was fifteen. Likewise, Lucy was preparing to return to high school after a vacation at home when her mother's scolding became too much. Looking back, she explains: 'My mind was confused by the scoldings. Mando and I were not sweethearts, but in my irritation I decided to leave the house and talked him into eloping. He just followed my decision.'

Marriage: a lifetime commitment

Marriage is a sacred social institution in the Philippines, reflected in the fact that divorce is still illegal. The idea of the inviolability of marriage pervades Philippine society. As Didi, a 43-year-old mother in Rama, told her mother: 'It is my fate. If you had sent me to school, this would not have happened. I wanted to work as a housemaid but you wouldn't allow me. There is no other option but to marry.' Lina, only twenty-one, shows that this view crosses generations. 'Marriage is learning to live with a man for the rest of your life, never to be parted again,' she said. Although many respondents worked before marriage, all agree that women are eventually fated to enter marriage and motherhood. Almost all respondents are legally married, while six, mostly from Bagbag, have a 'live-in' or domestic partner arrangement. Most have had only one long-term relationship, regardless of generations.

While not every marriage (*pag-aasawa*) starts with a wedding (*kasal*), which can be very expensive and is usually paid for by the man's family, people in live-in arrangements are considered married, and one may call the other *asawa* ('spouse'). Thus women grow up expecting their right to marry and have families. Marriage is the primary way in which poor women forge a social identity; as the life stories reveal, grassroots women enter into marriage because it is expected of them. Alice, seventy-two, recalled that her father had pulled her out of school, saying, 'She is just a girl; she will not follow any career but marriage.'

Among the life story respondents, seven had taken part in arranged marriages, five of these among the mothers' generation. Most were the result of the parents' desire to protect their daughters' chastity. Daughters shared this concern with virginity; thus Leila eloped with her boyfriend in Tabi despite her father's opposition because she had engaged in sexual relations with him. Isabel and her daughter Ludy, also living in Tabi, had both entered marriage after their boyfriends tricked them into spending a night in their homes. Pregnancy and rape were further inducements. Rape is no longer a crime in the Philippines if the man offers marriage; thus Laida's mother, Pining, who feared her daughter would be raped, herself almost married a boy who had tried to rape her.

A majority of the life story respondents had attempted to forge their own identity before marriage, either through work or through continuing their schooling; one-third of them saw marriage as a way to become independent of their parents. But for the most part, those who entered marriage in the hope of improving their lot or escaping their mother's control, have been disappointed, as their husbands held irregular or low-paying jobs. Moreover, parental control does not end with marriage, as most respondents live with or near their family or in-laws. The norm is to reside with the husband's family since it is their responsibility to provide shelter, although younger respondents preferred to live with their own parents, especially in Bagbag. However, it is notable that in all three communities the mean age at marriage has increased from the mothers' generation (18.1) to the daughters' generation (20.4), a significant shift. Cecilia, a young woman in Bagbag, cited her mother's stormy marriages and eight children as a reason for waiting to marry until she was twenty-six years old.

Motherhood: 'You are now responsible for a life'

Respondents stated that a woman becomes *ganap na babae* (a whole woman) only when she has given birth. As a participant in the validation survey stated: 'It is only when you have children that you have proved that you are really a mother.' With the birth of the first child, a woman is accorded a new status, having completed one part of the life cycle, childhood, and entered the next, motherhood and adulthood. The weight given to motherhood can be gleaned from the expression often directed to mothers: *Magaalaga ka na ng buhay* ('You are now responsible for a life').

All the respondents had their firstborn almost immediately after marriage. For women in both generations, it was quite unthinkable that a married woman would not want to get pregnant. As Ludy, who had just given birth to her second child, asked, 'When one is married, why should one be ashamed to get pregnant?' The apparently easy transition from marriage to motherhood can be explained in part by the fact that most engaged in reproductive work from an early age, taking on housework and the responsibility of caring for their younger siblings while their mothers earned a living outside the home. Upon reaching adulthood, respondents in both generations also worked as domestic helpers to assist their families financially. Mothers were also usually on hand during their daughters' pregnancies and in critical moments of their married children's lives. Hence, women define reproduction as a lifelong process, woven into their lives. Of the fourteen women in the mothers' generation, half are taking care of grandchildren on a permanent basis. They laughingly refer to this as taking a 'back subject' (like repeating a course in school).

Since culture and tradition assign the roles of childbearing and mothering almost exclusively to women in the private sphere, women usually raise their children alone, with little support from government and the larger society. Motherhood for many women thus consumes much of their adult life, defining who they are. Nevertheless, precisely because these roles are considered vital not only to the women but also to their children, they also represent spaces from which women can assert their rights. If the women's sense of identity as autonomous individuals is strongest during their working *dalaga*, their sense of what they are entitled to is clearest during pregnancy and childbirth.

Pregnancy and childbirth bring together the women from both sides of the family, are a time when the daughter and mother (or mother-in-law) experience a special bond. Often, her mother by her very presence provided the confidence and strength a woman needed to face childbirth. Tisay's experience of labour pains reminded her of the pains she gave Alice, her mother. Because of this special event, four women had reconciliations with their mothers; Julia, who was having a difficult first delivery, could only relax upon the arrival of Tasing, her mother, with whom she had had an earlier dispute. Her relief may also be partly connected to the popular belief that difficult births are caused by the lack of forgiveness or unresolved conflict, and that the birth could only be eased by obtaining the other party's forgiveness or understanding.

Respondents viewed the thought of bringing up a new life, which they can unequivocally claim as their own achievement, as thrilling and challenging. Minia, fifty-five years old, said of her first childbirth: 'It is wonderful to be a mother at last, with a child that will occupy one's attention. It feels even better than being newly married.' Basyon, now sixty-two, has eleven children. Recalling her first pregnancy, she said: 'I am now a mother. I will start to experience all the hardships of a mother and I accept this.' Thus respondents generally greeted the news of their pregnancy with mixed emotions: joy at having a child combined with apprehension about the new responsibilities and inevitable changes in their lives. As Ludy, twenty-six years old with two children, said: 'It is okay for a mother to be able to bathe and comb her hair, but children need to be looked after otherwise they will go hungry. It is the obligation of the mother to clean her children even if she herself is dirty.' But none expressed regret. Julia, a daughter in Tabi who at twenty-seven recalls mainly tragic experiences from her past, says: 'I only remember that I was happy when I became a mother.'

Respondents accept the burdens of motherhood because they know that it is the source of their completeness as well as achievement. A successful family is a reflection of a successful woman. Mothers generally also expect children to help them when they get older, not only providing material assistance but becoming caregivers: 'There will be children one can lean on when one grows old,' explained a survey respondent in Rama. 'When a woman grows old, no one will attend to her if she does not have children,' stated a focus group member in Tabi. And in Bagbag, a woman in the validation study said: 'Children are the hope of their parents, for children will help their parents.' Indeed, for mothers with grown-up children, their own self-worth is measured in terms of the care accorded by their children. Divina, fifty-nine, who has eight living children, says: 'If you have taken care of your children well, then your children will also be good to you.'

Negotiating economic autonomy through motherhood

Even as they labour under traditions and norms, most respondents attempt to redefine motherhood through negotiation, to parlay the ideology of motherhood into a broader range of entitlements. The extent to which they are able to do this depends on several factors, primarily their ability to work outside the home. The ability to earn their own money and the knowledge acquired through work or community participation allow women to challenge the power disparities enshrined within the tradition of motherhood.

A majority of life story and survey respondents had worked at some point in their lives, many starting in their mid-teens. Typically they became domestic helpers and laundry workers, extensions of their homemaker roles, although service occupations – including sales clerk, cashier, waitress, cook, and health worker – have become more common among the daughters, reflecting urbanization and the growth of the service economy. Among those who were not working, most cited family responsibilities. 'No matter how much I wanted to work, there is no one I can leave my children with,' said a survey participant in Bagbag. Child care is a problem for women in cities, where they lack the support of relatives to take care of children.

Cecilia, a young woman in Bagbag who defined herself as a full-time housewife, also took charge of the meals for workers in her husband's cottage industry. In so doing, she avoided opposition from her husband, another reason women cited for not working. Despite the recently enacted Family Code, which protects women's right to work, men still view any movement outside the domestic sphere as cause for alarm.[13] In order to avoid this, a number of life story participants found work within their husbands' geographical and psychological domain, engaging in farming, gardening, livestock raising and the like. Laila told her husband that she wanted to help out in the rice fields so that he could avoid paying for extra labour. Others started working when their husbands could not find work or had lost a job. This was especially true in Bagbag: when Dada was living with her first husband, for example, she found it impossible to feed six children on his income as a shoemaker so she went to work as a laundrywoman. So did her daughter Jean, whose husband could not find a job during the first years of their marriage.

Almost all respondents had worked to support their families before marriage. Alice, seventy-two, was able to escape her father's control over her life when her aunt arrived from Manila when she was fifteen. The aunt managed to get Alice away from home in Rama, saying that she needed someone to help care for her children, just for three months. The three months became three years. Alice was happy: she felt that she was making her own way in the world, earning her own money, choosing her own friends.

In fact, despite compelling economic circumstances, many respondents associated working with nonmonetary returns: joy in seeing a new place, learning new things, having new experiences. Terya, now sixty, as a young women in Rama dreamed of working in Manila, 'just to set foot in Manila, as the others said it was a nice place'. Many of the women have become active in community organizations. Tisay, forty, is secretary of a local peasant organization and a women's health group and is public relations officer for a district committee for the disabled in Tabi. She finds fulfilment in thinking about others and is stimulated by learning about national issues. Isabel, forty-two, recently started to work as a health worker and joined a community organization in Bagbag, despite her husband's objections. As a health worker, she says, 'I enjoy learning a lot of things. The knowledge that I gain from attending seminars and conferences gives me a sense of fulfilment, something I'd missed in formal schooling.'

Respondents dream of starting small businesses. As their children grow up, many start small neighbourhood stores called 'sari-sari' stores or engage in small-scale trading. Most do so to augment the family income, either for a special purpose, such as study, or to buy necessities like gas, groceries, or clothes. Pining, a Rama woman whose husband's drinking is the cause of continual conflict, explains:

> I used to sell shorts. In one month, I travelled three times. Every time I was away for five days selling these shorts, I earned about P300, sometimes P400 in one week. When I came home I would buy rice, coffee, sugar, things for the children, school supplies, slippers. Now that I don't have any business, I can't give my children anything.

Lucy, who lives in Rama, saw work as a way to occupy her time, apart from the domestic world, while supplementing the family income. Recently she joined her mother Divina in a small handicraft business, dealing in hand-woven mats. When her husband wanted to build a fishing boat, she pretended she had borrowed money:

> But I had money saved and put away inside the hem of my dress that I never wear.... The following day, I gave him a thousand pesos and told him to go and order the hull. Afterward, he worked hard to save money to pay our debt. He would not even drink. He was a heavy drinker. He said, 'Since we have a debt to pay, I will not drink for the time being.' He would drink only once a week, a bottle of beer before going to sleep. The money that he gave me to pay our debt, I would sew again into the hem of my dress.

Women working outside the home gain the skills and the financial resources to exploit opportunities that enhance their position within and outside the household. Economic independence expands options, enabling them to push for more equitable relations with men, especially in relation to the household finances and the right to be free from violence. From there women might be able to decide the timing or circumstances of their pregnancies, the number of children, and the enjoyment of their own sexuality. Asked about how work influences women's right to decide the number of their children, for example, respondents stated clearly that if women do not work outside the home and contribute to the family income, they are constrained to have as many children as their husbands wish. While working does not convey this right automatically, a woman who does not earn cannot put any conditions at all on the marriage, they said. These women know they derive happiness, satisfaction, and health from having jobs.

Life story respondents confirmed that women are 'allowed' to engage in the arena of work only so long as it does not explicitly challenge the norm that women are meant for the home and reproduction. As such, it is an acceptable arena where women can stretch their wings. Working is seen as less forgivable if the woman declares that she wants her own life. The findings suggest that the women at least instinctively realize this. They know they can pursue a job outside the home without fear, because it is not seen as too threatening to the women's responsibilities in motherhood and domesticity.

And yet the experience of some women suggests the power of work to undermine this ideology of domesticity. When the women became the sole breadwinner, for example, there was usually a shift in roles. Cecilia's husband, for instance, took care of the household tasks in order to enable her to leave early for the market to sell her wares. While decision making for most respondents was limited to household management and childrearing, those who were more or less major earners took on more authority. Lucy illustrates how her status also changed the power relations in the family.

While resting from her business after giving birth, she said: 'Now that I am not doing any business, I still have control over the earnings. I am the one who tells Mando to go on a (fishing) trip; if I tell him to go fishing, he will go fishing. If I tell him to buy and sell dried fish this week, he will do it.'

It is clear that for some women, waged work can provide at least a short-term alternative to early marriage. Although it may be temporary, the possibility of new life situations for women prior to marriage and therefore outside marriage, and thus even the possibility of leaving an oppressive marriage, has been created. Ludy, who lives in Tabi, started to work when she was seventeen, in part to earn her own money, in part to meet other people and learn how to deal with them, and in part to add to her knowledge through additional experience. First she cooked, cleaned, and did the laundry in her aunt's house. She made friends with other young women from Gubat who were trying their fortunes in the big city and found work in a garment factory. But the employer's wife was too critical, and she left after three weeks. She was not worried: 'Anyway, I am still a young girl, with no family to think of.' In this way, work offers a potential challenge to the institution of marriage and family.

Work experience in itself, however, does not guarantee a woman's power within the household. For instance, Laida, twenty-four, who started working as a housemaid in Rama at age fifteen, obediently allowed her parents and grandparents to marry her off to a man she hardly knew. 'It didn't matter to me,' she said: 'I felt I was immature so I just followed my grandfather.' On the other hand, Julia, twenty-seven, who went to Manila and became a sex worker, finds herself retreating in a marital conflict so as not to provoke her husband's ire. In both cases, the women never went outside the patriarchal authority structure.

This implies that not merely earning income but the kind of income-generating activity women engage in and their economic activity after marriage are critical factors in determining whether work becomes part of an empowerment process. The women who are either self-employed or are engaged in nontraditional economic activity appear to have a greater sense of their personhood, giving them more latitude in decision-making processes at home. Marla, twenty-two, who earned an independent income as a factory worker in Bagbag, appears to have no major complaint regarding her marriage. She has had no experience with domestic violence, unlike the other respondents; the one time her husband joked about hitting her, she fought him.

'Puno na ako' – *negotiating respect and freedom in marriage*

While motherhood helps to motivate women to negotiate the right to work outside the home, or take decisions about family resources, it also serves to keep them in unhappy marriages. Some accommodated their husbands' drinking, for example, so long as the men were responsible or drank only at certain times. Pining first resisted her husband's drinking by not letting him inside the house, and later by not speaking to him. She left him, but was forced to reconcile after her children pleaded with her. As Tisay, now forty, who endured domestic violence for about thirteen years, put it: 'Marriage entails a lifetime commitment for the children's sake.'

Respondents resisted their husbands' downgrading of their self-worth. Divina was insulted by her husband's complaint that she was always eating when she did not have any work. She was furious and answered back, 'I don't have any work!? How about these childbirths, childrearing, and housework? Even if you pay me thousands of pesos, I don't enjoy having to give birth so often.' Her husband tried to reconcile with her, saying that she could get his salary. Instead, Divina brought their children to him and said, 'I did not come here to get your salary because I will not eat or live on your salary; I know how to earn a living.'

Above all, all life history respondents insisted that husbands have no right to be violent with them and wives have the right to protect themselves against domestic violence. When beaten, some fought back, even if it became a scandal in the community. Tisay threw stones at their house while Julia, after being beaten up by her husband, insulted him publicly, then ran and hid, later seeking refuge in her parents' house. Madel's mother-in-law, herself a victim of wife battering, encouraged Madel to get a weapon. When Madel took her advice and started sleeping with a knife beside her, her husband no longer dared to hit her.

Those who could not find a way to stop their husbands' violence eventually left them. Neither the law nor the Catholic Church recognizes divorce, while annulment, which is recognized, is a tedious process and entails money, time and effort. Walking out, while looked down upon as a transgression of Catholic values, is the only alternative; among the twenty-eight respondents, four mothers and a daughter had permanently separated from their husbands. Two mothers separated for a time (one for one year, the other for four years) but later reconciled with their spouses.

Tisay decided to leave her husband after six children and thirteen years. She faults her husband for his excessive drinking and the little support he gave the family financially as well as in the house. By the time she left him, their fights had got worse, and he had begun to beat her up. She concluded: 'If the husband and wife do not get along at all, it is very difficult for them to live with each other. In this case, it would be better to separate than to go through too much pain and trouble.' Now single, she would think twice about remarrying, even though she has a boyfriend. 'Women do not deserve to be abused by men,' she says.

Her mother, Alice, also left her husband. He was always scrounging around for money, Alice explained, because he used up the rice production money to buy liquor. Worse, when he got drunk, he would try to hit her. He also never helped around the house. She put up with all this for twenty years, but when their only child stopped schooling and got married, she decided there was no more reason for her to stay. Fatima left her husband when he began to gamble and lose all his money, leaving nothing for family expenses. After landing a job to support her children, she decided to separate from him. For Dada, now sixty-one, it was her husband's womanizing, which began after only a few years of their living together, that became the source of conflict. Though he never physically hurt her, she could not tolerate his infidelity and finally left him, even though they had six children.

For all these women, the breaking point came from a combination of several factors: their husbands' vice, usually linked to a dwindling capacity to provide and a propensity towards violence, emboldened them to leave. It seems that no one of these factors by themselves would be enough to provoke such a monumental decision. Together, they enable the woman to stand up for her entitlement: *Puno na ako* ('I'm fed up') is how the women talked about this point. Validation survey participants emphasized that becoming the husband's possession extended only to the body and not to the *kalooban*, or inner self. Above all, it does not give men the right to inflict violence. When this happens, said one, 'I fight back; he doesn't own me anymore.'

It should be noted that, except for Alice, all the women who had left or tried to leave were from twenty to thirty-five years old. Divina, in challenging her husband for a separation, said: 'I will not go after you, I am still young, I can still find a man better than you.' And while families often try to persuade their daughters to stay in bad marriages, their support is also critical in enabling the women to flee. When Tisay's parents promised support after yet another fight with her husband, she never returned. All the women who separated went back to their parents. Finally, a critical element in their ability to resist violence is the ability to support themselves. Though Madel's husband stopped hitting her when she got the knife, they both recognized that, by that time, she had also begun to raise pigs, so she could support her child by herself. Cecilia, who managed the family finances, could not stand arguing about them, especially as the fights became serious. She decided not to take any money from her husband and went back to vending so that she could support the family. And when Lucy's husband hit her during a serious fight she grabbed him and pointed a knife at him, driving him out of the house. Although her in-laws persuaded her to take him back she knew she could manage without him: 'I can say that I am now economically independent from my husband, for I already earn my own money,' she concluded.

Sexuality and fertility - still only sanas

Women's ability to negotiate *dapat* is far less successful in the realm of sexuality and fertility than in that of working outside the home or resisting violence. Their relative powerlessness in this arena stems from the strict expectations and restrictions surrounding the institution of marriage in the Philippines, laid down by the Catholic Church and cemented by state and community norms and tradition. In the main, husbands are believed to have a sexual right to their wives, while this does not hold true for wives. Instead, virtually all the life story respondents stated that women are duty bound to provide for their husbands' sexual needs regardless of their own preferences. Tonyang, who has seven children, said, 'If it were not for the fact that he is my husband.... I really do not want to have sex with him anymore.' Alice, who was forced into marriage by her father, refused to have sex with her husband on their first night, but because she had given herself to the man in marriage, subsequently she abided by his wishes. These attitudes were confirmed by the follow-up survey; more than half the respondents said they give in to their husbands' sexual demands because they view it as their obligation.

Although sexual relations with their husbands left much to be desired, few respondents gave sexual satisfaction high priority. Most said they felt embarrassed by initiating sex, let alone demanding satisfaction. The Catholic Church teaches that sexual relations occur only within marriage, and solely for the purpose of procreation; thus women are supposed to be passive recipients and not to be obsessed with sex or satisfaction. Few husbands bothered to understand the wife's feelings and body. Only one of the life story respondents said that her husband waited a while after marriage before they had sex to give her time to get used to him. No one expressed any regret for not having an active sex life for many years, and most were evasive when the issue of sexual dissatisfaction was raised. Moreover, fear of pregnancy and the financial difficulties entailed, plus the added burden of another child to rear, generally obliterated their desire for sexual satisfaction.

For all but two of the life story respondents, the first experience with sex was with their husbands. Though some indulged in premarital sex, they eventually ended up marrying the same men. Many were not prepared for sex on the first night of their marriage. Terya, who eventually gave birth to fourteen children, recalled that at first she could not sleep because her husband wanted to sleep beside her. When she told her parents, they laughed and told her, 'That is why he married you, because he wants to sleep with you.' It was over two weeks before the marriage was consummated.

In spite of the difficulties, some notion of entitlement to sexual pleasure sometimes managed to survive. Ana, a 46-year-old mother from Bagbag, and Terya, a 60-year-old mother from Rama, said that one of the reasons for marrying is to be able to indulge in sex, so naturally they want to enjoy it. The daughters' generation fared slightly better. Most of them knew about sex prior to their first sexual intercourse. Some had some sex education in high school, although limited only to its biological aspect. For the most part they picked up what they knew about sex from romance novels or videos. Lucy, who is thirty-eight, admitted: 'I enjoy sex, for sometimes one is relieved of one's problems.' Some of these younger women, like Tisay and Julia, believed that women may initiate sex as well, although in practice they rarely did so themselves, and never directly. Julia insisted, 'Of course a woman has the right to be made happy during sex, not only the man.' Minia, married with seven children, cautiously stated that she didn't think it was bad for women to be able to say when they want to have sex.

For many poor women, however, sexual relations simply reinforce the sense of belonging to the husband. Over three-quarters of those in the follow-up survey said that by virtue of marriage a woman is her husband's possession, or *pag-aari*. Basyon, sixty-two, who eloped at sixteen, was not allowed to sleep with her husband because she had not yet menstruated. When the time came, she was happy that she could engage in sex. But there was sadness too:

> With the commencement of sexual relations and its pain, it came to me that I belonged from that time on only to my husband. It hit me that marriage meant that I was tied to my husband and that the time of hardships would come.

Overall, respondents' attitude toward sex is captured by the phrase *basta makaraos*, 'so long as one gets it over with'. Women seem to weigh the cost of refusing their husbands' sexual demands against what they may gain from giving in. A peaceful relationship within the family is highly valued. Thus many concede to sex in order to avoid their husbands' anger or jealousy. Help with household chores is also important, and the wife's agreeing to have sex usually puts the man in a cooperative mood.

What was clear, however, is that in practice the women often are ready to assert their own needs and to evade their 'duty' when it comes to unwanted sex, and they employ many tactics to do so. Almost all the life history respondents, especially among the older women, said that if they are really tired they defy their husbands' expectations and accept the consequences. In order to resist the advances of her drunken husband, one woman refuses to let him lie down with her, while another lies down flat on her stomach. Some take their babies to sleep with them, thus forcing the husband to sleep elsewhere. Minia, who is fifty-five with seven children, has used her weak health as an excuse to avoid sexual relations for several years. Clara, also fifty-five, wears sanitary napkins to send the message that she has her period, or contorts her body while sleeping so as to avoid arousing her husband. Sometimes, the women feign frigidity. Tasing, who got married at sixteen and has fifteen children, said, '[My husband] complains that I am like a corpse.' Others refuse to take a bath at night or sleep only when their husbands start to snore. One usually starts a quarrel with her husband so he sleeps by himself. This willingness to face the consequences of refusal becomes a form of entitlement for these women, even in this difficult area. It can be heard in the frequent expression *Pag sinabi kong ayoko na, ayoko na!* ('When I say I don't want it, I don't want it!')

Fertility control: 'I am the one who is burdened'

Sustaining their determination in resisting their husbands' desire for sex is the fear of becoming pregnant. Didi, who at age forty-three has eleven children, asks, 'How can you enjoy when it means more children?' Ironically, while women are seen as mainly responsible for reproduction, they have little power to control it. On the one hand they are expected to gratify their husbands' frequent demands for sex, and on the other they are expected to bear the main worry over the quality of their children's lives. Compounding this problem, especially for women in poor communities, is the difficulty of obtaining satisfactory methods of birth control and accurate information about various options. Because of the continued hostility of the Catholic Church, social and community norms still discourage family planning; frequently women are told that all kinds of birth control are 'a sin against God'. Basyon recalled how the elders used to say, 'Don't use family planning because it involves dissolving a child within you.'

Lack of control over reproductive decision-making resulted in many unwanted pregnancies. Though both mothers and daughters said that they did not want 'many mouths to feed', they were unable to realize this preference. More often than not, pregnant women were resigned to having the baby. As Basyon put it: 'I felt there was nothing left to do but wait for the baby to come out and grow up. One cannot return it once it's there.' This attitude is shared by both mothers and daughters, who see children as 'gifts from God'.

All these factors resulted in large families among all of the life history respondents.[14] They were largest in Rama, with 8.5 births on average to each woman, while in the other two communities the average was 6.5. There is also a marked difference between the mean number of births for the older women (10.3) and their daughters (3.2). While it is true that the latter's reproductive years are not yet over, and in fact four of this group were pregnant at the time of the interview, it is also true that the younger women are endeavouring to use birth control much earlier in their reproductive careers, often with the agreement of their husbands.

A large majority of the life history respondents have used some form of contraception at some time in their reproductive lives: fifteen had used the pill, three had had IUDs, and three had been sterilized, while eighteen had used various natural methods, including the rhythm method, withdrawal, herbal preparations, or abstinence. But at the time of the study, only nine of the twenty-one nonmenopausal women used any form of birth control, all of them natural; those who were not pregnant mostly tried to avoid sex. Women who had stopped using contraception explained that their efforts had met with varying degrees of success; some noted side effects or husbands' hostility as a reason for not continuing to use it. Older women mentioned the absence of family planning awareness during their reproductive years as a reason why they had more children than they wanted.[15]

While the types of contraceptives used do not differ significantly between the older and younger women in this study, younger women tend to use these methods earlier; eleven of the younger women used some form of contraception after the first, second, or third child, while only four of the older women did so. Some of the younger women feel their lives were constrained by the lack of family planning by their own mothers. Julia views her rape and initiation into the sex industry when she was sixteen as the direct consequence of coming from such a large family:

> If only we had not been poor, I would not have thought of going to Manila to work. And if I had not gone to Manila, then that tragedy would not have happened to me. It's as if everything that happens has a root. So the root is being poor. Look at us, it's because there were so many of us.

Before she got married she wanted 'only a few children, around four. But after I had experienced the difficulties of pregnancy and childbirth, caring for the baby, washing the diapers ... my goodness, two are enough!' Julia now uses the pill; although she has tried relying on natural methods, she says that refusing her husband's advances simply fuelled his suspicions that she was having an affair.

Julia is one of two women who reported having had an abortion. She became pregnant when she was a sex worker and decided on an abortion in the sixth month, a decision that still haunts her:

> I only saw her when she came out. I wanted to put her back, but I could not do anything anymore. I can still see how she looked, especially when I am alone. The midwife who performed the abortion even said, 'This one would have been beautiful.' ... I never knew what they did with the baby....

For women in the older generation, this kind of decision could only be made after having many children. Isabel, for example, always viewed abortion as a sin. She tried using the pill early, after her first child, but was advised to discontinue using it when she started to lose weight. She then had seven more children in quick succession. When she got pregnant for the ninth time her youngest was less than a year old. So she decided to have an abortion. 'I cannot continue with this pregnancy. I am already forty-two, too old to conceive another child. Besides, it is embarrassing to be bearing a child when two of my daughters are at the same time pregnant.' Younger women, who are using contraception earlier, may not have to face such decisions, at least not yet. Isabel's daughter Marla, for example, whose inability to get regular supplies of the pill resulted in her third pregnancy, would not consider having an abortion.

While economic independence enables women to demand the right to more control over household decisions, this is greatly limited when it comes to fertility. Divina and her daughter Lucy, whose successful handicraft business has allowed them to assert some independence *vis-à-vis* their husbands, illustrate this. As Divina says, 'That's why we were married, to have children. But sometimes I would have liked to have been able to control my pregnancy. I would have liked to have only six children. For me, six is just the right number I can attend to.' At fifty-nine, she has had eleven children, eight of whom are still living. Her daughter wanted five children. After their fifth child, Lucy thought of taking the pill but her husband objected, saying they still did not have a son. At thirty-eight, she has had nine children.

Thus while there are differences between the generations, these are less significant than one might expect, reflecting the fact that options are still very limited for women in poor communities. Life history respondents, for one reason or another, got married and settled down in the same community. Their attitudes toward reproductive health, like health in general, are framed by the conditions of poverty that still constrain every aspect of their lives. In Tabi, for example, women ask themselves, Can I still do what I have to do? If the answer is yes, they do not define themselves as sick. Moreover, despite the fact that reproductive health and family planning are now a central part of state policy, providers at the local level often subvert the policy. The midwife in Tabi, responsible for making contraception available, admits she opposes contraception. In Rama, when Divina went to see what she could do to prevent another pregnancy after her tenth child, the doctor told her: 'Your uterus is still thick. You can have sixteen children!'

The paucity of health clinics makes poor women more susceptible to hearsay, usually based on community norms that frown upon artificial fertility control methods. For instance, Alice had heard stories that a neighbour's IUD got dislodged and found its way to the woman's heart; Tasing was afraid of the pill because of the 'horror stories' about side effects; and Laida would not take it because they were poor and often hungry, and a recent public health campaign had stressed that one should not take pills on an empty stomach. Respondents in the validation survey voiced similar fears. One shared a frightening story of a woman whose belly swelled up; when she had it operated on, it was said to have been full of the pills she took.

Still, giving birth to a child each year, year after year, women become tied to the home. As women become entrenched in the role of lifebearer and caregiver, they are frequently pushed to the point of exhaustion and weakness. At the same time, their rights as mothers to ensure a better life for their children is curtailed when they have too many children to care for. In this light, Ludy stated, 'It is not just a matter of giving birth. What I am after is a good future for the children.'

Thus, more and more respondents had begun to think about birth control. Five mothers and three daughters saw it as their right to refuse their husbands' sexual advances, especially since it is they who would be burdened with childbirth and child care. When this failed, they began to use artificial methods. Consultations with health workers regarding contraception then become both a right and a form of resistance. Basyon, after giving birth to her seventh child, went to the health centre and asked for birth control pills, asking the nurse to keep it a secret from her husband: 'One must think, what is more destructive, having children you cannot care for properly, or planning not to have them?' Some women who would not consider abortion nevertheless resorted to traditional methods to which the community subscribes. Tasing took *maravillosa* (a concoction from the root of a bitter plant that, in traditional knowledge, is an effective abortifacient). Two other life history respondents took *papaitan*, a native concoction used 'to regulate menstruation', at the urging of their mothers-in-law.

Ultimately, respondents have learned that it is they who bear the responsibility for their children's lives. As a woman in a focus group in Bagbag explained: 'My husband wants more children but I tell him that he should be the one to bear them.... After all, I am the one who gets burdened at home.' In this sense, therefore, motherhood itself taught these women the right to say no to unwanted sexual relations and unplanned pregnancies. For some respondents in the validation survey, this sense of entitlement extended even to challenging the church's interference in family planning policy. When asked whether the church should interfere in the use of contraceptives, almost half said no. 'Religion and health are two different matters,' said one woman in Bagbag; 'This is not in the church's domain,' said another; and a third remarked, 'It is not the church that will go hungry and experience poverty.'

Accommodation, resistance, and the negotiations in between

All these findings indicate that women's ability to negotiate entitlements depends on several conditions. First, while access to economic resources does not automatically empower women to assert their entitlement to make decisions about their own bodies and sexuality, it is a necessary starting point. Some respondents have clear conceptions of their entitlement but do not possess the resources necessary to try to assert these conceptions openly. In their recourse to subterfuge, these women in effect are negotiating the difference between what they want (*sana*), and what is in their power to achieve. On the other hand, other women have vague ideas of their rights, but fall prey to the ideology of domesticity and its internalization by virtually everyone in their family and community – a powerful resource in a traditional society. These accommodations have little to do with the norms of reproductive rights that most of the women share. Rather, they demonstrate the effect of differences in power and resources on the women's abilities to put those beliefs into practice. Looking across the categories in which grassroots women negotiate entitlements, three interrelated areas of family life emerge as arenas in which accommodation and resistance operate in different ways, namely: the sexual division of labour, sexual relations and fertility control, and the right to be free of violence.

The sexual division of labour, which by tying women to motherhood and caregiving has long deprived women of their right to develop their full potential, simultaneously provides some women with leverage *vis-à-vis* their husbands to improve their own and their family's plight. The husbands' inability to perform their traditional provider role, along with the women's increasing ability to take on this role, enables women to negotiate for greater authority within the household. Some were even able to extend these negotiations to family planning; Laida's husband eventually relented in his opposition to birth control upon realizing the difficulty of raising too many children. Women can work within the sexual division of labour and the ideology of domesticity to assert their *sanas*; in so doing they acquire the moral agency to pursue their right to share household decision-making and even a level of autonomy without provoking a confrontation with their husbands or stirring controversy in the community.

In negotiating rights within marriage, on the other hand, respondents typically went back and forth between accommodation and resistance. Despite the fact that Philippine women of all classes are raised to believe that marriage strips them of the right to refuse the husband's sexual desires, a few of the respondents have gone beyond the use of subterfuges to avoid sex and have begun to talk to their husbands about their visions of sexual entitlement, while others have begun to acknowledge the importance of their own desires even if they still express them through limited hints rather than more direct assertions.

Negotiations on fertility are also characterized by a mix of accommodation, subtle resistance, and overt resistance. Women opt for accommodation and muted resistance when they cannot dismiss their husbands' sexual demands, even during their fertile days. Within these interrelated sites of negotiation, some women revealed a growing sense of entitlement, due to their accumulation of resources, whether material or social. Only when it comes to violence and resisting unwanted sex are women empowered to act on their entitlement, eventually even leaving their husbands, usually after they have tried every other form of negotiation. To recognize that 'he doesn't own me anymore' is a reclaiming of the self and an assertion of personhood.

Nevertheless, such a progression does not fully determine women's status. As noted, it is difficult to identify factors that might allow women to shift the power balance. Economic autonomy, while it gives women greater confidence to negotiate for greater respect and the right to make household decisions, does not translate automatically into power to determine how many children they will have. Women may gain some power in some areas while retaining their vulnerability in others. This suggests that grassroots women make strategic calculations about the cluster of strategies at their disposal; different degrees of success reflect women's specific cultural and material situations, the degree to which they can depend on family or community organization or their ability to earn their own income, rather than different levels of awareness.

Despite the vicissitudes of married life, women continue to struggle to hold on to their dreams, which usually translate into a mother's desire for a better future for her children. The bulk of women's aspirations were not for themselves but for their children and their children's children – especially regarding education. Though some life history respondents complained of mothers who prevented their education, others in both generations resisted life's difficulties and their unfinished schooling by advising their children to study. They also tried to pass on their lives' lessons to their children. Tonyang advised her daughters not to go out with a gang while Minia reminded her daughters not to be *magaslaw* ('crude'), which she says gives men reason to abuse them. Both mothers and daughters hope that their children will not travel the same route as they did. Alice hoped her daughter would have 'a quiet life and a husband who knows how to live in the right way', and Fatima warned her daughter 'not to expect married life to be rosy'.

Women in both generations asserted their right to be able to give their children a good future. Like the decision to work outside the home, this can be seen as a form of self-assertion. Resistance to their life situations is also expressed through the lessons they shared with their children. Cautioning their daughters against the possible pitfalls a woman may encounter and suggesting coping and fightback mechanisms that are open to her can be seen as a form of healing for the mothers and an entitlement for the daughters.

Conclusions

Our research findings suggest several conclusions about reproductive rights in grassroots Philippine communities. The first is that underpinning the repeated acts of subterfuge and resistance lies a persistent assertion by the women we interviewed of their own rights to reproductive freedom. As the women's life stories reveal, grassroots women's pursuit of their entitlements begins when they feel a gap between what they want (*sana*) – the basis for identifying their entitlements – and what is accorded them in a given situation. Such a gap breeds a feeling of discontent, prompting the women to begin a process of negotiation to attain a better situation for themselves.

The respondents' use of subtle subversions and muted struggles as well as their oscillation between accommodation and resistance can be seen as falling within the disempowered's tradition of everyday resistance, as elaborated by James Scott (1990). Scott argues that subordinated groups, aware of their relative powerlessness and the danger of direct confrontation, typically employ indirect, veiled, and tactical forms of opposition ('practical forms of political struggle') against dominant forces. As he points out, 'all political actions take forms that are designed to obscure their intentions or to take cover behind an apparent meaning' even as such actions constantly test 'the limits of the permissible'.

The entire debate over reproductive rights in the Philippines has been laced with assertions that Catholicism, which defines women's role within the family, makes women unwilling to exercise their rights in the reproductive process. This research demonstrates that despite the power of tradition – especially regarding women's roles – it nevertheless exists alongside a vibrant and counterhegemonic tradition, according to which women assert these rights through various strategies, usually covert or camouflaged but sometimes openly resistant. Anyone who takes seriously the words and stories of the women in this study must question the assumption that a woman's silence is the same as her acquiescence, that a failure to construct a better life is the same as a failure to try. Moreover, far from sustaining the idea that Filipina women do not value their ability to control their own reproduction, this study suggests that a conception of reproductive rights dominates women's thinking about their sexuality and roles in society.

This recognition is directly related to another important conclusion: that the sense of reproduction that informs grassroots' women's decisions extends far beyond biological reproduction. The role of the mother is constructed in broad social terms, to extend to issues of care giving and social reproduction. Hence, when these women engage in struggles in their families and communities about ostensibly economic matters, they are doing so according to the terms of this expanded and social definition of motherhood, one in which fertility management plays an integral part. Rather than accepting the traditional conception of motherhood, women in this study worked with their own, counterhegemonic conception, which at times gives them the impetus to pursue activities and roles outside community norms: becoming primary breadwinners, for example, or resisting violence with weapons.

Nevertheless, the fragmented and subtle assertion of entitlement by grassroots women also reveals how vulnerable they are, how easily they may fail, and how well aware they are of this vulnerability. While women may advance in certain areas, such as work outside the home, this power does not necessarily translate to other more intimate areas, such as marital relations. Moreover, everyday resistance, precisely because of its nonconfrontational nature, by itself can work only at best to ameliorate oppression and at worst to distract women from engaging in collective, open, political actions. Women's lack of power in the household cannot be isolated from the constraints imposed by the larger society. Poverty, lack of access to health services, and the pervasive ideology of domesticity and passivity, upheld not only by the church but also by state and community officials, doctors and health workers, and members of the community and family, all have a direct bearing on women's appreciation and exercise of reproductive rights.

While the efforts to act on their *sanas* show that in many ways the Catholic Church can no longer dominate their decisions (few of the women attend church regularly or go through Catholic ceremonies for marriage or childbirth), in the reproduction of tradition one sees the influence of generations of church teachings – upheld by state policy and legal norms –

on the ideology of domesticity. That ideology virtually defines women in terms of producing and reproducing children, and, though it affects the lives of women of all classes, it flourishes in the poverty and hardship of poor communities. In these communities, moreover, as in poor communities everywhere, church doctrine also does much to reinforce the attitude that people, and poor people especially, cannot control their destinies.[16]

This analysis of grassroots women's efforts to negotiate entitlements in reproductive and sexual domains points to the important role that the women's movement can play to advance women's overall position in society. The women's movement, insofar as it offers a gender analysis of women's marginalization as well as services to meet specific women's needs, represents a powerful resource for grassroots women in their pursuit of self-determination. As feminist organizations attempt to bring public policy into line with the norms and values expressed by women themselves, they can likewise deepen grassroots women's understanding of their own situation and expand their capacity to transform it. Appreciating the negotiated order wherein women are subsumed presents a challenge to feminists, however. Advocates of women's empowerment have worked to broaden opportunities for women's growth in the social, political, and cultural spheres. Yet women's empowerment also entails the recognition of every woman's right to choose the kind of life she wants for herself as well as her right to a space wherein she can reflect on her life and construct its meanings. Thus, while feminists work to advance an enabling environment for women, they must leave the question of choice to the women themselves. If grassroots women's negotiated entitlements demonstrate a conception of rights that differs from those of the dominant discourse, both advocates and policy makers must begin to account for such contextually specific readings of rights. Clearly, the conception of rights expressed in the voices and stories of the women represented in this study differs sharply from those that inform the construction of public policy. One can only assume that if the policy does not conform to women's conceptions of their own rights, it is because policy makers have been working under false assumptions of what those rights entail.

Reproductive and sexual entitlement comes precisely from women's self-generated ideas of what it means to be a woman and a mother in their communities. In turn, those meanings, as illuminated through the voices of the women whose life stories inform this research, are constructed out of the contradictory pulls between harsh material realities, patriarchal traditions, and a burgeoning sense of self. Hence, again, the significance of *sana*, for it marks out the difference between what these (particular and contextually specific, rather than universal and generic) women are, and what they feel they should be.

Table 7.2 Women Interviewed

Rama

NAME	AGE	EDUCATION	MARITAL STATUS	WORK OUTSIDE THE HOME	NO. OF CHILDREN (NO. LIVING)	BIRTH CONTROL METHOD
Mothers						
Divina	59	2 years High	Married	Variety store	11(8)	Menopause
Didi	43	Grade 6	Married	Laundress	11	Avoids sex
Terya	60	Grade 5	Married	Raises pigs	14 (7)	Menopause
Pining	49	Grade 5	Married	Vendor	10	Avoids sex
Daughters						
Lucy	38	1 year High	Married	Vendor	9 (8)	Avoids sex
Madel	22	Grade 5	Married	Raises pigs	1	Pregnant
Rona	31	Grade 4	Married	Food vendor	4	Pregnant
Laida	24	Elementary	Married	Raises pigs	3	Pregnant

Bagbag

NAME	AGE	EDUCATION	MARITAL STATUS	WORK OUTSIDE THE HOME	NO. OF CHILDREN (NO. LIVING)	BIRTH CONTROL METHOD
Mothers						
Dada	61	Grade 5	Live-in	None	19 (13)	Menopause
Isabel	42	2 years High	Married	Health worker	8	Rhythm
Clara	55	Grade 4	Live-in	None	8	Menopause
Fatima	37	Grade 6	Married	None	9 (4)	Rhythm
Ana	46	High school	Married	Variety store	5	None
Daughters						
Jean	29	Grade 4	Live-in	Laundress	3	Withdrawal
Marla	22	High school	Live-in	–	2	Pregnant
Cecilia	31	Grade 4	Married	Food vendor	4	Pregnant
Daisy	18	3 years High	Married	–	1	No sex*
Maricar	22	2 years High	Live-in	None	3	None

* Just given birth

Table 7.2, continued

Tabi

NAME	AGE	EDUCATION	MARITAL STATUS	WORK OUTSIDE THE HOME	NO. OF CHILDREN (NO. LIVING)	BIRTH CONTROL METHOD
Mothers						
Tonyang	46	Grade 6	Married	Raises pigs	7	None
Minia	55	Grade 6	Married	Raises pigs	7	Menopause
Basyon	62	Grade 6	Married	Helps with farm	11 (10)	Menopause
Alice	72	Grade 3	Widow	Farming	4 (3)	Menopause
Tasing	45	Grade 6	Married	Variety store Billiard hall Farm	15 (14)	Withdrawal
Daughters						
Lina	21	High school	Married	Raises pigs Small lender	1	Ovulation
Leila	34	1/2 year High	Married	Helps with farm	3	Withdrawal
Ludy	26	2 years High	Live-in	None	2	Not menstruating
Tisay	40	3 years College	Separated	Admin. assist.	6	None
Julia	27	2 years College	Married	None	2	Pill planned

Notes

1 A *barangay* is the smallest unit of government, usually equivalent to a village.

2 In Bagbag and Tabi, local women's groups provided a shortlist of names of women who were qualified for the study; in Rama, where there is no women's organization, the researcher lived with the local midwife and was thus able to meet the women in the community.

3 Other religions include Protestant (9 per cent) and Muslim (5 per cent), the latter primarily in the southern island of Mindanao (US State Department 1995).

4 While exports rose by 18 per cent in 1993, imports grew by 22 per cent (Barr 1995).

5 High urban unemployment has forced many women to leave the country. By 1994 they made up 60 per cent of the overseas workforce, working primarily as domestics and entertainers, where they are forced to work long hours and are subjected to sexual abuse (NCRFW 1995).

6 Women in both occupations are subject to frequent abuse. The highly publicized cases of two Filipina domestics, one charged and summarily executed in Singapore for killing a child in her charge and one in the United Arab Emirates who killed an employer who had raped her, brought attention to a widespread problem. A study of

women entertainers in two Philippine cities showed that 22 per cent suffered from sexual violence (POPCOM 1994: 14).

7 A bill to amend the Civil Code, making rape a crime against the person, has passed the Senate but is stalled in the House of Representatives, which rejects the inclusion of marital rape. Two bills recognizing domestic abuse as a crime are currently before Congress, but both require the victim to prove she has been beaten at least twice during the year.

8 The Philippines also has the world's highest incidence of breast cancer, which prompted the World Health Organization to undertake a campaign for early detection (WHO 1997).

9 The same study found a close correlation between use of contraception and the level of education: over 40 per cent of women who complete high school or college use contraception compared with 35 per cent of those with elementary education and only 11 per cent of those with no education.

10 An illustration of what supporters of women's reproductive health are up against: a bill currently before Congress, supported by the government, would increase the maximum penalty for women who have had abortions (and doctors who performed them) to life in prison or death (Easton 1997).

11 A progressive group, Samakana, mobilized urban poor women around issues of housing, water and electricity, day care and other social services.

12 After inviting women to submit nominations for membership in key committees of the technical secretariat of the PFPP, the health department chose only a few, prompting a debate about who should determine the so-called experts.

13 Thus during the validation focus groups, husbands would check up on what was going on and would fetch the women if they went beyond the expected time away.

14 Fertility rates in each location were higher than national norms, for both urban and rural areas. While this partly reflects the fact that the national family planning policy has reached mainly the middle class, leaving poor women with the same limited options, it also reflects the large number of older women in the study, whose childbearing was unaffected by the new policy.

15 It is also worth noting that nine of the women interviewed had given birth to many more children than were currently living; some of them up to five, six, and even seven more. While most of these women were over sixty, three were in their thirties and forties, indicating that infant mortality remains high in these communities.

16 This common belief is summed up in the expression *bahala na* (come what may). Once dismissed as passive fatalism, *bahala na* can also be seen as enabling people to actively confront situations that are full of uncertainty and lack of information rather than run away from them (Enriquez 1992: 49ff).

8 The South Within the North
Reproductive Choice in Three US Communities

DIANNE JNTL FORTE AND KAREN JUDD*

> Twixt the Negroes of the South and the women of the North, all talking about rights, the white man will be in a fix pretty soon.
>
> Sojourner Truth, 1851

The United States is a country of great social, cultural and regional diversity built by successive waves of immigrants. It may be said to be a land of many nations, many peoples. The situation of women – and their attitudes, beliefs, and behaviour concerning that situation – reflects this diversity. Any study of US women's perspectives on reproductive rights can capture only part of this mosaic; this study looks at the terms in which particular groups of women, primarily women of colour, within the small-town South as well as the diverse neighbourhoods of the urban North, express a sense of personal entitlement regarding rights.[1] In so doing, it seeks to give voice to some of those who for too long have been voiceless in discussions about reproductive rights in the United States.

This chapter contrasts women's reproductive lives in three communities, variously defined: Soperton, a rural community in the southern state of Georgia; Washington Heights, a New York City neighbourhood which includes a majority of immigrants from the Caribbean island nation of the Dominican Republic; and District Council 37, a New York City union of municipal employees. All of the communities studied are tied together through migration and immigration. Together they represent a particular instance, one of many such instances in the United States, of what we have called 'the South within the North': women of colour, poor, migrant and immigrant women of all races, indigenous women, or women trapped in pockets of time in places such as Appalachia or the Deep South, illiterate and

---

* This chapter was written in collaboration with Eugenia Acuña and Evelyne Long-champ. It benefited greatly from background research conducted by Dana Ain Davis and Jennifer Nelson as well as Joanna Gould Stuart, who prepared the longer report on which it is based.

without jobs, their lives constrained by church and state 'gatekeepers' invested in maintaining the status quo.[1] All of the women in this study share backgrounds of poverty and limited job opportunities; with the exception of those in the union, now enrolled in a college credit programme, they have few skills and limited education, and their lives are dominated by the struggle to provide for their families. Their voices, confined to silence by the myriad forms of racial and class bias that permeate public policy discussion, reveal some of the terms and categories in which poor women and women of colour understand and give meaning to the idea of rights, including reproductive rights, and within this framework adopt strategies to act on them.

All the women in this study are participants in groups, albeit in different ways and for different goals. Respondents in Soperton, all African American, are involved to varying degrees in a sewing shop and training centre set up by a charismatic activist, Cora Lee Johnson, to enable them to get piecework at factories in adjacent towns. Johnson learned 'the law and the system', as she puts it, and now advocates for food stamps, housing and welfare benefits for her community.[2] Dominican respondents in Washington Heights are members of two different groups: Alianza Dominicana, a large cultural and service organization serving both men and women, and a feminist health and empowerment project located at a Dominican women's centre. In addition to their decision to come to the United States, the women in both groups share a history of rural–urban migration within the Dominican Republic. Often it is they who have initiated this process. As one respondent explained, 'Whoever progressed would take the others.... If one of us got out of a place and did well, she would tell the others and they would follow.... I studied, I started to work and then I started taking everybody to the city.'

Respondents from District Council 37 are all enrolled in a college degree programme sponsored by the union.[3] They reside in different parts of New York City, and include African American, Caribbean, Latina, and white women. They too reflect the country's history of immigration and migration. Some came from the US South, others from Puerto Rico or the Caribbean. Their family histories reflect the economic and social transformations of the last fifty years: 'My parents came from South Carolina,' one said. 'My father was the first to come to New York City. He brought along my mother. He married her here when she was of age, because she came up here when she was sixteen. They brought along with them their culture and their background and that is how they raised their kids.' Another recalled: 'My father and mother came from Virginia and South Carolina. [Life] was difficult because they were sharecroppers. They had to depend on someone else for their money.' Still another: 'I came here with my parents ... my great-grandparents were brought from India as indentured labourers to Guyana, who after abolition started a coconut oil business.'

Despite shared backgrounds of poverty, women's life choices were very different in each of the three communities. The primary factor in shaping these choices was economic: while few have middle-class incomes and most work in nonprofessional jobs, those in the union have steady jobs, with guaranteed health and retirement benefits, while those in the other two communities rely on part-time or seasonal work with no benefits. Second, while all the respondents were participants in some kind of group, it became evident that the nature of the group influenced the awareness women had of themselves as citizens as well as women, and thus too their perception of rights. In general, those who came together to access services or share experiences were less confident of themselves and less certain of their rights than those who participated in groups that politicized the context of work, education and women's roles. A third factor was the nature of the relationship women are able to form with the communities in which they live; for some, survival depends on family and community, while for others it demands a break. Thus, in spite of shared backgrounds of poverty and hardship, the lives of women who stayed in the small-town South are very different from the lives of those who moved to the city, offering a vivid contrast between those who are able to act on their dreams and those who are not.

The chapter draws out these patterns of relationship between education and employment access, participation in organized groups, and the choices poor women make when they have opportunities and those they make when they have none. Issues of rights and identity are deeply entwined with overlapping issues of race, religion and culture as well as jobs and education, poverty and welfare. In deconstructing the women's stories, this chapter seeks to disentangle these forces in order to learn how women view their rights, particularly concerning reproduction; what gives them strength to challenge the odds in order to get what they feel entitled to; and what makes them submit to those odds that seem insurmountable.

The Research Process

The US research team comprised social scientists, women's advocates, grassroots health activists, and health professionals.[4] Recognizing that the attitudes and beliefs of poor women, especially women of colour, are often lost in discussions of reproductive rights, team members decided to focus on women who are participating in organized groups in the belief that they could best articulate such beliefs in ways that might influence the terms of the discussion. Selecting communities that they knew well or in which they had working relationships, researchers conducted in-depth, open-ended interviews and life histories, supplemented with focus groups with volunteers from each organization.[5] They encouraged women to speak about their reproductive histories; their family, employment and educational backgrounds; their cultural and religious ideals; their personal aspirations; the problems they face; and the full range of their needs.

Team members agreed that public discussion of reproductive health and choice in the United States often fails to recognize that reproduction is not limited to fertility control. Rather, in crucial ways, it is determined by the presence or absence of other options to define adulthood for women. Reproduction is 'embedded in a woman's life situation and is shaped not just by medical conditions, but also by social forces and power relationships that range from the level of the family to that of international institutions' (Obermiller 1994: 42). We agreed with Petchesky (1990) that structural conditions contribute heavily to the high rates of abortion and teenage pregnancy that set the United States apart from most industrialized nations: lack of universal health care, enduring poverty and inequality that lead to hopelessness for the future, and a pervasive ambivalence towards female sexuality in the media and political culture. For these reasons, race, class and gender dynamics remain critical factors in the discussion of rights regarding reproduction and sexuality.

At the same time, the US team understood that the women studied might not interpret their specific reproductive experiences as having been shaped by public policies and economic, educational, and social conditions, and that it was our challenge to make the connections between women's lives and reproductive choices and the broader context in which they take place. Too often, feminists have looked at poor women as powerless, not seeing how these women create their own ways to assert their power. The women whose voices are presented here challenge traditional views of poor and marginalized women as helpless victims of sexism, racism and class inequality. They are survivors, fighting to avoid being crushed or paralysed by the enormous daily struggle for survival, dignity, and their sense of self.

Race, Religion and Culture

Historically, the US rural and small-town South has had a self-conscious and identifiable culture, which persists today as a coherent collection of assumptions, values, traditions and commitments. It is characterized by localism, violence, religiosity, political conservatism, racism, poverty, and the legacy of the plantation system, which was sustained by two hundred years of African slavery, beginning in the seventeenth century (Hill 1988: 37). Throughout this history, the South maintained order through deference and customary authority in which all whites had informal police power over all blacks. Throughout the region, which contains a disproportionate number of the nation's poor, the majority of rural blacks are still very poor and undereducated, some remaining quite isolated from mainstream society.

Thus the issue of race is central to understanding how rights are constructed in the rural South. Nowhere is this more true than in Soperton,

Georgia, a town of three thousand people located in Treutlen County, three and a half hours from the state capital, Atlanta. Although on the surface blacks and whites coexist peacefully, one resident said you had to live there to see the reality:

> If you go to the bank and look around there are no blacks in the banks. They had one black girl … they say some money was missing so they fired her. After they fired her the money showed up…. Only two stores in town have any blacks working for them. In the plant where I work there are no black supervisors and some blacks have worked there for thirty years.

Although whites comprise 66 per cent of the county and almost 78 per cent of the South as a whole, Soperton's population is evenly divided between whites and blacks.[6] The town has been run by the same three white families since its inception, and schools were integrated only in 1970. School integration prompted some fights and name-calling but no large-scale overt violence. Soperton continues to have a black school prom (graduation dance) and a white school prom, the latter said to be secretly funded by the school. Segregation in housing is marked, and the black 'elite' has not moved into the exclusive white neighbourhood but has its own residential area. Blacks and whites also attend separate churches. Another aspect of racism shows up in interracial marriage. One respondent remarked: 'In Soperton, there are no interracial marriages but a lot of interracial going together. If a black guy was going with a white girl some of the white people want to put the police after them. But if a black girl is going with a white guy, they don't say anything.'

In the courts, according to some residents, sentencing has the imprint of race; a white person will get probation and a black person will go to prison for the same crime.[7] In 1994, Soperton's only public swimming pool was white-only. In an unusual act of resistance, a petition was signed by blacks to get a black swimming pool. Money was allocated, but no swimming pool was built. Other attempts to alter the status quo have also failed. In many ways, it is as if the civil rights movement has skipped over this town.

Washington Heights, a New York City community district of just under 200,000 people, is extraordinarily dynamic by contrast. A full 44 per cent of the population come from the Dominican Republic, a predominance that has earned this vibrant community the name 'quisqueya heights', after the indigenous name of their island homeland. The streets of Washington Heights are a virtual marketplace, offering yucca and pumpkin, mangoes and papaya, candles and flowers, toys and batteries outside an array of Dominican-owned small shops, money transfer services, driving schools and travel agencies. The Spanish language dominates the streets, orchestrated by *merengues* (dance music) blaring from variety shops or parked cars. Located in the heart of the country's largest urban area, where civil rights struggles have a long history, the Dominican community is intensely political. The first wave of Dominican immigrants followed the US invasion of the Dominican Republic in 1965, when an uprising to restore a populist president ousted by the military prompted fears among the ruling elite of a 'revolution'. Reflecting their highly politicized culture, many Dominicans bracket their lives in terms of 'before the revolution' and 'after the revolution'. Many dream of going back home, and many of them do, once they have finished their education or have saved enough money to build a house.

In 1990, 30 per cent of New York City's population of over 7 million were recent immigrants. While prior to the 1965 US Immigration and Nationality Act the majority of immigrants arrived from Europe and other parts of North America, since 1965 the proportions of immigrants from Asia, South America, and Africa have soared, with the largest increase coming from the Caribbean and Central America. Moreover, a full 40 per cent of Caribbean immigrants and 35 per cent of South American immigrants settled in New York City, including 60.8 per cent of all Dominican immigrants. Dominicans represented the highest proportion of immigrants to New York City during the 1980s – slightly more than one-sixth of the total (NYC DCP 1992a).

Although sex ratios vary by sending country, overall female migrants outnumbered male migrants to New York City during the 1980s, primarily because of the demand for domestics and garment workers. Among Dominicans, the ratio of women to men was 100:94 in 1989. According to the New York City Department of City Planning (NYC DCB 1992a:73), women are increasingly the 'pioneer immigrants, establishing "beachheads" for further immigration'. These women then save the money to sponsor their families and other immigrants. Unlike earlier women immigrants, they are not dependent on their husbands to obtain a 'green card', the US residency and employment permit. Instead, their pioneer status, however difficult, contributes to a sense of positive identity and authority for immigrant women.

Organizing is a way of life in the Dominican community, for women as well as men. Even those who cannot vote participate in campaigning and leafleting. Already they have elected a member of the New York City Council. Women have also formed their own organizations, including the Dominican Women's Development Center and the Dominican Women's Caucus. A few are active in LatiNegra, a Latin American black women's organization in New York City. Thus while the community still expects that women should spend their lives taking care of men, women's expectations of themselves are changing; 'women should be out organizing', respondents said; or 'women should be in school'.

Perhaps surprising in this highly political community, respondents, many of whom are black, said that racism is not a major issue for them. With the second highest population of Latinos in the city (64.4 per cent), the neighbourhood is home to Puerto Ricans, Cubans, Mexicans and Central

Americans as well as Dominicans. Latinos also share the district with African Americans and whites, including increasing numbers of Russian Jews (Garfield and Abramson 1994). Thus unlike the South, where racism is black and white, in Washington Heights discrimination operates along different lines, including language, culture and religion as well as skin colour. Asked about racism, respondents there said they experienced discrimination mostly in terms of language.

The role of religion in Dominican immigrant life is subtly changing. Although virtually all the women were raised as Catholics, many are moving away from the church; they may attend services, but the church no longer determines their decisions, including those related to marriage and children. At best, it offers them a general sense of social identity. Thus, one Dominican woman who was no longer a practising Catholic said: 'I am a single mother ... but if one day I get married, it's with a man who's from the Catholic Church.' For many, the teachings of the church are mediated through the family. Women who need advice seek it from a relative or friend rather than a priest. For younger women, more influenced by their peers, even the problems are changing. Girls growing up in New York are not so sheltered as their mothers were in the Dominican Republic; they take classes in leadership and sex education that would not have been possible back home.

In Soperton, on the other hand, where the majority of residents belong to either Baptist or Pentecostal Protestant sects, religion plays a crucial role in maintaining community norms. A Pentecostal minister acknowledged racism in town, but went on to say 'the real enemy is the devil'. After observing how much land blacks have owned and lost, he said, 'in Christ there is true freedom ... through Christ there is justice'. This man apparently believes that white people and men of all races have a god-given right to rule: 'You can look around and see who God has placed in position,' he said. 'One particular scripture I'm reminded of says promotion comes from the Lord – some of them are wicked but God has a hand in it.' When it comes to the family, he says, 'the man should have the final say'.

For African Americans, especially in the South, the black church historically represented not only the primary social, health, education, and welfare agency, but also the locus of resistance to white domination and, for many, the only arena in which they could make decisions for themselves (Quarles 1989). Today, while it has lost many of these functions, it remains a bedrock of religious salvation as well as the social and cultural nexus of black life. This is especially true in Soperton, where there is no movie theatre or recreational centre and, apart from an annual crafts festival put on by a foreign timber company, only church-sponsored social activities. Not surprisingly, many respondents saw religion as a part of rights; one stated that 'a right is only a right if it is *right*', while another claimed 'a right to Jesus'. Women's groups never really developed in Soperton and women rarely socialize outside the church.

Employment, Poverty, and Welfare

Despite their religious and cultural differences, women's education and employment opportunities in Soperton and Washington Heights are remarkably similar, constrained by the same economic forces that increasingly separate the country's rich and poor. In fact, the United States is now characterized by one of the largest gaps between rich and poor and one of the highest poverty levels in the industrial world. From 1979 to 1993, with successive waves of corporate and public sector layoffs, the real wages of the top 20 per cent of income earners rose by 10.4 per cent while that of the bottom 20 per cent has actually fallen (Gordon 1996). Today the number of Americans living in poverty is nearly 50 million, or 19 per cent of the population (UNDP 1997). More and more women have entered the workforce, clustering primarily in low-wage service industries and increasingly in part-time, temporary, or contract jobs, taking on two and even three jobs to make ends meet.[8] During the 1980s, as manufacturing jobs disappeared, the wages of male workers dropped steeply, gradually reducing the gap in wages between men and women over this period (Mishel, Bernstein and Schmitt 1996). Even so, in 1995 the annual earnings of full-time women workers were still only 71.4 per cent of those of men, while those of black women were 64.2 per cent and those of Latinas only 53.4 per cent of those of white men (US Department of Commerce, Bureau of the Census 1996).[9]

Since the 1950s, the South has been a hot spot for both foreign and domestic manufacturing, lured by cheap labour, low taxes and few unions (Foust 1993). The US South reflects the same dynamics of international trade and global corporate capital that characterize developing countries. In today's South, where employment growth has outstripped the nation as a whole, one out of every four manufacturing workers receives a pay cheque from a foreign employer. Yet restrictions on unions help maintain low wages and a high rate of part-time and seasonal jobs that lack benefits. Today, southern states still rank among the nation's worst in terms of social progress indicators, such as literacy, public expenditure on education, and infant mortality.

Low-paying work is also a staple of the Dominican community in Washington Heights. In 1996, New York City as a whole was still emerging from a severe regional recession. Employment dropped 9.3 per cent from 1989 to 1993, a loss of 334,000 jobs (US Department of Commerce, Bureau of the Census 1993), widening the gap between the educated, skilled workforce whose earnings have actually increased, and the poorer population, more frequently unemployed and with few of the skills required for employment in the city's high-technology industries.

Over the last three decades, as New York City became a major centre of global technological expansion, immigrants have filled its growing demand for low-wage domestic and service jobs, especially in the garment industry. Unions have been slow to try to organize in these sectors, which are heavily dominated by women and immigrants. Unlike public sector jobs, which have offered new economic security to many women, especially black and Latina women, the informal labour market open to immigrant women provides far less steady employment, at much lower wages and without any benefits. In Washington Heights, 59 per cent of men and 39.3 per cent of women reported they were working: 49 per cent in service jobs (hospitals, home care, hotels, restaurants, child care); 18 per cent in factories, and 10 per cent in administrative support. Moreover, 44 per cent of Washington Heights households were headed by a single woman. As a result, 30 per cent of the district population had incomes below the poverty level and 34 per cent received some form of government income support (Garfield and Abramson 1994).[10]

Thus a large percentage of the population in both Soperton and Washington Heights would be officially categorized as 'poor' – a growing category in the United States. In the country as a whole, the proportion of the population living in poverty in the 1990s exceeded that of the preceding three decades. In 1992, 14.5 per cent of the US population (over 36 million people) were classified as poor, based only on cash income before taxes. Although the numbers of whites living in poverty exceeds the numbers of other ethnic groups, the proportions are much higher for these groups. Compared to 11.6 per cent of whites, 33.3 per cent of blacks and 29.3 per cent of Hispanics live in poverty. The rate of poverty is highest among female-headed single-parent households; half of all single-parent families now live in poverty; female-headed households make up 38.7 per cent of all families in poverty. In New York City, the largest number of welfare recipients are single-parent families with children; almost 30 per cent of the city's children are poor (US Department of Commerce, Bureau of the Census 1993).

The primary welfare programme, Aid to Families with Dependent Children (AFDC), has since 1950 provided funds for dependent children as well as the poor mothers who care for them. At the time of the research, federal legislation guaranteed that all those deemed eligible for public assistance were guaranteed monthly payments, although the amounts varied greatly depending on the state.[11] Since then, a punitive national Welfare Reform Act, passed in 1996, gives states a fixed sum to spend on welfare, based on a one-time assessment of need, places strict lifetime limits on benefits, denies benefits to drug users and illegal immigrants, and allows states to deny them to legal immigrants.[12]

But support for poor women with children has been a source of contention almost from the programme's inception. Then starting in the late 1970s, at the same time as the income gap between the rich and the poor began to widen, attacks on welfare – known as an 'entitlement programme' –

and its recipients became more concerted, resulting in a widespread acceptance of poverty as an individual rather than a social problem, a sign of personal failure and inadequacy. Benefits have been increasingly tied to work requirements, reinforcing the message that those who receive them are unwilling to work rather than unable to find work. All of this has engendered profoundly ambivalent feelings among many recipients, an attitude that spills over to their view of any form of personal entitlement (Abramovitz 1996). In this study, not surprisingly, few respondents acknowledged being on welfare, unless asked directly. In Soperton they defined themselves in terms of the job they once had, or hoped to have, like garment workers or secretaries, even when they were unemployed or received welfare.

Union Membership and Job Security

In this context, trade unions, which after decades of combined business and government attacks now represent less than 15 per cent of the country's workers, have begun to focus on organizing women and minorities – who increasingly make up New York City's workforce. Some of their greatest strength is in the public sector, where in consequence of government affirmative action policies, women and minorities have found relatively good jobs with secure benefits; by the mid-1980s, 24 per cent of women employed in government were women of colour, compared with 14 per cent of all employed women (Bell 1985).[13]

While women work in all areas of government, most have jobs in education, health, social services and administration. Because of the public sector character of certain traditionally female professions – teaching, library sciences, and social work – women employed in government are much more likely to have jobs classified as professional than women working in the private sector. But clerical workers also are overrepresented in the public sector, making up 42 per cent of its female workforce compared with 35 per cent in the economy as a whole, and the median salary for full-time women government workers is the same as that for all full-time women workers. Even so, women's jobs in government offer greater job security and better benefits than do jobs held by women in manufacturing or the service sector (Eaton 1992).

Although organizing efforts directed specifically at women workers were almost nonexistent until the 1970s, women have quickly assumed leadership roles in public sector unions, and issues of concern to women workers have become more prominent on public sector union agendas. Women's success here reflects not only the strength of unions in the public sector and women's increased entry into this sector, but also the vision and determined efforts of feminists within the labour movement. By the late 1980s, over 40 per cent of the 7.7 million female workers in the public sector were represented by a union or labour association – more than twice the level of organization among women workers in the US economy as a whole (Eaton 1992).

District Council 37, the nation's largest local union of public employees, represents 130,000 New York City workers, the majority of whom are women working in clerical, administrative, and paraprofessional jobs. Carrying on the union's tradition of progressive struggle, women have succeeded in drawing the leadership's attention to a number of issues, including equal pay for equal or equivalent work, equal opportunities to access non-traditional, often higher-paying jobs, flexible work schedules, and the creation of career ladders for promotion, training, and skills upgrading.[14] Recently, a Committee on Lesbian and Gay Issues successfully pushed the union to negotiate an agreement with city government to include domestic partners in union members' health coverage.

Today, with cuts in government programmes, public sector unions are focusing more on 'bread and butter' issues of jobs and benefits. Because women, including women of colour, are the most recent entrants into public sector employment, they are the most vulnerable to layoffs. Just at a time when women have gained leadership positions in unions, they do not have the 'luxury' to argue for the particular needs of women workers, and such issues often take a back seat. At the same time, however, public sector unions remain strong on issues of racial discrimination and have become more outspoken on issues of affirmative action. Respondents in the education programme all appreciated the security this gave them. As a respondent who had experienced racial discrimination at a former job said, 'With the union you have someone to fight back for you. In a nonunion job, you are there … you just work, you just do what they tell you to do, you don't have any rights.'

Reproductive Rights: An Overview

US feminists coined the term 'reproductive rights' at the end of the 1970s, emphasizing the conditions and resources that make individual reproductive decisions possible. The term reflected an understanding of the diverse perspectives among women of different class and racial backgrounds and recognized that meaningful control over reproduction goes far beyond the right to abortion. Radical feminists had insisted that only free abortion would guarantee the most oppressed women control over their reproduction and had made explicit the connection between a liberated female sexuality and authority over female reproduction (Echols 1989; Fried 1990). Later, however, largely owing to the leadership of women of colour, almost all reproductive rights advocates realized that abortion could not be separated from the right to safe childbearing, the right not to be sterilized, or the right to affordable health care. They campaigned for all of these rights for poor women, rural women, and women of colour, insisting that all women should have 'the ability to choose whether, when, how and with whom one will have children' (Davis 1990; Tervalon 1988; Fried 1990). A reproductive rights agenda now includes access to education and work, child care, housing, and health care, as well as abortion, contraception and freedom from sterilization abuse.[15]

As the reproductive rights movement framed the right to choose in terms not only of the legal freedom but also of the economic resources and social conditions that make it possible to exercise choice, it increased its ability to influence public opinion. However, its success was matched by a strong, organized opposition, galvanized in the wake of laws legalizing abortion in New York and California in 1970 and 1971 and especially following the 1973 Supreme Court's decision legalizing abortion under a constitutional right to privacy. This opposition, led by an unprecedented coalition of Catholic and fundamentalist Protestant churches and united around a traditional patriarchal family model, gained in strength throughout the 1980s (Petchesky 1990, 1987; Shapiro 1985). Indeed, the same social changes that fostered the resurgent feminism of the 1970s, including an increasing number of women in the workforce, the dramatic increase in divorce, and the rise of single parenthood, contributed to the ability of this right-wing, Christian movement, the so-called 'right to life movement', to mobilize in defence of traditional family and sexual norms. The more atypical these so-called norms become (two-parent families with children constitute fewer than half of US families), the more fiercely they are held up as ideals of American life. Increasingly, those who are seen to violate them – through single parenthood, divorce, extramarital, gay or lesbian sex, or abortion – are judged undeserving of public support. Recent Supreme Court decisions have upheld numerous state-imposed restrictions on abortions, making them increasingly difficult for poor women or teenagers to obtain. Pro-family rhetoric and religious morality have today become synonymous with the eradication of social welfare programmes for the poor.

Today, despite feminist efforts, reproductive rights in the United States remain constrained, particularly for poor women, rural women, young women, women of colour and immigrant women. Teenage pregnancy, sexually transmitted diseases (STDs) and AIDS, abortion restrictions and violence against women represent only a few of the barriers to women's reproductive self-determination. Poverty among single mothers, a sex-segregated workforce that depresses women's wages, sexual harassment in public and private, inadequate public health care services, and lack of access to education are all issues that need to be addressed before US women can achieve reproductive rights.

While the United States continues to have one of the highest abortion rates of all industrialized countries, with 1.4 million abortions per year (88 per cent in the first three months of pregnancy), decreased public funding, restrictions on minors, mandatory counselling regulations, and intimidation through violence and threats of violence have taken a toll: by 1993, 84 per cent of all US counties and 94 per cent of all counties outside a metropolitan area had no abortion provider. Medicaid (state-supported health insurance) is available for abortion in only fifteen states, nine of these only with a court order (Lerner and Freedman 1994). Only 12 per cent of obstetrics/ gynaecology residency programmes require training in abortion procedures (Westhoff 1994).

Not surprisingly, the poorest prenatal and child health services are found in low-income communities, African American and Latino communities, and immigrant or transient communities. Almost 4 million people in the United States cannot afford health insurance, including 9 million women of childbearing age (Lerner and Freedman 1994). Among people of colour, 31 per cent lack such coverage compared with 14 per cent among whites. As a result, high rates of infant mortality, low-birthweight babies, and communicable childhood diseases plague the poorest communities (Carnegie Corporation of New York 1994).

Compared with other industrial countries, the United States has a higher proportion of low-birthweight babies, a smaller proportion of babies immunized against childhood diseases, and a much higher rate of babies born to adolescent mothers. This is true despite recent progress in reducing infant mortality, primarily as a result of a drop in Sudden Infant Death Syndrome, and a five-year decline in the rate of births to teenagers. Rates of neonatal and infant deaths among African Americans are still almost twice those among whites, and although the decline in births to black teenagers (21 per cent) is greater than that to white teenagers (12 per cent), mainly due to increased use of contraceptives, the rate for black teenagers is still nearly double that for white teenagers (Ventura *et al.* 1997).

African American women have inherited a legacy of reproductive violence ranging from coerced childbearing to forced sterilization, experimentation and dangerous reproductive technologies. In turn, they have adopted a number of strategies to gain control over their own reproduction. Many black women for a long time refused to bring children into a world of brutal exploitation; forms of birth control, including abortion, were known and practised during slavery and subsequently (Hine and Wittenstein 1981). While researchers have documented birth control measures in southern communities since the early twentieth century, in many rural areas, where lack of Medicaid coverage and few service providers make abortions particularly difficult to obtain, black women still perform them at home by using quinine pills and brewer's yeast and even by drinking turpentine (Ward 1986; Rodrique 1990).[16] In 1967, the death rate resulting from illegal abortions was 14 times higher for black women in Georgia than for white women (Tervalon 1988).

Black feminists observe that reproductive freedom has been part of the civil rights movement since its inception in the 1800s. Recent scholarship has documented the efforts of African American women to control reproduction, not only limiting their own fertility but promoting efforts to set up local clinics and engaging in the birth control debate (Jones 1990: 222; Rodrique 1990: 333). In the early twentieth century, African American leaders, especially through the Black Women's Club Movement, supported these efforts, linking reproductive rights to racial advancement (Giddings 1984). Thus black women were not the passive victims of the population control establishment, though the latter undoubtedly had its own agenda, but active agents of their own reproductive destinies (Ross 1996: 146).

In the mid-twentieth century, attempts to control the fertility of poor and nonwhite groups, including African Americans, immigrants, and Native Americans, embraced both 'positive' methods such as tax incentives and education for those considered 'desirable', and 'negative' methods such as sterilization, involuntary confinement, and immigration restrictions for the 'undesirable' (Ross 1996; Petchesky 1990, 1981; Lopez 1993). The USA became the first nation in the world to permit mass sterilization as part of an effort to 'purify the race'. By the mid-1930s, about 20,000 people had been sterilized against their will and twenty-one states had passed eugenics laws. In 1939 the Birth Control Federation's so-called Negro Project asserted:

> the mass of Negroes, particularly in the South, still breed carelessly and disastrously, with the result that the increase among Negroes, even more than among Whites, is from that portion of the population least intelligent and fit, and least able to rear children properly. (Gordon 1974: 332)

As a result of this history, as Ross and others have argued, African American women were the first to envision the concept of reproductive justice: 'the freedom to have, or not to have, children and the right to raise them free from racism, sexism and poverty' (Ross 1996: 141). In general, black women have a complex view of reproductive rights: they want individual control over their bodies while remaining suspicious of government programmes that have targeted their communities for medical experimentation and population control.[17]

Today, throughout the rural South, drugs and HIV/AIDS are serious public health problems, along with sexually transmitted diseases. Alcoholism, now recognized as a cause of increased morbidity and domestic violence, is a major health issue for blacks. In Soperton, crack and cocaine addiction is rising, and townspeople correlate this with increases in burglaries and crime, syphilis and AIDS. In 1991, following the construction of a new prison the number of known syphilis cases in Treutlen County rose to 212, from 8 four years before, then dropped to 142 in 1992. Since 1984 there have been 34 cases of AIDS and 22 deaths in Treutlen County, two-thirds of these among African Americans. In Soperton, where migrant work patterns leave women particularly vulnerable to sexually transmitted diseases, women are becoming more aware of the danger, especially younger women. The public health nurse reports that they have learned to be aware of symptoms, and inquire about such changes as vaginal discharge, adding that teenagers do not talk with their mothers about private matters.

In New York City, while rates of STDs have been declining, drug-resistant tuberculosis and HIV/AIDS are continuing health crises. AIDS, the leading cause of death for New Yorkers between twenty-five and forty-four years of age, is on the rise in Washington Heights, and HIV infection rates are higher there than in the city as a whole: 232 compared to 87 per 100,000 in 1990. Women are particularly vulnerable: Latina infection rates in the district were about 40 per cent higher than for Latinas citywide (73 compared to 45 per 100,000), although the rate for males was lower than for Latinos citywide (180 compared to 331 per 100,000) (NYCDOH 1993). Heterosexual intercourse and intravenous drug use were the principal risk factors for women in 1990–91 (Daykin, Eu and Zimmerman 1994). Moreover, while STD rates in the district were generally lower than in the city as a whole, gonorrhoea rates were higher, especially for women (Krasner, Heisler and Brooks 1994).

Nationwide, women are the fastest growing HIV-infected population; over 18 per cent of the HIV-infected population were women in 1994 compared to 7 per cent in 1985. Of 80,691 new cases of AIDS reported in 1994, 41 per cent were infected through intravenous drug use, and 38 per cent through heterosexual intercourse. Women of colour accounted for more than three-fourths of all AIDS cases among women – African American women represented 57 per cent and Hispanic women 20 per cent of the total (CDC 1994; 1995).

In addition, a recent study shows that rape survivors are more likely to become infected with HIV or other STDs than women who have not been raped (National Center for Health Statistics 1995). According to some estimates, nearly one-fifth of US women are subjected to a rape or aggravated assault or both during their lifetime. Among teenagers, 60 per cent of females who had sex before age fifteen did so involuntarily (AGI 1994). Yet despite the rapid increase in the number of HIV-infected US women, the medical community as well as public policy and education have been slow to respond, failing to recognize that women often are not able to control how, when and where they have sex. Racism and gender bias clearly intersect here, contributing to the vulnerability of low-income women of colour to sexual violence and HIV/AIDS (see Williams 1991).

'No One Ever Asked Us to Tell Our Stories Before'

In all the women's stories contradictions abound, and pain and joy often are two ways of looking at one experience. Among respondents in the union college programme, for example, many remembered growing up as a happy time, despite being poor. One woman from South Carolina, who came from a family of twelve, explained: 'What else did we know? We had each other, we were close.' Like the women in Soperton, their most pleasant or unhappy memories, both as children and adults, are remembered in terms of family: time together, separations, accidents, illness, deaths. Because of the dynamics of immigration and migration, contemporary urban families, like families in the rural South, are most frequently not 'nuclear'. Indeed, they are almost everything else: single women or couples with children left behind, single women with children, or multigenerational families with children and their grandparents. Yet for most of the women interviewed, family is still the key to happiness.

Few respondents were able to achieve what they perceived to be their ideal social roles. Keisha, a 32-year-old Soperton woman, expressed her aspirations in these terms: 'When I was a child, I always felt like I was going to live for God. Then I loved to play basketball with a passion and I always wanted to be a basketball player and go to college.... I was good at it and could have been better if I could have had the place to set down and be still.' Others in the sewing shop aspired to roles inspired by television: model, singer, basketball player, cosmetologist, nurse. Even the union women, who had greater opportunity to realize their goals, had made wide detours from their stated aspirations – to become psychiatrists, social workers, college professors, police officers, nurses, teachers, lawyers, real estate brokers – because of early circumstances or choices.

Most respondents had their own dreams, but even at forty or fifty years old many of them still carried the burden of parental expectations. A respondent in the union college programme, now forty-seven, was a housewife for many years: 'I didn't do what I wanted to do because my parents thought a young lady should get married and raise a family,' she explained. A classmate, who got pregnant as a teenager and did not finish her education, says: 'I feel a little bit disappointed that things didn't work out the way it was planned for me, but everyone is entitled to their mistakes. And then you just have to fix them one day.' A 36-year-old woman who grew up with her grandmother in Soperton while her mother migrated to Atlanta has not come to this point. She wants to go 'be with my mama, but I can't do it, she expects too much ... she wants me to be someone I'm not.... It's like, when her birthday come, she'll say "don't buy me no kinda jewelry, because you can't afford what I wear." ' Even so, respondents in all three communities, but especially among immigrant families, recalled their strict upbringing with pride: we 'weren't allowed to do what other people were allowed to do', they said, listing the prohibitions as if these somehow made them different from other people.

An important factor in women taking control of their lives seems to be their ability to break away – from the expectations of family or community about how women should behave and live, and often from the family and community themselves. Keisha, who had been a drug addict, told how she had struggled to take control of her life since she was nine years old, going from one house to the next and virtually raising herself. She dropped out of high school but got her high school equivalency certificate and began a nursing assistant course. When trying 'to act like a woman' did not work she tried to act like a man: 'I worked in construction, tried to supply for the family, I just couldn't hit it off right. I was like in jail in my own house.' She went to jail, tried to kill herself, became an alcoholic. She became addicted to crack cocaine while pregnant and then 'kinda slowed down'. Finally, she found her peace and power in religion and has taken on struggles against racial discrimination and with the school board: 'They said children on welfare don't learn like children that's not on welfare,' she related, adding, 'I'm proud of mine.'

Barbara, an African American in the union college programme who is now in her fifties, came from a sharecropping family in North Carolina, in which education was not valued. As a teenager, she told her three sisters, 'When I graduate [from high school], I'm out of here. I'm going to save my money and I'm leaving; whatever happens, happens. They said they were afraid, that's when we made a pact that we would leave.' In order to help the younger ones leave, she said, 'I'm trying to set up a scholarship fund within my family.' Few women from Soperton talked about leaving, though a younger woman, who later had a nervous breakdown, said: 'If I could live my life all over again I would move away from home.'

But most of the older Soperton women were not able to imagine leaving. Most said, 'I wouldn't know where to go, or what to do.' One woman said, 'It's a small town. And you're not just a number. If you fall out there on the street whether you're black or white, somebody gonna stop'. Only Suzanne, thirty-nine, who has been married twice and now has her own beauty shop, still fantasizes about getting away: 'If I had it to do all over again, I would not get married and I would not have children,' she says, adding: 'I would buy a black Lexus and drive into nowhere. I've always wanted to go to Wyoming … wide, open country.'

Immigrant women as a whole were less afraid of the world's uncertainty. A respondent in the health empowerment group in Washington Heights said: 'I worked for fourteen years in the same place as a nurse's aide. I don't feel frustrated because I didn't become a doctor. At least I got close to what I wanted, I didn't get stuck in one place, because as I said I had to move forward and not get stuck in the countryside like some of those girls who got married and stayed there only having children. I thank God who gave me intelligence to move ahead, and I did not stay in the countryside.'

But getting away is not simply a matter of intelligence; it also requires the ability to recognize opportunity and the courage to take risks. One woman in her late twenties, who came from Alabama, had passed up an unusual educational opportunity afforded her because her parents worked for better-off white folks. She said if she could do it again, 'I would've finished school with my parents paying for it.' She added: 'I tried to satisfy the whites, I tried to satisfy the blacks and ended up satisfying no one. It took me this long to learn my lesson: take care of me and my son.' A classmate said she too would have taken the chance to stay in school. 'Not saying I would wait for marriage, but I would stay in school just a little bit longer.... I wouldn't have had my daughter when I had her. I would've went away and went to college.'

Education: 'It Was Practically Like the Die Was Cast'

As these remarks indicate, education is the opportunity respondents felt they missed the most. A respondent in the union college programme, who dropped out of school at age fourteen and is now thirty-four, summed up a common sentiment: 'If I could live my life all over again I would get a good education.' But for most of these families it was hard to find the resources. Her classmate Barbara, now in her fifties, put it clearly: 'When I came up, it was practically like the die was cast.... The families that went to school, went to college. But the ones that didn't go, didn't go on, no one breaks that.'

Though equal education for blacks has been a central part of the civil rights struggle, opportunities in the rural South remain limited; only one Soperton respondent had completed college. Older respondents especially see school as a right that economic circumstances denied them. They could not stay in school, they explained, because they had to take care of younger children and do the household chores, then work in the fields. Cora Lee Johnson, who grew up in a sharecropping family in Soperton, remembers picking cotton even before she could walk ('because the cotton was so distinct even a little girl could pick it'), so she got four years of school and only when it rained. For the younger women the situation had improved: sixteen had graduated or obtained a high school equivalency certificate, while one had finished college.

Soperton respondents are keenly aware of the ways in which their limited education has held them back. A woman in the sewing shop was very bitter about her mother not doing more to ensure that she got an education: 'Look like she should have kept pulling until they let her put us in school, I don't care what it took.' Another explained that her current ability to get an education was limited by her children: 'They all say a woman should do what she wants to do; I guess my children are stopping me.' Still another would help her daughter finish school even if it meant challenging the community's strict norms against abortion: 'If my daughter got pregnant and wanted to finish school, I would do everything possible to help her get one,' she said.

In general, respondents viewed education as a passport to work. But it was the one woman who had obtained a college degree who expressed a sense of entitlement to *meaningful* work: 'A black woman is entitled to a choice of jobs,' she said, as opposed to 'just a job'. Another woman in the group, now twenty-nine, had wanted to be a nurse: 'My biggest goal was finishing school, that welfare was not gonna be my life. I was going to do something more than when they ask you, "Your parents finished school?" and you gotta like, "Naw, my mama ain't finish; naw, my daddy ain't finish."' But she got pregnant at fifteen, left school and went on welfare. She looked for two years before she found a job. You can't blame welfare mothers, she says, 'because there ain't jobs out there'.

Dominicans, like many immigrants to the United States, view education as a way to improve employment options, especially for their children. Education is highly valued in the Dominican Republic, which prides itself on having the first university of the Americas; but at the same time the country has the Caribbean's second-highest illiteracy rate (only Haiti's is higher). In 1990, 56 per cent of the Washington Heights population had less than a four-year high school education (Garfield and Abramson 1994). However, the Washington Heights school district operates at 122 per cent of capacity (Daykin, Eu and Zimmerman 1994), and Dominicans make up the highest per centage of Latino students in the City University of New York.

Dominican women in this study, having grown up with the idea that education was important, said they planned to continue with their own education as well as to help their children attain this goal. Respondents in both groups were still trying to make this a reality, however difficult. Few of those over forty in the health empowerment group had had more than an eighth-grade education and only one had reached the tenth grade; while the younger ones did better, only two had graduated from high school. In the Alianza group, of those over forty, again, most went only up to grade eight, but three of ten graduated; of the younger women, twelve of nineteen had graduated from high school, and nine of these had some college or technical training. A member of the Alianza group explained: 'As far as education goes, our father, for example, didn't concern himself with what the children did.... To them it wasn't important if we did our homework, if we studied, if we went to school, if we arrived early, late.... What did my parents expect from us? That's what I ask myself.'

The opportunity for union women to participate in the college degree programme sets them in sharp contrast with the other women in this study. For many, who shared similar stories of growing up poor in the South and working in the fields, it was an opportunity they got late in life. A focus group member said, 'We were expected to work on the farm and that was it. Education? We went to school off and on.... Education was like you get it if you get it, and if you didn't, you didn't.' One, whose father had never finished high school, said he 'knew by working so hard that the only way you were going to be free, you had to have that education'.

Employment: 'A Lotta People Working Out There to Survive'

Along with education, the right to a job and an income registered high on respondents' lists of rights in all communities. Most respondents referred to economic well-being in ways that conveyed a sense of social justice or entitlement. They spoke of wanting to be able to earn a living, wanting a secure job, wanting the means to start a small business enterprise. Those who lacked these things felt that government should give them the training to get them, along with public support and child care in vulnerable periods. Dominican respondents were outspoken about the right to work: 'illegal immigrants should be allowed to work like everyone else, and to better their lives', said a member of the health empowerment group.

In both Soperton and Washington Heights, women put together a living through many kinds of work, formal and informal, part-time and full-time. Soperton, like many southern towns where freed slaves first worked as sharecroppers and later as factory labourers, offers limited employment options for both men and women. There are only two factories, specializing in garment manufacturing and vacuum cleaner bag manufacture. Neither has a union.[18] The town does have several small businesses, nine of which are owned by blacks. However, most men seek employment in out-of-town construction jobs, which pay $14 to $15 per hour, and many work as inter-state truck drivers – with the result that Soperton is an infrequent 'home'. Women seek contract work in garment factories outside town that pay $4.25 to $4.50 an hour, even after ten years of work.[19] The work is available only on a daily basis, and many days they return home without a day's work. There are three day care centres in town, but for most respondents, child care is provided by other female family members, especially grandmothers.

The constants in Soperton women's lives are work, prayer and children. These women work hard and long; when they are not working they are looking for work. Yet all of their time and effort merely brings them food for their families. They are constantly trying to break out of the welfare trap. Keisha, raising four children, says:

> You can work in the fields. Long as you stay out there nobody don't go and tell [the welfare office] on you, they ain't gonna go looking for you.... This month we're not going to get no Medicaid, no welfare cheque and my food stamps went down to $175 a month. If you get $50 work, they take part of it out of your food stamps. You never get ahead.... I am a Christian, you know, so it's kinda hard. I gotta do something. They don't need to know everything about you no way.

The same is true in Washington Heights, where many respondents combined public assistance with part-time factory or department store jobs or informal activities in the home, baking, cutting hair, or babysitting. Yet the study indicates that an important function of work is that it allows women to break out of their isolation, offering access to new ideas, awareness and information. A respondent in the Alianza group linked it to entitlement in the family: 'Work, you feel more liberated,' she said. Lack of economic opportunity, on the other hand, limits not only relationships but aspirations. In Soperton it was teenagers who were most able to articulate a sense of entitlement in terms of the right to have money to live well, to have an education and a good job in order to delay starting a family. As one teenager insisted, 'living on a fixed income which cannot meet my basic needs is violence'.

In this regard the union women represented the range of choices the other women wanted to have. While most are clerical workers, other jobs include counsellor, social worker, computer specialist, researcher, day care worker. Their salaries ranged from $10,000 to $50,000, and all included paid vacations and medical benefits. Work also provided more varied roles as women: several were union officers or shop stewards and some had represented the union at national conferences. In addition to attending regular union meetings, many were involved in the Women's Committee, which organizes education events. While most said that being female limited promotion opportunities, they were keenly aware that without the union they would be far more vulnerable, especially as women of colour. Barbara cited her experience in South Carolina, where people worked for a company for years, then were simply fired or demoted. 'There's nothing you can do about it,' she said, 'they can do whatever. But the union gives you some kind of security, it gives you a chance to have arbitration.' Estelle, also from the South, agreed: 'I look at it as a dog-eat-dog world. You are in today and you may be out tomorrow,' she said: 'You definitely need some type of security, especially being a minority. And it's more security with the union.' Indeed, those who were critical of the union felt it should fight harder, not just when 'they know they are going to win'. 'The union is supposed to protect a person from being fired, and protect the rights of the person,' said 56-year-old Claudia, born in Puerto Rico. 'And they have all sorts of things that they offer, right? … that's something I was looking for, too.'

Above all, however, the women in this programme valued income and job security. And most of them had been determined to get these things from an early age. Estelle, who works at two jobs to pay for what she wants in life, described her most powerless moment as joining her husband in the South after finishing junior college and being told she could get a job at a fast food chain or babysit. She left and went back to New York. 'I'll come out here every week', she told her husband, 'but I got to go back to New York City. I'm attending school and I gotta get a job that makes me feel complete.'

Marriage and Relationships: 'I Ain't Fixin' to Be Dogged'

As is shown in Table 1.1, a large number of respondents in all three communities were unmarried. As with early childbearing, many saw early marriage as a mistake of their youth. This conviction crossed ethnic as well as rural–urban lines. A respondent in the Dominican health group asserted: 'I wouldn't let anyone humiliate me now as before. For example, that the men humiliate me and make decisions ... they spent many years of my life deciding for me, but never again'. In Soperton, too, respondents are sceptical about marriage. Lulu-Mae, who got married at age seventeen, said, 'I wanted some children but I didn't want to get married. Cause I don't like to cook and I figured if you have a husband you have to cook, and I don't like to sleep with nobody.' And Keisha, who has never been married, said, 'I just ain't gonna put up with nobody. I know some women who got nice houses and things but their husbands cheat on them and treat them like dogs. I ain't fixin' to be dogged. I mean, I rather be by myself.'

Table 8.1 Demographic Indicators, All Respondents

INDICATOR	SOPERTON SEWING SHOP (35)	DOMINICAN HEALTH GROUP (16)	ALIANZA DOMINICANA (29)	UNION GROUP (50)
Mean age	34	44	33	32.5
Mean age 1st pregnancy	18.7	22.7	21.6	20.2
Mean fertility rate	2.8	1.8	2.0	0.7
30 and under	2.0	0.5	1.2	0.1
Over 30	3.5	2.3	2.9	1.6

The reasons for not marrying varied. Respondents in all the communities stated that children and marriage do not assure male loyalty; women in multigenerational female households, such as those in Soperton, often felt greater support in their childbearing than did many of the union women, even those who were married. They understand the reasons for this are complex, especially when there are no jobs for the men. Vera, a 47-year-old woman from Guyana who entered the workforce late in life and is now in the union college programme, observes: 'People don't have incomes, and that alone deteriorates family life.'

Another reason is the way welfare is structured in many states. Although at the time of the study Georgia allowed benefits to families in which a father has lost a job, the complex criteria still limited a woman's ability to receive aid if there were a man in the household. As a result, men remain tangential in the women's lives. Relationships are unstable and live-in boyfriends often break off a relationship once a child is born, as their inability to give financial support ruins many relationships and state authorities come after them for child support. Women in Soperton said that if they waited to get married before having children, they would never have children. This might mean denying themselves the status of motherhood, the primary component of their adult identity.

Men were also largely absent from the lives of urban women in the study; half of the respondents in the union programme and over half those in the health empowerment group did not have a partner at the time of study. While this may in part reflect decreasing employment and income conditions for black and Latino populations, in part it also reflects a sense that women can do better on their own. As Milagros, a member of the health empowerment group who has separated from her husband, said: 'más vale estar sola que mal acompañada' (better to be alone than in bad company).[20] One question, designed to elicit personal entitlements, was 'what do you do only for yourself?' Fully half of those in the Alianza group replied 'nada, nothing.' Other responses ranged from cooking or sewing to shopping, working, and reading books. One reached for something different: 'I keep my own personality and not let anybody come into my own personal life.' Women in the union and health empowerment groups overwhelmingly claimed entitlement to personal development and leisure, including vacation, exercise, dancing, friendship, enjoying nature, journal writing, helping others, or being alone. Few of those in Soperton seemed able to take the time for doing things that could lead to the fulfilment of their aspirations.

Respondents in the education programme talked about being trapped in their relationships. Barbara, who remembers her marriage as the most painful period in her life, explains: 'I didn't like married life, too confining.... I didn't want my family to know that we didn't get along.... I was afraid of failing.' She tells her daughter, when she gets into a relationship, 'Don't be intimidated. Don't feel you can't breathe without his existence. Have your own pay cheque. If things do not work, hey, move on.' Estelle, who has two jobs, paid for her own wedding: 'This way if it doesn't work, me and him can kiss and walk away and I can say, I don't owe y'all anything.' Among Soperton respondents, such confidence is harder to come by; while few were married, it was the one with a college degree who observed that 'Every woman should be able to do what she wants to do, married or not.'

Others in the sewing group know it is not so easy. Suzanne, who dreams of getting in a black Lexus and driving away, talked about her sister's abuse: 'We tried to get her to leave, but this man had her thinking she couldn't make it without him ... that she did not have sense enough to buy groceries ... to raise her children. Me and mama had to help raise the children because he was running around with other women.' After sixteen years of abuse, Suzanne's sister left. But her husband found her at her mother's house and killed her, stabbing her thirty-five times and shooting her twice. The shock killed her mother. 'That Sunday, me and she went to church, just before services was over she had a massive stroke and died. So I lost everything in about two months. And I inherited some children.'

Drugs and violence have ravaged the lives of women in all the groups studied. More than half of the Washington Heights respondents and nearly two-thirds of the Soperton respondents felt affected by the rise of crime and drugs in their community, while seventeen of the fifty women in the union programme reported being victims of violent behaviours: two women were raped, one was sexually molested as a child, several were victims of date rape, or were violently robbed and violently abused. Nearly two-thirds of the women reported verbal abuse and slightly fewer reported physical, child, and sexual abuse.

When asked about abuse, and the right to decide when to have sex, all the respondents stated that women should not stay in abusive relationships; not a single respondent said a husband had the right to have sex with his wife without her permission. They differed on how to resolve such problems, however. Among the women in the Alianza group, respondents over-whelmingly said an abused woman should 'leave him' or 'get out and get help'. Only two said that women should talk it over. A respondent in the college credit programme said it is best to just 'leave, get the hell out, but this is easier said than done as women don't feel that they have the emotional support to do it'. Only half the respondents in this programme felt counselling was worth trying. Respondents in Soperton and Washington Heights told stories of resisting the physical abuse of their partners; in fact, several women in Soperton thought of themselves as abused only when they did not fight back: 'We got into one fight,' she said, 'but after I cut him he left me alone.' Milagros, in the Washington Heights health group, explained when she decided to divorce:

> What I would do is go to bed and tell him, 'Try and see if you can.' He would tell me, 'you're as cold as ice' ... and I would tell him, 'If I don't have a man at home (because he wasn't working at the time) then I won't have a man in the bed.' Once he tried to hit me, so I hit him and cut him ... I realized this could turn into tragedy ... so I decided to divorce him.

Not all of the women were living alone. Among the union women, Estelle, who was engaged at sixteen and married at twenty, has been married for nine years. Her husband, she said, 'is the backbone of the relationship'. A classmate, who raised her child alone, would like her daughter to get married first: 'Not because it is harder if you're not married but because it doesn't have a backbone,' she mused. Those women who felt that they were the 'backbone' often were less willing to play that role after children arrived. 'I had gotten a good husband, I can actually say I was his wall,' said Edna, thirty, who left her husband. 'When you have to be someone's mother you don't have time to be a grown man's mom.'

Motherhood: 'Having Children Made Me Proud of Myself'

Consistent with US data as a whole, births to all of the women in this study have declined, falling by half for each generation (see Table 8.1). But tables do not tell the whole story. Women in this study, primarily rural and immigrant women, more often than not have been mothering early and long; for them motherhood is not something that starts or ends with their own children. Many had dropped out of high school to take care of siblings and many had babies themselves while they were still teenagers. Some deliberately delayed birth control until after the first birth. This was especially true in Soperton, although the health clinic pushes the pill aggressively among teenagers. With few marriage possibilities because of the way men leave town for jobs, motherhood remains a choice within a context that offers so few choices, and is seen as an entitlement independent of marriage. 'We were put here to multiply,' one women in the sewing shop explained.

For nearly two decades, policymakers have decried the 'crisis in teen pregnancy', primarily because of the close link between adolescent parenthood and poverty. In 1989, one-quarter of all US children were born to unmarried women, over one-third of these under twenty years old; 83 per cent of teenagers giving birth are from poor or low-income families (AGI 1994). Yet in Soperton, the welfare system is structured in such a way that young single mothers can get subsidized apartments that are not available to women without children. To many, therefore, motherhood represents an opportunity to use socially supported avenues to improve their lives. An older woman said that her daughter was courted by a man who wanted to live with a woman who had a child, so as to be guaranteed an apartment: 'That's the only way you can get an apartment of your own,' she said. The other side of this 'asset' however, is that it is often hard for the woman to get the man to leave once the relationship has soured.

In all locations, including Soperton, respondents spoke of great conflict about out-of-wedlock motherhood. It is possible that by having children women hope to gain the respect, concern, and some measure of support from other kin, and from other churchgoers, that they had not felt before. The reality of an unplanned teenage pregnancy is that the rise in status and prestige expected may not be forthcoming, posing serious emotional problems. One unmarried woman in her early twenties had made plans for her life and was vocal about her rights, but got pregnant and had an emotional breakdown. She said, 'I got depressed because of the reality of being on welfare, being responsible [for my children], and being judged.'

For many of the women in the study, however, motherhood seems to give them authority to assert rights. Even those who would not stand up for their own rights will fight for the rights of their children. One of the few instances where Soperton women challenged racism was when they took action as mothers against what they saw as unfair treatment of their children in school. When asked to isolate the most important thing every woman is entitled to, a respondent in the Alianza Dominicana group said it was 'to be an unconditional mother'; another said, 'to be a mother, to take care of her children'. A third struggled with the idea of rights, saying, 'Right is in general something that we don't know.... It's to defend something that is your own, it's to defend something that's mine, but you don't know what that is.' Eventually she concluded: 'Right is to care for your children, give them what they need.'

For many Dominican respondents, the right to motherhood seemed to carry a conviction that they should be supported in their efforts to raise children properly, since they were fulfilling the roles expected of them. Most did not actively choose motherhood; it was normal; it happened. Especially where other means of claiming maturity are absent (work, education, home ownership, marriage, financial independence), motherhood seemed to become a rite of passage, a way to establish adulthood, offering something over which respondents felt they were in control. In the Dominican community, they explained, women who have not 'satisfied' this role could be considered 'less of a woman'. Older respondents in the Alianza group saw women who do not bear children as 'very frustrated, sad'. A woman in the health group said, 'A woman who hasn't been a mother I don't believe can feel the same as one who has had children. I don't think she can be equal.'

Respondents in the union programme, on the other hand, looked upon motherhood more as an option than a duty, and viewed it very much as a personal responsibility. Thus many expressed their determination to avoid any form of public assistance: 26-year-old Violet, a black woman born in the South, raises one child by herself, 'because, the welfare system, I don't think that's for me. I couldn't see myself sitting home, waiting for somebody to give me money.... At least if I made a couple of dollars, I earned it on my own.' Edna, now thirty and raising her daughter alone, says, 'my mother and father never went to welfare or anything. Because my father always said he don't want nobody telling him what he can do with his kids. So if you don't want nobody telling you what to do, you don't take any money from the government.'

Respondents in all locations reported that after having their first child, they adjusted their aspirations and drew power from their mothering. A woman in Soperton said, 'Having children made me proud of myself.' Perhaps not surprisingly, a number of respondents seemed to find more certain fulfilment in their children than in unsupportive early marriages. This was also true of women in the union education programme, though few had had children. Those who did described motherhood as the impetus needed to push their own self-fulfilment: 'Having this child will probably give me a little more energy to do the things I've always wanted to do for myself,' one explained. 'It makes me see why my mother did or said a lot of things she said to me and it makes me struggle personally for more.' Edna recalled: 'An old saying goes "never snob a person when you have children, because you may have to knock on that person's door to get your kids some food."'

Reproductive Health:
'You Do What You Have to Do to Make Your Life Better'

Despite the importance of motherhood in all respondents' sense of their rights as women, the mean number of children varied widely among the women in each of the three communities. Those in the Soperton sewing group had by far the largest number of children, while those in the union college programme had the fewest; even separating out women under thirty in this programme, who might be waiting to have children, the number is strikingly low. When asked why they had not had children, even those who wanted them, respondents indicated they needed to make more money, in order to be able to support children in the way they thought was necessary. One young woman, who has a three-year-old child, said that the most powerful moment in her life was the day she gave birth, yet still she feels most powerless when her daughter asks her for something and she can't afford to give it to her. Though few spoke of it, it is also likely that they viewed their own large families as making it more difficult for them to finish school as girls; the mean fertility rate among the mothers of the fifty respondents in the union education programme was 4.7.

In New York City, where foreign-born women had nearly twice as many children as native-born women in 1991, live births in Washington Heights were 91.2 per 1,000 women aged 15–44, compared to 54.8 per 1,000 women in Manhattan overall (Krasner, Heisler and Brooks 1994). Yet the total fertility rate for Dominican immigrants in both groups in this study was 1.9, below that for Hispanic women statewide, which was 2.6 in 1990 (Clarke and Ventura 1994). Averaging in union programme respondents, many of whom are immigrants, the average number of children born to immigrants in this study is even lower. Respondents mentioned economic concerns as primary in the decision to limit family size, often related to the desire to give children a good education or to continue their own education.

In rural Soperton, by contrast, most respondents began having children as teenagers, and most had already had two children by the time they were in their twenties; thus the differences between those over thirty and those younger to some extent reflects the fact that the younger women had not finished having children. Yet despite the fact that Soperton teenagers are still having children, there is some evidence that they will stop after one or two. Use of contraceptives among adolescents is increasing, as is condom use in adult males, primarily due to fear of AIDS. Sex education is taught in school, and the public health clinic – where contraceptives are actively encouraged and provided free of charge – is widely used. Some teenagers said that they were routinely given birth control at about fifteen years of age, even before they became sexually active.

The adolescent pregnancy rate is obviously of concern in Soperton, as reflected in the fact that tubal ligations are widespread and frequent before age twenty-five. Among Soperton respondents, sterilization was by far the most prevalent method of contraception; fully half had had tubal ligations in their early to mid-twenties. How freely this decision was taken is not clear. The nearest hospital is 17 miles away and some residents travel 100 miles to Augusta, or even to Atlanta for prenatal care and delivery. A few who had decided to have tubal ligations expressed regret, saying they had mistakenly thought the procedure was reversible or that they did not feel well afterwards. Moreover, most of the older respondents did not know of any other contraceptive method but the pill and sterilization. The clinic does not do abortions or provide abortion counselling. Most of those who chose a tubal ligation, however, while aware that women of colour have historically been targeted for sterilization abuse, felt it was a liberating option and a good decision. One respondent, a mother of two, described her decision after getting pregnant on the pill: 'I told that doctor, "I want you to cut them in half, clip them, bind them, tie a bow in them if necessary."'

Sterilization was prevalent among respondents in both Washington Heights groups, who said it was also a common method in the Dominican Republic. Of eight sexually active respondents in the health empowerment group, seven had chosen this method. And in the Alianza group, of twelve who were sexually active, five had been sterilized. Several members of this group voiced dissatisfaction with reversible methods, saying they were messy or unreliable, or they had heard about negative side effects. In general, sterilization was easier, but not always. As a respondent in the health group explained: 'Economically I was bad off, I wasn't ready to have more children, and my marriage was falling apart. It was a difficult decision because I had been married in the church and the church didn't accept my decision.' Among respondents in the college credit programme, only five of the twenty-two who were sexually active had chosen this method; the rest used either the pill or condoms.

In the United States as a whole, the percentage of women at risk of an unintended pregnancy who are currently using contraception remained steady at sixty-four per cent from 1984 to 1995. During that time, sterilization use increased from twenty-three to twenty-eight per cent while both IUD and diaphragm use declined and the pill remained fairly constant (AGI 1997). The reasons for this increase are various, but reflect pressure to become sterilized on poor or abused women, drug users and women in prison, as well as those exposed to toxic chemicals. Medicaid, the state-funded medical insurance for the poor, covers 90 per cent of the cost of sterilization, unlike other forms of contraception. In addition, the larger the family the more likely the woman will use more permanent methods of contraception, such as sterilization. In general, women most likely to become sterilized are aged 30–44, previously married, black and Hispanic, with the least education and lowest incomes in the country (AGI 1993:1).

Immigrants rarely have jobs that provide comprehensive health coverage. Instead they rely on municipal health services, which are typically over-crowded, with inadequate resources and overworked staff. Thus immigrants frequently delay seeking healthcare services and often forgo preventive and prenatal care entirely. In Washington Heights, almost one-fifth (18 per cent) of pregnant mothers have late or no prenatal care; 54 per cent of births are to unwed mothers, compared to 44.8 per cent for the city overall (NYCDOH 1993). Citywide, it is estimated that two-thirds of women who do not use a birth control method are poor and low-income; they are likely to be among the approximately 50,000 women in need of family planning services who are not receiving them (NYCDOH: 1993).

Introduction of long-acting contraceptives such as Norplant and Depo Provera in recent years has created a new area of vulnerability for women. Women in the Soperton focus group reported that Medicaid would pay for Norplant implants but not to remove them except for 'medical reasons'; they were told they would have to pay $300, and reimburse the state the cost of insertion, if they had implants removed before the end of two years. On the other hand, they said that when they complained of headaches, continuous bleeding, massive hair loss, or palpitations, the local medical authorities called these 'inconveniences' and not medical problems. One young woman who has a history of migraines, high blood pressure, and dysplasia was given Depo Provera without any warning of side effects.

Few respondents were unequivocally in favour of abortion. In Soperton, respondents almost without exception were negative. Yet some of the older women reported jumping off the porch or down the stairs to try to terminate pregnancies. And the public health nurse reported a high incidence of miscarriage in the town, since between twenty-five and thirty women per year with a positive pregnancy test do not return for prenatal care. It is said that people used to go to Atlanta or Florida for an abortion, but now they can get an abortion in Dublin, twenty-five miles away. In Washington Heights, respondents in both groups were also fairly negative, although much less so. Only seven of the twenty-nine women in the Alianza group supported abortion, while sixteen opposed it and four did not have a position. Of those opposed, however, only nine did so in all circumstances; when asked about a therapeutic abortion, seven said they would either have one or consider having one. Among the health empowerment group, while many said they opposed the procedure, when asked about a therapeutic abortion nearly one-third admitted that they had had such an abortion, and four of them had had more than one. Asked about decisions they felt good about, one member of the group mentioned the 'decision to have an abortion, because I was sick and alone'. Even those most strongly opposed admitted some tolerance, understanding that sometimes women felt they had no other options.

Given the tendency of respondents in both communities to define themselves largely in terms of motherhood, the pervasive influence of religious teachings against abortion, and perhaps more insidiously the increasing tendency in media and public policy discussion to portray unwed mothers, especially women of colour, as irresponsible and a drag on the ethnic or cultural group as a whole, the extent of opposition is not surprising. But given these women's simultaneous efforts to work outside the home and achieve greater status within it, neither is their tolerance when it comes to practice.

In general, respondents in the union education programme were more outspoken in favour of choice, although more than one-third said they would not consider an abortion. 'If a woman needs it it's up to her,' said one; 'You do what you have to do to make your life better,' said another. But Edna, in her late twenties, who would have an abortion in 'a second' to avoid an unwanted pregnancy, said it was different for people who were married: 'If you are taking birth control and you become pregnant it is because God meant for it to be there,' she said. And Claudia, who feels guilty about leaving her husband, had this advice for her daughter: 'Stay married, go to church, plan your babies.'

Sexuality: 'Do you want to be a good girl or a bad girl?'

Ultimately, conflicting views about childbearing and abortion reflect the deep ambivalence about sexuality that pervades US culture and society, especially concerning women. At a time when the popular media bombards audiences with sexually explicit talk and images, the policy debate revolves around admonitions to 'just say no', especially for young women. Public and media discussion virtually never starts from an affirmation of women's sexual rights, including the kind of support that would allow them to choose healthy sexual expression without fear of disease or censure. Religious and political conservatives have mobilized to limit access to reproductive health and limit the terms of sexual education to pregnancy prevention while eliminating all discussion of sex and sexuality outside the context of marriage. It is hardly surprising that the US has one of the highest incidences of sexually transmitted disease in the developed world; an estimated 12 million new STD cases occur each year, one-quarter of these among teenagers (National Center for HIV, STD and TB Prevention 1996).

Not one woman in the entire study said that her parents or guardians spoke to her of sexuality in terms of the right to pleasure. Rather, older sisters and aunts usually provided information on menstruation or admonitions against getting pregnant. 'Sexuality was taboo; my mother was very shy,' said one respondent, now fifty-six. But responses of younger women suggested that things had not changed: 'I didn't know what menstruation was until I got mine,' said Joy, now thirty-four. 'Till I was a teenager, I thought airplanes brought babies.' 'My mother handed me a box of [sanitary] napkins and said you know what to do with it right? and I said yeah and read the directions,' recalled Edna, now in her mid-twenties.

Even Latina respondents, whose families celebrated menstruation as a sign of womanhood, stated that it was also the beginning of their sexual isolation. 'I could no longer sit in my father's lap,' recalled one young woman in the health empowerment group. 'And if you told them they tell you, "You can't go swimming and you can't do this." And you weren't allowed to go in the garden. My Papa used to say, "You can't get near the beans, it will kill your beans … It will kill your garden." '

The same taboos surrounded virginity. Of the sixteen respondents in the Dominican health group, thirteen said they were taught that women must be virgins before marriage, yet 54 per cent of these women had their children while unmarried. Although more than three-quarters of the union women said they were expected to be virgins at marriage, they recognized this as an 'ideal, but unrealistic with late marriage'. Some believe that remaining a virgin makes life easier: 'That's what I was taught since I was a little girl,' one woman in the health empowerment group explained: 'One can avoid many problems.' Many of the women in this group were questioning these teachings, however, and some rejected them outright: 'The message came from my grandmother, my mother, very traditional … I think it's absurd. I don't recommend anyone to marry like that,' one said. Another agreed: 'I think it is very negative, you don't need to be a virgin, only to be sure of the person you want to marry.'

Among Soperton respondents, while few valued virginity, and none were virgins after the age of twenty, very few felt free to speak of sex with pleasure. In focus groups, sexual relations were frequently recounted in terms of pressure and pain, emptiness and deception; most did not know what an orgasm was, or if they had ever had one. Teenagers were the only ones in this community who expressed a sense of entitlement to sexual pleasure and orgasms, perhaps as a result of sex education from a less embattled period or, more likely, frequent television and film messages of sexual pleasure for women as well as men.

But AIDS has made respondents in all groups aware of the dangers of sex. As one member of the union programme put it: 'It's very dangerous out there. And the best way to avoid that is to keep it to yourself.' While stressing the importance of knowing their partners and using condoms, many simply avoided sex: over half the respondents in the Dominican health group and almost half the women in the union programme did not use birth control because they were not having sex. A participant in a union focus group said: 'When I got married, the norm was that people were virgins. Shortly after I got married was the sexual revolution. So I missed that. Now, of course, we have AIDS. So I am like screwed.' She says she admires young girls today, who understand 'you don't have to get married to have sex'.

Focus group participants also voiced uncertainty about masturbation:

'You taught yourself that it was a bad thing, because in your mind, it was wrong. Because it felt good, it is wrong,' said a member of the union programme. Another agreed: 'I think the first time I heard this subject discussed openly and freely, was when I heard Dr Ruth [a television sex therapist] give women permission, saying "It's okay. Do it! It's fun!" I think it was the first time I heard a woman say that.'

Many expressed the same difficulty overcoming ignorance or guilt about seeking sexual pleasure. One union focus group participant recalled her own experience:

It wasn't until I got my hysterectomy, and maybe I became more mature, that I began to say: "I have to 𝗅₋₋ 𝖽 out what this is all 'bout. What's the pleasure in it?" I still didn't ask my husband.... I just couldn't. I remember the first time it happened. I was so afraid. I went to the bathroom and I looked at myself in the mirror, and I said, "Dear God!" I felt something weird, something funny, something I never felt before. Maybe that was my first orgasm. And I was thirty-something already. And here I am, looking in the mirror and asking myself, Why did I feel so good? What happened? How did he do it? And, then I couldn't wait for him to do it again.

Her colleague agreed. In the public housing community where she was raised, she explained, 'all of these girls were having babies, and everybody was ashamed.... I didn't realize that you had to free yourself [to achieve orgasm]!'

Talk about sexuality was more restricted when it came to gay or lesbian sexuality. Most respondents stated that they grew up believing that homosexuality was taboo, a sin, or abnormal. Homosexuals within the Washington Heights communities are largely rendered invisible, as they are in rural Soperton, where respondents said, 'We don't have any homosexuals in our community.' Yet most of those in the health empowerment group felt that homosexuality was normal, while only four disapproved or said it was 'abnormal'. And a Soperton community leader told researchers: 'In one household alone, there are several gay men.' Clearly struggling with attitudes she grew up with, a union group member said: 'I don't support that [type of] relationship. It is abominable. But I respect each person's decision.'

Outside of the issue of identity, focus group participants were comfortable about same-sex relations and talked about their experiments as girls: 'I remember practicing kissing with my girlfriends because we couldn't kiss the boys,' said one.

Thus sexual pleasure, however imagined or sought after, seems to be a right women claim as they come to terms with their conditioning as well as the virgin/whore images perpetuated by religion and the media. A focus group participant summed up what many felt.

So you had to make a decision. Do you want to be a good girl or a bad girl? If you were a bad girl, your name was posted, and everybody knew you were a bad girl, and everybody knew what you were doing. So I decided to be a good girl.

Made everybody happy. I got married, had five pregnancies, and four babies. Did I want to get married? Did I want to have babies? No! But that was the thing to do. I've been married thirty-one years. You learn over the years to make changes and adjustments, and that's what I've done.... In the beginning of marriage, he wanted sex every moment of the day. I dreaded it. I didn't want it, I didn't like it. After you heard all these years that it is taboo, you don't do it, and it wasn't something you talked about as a pleasurable thing.... I think it took years before I was able to relax myself to where I could just enjoy sex.

Conclusions: Getting Away – and Getting Organized

Listening to respondents talk about their reproductive and sexual lives sheds light on the complex process by which women in poor communities, and particularly women of colour, learn to value themselves as independent adults as well as women with rights. In all locations, it emerged that a sense of entitlement to specific rights as a woman was closely tied to a belief that different opportunities were available in different communities. That is, which 'people' a woman saw herself as belonging to, in cultural and ethnic terms, seemed to influence how much authority each situation gave her to 'do what I want to do and go where I want to go'. For respondents in all locations, finding an autonomous identity and meeting basic needs in communities that are also struggling to survive involves complex trade-offs between the need for the security and support of family and the desire for freedom to live their own lives.

In African American and Latina communities, in Soperton as well as New York City, women were struggling with their relationship to these communities, which have both nurtured their identity and often seemed to limit the terms in which they are able to value themselves. Younger women in Soperton expressed frustration with the 'stand by your man' values the community tells its women: 'Some women think about the man rather than herself,' one said. 'The role of the woman is to think for herself.' And another felt she might be more supportive if she learned to think of herself first: 'I can't do much to improve my community, I need to improve myself – start with myself and then I'll think of them.' Latinas in Washington Heights, having left the security of family and community in their country of origin, are shaping a personal and social identity through a community of culture and language they themselves helped to (re)-create. Within the health empowerment group, participants moved from concerns about their personal health and that of their families to think about their role as women. 'Women are taking interest in educating themselves to free themselves and to feel useful to themselves and to their community,' explained one. For another, this is the meaning of entitlement: to 'create groups, raise women's consciousness ... to learn to struggle for our rights as women.'

The terms in which women in the different communities are able to make decisions as women depend on their ability to define what we call their 'social citizenship', meaning the ability to be fully functioning adults. All respondents, through their choices if not their words, expressed a right to define themselves as adults. Thus they viewed 'rights' in terms of what they saw as necessary to their self-determination and expressed them primarily in terms of what they did not have. Those without jobs or adequate education expressed a right to both of these, along with such basic needs as housing, food, and health care. Those who had steady jobs and housing, primarily the women in the union college programme, viewed their rights in broader terms, including leisure and self-care activities, a loving partner, freedom to make decisions about their own bodies, space and privacy, respect and equality.

For respondents in the union college programme, many of whom have left the families and communities in which they were brought up, the union functions as a replacement, one which provides opportunities as well as security. In contrast to other women in the study, these women's lives are characterized by three essential elements: job security, educational opportunity, and the experience of union membership, which stresses collective organization as well as individual rights. These factors, the study suggests, provide the bottom line that enables women to move from a sense of personal entitlement to rights to the capacity to take risks, to act on opportunities.

The sense of social citizenship observed in this study thus differs from the concept of 'cultural citizenship' observed by Benmayor *et al.* (1992) among Puerto Rican women in New York City. In bringing together culture and citizenship, the authors assert, 'cultural identity comes to bear on claims for social rights in oppressed communities, and at the same time, identity is produced and modified in the process of affirming rights'. Social citizenship, by contrast, is both more tentative and more limited. In Soperton, for example, the will to articulate, let alone demand, rights is constrained by fear of losing jobs, welfare benefits, or social support. Thus despite her passionate commitment, Cora Lee Johnson has not succeeded in moving other women to become activists in the community.

But even in Soperton it was apparent that rights, including personal rights, are sustained in the course of participating in a group, however loosely organized. Any opportunity to work together in a group, even if it is only to socialize, allows women in poor communities to break patterns of isolation, and for many women this study was their first opportunity to examine and share their thoughts on sexuality, contraception, pregnancy, and abortion and to hear each other's thoughts on reproductive health issues and begin to perceive them as rights. The 'unsteepled places' (places other than churches) where women are able to meet and break their isolation seems important to enable women to feel that they can take the risk to change their circumstances. Respondents in the Soperton sewing shop, reluctant to take such risks, rely on those who have devised ways to negotiate around the gatekeepers (church, welfare agencies, family planning clinics).

Respondents in all locations expressed a concrete right most clearly with regard to childbearing or mothering, indicating that for poor women across racial and cultural as well as geographical lines, motherhood is often synonymous with family and intimacy as well as a symbol of their struggle to establish personhood and adulthood. Women in all the locations spoke of motherhood as a source of affirmation and fulfilment. For those with few opportunities, motherhood gave them some authority to assert rights, for their children if not for themselves – as shown by young mothers in Soperton who stood up to school officials when they felt their children had been discriminated against. Yet even those who saw motherhood as critical to their identity also voiced yearnings for meaningful lives before, after and during motherhood, the opportunity to become the women of their imaginations.

This finding takes on greater meaning alongside the observation that most of the respondents, in all locations, were living without men. Respondents in Soperton, most of whom had never been married, lived with their children in multigenerational female households, where men were at the most visitors. Those in Washington Heights, many of whom were the first family members to immigrate to the United States, got fed up with taking care of husbands as well as children, especially as many had also become primary breadwinners. Several had left their husbands, while others remained unmarried after their husbands had died. This was also true of women in the union programme, although a few had happy marriages. These women are tired of men who cheat on them, or insist on making family decisions, while leaving the women to take care of the children. Like Barbara, who tells her daughter to get her own pay cheque so if things don't work out she can move on, they were deciding they were better off on their own.

The decision to live in families without men may shed light on another finding of this study: the choice of so many women to become sterilized or use long-lasting contraceptives such as Norplant, even though they may not have had as many children as they may have liked. While in part, as we have noted, this reflects the attitudes and biases of medical providers in poor communities, who try to get women to limit their childbearing, it also reflects the women's decision to be free of the burdens of pregnancy and childrearing, one which they find profoundly liberating. In this respect, respondents demonstrated a capacity to separate sexuality from motherhood, an implicit assertion of sexual rights. Instead of devising ways to avoid sex, they are free to think about enjoying it, and even initiating it. And despite community opprobrium, a few even talked about masturbation and lesbian sexuality.

To some extent these findings express the contradictions of life for poor women in the US: the opportunity – and the stigma – offered by welfare benefits for poor women to choose motherhood, and to live without men; the freedom – and the potential regret – offered by long-term birth control and sterilization; the ability to imagine – if rarely demand – sexual pleasure. The terms in which they express these things, like the articulation of a sense of entitlement, reflect their differential abilities to organize for economic security and personal and community needs. Beyond this, however, they reflect the extent to which poor women in all regions of the country are influenced by the wider popular culture, especially the media, as well as the social and economic policy context. The nature of public policy – and the vehemence with which it is contested – oblige women in poor and immigrant communities to negotiate with state and medical authorities on a daily basis, transforming the boundaries of private and public domains, turning personal decisions into matters of economic and social justice. In all locations, women's survival struggles go beyond the intensely private contests of husbands and family to the articulation of claims *vis-à-vis* the state and the wider society.

These findings about the ways in which poor women and women of colour think about their rights as both women and as social citizens support those in the reproductive health and sexual rights movement who have long struggled to integrate a vision of personal autonomy with community solidarity and responsibility. Like their counterparts in the global South, these women in the South within the North are striving to find ways to meet their own needs as well as those of their communities. But asserting their personal and collective rights and identities is only a beginning. If a movement for women's sexual and reproductive rights is to evolve with the strength and ability to fight the forces that would keep women 'in their place', it must constantly define and redefine its issues in the terms in which they are experienced – by poor as well as more affluent women, by women of colour and immigrant women as well as white women – not outside work and community but solidly within them.

Table 8.2 Education

EDUCATION	SOPERTON SEWING SHOP*	DOMINICAN HEALTH GROUP	ALIANZA DOMINICANA	UNION GROUP
Mean years	10.8	8.5	10.9	14.4
Grade school	3	6	4	–
Junior high	13	8	9	–
High school/technical	16	2	16	–
Some college	1	0	0	50

* Education information was not available for two women in this study.

Table 8.3 Median Income, All Respondents

SOPERTON SEWING SHOP	DOMINICAN HEALTH GROUP	ALIANZA DOMINICANA	UNION GROUP
<$10,000	$12,000	$10,000	$20,000

Table 8.4 Birth Control Use

METHOD	SOPERTON SEWING SHOP	DOMINICAN HEALTH GROUP	ALIANZA DOMINICANA	UNION GROUP
No. using*	24	8	12	22
Sterilization	14	7	5	5
Norplant/Depo Provera	2	0	1	0
Pill	6	1	5	15
Condom	2	0	1	13
Nothing	2	5	6	17
Other**	9	3	11	13

* Where totals are greater than this entire category it reflects use of more than one method

** Includes hysterectomies, menopausal and pregnant women, and those for whom data is unavailable.

Notes

1 The term 'people of color' has been widely adopted in the United States to refer to people of indigenous, African, Latin American or Asian heritage or culture.
2 Food stamps are state-issued vouchers equivalent to a fixed value, which can be exchanged for basic food items in grocery stores or local shops.
3 District Council 37, the largest union within the American Federation of State, County, and Municipal Employees (AFSCME) comprises many locals, including the civil service clerical workers union, and the majority of its members are women.
4 Field research was designed and carried out by Dianne Jntl Forte, Junee Barringer Hunt, and Gejuanna Smith in Georgia; Eugenia Acuña and Graciela Salvador-Davila in Washington Heights; and Evelyne Longchamp at District Council 37, with institutional support from the National Black Women's Health Project. Vilma Ramirez, Rosa LaVergne and Margarita Asha Samad-Matias assisted in different ways with the research, while Tola Olu Pearce provided valuable advice as research consultant. A pilot study in Appalachia, conducted by Patricia Antoniello, contributed valuable comparisons with poor white women (see Antoniello 1994). Mary Lefkarites,

Nondita Mason, Patricia Antoniello and Dianne Jntl Forte served as country coordinators at different stages.

5 Complete information was gathered from 35 women from the Soperton sewing shop; 29 from Alianza Dominicana; 16 from the Dominican health project; and 50 from two separate classes in the union college credit programme. In order to capture a range of views and experience, an additional seven community leaders from Soperton were interviewed, ranging from the sheriff to a health care clinic administrator, though they are not included in the database. Respondents include teenagers as well as older women and all but two are women of colour.

6 The US South consists of eleven states: Alabama, Arkansas, Florida, Georgia, Louisiana, Mississippi, North Carolina, South Carolina, Tennessee, Texas and Virginia, with a total population of 85,446,000, of which 76.8 per cent are white, 18.5 per cent black, 0.7 per cent Native American, 1.3 per cent Asian Pacific, and 7.9 per cent Hispanic (US Bureau of the Census 1991) Since the late 1960s, the rate of population growth in the South has exceeded that in all other regions in the country.

7 This is a common and well-documented pattern in the United States, where one in three black men aged 18–25 have had some experience of the criminal justice system.

8 While women now make up 46 per cent of the workforce they comprise two-thirds of part time and temporary workers (US DOL 1996). Women account for 85 per cent of the increase in multiple job holders from 1989 to 1995 (Mishel, Bernstein and Schmitt 1996).

9 Calculated on a weekly rather than an annual basis, women's earnings were 75.5 per cent of men's, but these figures fail to include bonuses and overtime, which primarily benefit men (US DOL 1996).

10 The federal poverty level was estimated at $15,141 for a family of four in 1995. Because of New York City's high cost of living, its poverty level is set at 125 per cent of the federal level.

11 Eligibility and benefit levels have always been determined by the states. In 1992, the average AFDC benefit for a family of three paid $372 per month, about 40 per cent of the official poverty level (National Commission on Children 1993).

12 Lifetime limits vary depending on the state; in New York it is five years, while in Georgia it is two years. Legal immigrants are eligible for assistance in New York State, depending on date of arrival, and elderly and disabled immigrants can still get food stamp benefits.

13 Affirmative action policies, now under attack, mandate that race and gender should be regarded as additional qualifications for educational or employment opportunities.

14 In the 1990s, despite legislation mandating equal pay for equal work, women are still earning less than men, primarily because they are overwhelmingly segregated into jobs categorized as 'women's work' which are valued less than jobs done by men that require the same level of skills or qualifications. The campaign for pay equity seeks not only to equalize wages but to break down some of the persistent job segregation patterns.

15 Particularly influential were the National Black Women's Health Project, the Women of Color Partnership of the Religious Coalition for Abortion Rights, the Latina Roundtable, the National Latina Health Organization, the Reproductive Rights National Network, and the Committee for Abortion Rights and Against Sterilization Abuse (CARASA)

16 In many states, including most southern states, Medicaid coverage for abortion is limited to federally authorized cases of endangerment to a woman's life or cases of rape or incest.

17 In 1997, the US President publicly apologized to the African American community for a government research project that left syphilis untreated in poor, uneducated

black farmers for forty years (1932–72) in order to allow public health officials to study the untreated development of syphilis in humans.

18 Trade unions have been reluctant to organize in southern 'right to work states' such as Georgia, where legislation mandates that in companies where unions have successfully organized the majority of workers, anyone who does not want to join the union does not have to do so.

19 The minimum wage was $4.25 at the time of research; it was increased to $4.75 in 1996 and to $5.15 in 1997.

20 Since this group included a large number of women past reproductive age, the reality of many older Latinas who are not involved in sexual relationships is also reflected here.

9 Cross-country Comparisons and Political Visions

ROSALIND P. PETCHESKY

Comparing Across and Within Differences

What can we say about the seven complex narratives presented in Chapters 2 to 8 that will weave them all together yet acknowledge the contrasts and contradictions they bring to light? Any effort to draw comparisons across the seven IRRRAG country studies must contend with the great differences among the women who participated: in the methods of selecting them; their distribution by age, ethnicity, religion, marital and employment status and other variables; and of course the cultural, legal and political contexts of the countries and communities in which they live. The following discussion can only highlight a few of these differences in order to illustrate the challenges and opportunities they pose.

In a recent book, Nira Yuval-Davis develops a useful theoretical framework for analysing the various ways in which policies aimed at directing the biological and cultural reproduction of 'the nation' affect the position of women across very diverse societies and cultures – or 'transversally', as she puts it. Echoing a generation of Third World and women-of-colour feminists, she cautions us that attempts to situate local studies within such a framework must always encompass women's identities as 'members of national, ethnic and racial collectivities as well as of specific class, sexuality and life cycle positionings':

> Women are not just individuals, nor are they just agents of collectivities. 'Reproductive rights' campaigns should take account of the multiplexity and multi-dimensionality of identities within contemporary society, without losing sight of the differential power dimension of different collectivities and groupings within it. (Yuval-Davis 1997: 38)

Yet a good-faith effort to approach questions of reproductive rights and 'national reproduction' from a 'multidimensional' perspective may seriously challenge any comparative analysis across the seven IRRRAG studies, or even within each. How does one draw links between the reproductive strategies of a Hausa woman in northern Nigeria, a rural Chinese woman in Malaysia, or a Dominican immigrant woman in New York City (all of whom bind their identities more tightly around their ethnicity than any abstract notion of the nation) and respondents from countries like Brazil and Egypt, where the nationalizing project has had a much broader reach? How does one compare the impact of women's participation in local groups on their sense of reproductive and sexual entitlement, when in some settings, such as Brazil and the Philippines, feminists have had a long interaction with those groups while in others, such as Nigeria and Mexico, such interaction is newly developing?

Variations in national political and economic contexts among the seven countries also make comparisons hard. The severe repression and corruption that infest the current regime in Nigeria have no real equivalent in the other countries, although authoritarian and anti-democratic policies characterize others to different degrees. Likewise, while economic pressures and the impact of structural adjustments burden all the research communities, income disparities among the countries are vast, with Nigeria again in by far the worst situation and the US in a position of gross advantage (see the figures for GNP per capita in Table 9.1). While transnational movements promoting religious fundamentalism are ubiquitous, affecting all the countries to some extent, their influence over public policy is much greater at the moment in some country contexts (Egypt, Malaysia, Philippines and the US) than in others. These external conditions severely limit not only women's ability to realize any sense of entitlement, but also the ability of our respective teams to research this question, and that of women's movements to connect reproductive/sexual rights to broader issues of democracy, citizenship and development.

Differences in national laws also impact differently on women's sense of reproductive and sexual entitlement and thus complicate efforts at comparative analysis. To take one obvious example, abortion laws vary widely among the seven countries, as do the methods of enforcement and the practical effects on women's lives. At the most severe end of the continuum, in the Philippines (where the Catholic Church has the greatest influence over public policy among our countries) penal law prohibits abortion under any circumstances, even in the case of risk to a woman's life. In Nigeria, endangerment to the woman's life is the only exception permitted for a legal abortion. Next in line is Brazil, where abortion remains illegal with two exceptions: life endangerment to the woman and pregnancies caused by rape; but even in these lawful situations, the abortion must be approved by a hospital committee and performed only by a physician. These three countries, where abortion laws are the most restrictive, have significantly higher estimated maternal mortality rates than the other four countries where IRRRAG studies were conducted. (See tables 9.1 and 9.2.) In a middle range are Egypt, Malaysia, and Mexico, whose laws currently allow abortions

Table 9.1 IRRRAG Countries, Some Vital Indicators

COUNTRY	MATERNAL MORTALITY RATIO 1990*	TOTAL FERTILITY RATE 1990–95	INFANT MORTALITY RATE 1990–95†	CONTRACEPTIVE USE, MODERN METHOD 1990‡ (%)	CONTRACEPTIVE USE, ANY METHOD 1990‡ (%)	BIRTHS WITH TRAINED ATTENDANT 1986–90 (%)	GNP PER CAPITA, 1993 (US$)	PUBLIC EXPENDITURE ON HEALTH 1990 (AS % OF GDP)
Nigeria	1,000	6.4	96	4	6	45	300	1.2
Philippines	280	3.9	43	25	40	53	850	1.0
Brazil	220	2.5	57	57	66	73	2,930	2.8
Egypt	174	4.1 / 3.6§	57 / 72.9§	44	45	47	660	1.0
Mexico	110	3.2	35	45	53	45	3,610	1.6
Malaysia	80	3.6	14 / 11.6§	31	48	92	3,140	1.3
USA	12	2.1	8 (NYC 25)	69	74	99	24,740	5.3

* per 100,000 live births.
† per 1,000 live births.
‡ for married couples only, currently using
§ designates Egyptian Demographic and Health Survey or Malaysian Ministry of Health figures, where these differ from UN data on maternal mortality.
Sources: UNDP, *Human Development Report 1996*; WHO and UNICEF, *Revised 1990 Estimates of Maternal Mortality* (April 1996).

under certain limited circumstances, including risk not only to a woman's life but her health, pregnancies resulting from rape, and diagnosis of foetal defects. But implementation measures are severely lacking in these three countries, with very limited availability of services and a failure to provide any information about the law to women or health providers in both Malaysia and Mexico; and harsh criminal penalties in Egypt for both doctors and women who violate the law. (See chapters 2–8 and Ross, Mauldin and Miller 1993, tables 19 and 20.) Only in the USA is abortion officially a constitutional right for all women, yet even there various state and federal laws prohibit public financing of abortions for poor women and create barriers to access for minors. Moreover, many public hospitals, rural areas and, increasingly, private practitioners in the US – intimidated by an aggressive anti-abortion movement backed by the religious right wing – provide no abortion services at all (Chapter 8 and Petchesky 1990).

Table 9.2 Circumstances in Which Induced Abortion Is Legal in IRRRAG Countries

COUNTRY	ILLEGAL (ALL CIRCUMSTANCES)	RISK TO LIFE	RISK TO HEALTH	RAPE OR INCEST	FOETAL DEFORMITY	SOCIO-ECONOMIC HARDSHIP	ELECTIVE
Brazil		X		X			
Egypt		X	X		X		
Malaysia		X	X	X	X		
Mexico		X	X	X	X		
Nigeria		X					
Philippines	X						
USA							X

Source: Ross, Mauldin and Miller 1993, Table 19.

Finally, gender relations in all the countries are still, to be sure, characterized by a primarily patriarchal or male-dominant culture despite formal legislation almost everywhere supporting gender equality. Yet the daily impact of culture and tradition on the power men have over women and the form that power takes varies enormously. This becomes particularly evident when we look at differences in family composition and the meanings of marriage or domestic partnership in women's lives. A woman's sense of sexual and reproductive entitlement and her freedom to express it depend strongly on whether a decision to leave a marriage, or not to marry at all, is a practical option for her or a ticket to social ostracism and destitution.

Both across our seven countries and within them, the degree of manoeuvrability women experienced within and around marriage differed markedly. For grassroots women like our respondents in Nigeria, Egypt, and the Philippines, never to marry was nearly unthinkable because of the cultural unacceptability of childbearing outside marriage; divorce or separation was often fraught with agonizing consequences.[1] The burning issues around marriage were postponing the age of marriage for women and securing the right to the choice of partner and adequate support from a husband. For those in Brazil, Mexico and the US, on the other hand, the particular shape of urban and rural poverty made not marrying at all, or finding themselves single mothers (either divorced, separated or never married) without a man to support them, a more likely prospect; indeed, among the US respondents it was the norm. Instead of investing energy and resources in preparing daughters for marriage, mothers would warn, 'You can't depend on a man.'

Yet, however different their political contexts and cultures, the IRRRAG research sites also revealed striking commonalities that surfaced in the findings time and again – sometimes in words that echoed each other across chasms of language, culture and concepts of physical space. While sensitive to their different nuances, we were profoundly moved by such echoes. On this question of marriage and what it means, for example, recall Suzanne, the 39-year-old African American woman from rural Georgia who operates a small hairdressing shop: 'If I had it to do all over again, I would not get married and I would not have children. I would buy a black Lexus and drive into nowhere … [into] wide, open country.' And now listen again to Selma, the 27-year-old domestic worker from Rio de Janeiro:

> If I had to start it all over again, I would not marry. I would *namorar* [stay in a long-term relationship, non-cohabiting]. Personally, when I am alone at home, I feel better. You have your own space, freedom to think, to listen to music. You are more at ease and more self-determined. (Chapter 2)

Suzanne's fantasy of self-realization is suffused with the commercial television images of North American consumer culture (you too can be rich and 'do your thing'), to which even the most marginalized groups are susceptible. Feeling trapped in a small rural town, she dreams of 'wide, open' space and a free life without children. Selma's fantasy, on the other hand, reflects an urban habitat and above all the longing for a space of her own that comes from working daily in someone else's. And yet, both women – from subcultures that are more oriented toward community than self – express a longing for solitude, individual freedom and self-determination unassociated with reproductive and sexual activities. Similarly, in settings as diverse as Egypt, northeast Brazil and northern Nigeria, we repeatedly found women for whom control over their body meant physical mobility; who spoke of the freedom 'to come and go'. And not surprisingly, such images became especially salient during life stages that tend to be most sexually confining for women in all three settings: adolescence, pregnancy and early motherhood, and widowhood. Reproductive and sexual life experiences, we found, seem to create 'transversal' connections among women despite and through differences (compare Eisenstein 1994 and 1996; Yuval-Davis 1997).

Eight Findings from the Country Studies

Within this general overview, we have culled eight specific findings of common patterns across the diverse country settings that play out in culturally and socially distinct ways. Some of the findings are suprising, while others echo problems that researchers and activists have stressed for years. But even the familiar messages need repeating because most national and international policies still fail to address them seriously.

1. Women respondents in all seven countries aspire to control their own fertility, childbearing and contraceptive use, although social, institutional and legal barriers may prevent them from succeeding. Often this sense of entitlement is acted upon in conscious transgression of community and religious norms and – prompted by fear of violence or harsh reprisals – in secrecy from parents, husbands, partners and authorities.

We found women's sense of entitlement to be strongest overall in the area of decisions about whether and when to have children. In part no doubt, as the Mexico study observed (see Chapter 5), this reflects the legitimating influence of family planning programmes and women's health movements since the 1970s. Respondents in all our countries surely know about various methods of fertility control, either traditional or modern or both; and most have access to them one way or another. Even in those research sites where there is still a glaring gap between the women's family size aspirations and the reality of numerous unwanted pregnancies – most notably, among older women in the Philippines – the (unachieved) sense of entitlement is strongly apparent.[2] In other words, our studies confirm what women's health groups have been saying for years in response to narrow definitions of 'unmet need': that it is not a lack of will or access to methods of contraception that keeps women from preventing unwanted pregnancies successfully, but rather a lack of methods that meet their *social* as well as their biological needs *as they define them*. (Côrrea 1994; Dixon-Mueller and Germain 1992; García-Moreno and Claro 1994)

Respondents in all the countries complained about perceived risks and side effects of available hormonal contraceptives, the main reason they stopped using them. Even more, a depressing number were thwarted in their brave attempts to regulate their fertility by social barriers: uncooperative or belligerent husbands, mothers or other kin; insensitive or inaccessible service providers; and punitive national policies on abortion. The Brazil, Mexico, Nigeria and Philippines studies all relate stories of husbands who threw away pills, refused to sign consent forms for sterilization, or demanded that the woman produce a son. Sometimes respondents were directly threatened with violence, like the rural woman from northeast Brazil whose husband searched through her things for her hidden pills and, upon finding them, warned, 'If I see these pills again you will pay me.'

Reports of domestic violence, especially during pregnancy, came from respondents in nearly all our research settings (compare Heise 1995 and Heise, Moore and Toubia 1995). For many married or partnered women in the Philippines, northeast Brazil, Mexico and the US, endemic male violence aimed at curbing women's reproductive and sexual freedom – usually compounded by alcoholism – was an overt part of daily life. For respondents in the other countries, violence more often lay below the surface or took the form of verbal conflicts; threats of domestic turmoil or censure by the community and especially older females; or a gender-divided upbringing inuring women to habits of obedience and/or surreption. This was especially the case in Egypt and Nigeria, where respondents frequently resorted to strategic accommodations to pre-empt anticipated opposition from husbands, kin, or local authorities.[3]

Barriers to respondents' self-determination over fertility came not only from husbands and family members but from coercive laws and institutions. Among African-American and Latina respondents in the US, as well as many of the Mexican respondents and domestic workers in Brazil, husbands or partners were nonexistent or out of the picture – because of divorce, separation, migration, the built-in conditions of domestic work, or welfare policies that discourage two-parent families. For some of these women, the most serious obstacles to realizing their sense of entitlement regarding fertility were often institutional rather than domestic. They included efforts by clinicians or employers to impose sterilization, hormonal implants, or childlessness, as well as restrictive, antinatalist welfare policies in the US. In Egypt, researchers found that, though family planning services were physically accessible, insensitivity and disrespect by clinicians created deterrents to care; and the same was true for many respondents in Brazil, Malaysia and Nigeria (see finding 8, below). In the Philippines, on the other hand, the control the Catholic Church exercises over family planning still severely limits access to reliable methods and information. And in nearly all the country settings where punitive or restrictive abortion laws prevail, respondents' sense of entitlement to limit their childbearing was being forced underground. Thus IRRRAG's research confirmed the finding of other studies that, '[b]y limiting and intruding into decisionmaking processes, the law encourages individuals to search for clandestine services' – at great danger and cost (Paxman *et al.* 1993: 217).

The result of such intimidation is most often women's subterfuge: hiding, pretending, lying outright; getting some man off the street to sign the required sterilization consent form, getting an illegal abortion clandestinely (and unsafely) or pretending it was a miscarriage. In Egypt, women's deployment of such ruses seems developed to a fine art, and telling their husbands about their use of contraception or abortion, much less subscribing to any kind of 'male involvement' programme, is the last thing they would do.[4] In Brazil, Malaysia, Mexico, Nigeria and the Philippines as well, the majority of women who were using contraception or reported getting abortions did so without the knowledge of husbands or parents, using traditional or illicit methods. Yet in all these cases, the intent and sense of entitlement to control their own fertility is clear, even when existing power relations make it difficult to realize. Even in the Philippines, where fertility rates among respondents were higher than in any of the other research sites, women of all ages expressed a strong aspiration to avoid having 'many mouths to feed'. Although sexual abstinence was their most frequent contraceptive, our Filipina informants clearly saw it as their *right* to refuse or evade the sexual advances of partners in order to reduce the burdens of child care.

2. The primary justification women use for their sense of reproductive entitlement is motherhood: that they (not husbands or partners) suffer the greatest burdens, pains and responsibilities of pregnancy, childbearing and childrearing and therefore have earned the right to make decisions in these arenas. This awareness partly reflects the context of massive urban migration and diminishing social and familial supports for child care.

While the presence and influence of family planning programmes in most of the countries may be an important part of the context that legitimates women's sense of entitlement, this is not what they themselves invoke to justify their decisions. Rather, the women we spoke to cited their responsibility for children as the main ethical ground for their right to make decisions to abort, use contraception, or take over where children were concerned. Over and over again we heard the words 'pain', 'suffering', 'burdens', as though the pain they have gone through in motherhood represents a kind of currency they have paid out of their bodies to earn reproductive authority. This kind of *bodily accounting* may be the counterpart to the 'spiritual accounting' anthropologist Ruth Behar says 'is a constant theme in Mexican women's popular discourse': 'one pays for everything in this world' (Behar 1993: 289, 356). It surfaces in the words of Marta, a forty-year-old Yaqui widow from Sonora, telling her husband why she resisted his attempts to beat the children:

> Because it hurts, . . .because I paid the price for them, because they were born from me, from me they were born and it hurts if someone hits them. Look at you, you can leave this house any time and who is going to stay suffering with this child? Isn't it going to be me? (Chapter 5)

Marta's sentiments are similar to those of Lai Yin, the rural Chinese mother-of-four from Malaysia who insisted, 'I am the one to make the decisions where family planning is concerned.... He only plays with [the children], he does not take care of them.... He does not suffer, the suffering is all done by me' (Chapter 4).

But notice that Lai Yin's sense of reproductive entitlement, like that of so many other women we interviewed, is set in the context of economic hardship and survival (too little food to go around, lack of child care), not 'this is what *I* want, what I need for myself or what would give *me* pleasure'. Illustrating the interconnected, socially situated self (see Chapter 1), the context in which women appeal to the responsibilities of motherhood as ethical grounds for their reproductive authority includes not only economic necessity but also urban migration, break-up of extended families, loss of kin-based supports for child care and household maintenance, and the resultant increase of burdens on biological mothers – trends that are common to all the developing countries in our study. Respondents in Malaysia, Mexico, Brazil, urban Egypt and the Philippines emphasized as a reason for seeking to control their fertility the absence of viable means of child care. This reflects the well-known fact that family size norms are relative to historically changing values about what it means to raise children decently; but it is women as mothers who most often take on the job of enforcing such values (Dixon-Mueller 1993; Ravindran 1996; chapters 2–4).

In some ways, the tendency of women we interviewed to feel more comfortable justifying 'resistant' reproductive decisions in terms of the family's economic survival rather than their own personal needs (much less their 'right to control over their bodies') may be seen as a form of accommodation. At what point does the 'situated self' merge into the normative selfless mother? Yet the 'bodily accounting' conveyed in the statements of Marta and Lai Yin implies a very clear sense of self and a concept of justice in which excessive physical and mental burdens merit primary decision-making rights. Respondents in the US, on the other hand, particularly those who were welfare recipients, expressed a rather different ethical stance, describing motherhood not in terms of burdens and pains but rather in terms of the right to be mothers. As in the other research sites, the US women too appealed to their responsibilities as mothers to justify their reproductive entitlement, but they did so *vis-à-vis* not husbands or partners, but the state. Aware of the power of the state to define their lives and their children's lives, they saw motherhood not only as a way of establishing their adulthood in the community but also as a legitimate expression of citizenship, entitling them to adequate public support. As one Dominican woman put it, 'Right is to care for your children, give them what they need' (Chapter 8 and Benmayor, Torruellas and Juarbe 1992).

3. The extent to which respondents were both willing and able to

express and act on their own judgements concerning sexuality and reproduction varied significantly over the life cycle and between generations. But the patterns differed among the countries, with sometimes young, unmarried women exhibiting the strongest sense of entitlement and other times older women who had passed the time and test of motherhood.

Generational differences in women's sense of entitlement to make sexual and reproductive decisions on their own were evident in all the country studies. In part these differences reflect socioeconomic changes affecting all seven countries to various degrees, as a result of which younger cohorts of women are generally receiving more education, marrying later and having fewer children than their mothers and grandmothers (UN 1995). A new emphasis on the value of educating daughters was particularly important among our respondents in Egypt, Malaysia and urban Nigeria, where we found young unmarried women to be more willing than their mothers' generation to defend women's right to choose their marriage partner, to work outside the home, to make decisions freely concerning contraception and abortion, and sometimes also to abandon the old norms of premarital virginity. In the Philippines, where such generational differences between the mothers and daughters were less vivid, married daughters were none the less more likely than their mothers to use contraception effectively.

In several countries – notably Brazil and Nigeria – mothers seemed willing to express aspirations on behalf of their daughters that they would not claim for themselves, including a strong desire that their daughters should experience not only more education but more freedom than they had had. The São Paulo health movement activists were most vocal on this score – like Fernanda, who wanted her daughter 'at least to finish high school' and 'to have a more open mind'; and Maria, who had 'worked like a slave so [her daughters] could study', telling them, 'you can't depend on a husband'. Most surprising was the São Paulo mother who turned upside down the old maternal dictum to 'take care of yourself' and 'be a good girl'. Instead of warning her daughter to guard her virginity and the family honour, she urged, 'Even if you have sex, do it carefully, use a condom.' While all of this no doubt reflects a context of growing economic insecurity as well as awareness about the risks of HIV/AIDS, it also speaks to the ways in which a sense of sexual and reproductive entitlement may be experienced vicariously across generations.

On the other hand, in some country settings we found that it was older women who tended to be more assertive and self-defined about sexual and reproductive decisions. This pattern was especially striking in Nigeria, where a tradition of seniority by age gave older, and especially postmenopausal, women greater status and authority in the community than younger women, including a certain freedom to seek sexual pleasure without stigma. Sometimes the inter-generational power of older women had positive consequences – for example, the postpartum care given to young Nigerian mothers by older female kin; or the lessons in how to resist spousal violence and unwanted sex that Filipina mothers and mothers-in-law provided to their daughters. In other circumstances, however, older women's power was exerted at the price of perpetuating patriarchal values and the sexual subordination of young unmarried women. This was evident in numerous disturbing examples of mother–daughter conflict: Egyptian mothers who persisted in arranging their daughters' marriages; older women gatekeepers in Egypt and Nigeria who continue to administer FGM and other harmful traditional practices; Filipina mothers who refused to allow their daughters to continue school; and mothers everywhere who withheld vital sexual information from their daughters, imparting instead messages of danger, fear and shame.

What became clear in nearly all the country studies and research settings was that the least empowered stage of women's life cycle was that of early marriage and childbearing. Indeed, we found that women's sense of reproductive and sexual entitlement is strongly mediated through motherhood, especially among Mexican, Egyptian, Nigerian, and northeast Brazilian respondents and among immigrant and African American respondents in the US. At some point, having had children becomes both a rite of passage and a source of authority, after which women feel more entitled to speak their own mind, assert their views and needs regarding contraception or sterilization, fend off male violence and abuse, seek sources of personal satisfaction outside the home, or relax enough to 'just enjoy sex' (see finding 7). It is significant that many of the respondents who became active in community organizations in Brazil and Mexico, and in the immigrant groups in New York, did so only after their children were grown (or old enough to take care of themselves or each other). For them, as for many of the Nigerian respondents, motherhood as an ethical basis of entitlement means that their reproductive and sexual self-determination is postponed until later in life. Moreover, this maternal ethic comes freighted with other costs: it deepens generational conflicts, insofar as activist and working women must depend on older daughters or grandmothers to replace their labour in the home; and it further penalizes childlessness for all women.

4. Women we interviewed are in dialogue with religion but do not let it govern either their behavior or their ethical reasons with regard to fertility control. In Brazil, Egypt and the Philippines, they often imagine a forgiving God who understands their need to have an abortion, use contraception, or refuse unwanted sex with husbands. However, religious authorities still wield great power over women's ability to realize their sense of reproductive entitlement as well as their sense of sexual entitlement.

That people's behaviour often diverges from their publicly stated moral and religious beliefs, especially with regard to intimate matters concerning birth control and sexuality, has been well documented (CFFC 1994, 1997; Luker 1984; Petchesky 1990). We found this pattern often, and with regard to abortion in all seven countries. But we were also surprised and interested to find among our respondents that a practical morality, based on women's bodily suffering and social responsibility for children, as well as economic pressures, usually took precedence over religious belief and the teachings of the Catholic or Islamic authorities. Church authorities in the Philippines might be startled to know that poor women there are saying, '[Birth control] is not the business of the church' (Chapter 7). The church in Brazil, having long contended with popular liberation theology, would be less surprised but no doubt upset to hear our respondents justifying their abortions in terms of a forgiving and understanding God. This is another instance of women's words echoing one another across great cultural and geographic divides. For surely the Brazilian women would identify with the convictions of Soheir, a Muslim working mother in urban Cairo, when she reconciles her abortion with God's will, asking rhetorically, would God want the whole family to suffer if she had to quit work? (Chapter 3)

Soheir's question exemplifies the mosaic of adapted theology and situational ethics that characterizes many women's consciousness about reproductive decisions. Like the Filipina and Brazilian women we interviewed, she is asserting her reproductive entitlement through the invention of a benevolent deity,[5] and she is doing so on the basis of harsh economic conditions that constrain her on all sides. Unlike them, however, she is also accommodating to traditional norms of modesty in Egyptian culture that make breastfeeding on the job unthinkable. In a few cases, negotiating with religion actually led to appropriating aspects of traditional religious teaching that seem to work in women's favour – for example, Muslim respondents in Malaysia and northern Nigeria who based their sense of entitlement to divorce on Islamic law; or Christian respondents in southwest Nigeria who quoted the Bible to support their opposition to widowhood rites.

At the same time, religious authority operates to different degrees in most of our countries to influence state policy and clinical practice around abortion and contraception. The recent legal struggle over government regulations legitimating FGM in public hospitals in Egypt as well as church interference in family planning policy and programmes in the Philippines are the most blatant examples, but the power of religious institutions is only slightly more subtle in influencing legislation and the practical availability of services in the US and Malaysia. As suggested in finding 1, such influence may construct formidable practical barriers to women's realizing their sense of entitlement to control their fertility.

Religious teaching also reaches deeply into women's consciousness through diffusion as traditional norms in the family and community, especially around matters of sexuality and sexual pleasure. This was evident among respondents in Nigeria, the Philippines, and elsewhere. When Zenaib says that, as a Hausa (Muslim) woman, she should not enjoy sex lest her husband think her 'wayward', she replicates the views of Catholic women interviewed in the Philippines and in immigrant Latin communities in the US, as well as the African American respondents (who were Protestant, and also deeply religious). Indeed, attitudes of fatalism and of the inherent immorality of women's pleasure reverberate among at least some respondents in all seven country studies and might be traced in part to the power of religious ideology (see finding 7). Never mind that those attitudes have deeply cultural roots in patriarchal traditions predating organized religion and are sometimes even repudiated by religious authorities (as in Nigeria). The confusion among Egyptian respondents about whether FGM was a religious duty and similarly among Muslim respondents in Malaysia about contraception reminds us that the imprimatur of religion sometimes lends sanctity to traditions that historically had little to do with religion.

5. In most settings, women's empowerment to act on their sense of entitlement in reproductive/sexual decisions was significantly enhanced by having earnings of their own, whether through working outside the home or some kind of home-based work. Yet in all settings, women are still assuming the gender-linked responsibilities of the 'double day'.

On the one hand, we could say that Soheir's wage-earning job reflects the economic squeeze on poor families, but it also authorizes if not empowers her to make reproductive decisions. In all seven of our countries we found that the great majority of respondents, across age groups but particularly those under fifty, sought to work outside the home or, when husbands (or, in the US, welfare authorities) objected, surreptitiously to obtain part-time or home-based work. And most succeeded, as can be seen from the high rates of employment (including informal) among respondent groups listed in Table 1.1. While by no means guaranteeing 'liberation' or equality, the possession of independent earnings and, in many cases, their own marketable skill or small business functioned as a minimal enabling condition to give women not only additional income but a little more dignity, self-respect and space to assert their will in reproductive and sexual matters.

Defying the pervasive myth of men as principal breadwinners, married or partnered women raising children in nearly all our research sites saw acquiring economic resources of their own as a crucial strategy to help them not only to keep their families alive but also to negotiate conflicts with husbands, partners and employers regarding contraception, child care, the division of labour in the household, and unwanted sex or abuse. In urban Egypt, an employed wife like Zeinab derives sufficient autonomy from her status as a skilled seamstress to assert: 'A man who beats his wife lacks manhood' and 'My husband has nothing to do with this contraception issue.' Lucy in the Philippines found that her outside-the-home work gave her a little time of her own to go to the cinema and the means to divert her husband away from drinking into paying his debts. Maquiladora workers in northern Mexico, who have a strong consciousness of themselves as full-time workers and union members, were more likely than other Mexican respondents to use contraception early in their sexual life and to demand support from employers for child care. In Malaysia, where younger genera-tions of women now expect to pursue an education and continue working after marriage, a sixteen-year-old rural Chinese girl says confidently: 'It's better to work after marriage. If you stay at home your husband may bully you. If you are working you are not afraid, you are supporting yourself'.[6]

In Brazil, Miraceia and other married domestic workers, fortified by their earning status and outside-the-home identities, even succeeded in imposing a standard of domestic gender equality concerning household tasks and child care. However, in the majority of sites, married respondents were still contending with the 'double day', performing nearly all the tasks of housework and child care in addition to their outside jobs. In both Egypt and the Philippines, women we interviewed considered working outside the home a resource they must 'pay for' through proving they were not lax in their household duties. Because they acquire personal gratification and things they need from having jobs of their own, they feel they must earn this right; housework for jobs becomes a trade-off, not a question of gender equity.

At the same time, in most of the research sites, having access to independent earnings was a crucial factor that enabled women to fend off violence in the home or, if the situation became intolerable, to leave and support their children on their own. Ironically, this was the case even though working outside the home often exacerbated the women's risk of encountering domestic violence.[7] We heard numerous stories of women in the Philippines, Mexico and the US who confronted their violent, alcoholic husbands with knives or other weapons, who fought back or finally left when the abuse became too much. In Brazil and Malaysia too, a number of respondents walked out on abusive husbands, apparently for good. The critical element reinforcing the women's sense of entitlement in all these cases was their confidence in their ability to earn their own living, and sometimes additionally the support of parents or mothers-in-law. With Tisay in the Philippines (who, armed with a decent job, left her battering husband and took a boyfriend whom she refused to marry), they could say, 'Women do not deserve to be abused by men.' For the women in our research as in other studies, the bases of empowerment (sense of entitlement and ability to act on it) include human resources such as kin networks as well as material or monetary resources (George 1996; Batliwala 1994). Such empowerment correlated strongly among our respondents with not only acting on their entitlement but articulating it in terms of self-ownership and social rights –

like the Philippines respondent who asserted, 'I fight back; he doesn't own me anymore'; or Tisay, who linked her entitlement to that of women as a group.

6. In some settings, belonging to community groups or unions appeared to be one of the strongest factors motivating a sense of entitlement and, above all, the freedom to express it openly; but the latter cases are specific to certain local and political conditions.

Membership in an organization, union or community group was not a variable the IRRRAG project as a whole originally set out to study as one of the factors that might contribute to a sense of reproductive/sexual entitlement. Only in the Brazil, Mexico and US studies, reflecting the political context of those countries and their women's movements, was this a deliberate focus of the study. In Nigeria, Egypt and the Philippines, respondents' connections with local organizations served primarily as a mechanism for identifying and gaining access to interview subjects; and in Malaysia it was not a factor in either the research methodology or the findings. Yet in several of the countries, such affiliation seemed to make the difference between an implicit sense of entitlement, expressed mainly through actions, and one that is expressly articulated in terms of rights. Moreover, in some cases the research process itself became a dynamic vehicle whereby women (and, in Brazil and Egypt, men) began to see their reproductive and sexual entitlements, and their own identities, in a new light.

Like having an income of their own, belonging to an organization or union outside the home does not necessarily 'liberate' women, especially under conditions of increasing marginalization and job insecurity. But it does give them a social context in which to understand their situation and the possibility of seeing themselves as active persons in their own right; it makes the self more than just a body. This dynamic appeared most forcefully in another set of words that echoed across country contexts, with the São Paulo health movement activist who remarked, 'when I started to participate *I was Mary Nobody*, who was not aware of anything; a woman who looked after her husband…. Here in the movement I became conscious that we have to struggle for our rights.' We heard the same sense of transformed identity expressed by Natalia, the Zapotec single mother from rural Oaxaca: 'Before [joining the health organization], *I was nobody*, so to speak. Not now, nowadays everybody says, "let's go to her, she knows".' Likewise Isabel in the Philippines discovered her ability 'to learn something new' (to make up for poor education) and gain 'a sense of fulfilment' through her participation in the community health organization.

Respondents in all three research sites in the US study likewise indicated that belonging to an organized group provided a critical space where they could overcome isolation and talk to others about issues such as domestic violence, sexuality, and birth control. In some cases the expansion of identity beyond motherhood and daily work led to perceptions of group identity and the possibilities of collective action. Thus, for one of the women in the Soperton sewing group, the lesson was that 'Black women ... must accept and help each other'; and for one Latina in the health empowerment group, 'community involvement' meant '[learning] to struggle for our rights as women' (Chapter 8). Although the Egyptian study did not inquire about the role of community or group identity in determining women's sense of entitlement (except among the Islamist unmarried women), the correlation is suggested in the case of the Boulaq–Cairo respondents. In contrast to the other Egyptian research sites, the women there had all been working in a community-based development organization at the time of the study. Among all the Egyptian respondents, they consistently took the most outspoken positions with regard to such issues as their rights as women to marry whom they please, resist spousal violence, and make choices about their own fertility regardless of husbands' wishes.

In other country studies, the research process itself became an occasion for respondents to begin to question their own assumptions about gender, sexuality and reproduction and to experience a climate of support for making claims. This occurred most explicitly in the US, where respondents in group discussions told researchers that 'nobody has asked our opinion before' and expressed a desire to participate in such groups more often. In the Philippines study, a model of feminist participatory research projected from the outset that questions in the field would serve simultaneously as research instruments and interventions. There, follow-up interviews discovered that being asked questions they had never been asked before led to a kind of *conscientization* among respondents; in a rudimentary way, the research process served some of the same functions of opening up new values and identities as did organizational or union membership in Brazil, Mexico and the US.

Our country findings suggest that there may be a difference of magnitude between the kind of entitlement reinforced by women's income-earning activities and that associated with their participation in popular organizations (especially those with some kind of feminist presence). While earning income may empower women to make their own decisions about reproductive issues, activism in organizations may take them another step to form an identity as citizens and active claimants, not only within the household but *vis-à-vis* health providers and the state. But some forms of organization are clearly very different from others in the kinds of entitlement and self-expression they are likely to unleash. In Brazil and Mexico a recent political history of participation in popular, grassroots organizations – for women as well as men – has generated an activist form of citizenship through mobilization in social movements. Similarly, among the union members in New York, the idea of workers' rights, embodied in an organizational framework, was well ingrained and thus more readily transferable to the domain of personal rights. The older women leaders of traditional women's groups in Nigeria, however, like the young Islamist students in Egypt, are sobering reminders that organizational affiliation may result in a kind of assertiveness that is hierarchical, conservative, and reinforcing of patriarchal culture. Not only group participation *per se* but the *kind* of organization, and its ideology, may be key to the question of reproductive and sexual entitlement.

7. Most respondents express little entitlement to sexual pleasure, either to have it or to show need for it. This is in contrast to their strong and frequently articulated sense of entitlement not to be subjected to violence from husbands or unwanted sex. But the minority who do claim sexual enjoyment or autonomy do so unapologetically.

Women in our research communities are much more forthright in their opposition to the dangers involved in sexuality for heterosexual women than they are in expressing any right to sexual pleasure, especially outside the bounds of heterosexual marriage. As mentioned above, respondents in Brazil, Egypt, Mexico, the Philippines, and the US demonstrated overt and sometimes forceful resistance to spousal abuse and violence and more subversive or indirect but often effective tactics (for example, feigning their menstrual period or illness) to avoid unwanted sex. Malay and Indian respondents in Malaysia and Muslim and Christian respondents in Nigeria more frequently professed belief in a wife's duty of obedience to her husband and the husband's right to sexual satisfaction on demand; yet a number of them left their marriages when abuse became unbearable. And in Nigeria, where women are generally blamed for the spread of HIV-AIDS and other STDs, Zenaib, a Hausa Muslim housewife, argued strongly that 'If a man is infected with AIDS or any other STD, his wife should be free to refuse to sleep with him in order to protect herself.'

Yet, when it came to asserting their right to sexual pleasure and satisfaction, only a small number of the women in our studies found their voice. Though Zenaib insisted on protecting herself from the risk of infection, she also argued that a woman should be content 'to give her husband pleasure and get children out of the act', not bothering about enjoying sex. In the Philippines, Mexico and Nigeria, the traditional view of sexual accommodation as a wife's duty and sexual pleasure as a man's prerogative – images of women as passive receptacles or arable fields – seemed especially entrenched. Descriptions of the intimidating, shameful messages surrounding menstruation, puberty and sexual encounters (including even the wedding night) reverberated from one country study to another, across all the cultural diversities – messages that, while originating in religious ideology and patriarchal tradition, were often filtered through gender indoctrination of girls by mothers and other female kin. In Egypt and

Nigeria, painful rituals such as FGM, the *baladi dokhla* and menstrual taboos reinforced these verbal and symbolic messages. Some respondents, like those who stoically endured unwanted sex in the Philippines, viewed such torments as the price they must pay for peace in the home or respectability in the community.

While women in all sites lamented the unfairness of such indoctrination, and above all the failure of mothers to prepare them with accurate sexual information, most still expressed reticence about initiating sex and little awareness of sexual pleasure as a basic need for women as it is for men. Out of all the research communities, only in Egypt was the concept that women like men have a right to sexual satisfaction within marriage – a concept endorsed under *shari'a* law – commonly accepted among both women and men. And even there, initiating sex was usually thought to be something a woman could honourably do at best indirectly, through seductive ploys.

Not only religious taboos and rigid gender socialization explain why so many of our respondents found sexuality alienating and unpleasant. We also have to consider the harsher dimensions of their daily lives that make sexual enjoyment virtually impossible. Respondents in the Philippines like Tasing, with fifteen children, were very clear that constant drudgery, so many children, and a lack of space or 'our own room' made sex 'tiring and painful'. And no doubt, while Tasing's case is an extreme one, her conditions of hard work, fatigue, and lack of privacy are shared by many other women in all our research sites. Moreover, it seemed evident from the experiences reported in most of the countries that many husbands, especially in the early stages of marriage, had very little understanding of how to give a woman pleasure or even that this was something they ought to do. The experience of Wafa'a, a middle-aged married woman from Cairo who reported that her husband was 'nice to me' and 'usually [did] foreplay before the intercourse', seemed the exception. More typical were reports from other countries implying that enjoyment of sex in marriage came after many years if at all – for example, the trade union woman from New York who recalled: 'In the beginning of marriage, he wanted sex every moment of the day.... I didn't want it, didn't like it ... it took years before I was able to relax myself where I could just enjoy sex.' Other women had husbands or partners who remained crude and insensitive, like Gabriela, the bakery worker from Sonora: 'I guess he is like all men, they only care for their own satisfaction, and they want it all the time, every night, and you ... you get fed up ... they harass you so much with sex that you don't have the chance to like it.'

Given this pervasive pattern of sexual denial and harassment, the few strong voices we heard in favour of women's sexual pleasure were all the more remarkable. In nearly all cases these tended to be either young unmarried women or older women who were beyond childbearing and childrearing; though a minority, they emerged in nearly every country. Many of the young unmarried women asserted their entitlement to much more information about sex than their mothers had been given, and some mothers – like the progressive health activists in São Paulo – concurred. Urban young women in northern Nigeria rejected the double standard of virginity for women only, and one announced defiantly, 'Whenever I feel like sleeping with my boyfriend I go to him.' But most studies found respondents more likely to embrace their own entitlement to sexual pleasure in later years, presumably after they had proved themselves as wives and mothers (see finding 3) – for example, the postmenopausal women in rural northern Nigeria who insisted: 'We are not too old to have sex, and why should we give up anything? ... the older men still have sex.' In yet another instance of words repeated across continents, we heard one of these older Nigerian rural women advocating women's equal right to initiate sex on the ground that '*it is her body, she should be free to have control over it*'; an agricultural worker in her forties from northeast Brazil argued in nearly the same words that a woman 'doesn't need to ask for any permission; *it's her own body and she does whatever she wishes with it*'.

Practically the only open support for lesbian sexuality we heard in any of the IRRRAG studies came from another of the Brazilian agricultural workers, also in her forties: 'it's a matter of choice. If someone feels better with a man, she should keep to him. ... if I like a woman, it's my business. ... Everyone has the right to choose what is right for herself.'[8] Though the studies elicited very little evidence one way or the other among respondents regarding lesbian sexuality, and only the union women in New York raised the issue of masturbation, there was no dearth of women who were managing and in some cases choosing to live without men. This was true of the majority of US respondents as well as many in Brazil and Mexico. In Malaysia, a society where marriage is a nearly universal norm, it was particularly striking to hear Yati, an urban Malay woman in her twenties, declare unapologetically, 'I never worry about not getting married because I feel I can survive on my own ... without a man.' In Yati's case, as in that of the other voluntarily single, divorced or separated women in our study, including many who were raising children, surviving without a man was usually made possible by having a viable skill or means of earning a living (see finding 5). The structural context was critical here, as it was in determining other aspects of women's sense of entitlement.

8. With great consistency, respondents in all country settings complained about the poor quality, inaccessibility, and high cost of reproductive health and family planning services; above all they resented the disrespectful and abusive treatment they received from medical providers. Negative public encounters may enhance women's sense of entitlement, and for many women institutional claims may be easier to articulate than personal ones.

During the 1990s, dozens of studies, using different methods and indicators, have attempted to assess the 'quality of care' in reproductive health and family planning services in diverse countries from a 'users' perspective' (see Bruce 1990; Aitken and Reichenbach 1994; INDRA/HAIN 1996; Hardon and Hayes 1997; Jain and Bruce 1994; RHM/WHO 1997; and *Studies in Family Planning*, Vols 22–28). The IRRRAG project did not set out expressly to investigate our respondents' perspectives on the quality of care and service delivery (compare INDRA/HAIN 1996 and Hardon and Hayes 1997). Yet our enquiries about how women negotiate decisions concerning childbearing, contraception, abortion and gynaeco-logical problems invariably prompted a list of grievances about the bad experiences the women had had in clinical settings. If grassroots organiza-tions and independent earnings help to empower women, the health systems and services in our seven countries – all inadequate for and insensitive to poor women – certainly do not.

In most settings, particularly in Brazil, Egypt, Mexico, Nigeria and the US, respondents repeated the now-familiar complaints about the unsatisfactory quality, inaccessibility and high cost of hospital and clinic services. This was true at the same time as the presence of family planning programmes in these countries has undoubtedly been a crucially positive factor contributing to the women's sense of entitlement to control their fertility. In all the countries, problems of access were a direct reflection of the privatization of health services, documented in every chapter, and the rapid diminution of both public resources and government accountability for health care as a social right. Where services for reproductive health, family planning, emergency obstetrics and STD treatment are utterly inaccessible and unaffordable, as in Nigeria, women continue to use local healers, midwives, pharmacies or traditional methods. In the Philippines, as mentioned earlier, despite the longstanding existence of a government-sponsored family planning programme, Catholic Church opposition still prohibits many women, especially those in rural areas, from receiving the range of methods and information to which they are legally and morally entitled.

Yet even where public, low-cost services are available, as in most of Egypt and Malaysia, our studies found that the use of traditional or nonmedical methods for contraception, abortion and childbearing seemed to be a conscious choice on the part of many respondents. Very often this decision reflected inadequate counselling and the unpleasant and untreated side effects they experienced, or anticipated, from medical methods of contraception, as well as the persistence of legal and cultural restrictions on abortion.[9] But by far the most important barrier to genuine quality of care found in our studies was the demeaning and inhumane treatment respondents in all the countries received from health professionals. Certainly there were examples of women who had received sensitive counselling at local clinics and were using non-permanent methods of contraception successfully, like Lai Yin and

Karuthama in Malaysia. In Mexico City our research encountered extraordinary examples of women who knew what they wanted and how to negotiate the formidable world of public hospitals and family planning facilities, standing up to doctors and husbands alike to make sure their needs got met. But these seemed to be the exceptions. More typically, respondents in our study became discouraged and alienated by insensitive, often abusive treatment and gave up on medical services rather than exposing themselves to such abuse. Callous attitudes and practices on the part of providers, often rooted in class or race–ethnic as well as gender bias, operate as a *de facto* barrier to access, even destroying trust in all public services.

Stories of abuse by reproductive health providers did not just come from the global South, as the accounts by rural African American women who had been given Norplant attest. When they tried to have the implants removed because of side effects, local clinic personnel told them their complaints of excess bleeding, weight loss and palpitations were 'inconveniences' not 'medical problems', therefore not warranting removal under Medicaid unless they paid $300 to reimburse the state. Stories from respondents in Brazil and Mexico of abusive treatment by doctors and practitioners – including taunts, rude dismissiveness, and even sexual harassment of themselves and other women – are truly appalling, as well as confirming numerous reports of rampant involuntary sterilization, especially in Mexico. But while researchers voice the legitimate concerns of women's health movements about a medical culture privileging surgical and invasive methods (see Chapter 2), the palpable anger of the women in these studies is focused less on any particular methods than on the human aspects of the clinic. Sometimes respondents clearly wanted a tubal ligation, an IUD insertion, or a Caesarean section (like indomitable Emilia in Mexico City); but more than anything they wanted to be taken seriously, listened to and treated with respect. In Nigeria, Egypt, the Philippines and rural Malaysia, women seem less likely to protest verbally against clinical abuses but rather 'vote with their feet', refusing to go back to the clinic or hospital even if this jeopardizes their own health.

While poor quality and inaccessible services seem to be the reality for nearly all our study populations, these inadequacies are more severe in some country settings than others. A glance at differences in maternal mortality ratios, percentages of births administered by trained attendants, total fertility rates and contraceptive use rates among our seven countries offers the sharpest evidence of these national differences (see Table 9.1). Moreover, illegal or restricted abortion, though a problem in all seven countries (Table 9.2), clearly has more adverse consequences in terms of maternal mortality and morbidity for women in some of the countries.[10] Abortion remains a delicate issue in many of the research settings, addressed by most respondents with caution and often with a sharp discrepancy between what they are willing to say publicly and what they do in practice. As emphasized earlier, their reticence is the immediate and pragmatic result of punitive laws and religious and cultural sanctions, reinforced by the condemning attitudes of hospital personnel. Moreover, negative attitudes among respondents toward abortion often seem at least as motivated by fears of what they have heard about women suffering and dying as by any moral or religious feelings.

The long-term effect of such restrictions, however, like that of clinical abuses, may be to enhance women's sense of entitlement rather than suppressing it. We found that public encounters over such issues as abortion or involuntary sterilization aroused respondents' anger and made them aware of the injustices perpetrated by health officials and institutions. Increasingly, they are willing to speak out against the unnecessary price women have to pay in suffering and death because they are denied access to safe legal abortions. The focus group participants in São Paulo and northeast Brazil, who raged against doctors who 'don't give a damn' when they see women bleed to death every day from self-induced abortions or who scold you 'if you are poor' but not if you are rich, differ from respondents in Egypt and Nigeria in one critical respect: they belong to organized community groups that provide a framework in which anger may be directed toward collective action (see finding 6). Yet many of our respondents, whether organized or not, seemed to find it easier to articulate a sense of injustice and entitlement toward public institutions than toward partners and kin, those with whom they have to live. Perhaps negotiating public conflicts over reproductive and sexual rights will make it more possible for women to negotiate the private conflicts at home.

Summary

Over and over again, the IRRRAG research findings paint a picture of tremendous resilience and courage; women who not only cope patiently with meagre resources and intransigent cultural and social barriers to their reproductive and sexual freedom but who defy the tradition of female passivity: manoeuvring around, subverting, bending, or sometimes directly challenging those barriers. Fitting neither the image of victims nor that of staunch feminist warriors, they do express a sense of reproductive and sexual entitlement, but on some issues more sharply than others and in a context mined with obstacles – from husbands, parents, doctors and other clinic staff, religious authorities, and the state. Most of our respondents in all seven countries showed a clear sense of entitlement to make their own decisions with regard to marriage (when and to whom), fertility (number and timing of children), contraception, avoidance of domestic violence and unwanted sex, child care, and work (whether and when to work outside the home or seek economic resources of their own). While resenting the lack of male responsibility for safe contraception and children's care, they *seem to prefer relying on their own resources and control of things rather than trusting in the cooperation of men.* In this regard, they are clearly willing to go to great lengths to maintain secrecy, safety and self-determination in order to avoid the constant risks of domestic violence, marital discord, public shame, or clinical abuse. The reliance of our Egyptian respondents on risky, self-induced methods of abortion, or of those in Nigeria on local TBAs to administer childbirth, represents a kind of resistance, even a counterhegemonic morality, yet one in which women pay out of their bodies.

This suggests that strategic accommodations and trade-offs not only signify conditions of oppression; they also help to perpetuate those conditions, and they always exact a price. When a woman refuses to return for follow-up visits to a hospital or clinic because her complaints have been dismissed or condemned and her language, ethnicity or customs have been treated with contempt, she reclaims her dignity; but she also exposes herself to additional risks of infection, unwanted pregnancy, unsafe abortion, and thus reproductive morbidity and mortality. When a woman concedes to unsafe traditional practices such as FGM that damage her bodily integrity (or her daughter's) in order to purchase greater mobility and respect, she not only compromises her health and sexual pleasure but also buttresses a cultural context where notions of shame and honour turn on female virginity (Corrêa 1994). When a woman argues, 'I am the one who should decide because I am the one who bears the pains and responsibilities of motherhood,' she is definitely asserting a (consequentialist) ethical claim on behalf of her own entitlement as reproductive decision maker. However, her position falls short of demanding that others concerned with the wellbeing of children – the state, husbands or partners – share those responsibilities. In other words, she is still taking for granted the 'naturalness' of traditional gender divisions and defining motherhood as the core of who she is.

The harsh realities so many of the women in our studies are attempting to negotiate show clearly that having a sense of entitlement may be very distant from the ability to act on it effectively. This obliges us to ask, what is it that enables women to move from entitlement to action, from strategic negotiation to demands for social justice? What motivates them to address the structural conditions that govern their everyday strategies and that make the very terms in which those strategies are invented deeply unjust? The fact that so many women in all the countries studied routinely participate in the 'clandestine epidemic' of unsafe abortion, for example, reflects a perception of circumstances that may be unfair and oppressive but are also just 'part of life': poverty, lack of child care, angry husbands who threaten violent reprisals, state laws and punitive religious codes opposing legal abortion, and the unavailability of safe, acceptable contraceptive methods and sensitive care.

All the IRRRAG country studies have attempted to locate women's perceptions and decision-making within the wider context of social, economic and cultural conditions that constrain those decisions. Some of the studies – especially those done in Brazil, urban Mexico and the US – have pointed to a complex interface between organizational opportunities within community groups and unions and a commitment to collective action. For research to go beyond revelation to become socially transformative, we need to help women to connect their awareness of injustice – however articulated or implied through the daily negotiations of reproductive and sexual conflict – to demands for social and economic change. From this double perspective we can mobilize stronger, more grounded actions to redirect policies and transform societies.

Recommendations for Policy and Action

IRRRAG's research findings suggest a number of practical actions that should be given serious priority by (a) researchers and research groups; (b) women's health and rights movements; and (c) policy makers and donors in both national governments and international organizations.[11]

1. Researchers and research groups interested in women's reproductive and sexual health/rights as an aspect of development should value the *process* at least as much as the outcomes of their research (Benmayor 1991; Khanna 1996). They should consider the usefulness of a feminist participatory action approach to research. The Philippines team has described the dynamics of this process as it unfolded in their fieldwork, but the same experience was repeated more or less in all the IRRRAG country studies:

> The women knew that what they shared will be published, and they exhibited a sense of pride in learning that their words were in turn shared in both local and international forums. In some instances, these sharings were for them a dress-up occasion. In turn, the local women's organization was able to use its participation in the research to further project its existence and credibility to the community, at the same time that individuals within the organization gained valuable research, organizational and interpersonal skills. (unpublished communication)

Thus, the research process itself can become a way of validating women's experience, exchanging ideas, and engaging in action toward empowering women.

2. We encourage other researchers and research–action groups to follow up the IRRRAG studies in areas where our research design contained gaps or our findings point to the need for more data. In particular, we urge further investigation

- across divisions of class. How and when do middle-class and more educated women, at different life stages, express a sense of entitlement in the domains of reproduction and sexuality, and how do patterns among them compare with those of poor and working-class women?

- in relation to men. What do women feel entitled to in the way of support and responsibility on the part of male partners, sons and brothers with regard to reproductive and sexual tasks and decisions? In what ways would they – and the men in their communities – like to see men's involvement promoted, or not?[12]

- in relation to women kin and associates. How do mothers, mothers-in-law, sisters, other female kin, friends, co-workers, TBAs and nurses either reinforce or inhibit the sexual and reproductive entitlement of women and girls? Who among them is most influential?

- with regard to sexuality. To what extent does women's sense of sexual entitlement at different life stages and across diverse ethnic, class and other groups encompass the right to sexual pleasure, within or outside marriage, and the right to be a lesbian?

- with regard to work. Will further research validate the hypothesis (Chapter 7) that some types of income-generating work are more likely than others to empower women as decision makers and actors in the domains of reproduction and sexuality?

- in other countries and regions. Will similar studies, using IRRRAG's methods and framework questions, yield similar results in countries and regions not originally included in our project – for example, countries in Eastern and Western Europe, the Caribbean, Central America, East Asia, and Southern and Eastern Africa?

3. Women's health advocates and activists, in developing programmes that promote women's and girls' sexual health and rights, should emphasize not only the right and means to be protected from danger and STDs/RTIs but also the right to sexual pleasure and diverse modes of sexual expression. To counter the cultural and social hegemony of religious fundamentalists and traditional messages of shame, such programmes should provide women of all ages with positive images of their bodies, an awareness of erotic pleasure as a natural and joyful part of life, and knowledge that diverse sexual orientations and family forms are intrinsic to human societies.

4. In their educational and outreach work, women's health advocates and activists should focus more attention on generational differences among women and the role that older women play as gatekeepers, informants and mediators of reproductive and sexual entitlement, especially *vis-à-vis* young unmarried women. While remaining aware that older women may perceive accommodation to traditional norms and practices as their only source of dignity and respect, women's groups need to develop sensitive but effective strategies for providing alternative sources of respect for older women as well as improving intergenerational communication among women. Such strategies might include organizing discussion groups across generations on women's sexuality, sexual pleasure and danger;[13] developing feminist

educational materials, geared to older women as gatekeepers, concerning the health and social consequences for themselves and their daughters of traditional practices such as FGM, early marriage, son preference, etcetera, and presenting realistic alternatives; and recruiting older women as well as young women and girls into women's rights and health organizations.

5. Programmes and projects seeking to involve men in responsibility for reproductive and sexual health should first find out what women in the relevant communities want and need from men and whether involving men precipitously might have adverse consequences for women's empowerment and wellbeing. In particular, 'male involvement' programmes should not divert vital funds and resources away from programmes aimed at empowering women and girls, nor should they under any circumstances jeopardize the confidentiality women seek in their decisions and actions concerning fertility and sexuality (Berer 1996; Helzner 1996). Such programmes, rather, should place priority on counselling men and boys to prevent negative cultural attitudes, abuse and violence targeted at women and girls, which are among the most serious deterrents to women acting on their reproductive and sexual entitlement effectively. In addition, they should focus on increasing men's and boys', and alleviating women's and girls', responsibilities at all stages of the life cycle with regard to the daily tasks of child care and housework. (See FWCW Platform for Action, Paragraphs 28, 125–6, 276–7 and 283, and ICPD Programme of Action, Paragraph 4.11.)

6. In view of IRRRAG's finding that participation in grassroots organizations frequently contributes to women's empowerment in relation to reproduction and sexuality, governments, donors and intergovernmental agencies should foster the work of such organizations both through the allocation of resources and through creating a supportive and open political climate. Such support will carry out the Cairo Programme's objective to 'encourage the expansion and strengthening of grassroots, community-based and activist groups for women' (ICPD Programme, Paragraph 4.12) and should be aimed especially at women's health and rights organizations that are working toward implementation of the Cairo and Beijing documents. Toward the same end, governments, donors, international agencies, and women's advocacy groups should work to increase women's participation in unions and other associations in the public sphere that expand their members' sense of rights as women, citizens and members of civil society.

7. Governments, intergovernmental organizations, and women's health and rights groups should promote interfaith dialogues on issues of reproductive and sexual rights and should work to give the voices of feminist and alternative theologians more space in public policy debates over these issues. Support should be provided to groups like Catholics for a Free

Choice, Sisters in Islam and Women Living Under Muslim Laws to enable them to work more closely with grassroots rural and urban women to validate the women's ethical judgements and authority on these questions, *vis-à-vis* religious hierarchies, and to put them in touch with interpretations outside the religious mainstream.

8. IRRRAG's findings confim once again that women continue to get abortions even under conditions of extreme risk and illegality, and that this persistence implies a sense of ethical entitlement based on practical necessity. Governments and religious institutions should recognize the legitimacy of women's decisions by making abortions safe, legal, and less necessary (because offered as a back-up to the full range of contraceptive methods, provided in sensitive and caring facilities). They should do so not only on the basis of public health concerns (to lower maternal mortality and morbidity resulting from unsafe abortions), but also out of respect for women's personhood and moral integrity, for their knowledge as mothers and family caretakers, and for their need as moral persons to negotiate their reproductive rights openly and safely rather than through secrecy and subterfuge.

9. Both government and private clinics and hospitals have a responsibility, in guaranteeing 'quality of care' to all clients, to make sure that caregivers are sensitive and respectful of women's dignity, decision-making capacity and ethnic diversity. All providers should be required, as part of their professional training, to develop understanding of their patients' perspectives, from the standpoint of gender, age, sexual orientation, ethnicity and culture; they should also be prohibited from imposing their own moral or religious views in their function as caregivers. They should respect clients' own decisions as well as providing thorough counselling and information about and access to a full range of reproductive health services, without coercion, in keeping with paragraphs 7.3, 7.6, 7.7 and 7.13 of the ICPD Programme of Action. Such sensitivity, along with the resources specified in recommendation 10, should be an essential part of any programmatic definition of 'unmet need'.

10. The structural context and enabling conditions of women's reproductive and sexual rights must be linked programmatically to family planning and reproductive/sexual health services. Governments, donors and intergovernmental organizations should immediately implement the provisions of the ICPD Programme of Action and the Beijing Platform for Action that set forth strategic objectives to enhance women's economic and social development (for example ICPD, Paragraph 3.18 and FWCW, Strategic Objectives A.1–A.3 and B.1–B.3). Specifically, this means enacting policies and programmes that affirm the critical links between women's entitlement to make their own reproductive and sexual decisions responsibly

and effectively and their access, independently of husbands or partners, to economic and social resources, including jobs, skills, credit, education, and other vital means of securing a decent livelihood for themselves and their children. Such resources should be taken into account by demographers and reproductive health planners in programmatic definitions of 'unmet need'.

11. Regarding the enforcement of women's human rights, IRRRAG's research findings strongly support the principle of indivisibility among economic, social, cultural, political and civil rights, as well as the necessity of defining those rights through democratic and inclusive dialogue. Our studies show a direct link between women's ability to exercise their reproductive and sexual rights effectively and a wide range of enabling conditions that stretch from the highest levels of state power and law to the most intimate relations of the kitchen and bedroom. Governmental and intergovernmental agencies and NGOs should take account of these findings in their efforts to devise reliable indicators for measuring progress in implementing reproductive rights principles, as set forth in the Cairo and Beijing documents. Grassroots women in our research sites have, through their actions as well as their words, named several crucial indicators, including access to economic and vocational resources; access to sensitive, humane and responsive caregivers; access to information that would expand their choices; confidentiality, especially *vis-à-vis* husbands and partners; opportunities for involvement in women's groups; and access to safe abortions. Policies designed to implement reproductive and sexual rights principles, and to honour commitments made in Cairo and Beijing, should embrace what these women are saying.

Notes

1 In the Philippines alone among the seven countries divorce is still officially illegal. However, among the Philippine respondents counted as 'married', a good number were in unofficial, cohabiting relationships; and several had entered into permanent separations despite the legal and religious restrictions on divorce.

2 The form such aspirations take may differ from one country or region to another. For example, in four countries (Brazil, Egypt, Mexico and the Philippines) the majority of our respondents use methods to stop rather than to space or postpone childbearing; in Malaysia, Nigeria and the US a culture of child spacing exists among most of the study populations as well as the population at large. While Nigerian women, both in our study and generally (see Table 9.1), tend to have more children than those in the other countries (with the exception of the Philippines study), our qualitative data affirm that this corresponds to their desire – that is, the ideal family size for most Nigerian women we interviewed is 4–6 children. See Chapter 6.

3 A pervasive pattern of domestic violence is now also coming to light in Egypt. See Egypt, National Population Council 1995 and New Woman Research and Study Centre and El Nadim Centre for Rehabilitation of Victims of Violence 1995.

4 This finding of the Egyptian IRRRAG team contrasts strikingly with a recent study

based on data from the 1988 Egypt DHS emphasizing the cultural preference in Egypt for joint (husband–wife) decisions (Govindasamy and Malhotra 1996). See Chapter 3.

5 Poor rural women of the Brazilian Northeast draw on a longstanding history of popular opposition to Catholic Church teaching when they commonly regard their first-trimester abortions as 'trading with God'. Liberation theology, deeply entrenched among the poor in Brazil, provides them with an alternative vision – that of a merciful, kind deity who helps women through hard times – to justify their transgression of the clergy's moral views (Chapter 2 and Ribeiro 1994). We are not aware, however, of such a tradition among either poor Catholic women in the Philippines or certainly poor Muslim women in Egypt, and our researchers were fascinated to find this common theme across such different cultures.

6 Respondents' stories in Malaysia also illustrate the variety of ways in which women's work patterns may be constrained by parental fears about the immoral influences of town life, as in Aini's case, or a husband's sexual jealousy, as in Lia's.

7 Indeed, the very fear of such risk motivated some women, especially in Malaysia and the Philippines, to hide their income-generating activities from their husbands, through clandestine or home-based work. See Chapters 4 and 7.

8 It is possible that this recognizably feminist discourse is not completely coincidental but reflects the influence among the group of women agricultural workers in Pernambuco of feminist organizers from SOS-Corpo in Recife.

9 In Brazil, Egypt, Malaysia and the Philippines, many of our respondents had tried medical methods of contraception at one time or another but discontinued their use or were using them irregularly. From their perspective, the reasons were primarily the physical side effects they experienced combined with antagonism from husbands and kin (see finding 1), though these problems were clearly compounded by poor counselling, lack of follow-up, and illiteracy (inability to read the packet instructions).

10 According to recent estimates, unsafe induced abortion accounts for one-third of all maternal deaths and '800,000 hospitalizations annually' in Latin America, and abortion rates have been rising most rapidly in Brazil, especially in the Northeast (Singh and Sedgh 1997). In Egypt, where reliable hospital data on complications are less available, it is none the less well known that 'the country's hospitals ... receive a steady stream of emergency postabortion cases' (Huntington et al. 1995). See also Berquó 1993; Khattab 1992; Germain et al. 1992; and Younis et al. 1993 regarding excessive and unnecessary morbidity from poor reproductive health services.

11 Our purpose here is not to cover every possible implication for policy and action emerging from the IRRRAG studies but rather to highlight those that have until now, in our view, drawn too little attention and resources.

12 The IRRRAG project intends to follow up the present study with a second one that will address these questions about men in some of our research communities.

13 Discussions of sexuality and sexual pleasure have become a major focus of women's health groups and family planning programmes seeking to help women negotiate safer sex and to integrate HIV/STD prevention strategies into reproductive health practices (see, for example, Zeidenstein and Moore 1996 and Becker and Leitman 1997). Our concern here is that the focus of many programmes on young people should not distract from the importance of bringing older women, who play a key part in shaping younger women's attitudes and options, into the conversation.

About the Contributors

Amal Abdel Hadi is a medical doctor by training, a founder member of the New Woman Research Centre, and director of the women's programme at the Cairo Institute for Human Rights. She has been active in the Egyptian Task Force against Female Genital Mutilation.

Nadia Abdel Wahab is an internist and chair of the Department of Geriatric Medicine at the Palestine Hospital in Cairo. She is a founder member of the New Woman Research Centre and is active in grassroots mobilizations concerning reproductive health and rights in Egypt.

Ana Amuchástegui Herrera is a lecturer–researcher in the Department of Education and Communication at the Universidad Autonoma Metropolitana-Xochimilco in Mexico City.

Lourdes L. Arches is a chemist with training in the natural sciences and a member of WomanHealth Philippines.

Chee Heng Leng teaches community health in the Faculty of Medicine and Health Sciences at the University Putra Malaysia. Actively involved in women's issues, she was a founder member of the Women's Development Collective and the All Women's Action Society in Malaysia.

Simone Grilo Diniz is a medical doctor and also holds a master's degree in preventive medicine. She works as a researcher and activist with the Coletivo Feminista Sexualidade Saúde in São Paulo, Brazil, and was coordinator of IRRRAG-Brazil from 1992 to 1996.

Mercedes Lactao Fabros is the national convenor of WomanHealth Philippines, a nationwide organization that advocates on women's health and rights issues. She has served as country coordinator of the Philippines IRRRAG team.

Dianne Jntl Forte is editor of the Health, Reproduction and Sexuality section of the *Women's Studies Encyclopedia* and former director of international programmes for the National Black Women's Health Project in the United States.

Maria Teresa Guia-Padilla is completing her MA in anthropology at the University of the Philippines and has been involved in research, documentation and activism since the late 1970s.

Karen Judd has a PhD in anthropology and did her field research in Belize. A writer and editor specializing in women's economic and human rights, she currently works in New York City as a communications consultant for NGOs and foundations on gender-related policy issues.

Adriane Martin-Hilber holds a master's degree in public health and has worked as a consultant to numerous international development, environment, and women's health organizations. From 1995 to 1997, she was IRRRAG's international program manager in New York.

Cecília de Mello e Souza has been working in the field of reproductive health since 1988 and received her PhD in anthropology from the University of California at Berkeley in 1993. She is a professor at the Federal University of Rio de Janeiro in Brazil.

Adriana Ortiz Ortega is a feminist scholar with a PhD in political science, a technical adviser to international organizations on issues of gender and reproductive health, and a daydreamer for social change. She is the country coordinator of the Mexican IRRRAG team.

Grace Osakue is an educator and school principal in Benin City, where she has served as country coordinator of IRRRAG-Nigeria. She has been involved in the women's movement since 1984 and is a co-founder of Girl's Power Initiative, a group dedicated to empowering adolescent girls.

Aileen May C. Paguntalan works with organizations doing research and advocacy on behalf of both indigenous peoples and women's rights. She is pursuing an MA in anthropology at the University of the Philippines.

Rosalind Pollack Petchesky is professor of political science and women's studies at Hunter College of the City University of New York, and a

MacArthur Fellow. She has been active in the US-based movement for women's reproductive health and rights since 1977 and founded IRRRAG in 1992.

Ana Paula Portella has been a researcher and trainer with SOS-Corpo/ Gender and Citizenship in Recife, Brazil since 1991. She received degrees in psychology and political science in Brazil, where she has coordinated the IRRRAG team since 1996.

Rita Raj was a founder and co-director of the Asian Pacific Resource and Research Centre for Women (ARROW) and co-coordinator of IRRRAG's team in Malaysia. After many years working in family planning and reproductive health, she now studies traditional Chinese medicine.

Marta Rivas Zivy is a lecturer–researcher in the Department of Education and Communication at the Universidad Autonoma Metropolitana-Xochimilco in Mexico City.

Aida Seif El Dawla is assistant professor of psychiatry in the Faculty of Medicine at Ain Shams University in Cairo. She is a founder member of the New Woman Research Centre and the El Nadim Centre for the Rehabilitation of Victims of Violence and the coordinator of IRRRAG-Egypt.

Rashidah Shuib is Associate Professor of Medical Education at Universiti Sains Malaysia. She is chair of the Nursing Diploma Programme 354 and is active in local, regional and international family planning organizations on behalf of women's issues.

Bibliography

Abdullahi Ahmed, A. (1994) 'Towards an Islamic Reformation: Islamic Law in History and Society Today', in Norani Othman (ed.), *Shari'a Law and the Modern Nation State: A Malaysian Symposium*, Sisters in Islam, Kuala Lumpur.

Abramowitz, M. (1996) *Regulating the Lives of Women: Social Welfare Policy from Colonial Times to the Present*, South End Press, Boston.

Abu-Lughod, L. (1994) *Writing Women's Worlds*, University of California Press, Berkeley.

Ackerman, S. E. and R. L. M. Lee (1990) *Heaven in Transition: Non-Muslim Religious Innovation and Ethnic Identity in Malaysia*, Forum, Kuala Lumpur.

Acosta Díaz, F. (1992) 'Hogares más pobres con jefaturas femininas', *Demos*, No. 5.

Adamchak, D. and A. Adebayo (1987) 'Male Fertility Attitudes: A Neglected Dimension in Nigerian Fertility Research', *Social Biology*, Vol. 34, No. 1.

Adebanjo, C.O. (1992) 'Female Circumcision and Other Dangerous Practices to Women's Health', in M. Kisekka (ed.), *Women's Health Issues in Nigeria*, Tamaza, Zaria, Nigeria.

Adekunle, A. O. and O. A. Ladipo (1992) 'Reproductive Tract Infections in Nigeria: Challenges for a Fragile Health Infrastructure', in A. Germain *et al., Reproductive Tract Infections: Global Impact and Priorities for Women's Reproductive Health*, Plenum, New York and London.

Adetunji, J. (1997) 'The Quest for Healthy Childbearing in a Nigerian Community', paper presented at the Seminar on Cultural Perspectives on Reproductive Health, organised by the IUSSP Committee on Reproductive Health and University of Witwatersrand Department of Community Health, Rustenburg, South Africa (June).

Africa Leadership Forum, Federal Ministry of Health and Social Services (1992) 'Conclusions, Recommendations, Summary Report and Papers', proceedings of the Farm House Conference on Population, Gateway Hotel, Ota, Nigeria (November).

Afshar, H. (ed.) (1991) *Women, Development & Survival in the Third World*, Longman, London.

Agarwal, B. (ed.) (1988) *Structures of Patriarchy*, Zed Books, London.

AGI (Alan Guttmacher Institute) (1993) 'Sexually Transmitted Diseases in the United States,' *Facts in Brief*, AGI, New York.

AGI (1994a) 'Teenage Reproductive Health in the United States', *Facts in Brief*, AGI, New York.

AGI (1994b) *Clandestine Abortion: A Latin American Reality*. AGI, New York.

AGI (1997) 'Special Tabulations of NSFG 1995', *Facts in Brief*, AGI, New York.

Aitken, I. and L. Reichenbach (1994) 'Reproductive and Sexual Health Services: Expanding Access and Enhancing Quality', in G. Sen, A. Germain and L.C. Chen (eds), *Population Policies Reconsidered: Health, Empowerment and Rights*, Harvard University Press, Cambridge, MA.

Akhter, F. (1990) 'Issues of Women's Health and Reproductive Rights'. Paper presented at the Sixth International Women and Health Meeting, Manila, Philippines.

Akhter, F. (1994) 'Resist Reduction of "Population" Issues into Women's Issues', People's Perspectives, No. 8, March.

Alvarez, S. E. (1990) *Engendering Democracy in Brazil: Women's Movements in Transition Politics*, Princeton University Press, Princeton, NJ.

Amin, S. and S. Hossain (1995) 'Women's Reproductive Rights and the Politics of Fundamentalism: A View from Bangladesh', *American University Law Review*, Vol. 44, No. 4.

Antoniello, P. (1994) 'Pilot Study: Low Income Women in Appalachia', unpublished paper, Brooklyn College, Brooklyn, NY.

APPRR (Asia Pacific Population Research Reports) (1995), *Family Planning Policy and its Implementation in Eight Countries in Asia*, Research Reports No. 1, January 1995.

Arilha, M. and R. M. Barbosa (1993) 'The Brazilian Experience with Cytotec', *Studies in Family Planning*, Vol. 24, No. 4 (July–August). Revised version, 'Cytotec in Brazil: "At Least It Doesn't Kill" ', *Reproductive Health Matters*, No. 2 (Nov.)

Aromasodu, M. O. (1982) 'Traditional Practices Affecting the Health of Women in Pregnancy and Childbirth', in *Traditional Practices Affecting the Health of Women and Children*, WHO Regional Office, Alexandria, Technical Publication, Vol. 2, No. 2.

Askiah, A. (1993) 'The Reproductive Rights of Muslim Women: The Malaysian Case', Kuala Lumpur, unpublished.

Aslam, A. (1993) 'Beyond the Holy War', *Populi*, September 1993.

Atsenuwa, A. (1995), 'Effects of Structural Adjustment Programme on Women', paper presented at the NGO forum, African Regional Preparatory Meeting for the Fourth World Conference on Women, Dakar, Senegal (Nov.).

Ávila, M. B. (1993) *Direitos Reprodutivos: Uma Invenção das Mulheres. Reconcebendo a Cidadania*, SOS CORPO, Recife.

Ávila, M. B. (1993a) 'Modernidade e Cidadania Reprodutiva', *Revista de Estudos Feministas*, Vol. 1, No. 2.

Badiani, R. *et al.* (1996) *Avaliação Qualitativa Projeto Mulher-AIDS-Prevenção*, Clinica de Natal, RN, BEMFAM, Rio de Janeiro.

Badiani, R. *et al.* (1997) *Sexual Health and STD/HIV Prevention in a Salvador Clinic: A Qualitative Evaluation of Integrated Clinical and Educational Projects – Final Report*, BEMFAM, Rio de Janeiro.

Badran, H. (1995) *Women Headed Households*, National Population Council and National Council for Motherhood and Childhood, Cairo.

Badran, M. (1994) 'Gender Activism: Feminists and Islamists in Egypt', in V. M. Moghadam (ed.), *Identity Politics and Women*, Westview Press, Boulder/San Francisco/Oxford.

Bahey El Din, A. (1997) 'Equality before the Law: The Case of Egyptian Women', paper given to the Women, Law and Development Conference, New Woman Research and Study Centre, Cairo.

Bandarage, A. (1997) *Women, Population and Global Crisis*, Zed Books, London.

Bankole, A. (1995) 'Desired Fertility and Fertility Behavior Among Yoruba of Nigeria: A Study of Couple Preference and Subsequent Fertility', *Population Studies*, Vol. 49.

Barbosa, R. M. and W. V. Villela (1996) 'A Trajetoria Feminina da AIDS', in R. Parker and J. Galvao (eds), *Quebrando o Silencio: Mulheres e AIDS no Brasil*, ABIA/IMS-UERJ/Relume-Dumara, Rio de Janeiro.

Barr, C. (1995). 'Philippine Elite Prospers But Poor Still Scraping By', *Christian Science Monitor*, 9 February 1995.

Barros, F. C. *et al.* (1991) 'Epidemics of Caesarean Sections in Brazil', *Lancet*, Vol. 338, No. 20.

Barroso, C. and G. Bruschini (1989) 'Construindo a Política a Partir da Vida Pessoal: Discussões sobre Sexualidade entre Mulheres Pobres no Brasil', in M. E. Labra (ed.), *Mulher, Saúde e Sociedade no Brasil*, Ed. Vozes, Petropolis.

Barroso, C. and S. Corrêa (1995) 'Public Servants, Professionals, and Feminists: The Politics of Contraceptive Research in Brazil', in F. D. Ginsburg and R. Rapp (eds), *Conceiving the New World Order*, University of California Press, Berkeley.

Barsted, L. (1992) 'Decriminalization of Abortion in Brazil: Ten Years of Feminist Struggles', *Revista Estudos Feministas*, Vol. 0, No. 0 [*sic.*].

Basu, A. (ed.) (1995) *The Challenge of Local Feminisms: Women's Movements in Global Perspective*, Westview Press, Boulder, CO.

Batliwala, S. (1994) 'The Meaning of Women's Empowerment: New Concepts from Action', in G. Sen, A. Germain and L.C. Chen (eds), *Population Policies Reconsidered: Health, Empowerment and Rights*, Harvard University Press, Cambridge, MA.

Becker, J. and E. Leitman (1997) 'Introducing Sexuality within Family Planning: The Experience of Three HIV/STD Prevention Projects from Latin America and the Caribbean', *Quality/Calidad/Qualité* No. 8, Population Council, New York.

Behar, R. (1993) *Translated Woman: Crossing the Border with Esperanza's Story*, Beacon Press, Boston.

Bell, D. (1985) 'Unionized Women in State and Local Government', in R. Milkman (ed.), *Women, Work, and Protest*, Routledge, New York.

BEMFAM/DHS (1997) *Brazil National Demographic and Health Survey* (PNDS 1996), BEMFAM, Rio de Janeiro, and Macro International, Calverton, Maryland.

Benítez, R. (1990) 'Hacia el Siglo XXI', *Demos*, No. 3.

Benmayor, R. (1991) 'Testimony, Action Research, and Empowerment: Puerto Rican Women and Popular Education', in S.B. Gluck and D. Patai (eds), *Women's Words: The Feminist Practice of Oral History*, Routledge, New York and London.

Benmayor, R., R. M. Torruellas, and A. L. Juarbe (1992) *Responses to Poverty Among Puerto Rican Women: Identity, Community, and Cultural Citizenship.* Centro de Estudios Puertorriqueños, Hunter College, New York City.

Berer, M. (1996) 'Men', Introduction to *Reproductive Health Matters*, No. 7, Special Issue on 'Men' (May).

Berquó, E. (1993) 'Contraception and Caesareans in Brazil: An Example of Bad Reproductive Health Practice in Need of Exemplary Action', *Revista Estudos Feministas*, Vol. 1, No. 2.

Berquó, E., M. J. O. Araújo and S. Sorrentino (1995) *Fecundidade, Saúde Reprodutiva e Pobreza na América Latina. Volume 1 – O Caso Brasileiro*, Cebrap/Nepo-Unicamp, São Paulo.

Boland, R. (1997) *Promoting Reproductive Rights: A Global Mandate*, International Program/Center for Reproductive Law and Policy, New York.

Boland, R., S. Rao and G. Zeidenstein (1994) 'Honoring Human Rights in Population Policies: From Declaration to Action', in G. Sen, A. Germain and L. Chen (eds), *Population Policies Reconsidered: Health, Empowerment and Rights*, Harvard University Press, Cambridge, MA.

Brabin, L. *et al.* (1995) 'Reproductive Tract Infections and Abortion Among Adolescent

Girls in Rural Nigeria', *Lancet*, Vol. 345 (February).

Brazil Ministry of Health (1996) Program on STDs/AIDS, *Boletim Epidemiológico AIDS*, Vol. IX, No. 3, Semana Epidemiológica 23 a 35 (June–August).

Briggs, N. (1993) 'Maternal Health – Illiteracy and Maternal Health: Educate or Die', *Lancet*, Vol. 341 (April).

Brito de Martí, E. (1995) 'Liberalización, despenalización o legalización?', in A. Ortiz-Ortega, (ed.), *Razones y pasiones en torno al aborto*, EDAMEX and Population Council, Mexico City.

Bronfman, M. (1990) 'Evolución y tendencias recientes', *Demos*, No. 3.

Bruce, J. (1990) 'Fundamental Elements of the Quality of Care: A Simple Framework', *Studies in Family Planning*, Vol. 21, No. 2.

Bruschini, C. (1994) 'O Trabalho da Mulher no Brasil: Tendências Recentes', in H. Saffioti and M. Munoz-Vargas (eds), *Mulher Brasileira é Assim*, Rosa dos Tempos, Rio de Janeiro.

Bunch, C. (1990) 'Women's Rights as Human Rights: Toward a Re-Vision of Human Rights', *Human Rights Quarterly*, Vol. 12, No. 4.

Bunch, C. (1995) 'Beijing, Backlash, and the Future of Women's Human Rights', *Health and Human Rights*, Vol. 1, No. 4.

Cairo Demographic Centre (1992) *Quality of Family Planning Services in Egypt*, CDC, Cairo.

Cantú Gutiérrez, J. J. and J. Moreno Neira (1990) 'Continuidad y cambio en ciertos patrones migratorios en el plano nacional', in *Memorias de la IV Reunión Nacional de Investigación Demográfica en México*, Vol. III, Mexico City.

Carloto, C. (1992) 'Uma Análise Psico-Social dos Processo de Participação da Mulheres no Movimento Reivindicatório Urbano: Necessidades, Limites e Dificuldades', unpublished master's thesis, Social Psychology, PUC, São Paulo.

Carnegie Corporation of New York (1994) *Starting Points: Meeting the Needs of Our Youngest Children*, Carnegie Corporation, New York City.

Cavanagh, J., D. Wysham and M. Arruda (1994) *Beyond Bretton Woods: Alternatives to the Global Economic Order*, Pluto Press/Transnational Institute/Institute for Policy Studies, London and Boulder, CO.

CDC (Centers for Disease Control and Prevention) (1994) 'US HIV & AIDS Cases Reported Through December 1994.' *HIV/AIDS Surveillance Report*, Vol 6, No.2, Hyattsville, MD.

CDC (1995) 'HIV/AIDS Prevention: Women, Children and HIV/AIDS', Document No. 253, Public Health Service, Hyattsville, MD.

Center for Reproductive Law and Policy and International Federation of Women Lawyers/Kenya Chapter (CRLP/IFWL) (1997) *Women of the World: Laws and Policies Affecting Their Reproductive Lives – Anglophone Africa*, Center for Reproductive Law and Policy, New York.

Center for Women's Global Leadership (1995) 'From Vienna to Beijing: the Cairo Hearing on Reproductive Health and Human Rights', Rutgers University, New Brunswick, NJ.

CFEMEA (Centro Feminista de Estudos e Assessoria) (1993) *As Mulheres no Congresso Revisor*, CFEMEA, Brasília.

CFEMEA (1994) *Guia dos Direitos da Mulher*, CFEMEA, Brasília.

CFFC (Catholics for a Free Choice) (1994 & 1997) 'Catholics and Reproduction: A World View', Catholics for a Free Choice, Washington, DC.

CFFC (Catholics for a Free Choice) (1995) 'The Vatican and the Fourth World Conference on Women', Washington, DC.

Chee H. L. (1988) 'Babies to Order', in B. Agarwal (ed.), *Structures of Patriarchy: State, Community and Household in Modernising Asia,* Kali for Women, New Delhi.

Chiwuzie *et al.* (1995) 'Safe Motherhood: Causes of Maternal Mortality in a Semi-urban Nigerian Setting', *World Health Forum,* Vol. 16.

Cisler, L. (1970) 'Unfinished Business: Birth Control and Women's Liberation', in R. Morgan (ed.), *Sisterhood Is Powerful,* Vintage, New York.

Citeli, M. T. (1994) 'Mulheres e Direitos Reprodutivos na Periferia: Releitura Feminista de um Movimento de Saúde em São Paulo', master's thesis, University of São Paulo.

Clarke, S. C. and S. J. Ventura. (1994) 'Birth and Fertility Rates for States: United States 1990', National Center for Health Statistics, Vital and Health Statistics Series 21, No. 52, Hyattsville, MD.

Cohen, S. (1995) 'Encuestas de opinión pública sobre aborto', in A. Ortiz Ortega, (ed.), *Razones y pasiones en torno al aborto,* EDAMEX and Population Council, Mexico City.

Collins, P. H. (1990) *Black Feminist Thought: Knowledge, Consciousness, and the Politics of Empowerment,* Unwin Hyman, Boston, MA.

Comité Promotor para la Maternidad sin Riesgos en México (1993) 'De Cairo a Beijing,' *Maternidad sin Riesgos,* No.1, Mexico City.

Committee on Women, Population and the Environment (1994–97) *Political Environments,* Nos. 1–5, Population and Development Program, Hampshire College, Amherst, MA.

Cook, R. (ed.) (1994) *Human Rights of Women: National and International Perspectives,* University of Pennsylvania Press, Philadelphia.

Cook, R. (1995) 'Human Rights and Reproductive Self-determination', *American University Law Review,* Vol. 44, No. 4, April.

Copelon, R. (1994) 'Recognizing the Egregious in the Everyday: Domestic Violence as Torture', *Columbia Human Rights Law Review,* Vol. 25, No. 2, Spring.

Copelon, R. and R. Petchesky (1995) 'Toward an Interdependent Approach to Reproductive and Sexual Rights as Human Rights: Reflections on the ICPD and Beyond', in M. A. Schuler (ed.), *From Basic Needs to Basic Rights,* Women, Law & Development International, Washington, DC.

Corrêa, S. (1994) *Population and Reproductive Rights: Feminist Perspectives from the South,* Zed Books, London.

Corrêa, S. and R. Petchesky (1994) 'Reproductive and Sexual Rights: A Feminist Perspective', in G. Sen, A. Germain and L. Chen (eds), *Population Policies Reconsidered,* Harvard University Press, Cambridge, MA.

Cosío Villegas, D. (1974) *El presidencialismo en México,* Editorial Era, Mexico City.

Craske, N. (1993) 'Women's Political Participation in *Colonias Populares* in Guadalajara, Mexico,' in S. A. Radcliffe and S. Westwood (eds), *Viva: Women and Popular Protest in Latin America,* Routledge, London.

Curi, M. and A. Molina (1993) 'The Dominican Community of Lower Washington Heights: A Community Health Needs Assessment', unpublished paper, New York.

Dairiam, S. (1995) 'The Struggle for Women's Rights in Malaysia: A Review and Appraisal of Women's Activism in the Eighties and Nineties', *Canadian Woman Studies,* Vol. 15, Nos. 2 and 3.

DaMatta, R. (1987) *A Casa e a Rua,* Guanabara, Rio de Janeiro.

DANIDA (Danish Development Association) (1994) *Health Situation in Egypt,* DANIDA, Cairo.

Daniel, H. and R. Parker (1993) *Sexuality, Politics and AIDS in Brazil,* Falmer Press, London.

Davis, A. (1990) 'Racism, Birth Control and Reproductive Rights', in M. G. Fried (ed.), *Abortion to Reproductive Freedom: Transforming a Movement,* South End Press, Boston.

DAWN (1995) *Markers on the Way: The DAWN Debates on Alternative Development,* DAWN's Platform for the Fourth World Conference on Women, Beijing, September.

Daykin, D., H. Eu, and E. Zimmerman (1994) *Neighborhood Profile No. 5: Washington Heights/Inwood, Manhattan Community District 12,* United Way, New York City.

De Barbieri, T. ([1994] forthcoming) 'Cambio sociodemográfico, políticas de población y derechos reproductivos en México', forthcoming in A. Ortiz Ortega, (ed.), *Derechos Reproductivos en México?,* Colegio de México and Editorial Porrúa, Mexico City.

De Oliveira, O. (1988) 'Unidades domésticas y familias censales', *Demos,* No. 1.

Desai, S. (1994) 'Women's Burdens: Easing the Structural Constraints', in G. Sen, A. Germain and L. Chen (eds), *Population Policies Reconsidered,* Harvard University Press, Cambridge, MA.

Desser, N. A. (1993) *Adolescência, Sexualidade e Culpa: Um Estudo sobre a Gravidez Precoce nas Adolescentes Brasileiras,* Rosa dos Tempos, Rio de Janeiro.

DHS/Macro International (1996) 'A Profile of Teenage and Young Adult Women in Nigeria: Findings from the 1990 Nigeria Demographic and Health Survey', Africa Population and Health reports, Macro International Inc., Bureau for Africa, Calverton, Maryland, USA.

Diniz, C. S. G. (1996) 'Assistência ao Parto e Relações de Gênero: Elemento para uma Releitura Médico-Social', master's thesis, Faculty of Medicine, University of São Paulo.

Dixon-Mueller, R. (1993) *Population Policy and Women's Rights: Transforming Reproductive Choice,* Praeger, New York.

Dixon-Mueller, R. and A. Germain (1992) 'Stalking the Elusive "Unmet Need" for Family Planning', *Studies in Family Planning,* Vol. 23, No. 5.

D'Oliveira, A. F. P. L. (1996) 'Gênero e Violência nas Práticas de Saúde: Contribuição ao Estudo da Atenção Integral à Saúde da Mulher', master's thesis, Faculty of Medicine, University of São Paulo.

Easton, Adam (1997) 'Manila Seeks Death Law for Abortions', *Guardian* (UK), 5 December 1997.

Eaton, S. (1992) *Women Workers, Unions and Industrial Sectors in North America,* International Labour Organisation, Geneva.

Echols, A. (1989) *Daring to be BAD: Radical Feminism in America, 1967–75,* University of Minnesota Press, Minneapolis.

Egypt, Central Agency for Public Mobilization and Statistics (CAPMAS) (1991), *Yearbook 1991,* Cairo.

Egypt, Institute of National Planning (1994) *1994 Yearbook,* Institute of National Planning, Cairo.

Egypt, National Population Council (1992) *Demographic and Health Survey* (EDHS), Cairo.

Egypt, National Population Council (1995) *Demographic and Health Survey* (EDHS), Cairo.

Eisenstein, Z. (1978) *Capitalist Patriarchy and the Case for Socialist Feminism,* Monthly Review Press, New York.

Eisenstein, Z. (1988) *The Female Body and the Law,* University of California Press, Berkeley.

Eisenstein, Z. (1994) *The Color of Gender: Reimaging Democracy,* University of California Press, Berkeley.

Eisenstein, Z. (1996) *Hatreds: Racialized and Sexualized Conflicts in the 21st Century*, Routledge, New York and London.

El Baz, S. (1994) 'Women's Work in Egypt', paper presented to the Gender Task Force of the Egyptian NGO Forum in Preparation for the ICPD, Cairo.

El Hamamsy, L. *et al.* (1996) *Early Marriage and Reproduction in Two Egyptian Villages*, National Population Council, Cairo.

El Mouelhy, M. (1987) 'Maternal Mortality in Egypt', unpublished paper, Cairo.

El Mouelhy, M. (1993) 'Women's Lives and Health in Egypt', *Reproductive Health Matters*, No. 1 (May).

Elabor-Idemudia, P. (1994) 'Nigeria: Agricultural Exports and Compensatory Schemes: Rural Women's Production Resources and Quality of Life', in P. Sparr (ed.) *Mortgaging Women's Lives*, Zed Books, London.

Elias, C. (1991) *Sexually Transmitted Diseases and the Reproductive Health of Women in Developing Countries*, Population Council Working Paper, No. 5, Population Council, New York.

Elson, D. (1987) 'The Impact of Structural Adjustment on Women: Concepts and Issues', paper prepared for the Women and Development Programme, Human Resource Development Group, Commonwealth Secretariat, London.

Elu, M. C. (1970) *Mujeres que hablan*, Mexico City: Asociación Mexicana de Población.

Emembolu, J.O. (1990) 'The Early Marriage and Its Sequelae – Vesicovaginal Fistula: Social Implications and Prevention', paper presented at the Workshop on Vesicovaginal Fistula, Kano, Nigeria.

Engels, F. (1972) *The Origin of the Family, Private Property and the State*, International Publishers, New York.

Esu-Williams, E. (1991) 'Rural Women's Perceptions of their Health: A Study in Cross River State in Nigeria', Report prepared for Women in Nigeria–Cross River State, University of Calabar, Nigeria.

Eviota, E. Uy (1993) *The Political Economy of Gender: Women and the Sexual Division of Labour in the Philippines*. Zed Books, London.

Faria, V. E. (1989) 'Políticas de Governo e Regulação da Fecundidade: Consequências nao Antecipadas e Efeitos Perversos', *Ciências Sociais Hoje*, ANPOCS, Vertice, São Paulo.

Fatawi Al Azhar (1995), Vol. 9, No. 26, Cairo (published legal opinions of the Fatwa Council of Al Azhar University).

Faúndes, A. and J. G. Cecatti (1991) 'A Operação Cesárea no Brasil: Incidência, Tendências, Causas, Consequências e Propostas de Ação', *Cadernos de Saúde Pública*, Vol. 7, No. 2 (April–June).

Federal Republic of Nigeria (1988) *National Policy on Population for Development, Unity, Progress and Self-Reliance*, Lagos, Nigeria.

Federal Research Division (1991) 'Nigeria: A Country Study', Library of Congress website (June 1996) [http://lcweb2.loc.gov/frd/cs/ngtoc.html].

Fernández Vega, C. (1995) 'Música e inversión extranjera', *La Jornada* (Mexico City), 15 October.

FETAPE (1994) 'Acordo Coletivo de Trabalho – Sertão de São Francisco', Ms. Federação dos Trabalhadores na Agricultura do Estado de Pernambuco, Petrolina.

Feyisetan, B. J. and A. R. Pebly (1989) 'Premarital Sexuality in Urban Nigeria', *Studies in Family Planning*, Vol. 20, No. 6 .

Feyisetan, B. J. and M. Ainsworth (1995) *Contraceptive Use and the Quality, Price, and Availability of Family Planning in Nigeria*, Living Standards Measurement Study Working Paper, No. 108, World Bank, Washington, DC.

FIBGE (Fundação Instituto Brasileiro de Geografia e Estatística) (1996), *Pesquisa Nacional por Amostra de Domicílio – PNAD, Síntese de Indicadores, 1993,* FIBGE, Rio de Janeiro.

Figueroa Perea, J. G. (1991) 'Anticoncepción quirúgica, ducación y elección anti-conceptivo', in *Memorias de la IV Revolution Nacional de Investigación, Demográfica en México,* Instituto Nacional de Estadistia, Geografia e Informática y Sociedad Mexicana de Demografia, Mexico City.

Figueroa Perea, J. G. (1994) 'The Introduction of New Methods of Contraception: Ethical Perspectives', *Reproductive Health Matters,* No. 3 (May).

Figueroa Perea, J. G. , Y. P. Palma Cabrera, and R. Aparicio Jimenez (1993) 'Una aproximación regional a la dinámica del uso de métodos anticonceptivos', in Secretaría de Salud, *El entorno de la regulación de la fecundidad en México,* Mexico City.

FLACSO/CEPIA (1993) *Mulheres Latinoamericanas em Dados,* Instituto de la Mujer, Santiago.

Foust, D. (1993) 'The Boom Belt,' *Business Week,* 27 September 1993.

Freedman, L. P. (1995) 'Reflections on Emerging Frameworks of Health and Human Rights', *Health and Human Rights,* Vol. 1, No. 4.

Freedman, L. P. (1996) 'The Challenge of Fundamentalisms', *Reproductive Health Matters,* No. 8, November.

Freedman, L. P. and S. L. Isaacs (1993) 'Human Rights and Reproductive Choice', *Studies in Family Planning,* Vol. 24, No. 1, January/February.

Fried, M. G. (ed.) (1990) *From Abortion to Reproductive Freedom: Transforming a Movement,* South End Press, Boston.

Fried, S. T. (1994) *The Indivisibility of Women's Human Rights: A Continuing Dialogue,* Center for Women's Global Leadership, Rutgers University, New Brunswick, NJ.

Ganga, P. (1993) 'Fertility Trends and Differentials' in *Report of the Malaysian Family Life Survey – II, 1988,* National Population and Family Development Board, Malaysia and Rand Corporation, Kuala Lumpur.

García, B. (1993) 'La feminización en la actividad económica', *Demos,* No.5.

Garcia-Moreno, C. and A. Claro (1994) 'Challenges from the Women's Health Movement: Women's Rights versus Population Control', in G. Sen, A. Germain and L.C. Chen (eds), *Population Policies Reconsidered: Health, Empowerment and Rights,* Harvard University Press, Cambridge, MA.

Garfield, R. and D. Abramson (eds) (1994) *Washington Heights/Inwood: The Health of a Community,* Columbia University Health of the Public Program, New York City.

George, A. (1996) 'Gender Relations in Urban Households in Bombay: Challenges for HIV/STD Prevention', paper presented at the conference on 'Reconceiving Sexuality: International Perspectives on Gender, Sexuality and Sexual Health', Rio de Janeiro, April.

Germain, A. and R. Kyte (1995) *The Cairo Consensus: The Right Agenda for the Right Time,* International Women's Health Coalition, New York.

Germain, A. *et al* (eds) (1992) *Reproductive Tract Infections: Global Impact and Priorities for Women's Reproductive Health,* Plenum Press, New York.

Giddings, P. (1984) *When and Where I Enter ... The Impact of Black Women on Race and Sex in America,* William Morrow, New York.

Ginsburg, F. D. and R. Rapp (eds) (1995) *Conceiving the New World Order: The Global Politics of Reproduction,* University of California Press, Berkeley.

Gogna, M. and S. Ramos (1996) 'Lay Beliefs, Gender and Sexuality: Unacknowledged Risks for Sexually Transmitted Diseases', paper presented at the Conference on Reconceiving Sexuality – International Perspectives on Gender, Sexuality and Sexual Health, Rio de Janeiro, Brazil (April).

Göle, N. (1996) *The Forbidden Modern: Civilization and Veiling*, University of Michigan Press, Ann Arbor, MI.

Gonçalves, R. B. M. (1992) 'Práticas de Saúde: Processos de Trabalho e Necessidades', *Cadernos CEFOR*, No. 1, São Paulo Municipal Health Department, São Paulo.

Gordon, D. (1996) *Fat and Mean*, Basic Books, New York.

Gordon, L. (1974) *Woman's Body, Woman's Right: Birth Control in America*, 2nd edn. Penguin Books, New York.

Government of Malaysia (1985) *Fifth Malaysia Plan, 1986–1990*, Kuala Lumpur.

Government of Malaysia (1990) *Sixth Malaysia Plan, 1991–1995*, Kuala Lumpur.

Government of Malaysia (1995) *Seventh Malaysia Plan, 1996–2000*, Kuala Lumpur.

Government of the Philippines (1990) *Census of the Philippines 1990*, Manila.

Govindasamy, P. and A. Malhotra (1996) 'Women's Position and Family Planning in Egypt', *Studies in Family Planning*, Vol. 27, No. 6.

Greenhalgh, S., (ed.) (1995) *Situating Fertility: Anthropology and Demographic Inquiry*, Cambridge University Press, Cambridge.

Greenhalgh, S. (1996) 'The Social Construction of Population Science: An Intellectual, Institutional, and Political History of Twentieth-century Demography', *Comparative Studies in Society and History*, Vol. 38, No. 1 (January).

Grupo CERES (1981) *Espelho de Vênus: Identidade Social e Sexual da Mulher*, Brasiliense, São Paulo.

Guimarães, K. (1996) 'Nas Raizes do Silencio: A Representação Cultural da Sexualidade Feminina e a Prevenção do HIV/AIDS', in R. Parker and J. Galvao (eds), *Quebrando o Silêncio: Mulheres e AIDS no Brasil*, ABIA/IMS–UERJ/Relume–Dumara, Rio de Janeiro.

Gutiérrez, F. J. (1992) 'Algunos retos actuales', *Demos*, No. 5.

Hardon, A. and E. Hayes (eds) (1997) *Reproductive Rights in Practice: A Feminist Report on the Quality of Care*, Zed Books, London.

Hartmann, B. (1994) 'The Cairo "Consensus": Women's Empowerment or Business as Usual?', *Reproductive Rights Network Newsletter*, Fall.

Hartmann, B. (1995) *Reproductive Rights and Wrongs*, South End Press, Boston, revised.

Hatem, M. F. (1994) 'Privatization and the Demise of State Feminism in Egypt', in P. Sparr (ed.), *Mortgaging Women's Lives: Feminist Critiques of Structural Adjustment*, Zed Books, London.

Hathi, D. (1996) 'Speaking Out on Norplant', *Political Environments*, No. 4 (Committee on Women, Population and the Environment), Summer/Fall.

Heilborn, M. L. (1996) 'O Traçado da Vida: Gênero e Idade em Dois Bairros Populares do Rio de Janeiro', in F. Madeira (ed.), *Quem Mandou Nascer Mulher*, Rosa dos Tempos, Rio de Janeiro.

Heise, L. L. (1995) 'Violence, Sexuality, and Women's Lives', in R. G. Parker and J. H. Gagnon (eds), *Conceiving Sexuality*, Routledge, New York and London.

Heise, L., K. Moore and N. Toubia (1995) *Sexual Coercion and Reproductive Health: A Focus on Research*, Population Council, New York.

Hellman, J. A. (1994) *Mexican Lives*, The New Press, New York.

Hellman, J. A. (1995) 'The Riddle of New Social Movements: Who They Are and What They Do', in S. Halesbosky and R. Harris (eds), *Capital, Power, Inequality in Latin America*, Westview, Boulder.

Helzner, J. F. (1996) 'Men's Involvement in Family Planning', *Reproductive Health Matters*, No. 7 (May).

Hernández Bringas, H. (1990) 'Fatalidades han augmentado 150% en 25 años', *Demos*, No. 3, Mexico City.

Hernández Tellez, J. and E. Hernández Carballido (1995) 'Golpeará la crisis con mas fuerza a las mujeres', *La Doble Jornada,* March.

Hill, C. E. (1986) 'Anthropological Studies of the American South,' *Current Anthropology* 18.

Hill, C. E. (1988) *Community Health Systems in the Rural South,* Westview Press, Boulder, CO.

Hine, D. and K. Wittenstein (1981) 'Female Slavery Systems: The Economics of Sex', in F. Steady (ed.), *The Black Woman Cross-Culturally,* Schenkman, Cambridge, MA.

Hodgkinson, E. (1995) 'The Philippines: Economy', in *The Far East and Australasia 1995,* Europa Publications, London.

Hodgson, D. and S. C. Watkins (1997) 'Feminists and Neo-Malthusians: How Sturdy Are Their Alliances?', *Population and Development Review,* Vol. 23, No. 3 (September).

Huntington, D., L. Nawar and D. Abdel-Hady (1997) 'Women's Perceptions of Abortion in Egypt', *Reproductive Health Matters,* No. 9.

Huntington, D. *et al.* (1995) 'Improving the Medical Care and Counseling of Post-abortion Patients in Egypt', *Studies in Family Planning,* Vol. 26, No. 6.

Hussaina A. (1996) 'Wifeism and Activism: The Nigerian Women's Movement', in A. Basu (ed.), *The Challenge of Local Feminisms: Women's Movements in Global Perspective,* Westview Press, Boulder, CO.

IAC (Inter-African Committee on Traditional Practices) (1993) 'No Return to the History of Oppression of Women in Nigeria', *IAC Newsletter,* No. 14 (July).

Ikeji, N. (1996) 'The Emergence of the Silent Majority: Women NGOs Bridging the Health and Development Gap in Nigeria', paper presented at the Nigerian National Conference on International Health (June).

INDRA/HAIN (Institute for Development Research Amsterdam/Health Action Information Network) (1996) *Gender, Reproductive Health and Population Policies: Proceedings from the Zimbabwe Networking Workshop,* June 1995, Amsterdam.

INEGI (Instituto Nacional de Estadística, Geografía e Informática) (1992) *XI Censo general de población y vivienda,* INEGI, Mexico City.

INEGI and UNIFEM (1995) *La Mujer mexicana, un balance estadístico a final del siglo veinte,* INEGI, Mexico City.

IPPF Open File (1993) 'Nigerian Islamic Leaders Advocate Family Planning', *FHS News Update,* Vol. 2, Nos. 1 and 2 (Dec.).

Irwin, K. *et al.* (1995) 'Urban Rape Survivors', *Obstetrics and Gynecology* Vol. 85, No 5 (March).

Isiugo-Abanihe, U. C. (1994) 'Reproductive Motivation and Family-Size Preferences among Nigerian Men', *Studies in Family Planning,* Vol. 25, No.3 (May/June).

Ityavyar, D. A. (1984) 'Traditional Midwife Practice, Sokoto State, Nigeria', *Social Science and Medicine,* No. 18.

Jain, A. and J. Bruce (1994) 'A Reproductive Health Approach to the Objectives and Assessment of Family Planning Programs', in G. Sen, A. Germain and L.C. Chen (eds), *Population Policies Reconsidered: Health, Empowerment and Rights,* Harvard University Press, Cambridge, MA.

Jamilah A. (1994) 'Economic Development and Women in the Manufacturing Sector', in Jamilah Ariffin (ed.), *Readings on Women and Development in Malaysia,* Population Studies Unit, Kuala Lumpur.

Jiménez Ornelas, R. (1993) 'Cincuenta años de mortalidad o el resultado de la desigualdad social', *Demos,* No.6.

Johan, A. M. T. (1993) 'Country Situation on Abortion – Malaysia', paper presented at the International Planned Parenthood Federation, East and Southeast Asia and

Oceania Region, Kuala Lumpur.

Johnson, B. C. A. (1982) 'Traditional Practices Affecting the Health of Women in Nigeria', in *Traditional Practices Affecting the Health of Women and Children*, WHO Regional Office for the Eastern Mediterranean, Alexandria, Technical Publication, Vol. 2, No. 2.

Jones, G.W. (1994) *Marriage and Divorce in Islamic Southeast Asia*, Oxford University Press, Kuala Lumpur/Oxford.

Jones, J. (1990) 'The Political Implications of Black and White Women's Work in the South, 1890–1965', in Louise A. Tilly and Patricia Gurin (eds), *Women, Politics, and Change*, Sage Foundation, New York.

Ju S. H. (1983) 'Chinese Spirit-Mediums in Singapore: An Ethnographic Study', *Contributions to Southeast Asian Ethnography*, No. 2 (Aug.)

Jusidisman, C. (1997) 'Óptica de género: mujeres en las elecciones federales de 1997', *Fem*, Vol. 21, No. 175 (October).

Kabeer, N. (1994) *Reversed Realities: Gender Hierarchies in Development Thought*, Verso, London.

Kanidah, N. (1993) 'Status of Maternal Health Services in Malaysia', paper presented at the Technical Meeting on Maternal Health, SEAMEO-TROPMED, 25-27 May, Kuala Lumpur.

Kaplan, T. (1990) 'Community and Resistance in Women's Political Cultures', *Dialectical Anthropology*, No. 15.

Katz, N. L. (1995) 'Mexican Doctors' Tactics Criticized', *Dallas Morning News*, July 2.

Kelly, J. (1984) *Women, History and Theory*, University of Chicago Press, Chicago.

Khalipah Mohd, T. (1992) 'Marriage Trends Among Peninsular Malaysian Women', in *Report of the Malaysian Family Life Survey – II*, 1988, National Population and Family Development Board, Malaysia and Rand Corporation, USA, Kuala Lumpur.

Khanna, R. (1996) 'Research and Intervention: A Woman–centred Approach', paper presented at a conference on 'Reconceiving Sexuality: International Perspectives on Gender, Sexuality and Sexual Health', Rio de Janeiro, 14–17 April.

Khattab, H. (1992) *The Silent Endurance: Social Conditions of Women's Reproductive Health in Egypt*, UNICEF, Cairo.

Khattab, H. (1992) *The Silent Endurance: Social Conditions of Women's Reproductive Health in Rural Egypt*, UNICEF and the Population Council, Amman, Jordan.

Kisekka, M. (1992) 'Women's Organized Health Struggles: The Challenge to Women's Associations', in M. Kisekka (ed.), *Women's Health Issues in Nigeria*, Tamaza, Zaria, Nigeria.

Kishor, S. (1995) 'Autonomy and Egyptian Women: Findings from the 1988 Egypt Demographic and Health Survey', *Demographic and Health Surveys Occasional Papers* 2, Macro International, Calverton, MD.

Kolbert, K. (1990) 'A Reproductive Rights Agenda for the 1990s', in M. G. Fried (ed.), *From Abortion to Reproductive Freedom: Transforming a Movement*, South End Press, Boston.

Korayem, K. (1991) 'The Egyptian Economy and the Poor in the Eighties', Institute of National Planning Memo No. 1542, Cairo.

Krasner, M. I., T. E. Heisler and P. Brooks (eds) (1994) *New York City Community Health Atlas*, United Hospital Fund of New York, New York City.

Kuhn, A. and A. Wolpe (1978) *Feminism and Materialism*, Routledge and Kegan Paul, London.

Lamas, M., *et al.* (1995) 'The Growth of Popular Feminism in Mexico', in A. Basu (ed.), *The Challenge of Local Feminisms: Women's Movements in Global Perspective*, Boulder,

Westview Press.

Langer, A. *et al.* (1997) 'Improving Post-Abortion Care in a Public Hospital in Oaxaca, Mexico', *Reproductive Health Matters*, No. 9 (May).

Langer, A., R. Lozano and M. Hernández (1993) 'Niveles, tendencias y diferenciales', *Demos*, No. 6.

Leal, O. F. (1994) 'Sangue, Fertilidade e Práticas Contraceptivas', in P. C. Alves and M. C. Minayo (eds), *Saúde e Doença: Um Olhar Antropológico*, Editora Fiocruz, Rio de Janeiro.

Leal, O. F. and B. Lewgoy (1995) 'Pessoa, Aborto e Contracepção', in O. F. Leal (ed.), *Corpo e Significado: Ensaios de Antropologia Social*, Editora da Universidade Federal do Rio Grande do Sul, Porto Alegre.

Leary, V. (1994) 'The Right to Health in International Human Rights Law', *Health and Human Rights*, Vol. 1, No. 1.

Leete, R. (1996) *Malaysia's Demographic Transition: Rapid Development, Culture, and Politics*, Oxford University Press, Kuala Lumpur/Oxford/Singapore/New York.

Leete, R. and B. A. Tan, (1993) 'Contrasting Fertility Trends Among Ethnic Groups in Malaysia', in R. Leete and I. Alam (eds), *The Revolution in Asian Fertility: Dimensions, Causes, and Implications*, Clarendon Press, Oxford.

Lerner, S. and J. Freedman (1994) 'Abortion and Health Care Reform', *Journal of the American Medical Women's Association* Vol. 49, No. 5 (September–October).

Logan, K. (1990) 'Women's Participation in Urban Protest', in J. Foweraker and A. L. Craig (eds), *Popular Movements and Political Change in Mexico*, Lynne Rienner, Boulder.

López Austin, A. (1984) *Cuerpo humano e ideología: las concepciones de los antiguos nahuas*, Universidad Nacional Autónoma de México, Mexico City.

López, I. (1993) 'Agency and Constraint: Sterilization and Reproductive Freedom among Puerto Rican Women in New York City', *Urban Anthropology*, Vol. 22, No. 3–4.

Lugones, M. (1990) 'Playfulness, "World"-Travelling, and Loving Perception', in Gloria Anzaldúa (ed.), *Making Face, Making Soul/Haciendo Caras*, Aunt Lute Foundation Books, San Francisco, CA.

Luker, K. (1984) *Abortion and the Politics of Motherhood*, University of California, Berkeley.

Macías, A. (1982) *Against All Odds: The Feminist Movement in Mexico 1700 to 1940*, Greenwood Press, Westport, CT.

MacLeod, A. E. (1991) *Accommodating Protest: Working Women, the New Veiling, and Change in Cairo*, Columbia University Press, New York.

Madunagu, B. (1997) 'Women's Movements, Partnerships and Alliances: Experiences from Nigeria', paper presented at the 8th International Women and Health Meeting, Rio de Janeiro, Brazil (March).

Makinwa-Adebusoye, P. (1992) 'Sexual Behavior, Reproductive Knowledge and Contraceptive Use Among Young Urban Nigerians', *International Family Planning Perspectives*, Vol. 18, No. 2.

Malaysia Department of Statistics (1991) *Vital Statistics Time Series Malaysia (1911–1985)*, Kuala Lumpur.

Malaysia Department of Statistics (1992, 1993 and 1995) *General Report of the Population Census*, Vol. 1, Kuala Lumpur.

Malaysia Ministry of Health (1992) *Petunjuk-petunjuk Bagi Pengesanan dan Penilaian Strategi Kesihatan Untuk Semua Menjelang Tahun 2000* (Indicators for Monitoring and Evaluation of Health Strategy for All by the Year 2000), Kementerian Kesihatan Malaysia, Kuala Lumpur.

Marcos, S. (1991) 'Género y Preceptos de Moral en el México Antiguo: los Textos de Sahagun', *Concilium*, No. 6.

Marcos, S. (1992) 'Indigenous Eroticism and Colonial Morality in México: The Confession Manuals of New Spain', in *Numen*, Vol. XXXIX, No. 2.

Marcos, S. (1994) 'Género y Revindicaciones Indígenas', *La Doble Jornada*, December.

Marshall, T. H. (1975) *Social Policy in the Twentieth Century*, Hutchinson, London, 4th rev. edn.

Martine, G. (1996) 'Brazil's Fertility Decline, 1965–95: A Fresh Look at Key Factors', *Population and Development Review*, Vol. 22, No. 1 (March).

Massolo, A. (1989) 'Mujer y política urbana: la desconocida de siempre, la siempre presente', paper delivered at the Foro Nacional sobre Mujer y Políticas Públicas, Mexico City.

Megahed, H. (1994) 'Egyptian Women in Parliamentary Committees', paper presented at the Conference on Egyptian Women and the Challenges of the Twenty-first Century, National Council for Motherhood and Childhood, Cairo.

Mehrun Siraj (1988) 'Marriage and Divorce: The Law Applicable to Muslims', in *Women and the Law, Papers from a Seminar on Family Law*, University Women's Association, University of Malaya, Kuala Lumpur.

Mello e Souza, C. (1989) 'Gender, Class and Domestic Work: The Servant–Employer Relationship in Brazil', *Interchange*, Institute of International Education, Vol. 11, No. 1.

Mello e Souza, C. (1994) 'C-Sections as Ideal Births: The Cultural Construction of Beneficence in Brazil', *Cambridge Quarterly of Healthcare Ethics*, Vol. 3, No. 3.

Mies, M. (1986) *Patriarchy and Accumulation on a World Scale*, Zed Books, London.

Mies, M., V. Bennholdt-Thomsen, and C. von Werlhof (1988) *Women: The Last Colony*, Zed Books, London.

Minayo, M. C. S., (ed.) (1995) *Os Muitos Brasis: Saúde e População na Decada de 80*, Hucitec/Abrasco, São Paulo/Rio de Janeiro.

Mishel, L., J. Bernstein and J. Schmitt (1996) *The State of Working America 1996–97*, M. E. Sharpe, Armonk, NY.

Moghadam, V. (1993) *Modernizing Women: Gender and Social Change in the Middle East*, Lynne Rienner Publishers, Boulder, CO.

Molyneux, M. (1985) 'Mobilization without Emancipation? Women's Interests, the State, and Revolution in Nicaragua', *Feminist Studies*, Vol. 11, No. 2.

Morsy, S. (1993) *Gender, Sickness, and Healing in Rural Egypt*, Westview Press, Boulder, CO.

Morsy, S. (1995) 'Deadly Reproduction among Egyptian Women: Maternal Mortality and the Medicalization of Population Control', in F. D. Ginsburg and R. Rapp (eds),*Conceiving the New World Order*, University of California Press, Berkeley.

Mossa'ad, N. (1996) *Women and Parliamentary Elections*, Ed. Wadouda Badran, Cairo University Faculty of Economics and Political Science/Ebert Foundation, Cairo.

Mothercare (1993) 'Mothercare Nigeria Maternal Healthcare Project Qualitative Research', Working Paper No. 17B, John Snow, Inc., Arlington, VA.

Muñoz, H. and M. H. Suárez (1990) 'Educación y empleo: Ciudad de México, Guadalajara y Monterrey', *Memorias de la IV Reunión Nacional de Investigación Demográfica en México*, Bk. III, Instituto Nacional de Estadística, Geografía e Informática y Sociedad Mexicana de Demografía, Mexico City.

Musallam, B. F. (1983) *Sex and Society in Islam: Birth Control before the Nineteenth Century*, Cambridge University Press, New York/Cambridge.

Nagata, J. (1984) *The Reflowering of Malaysian Islam: Modern Religious Radicals and Their*

Roots, University of British Columbia Press, Vancouver.

Naguib, N. G. (1994) 'Gender Inequalities and Demographic Behavior: The Case of Egypt', paper presented at the Population Council Symposium on Family, Gender, and Population Policy, Cairo, 7–9 February.

National Center for HIV, STD and TB Prevention (1996) *The Challenge of STD Prevention in the United States,* National Prevention Center, Washington, DC.

National Commission on Children (1993) *Just the Facts: A Summary of Recent Information on American's Children and Their Families,* National Commission on Children, Washington, DC.

National Food and Nutrition Research Institute (1993) *Fourth National Nutrition Survey,* NFNRI, Manila.

National Task Force on Vesico Vaginal Fistula (Nigeria) (1994) 'Facts on Vesico–Vaginal Fistulae (VVF) in Nigeria', ABU Press Ltd., Zaria, Nigeria.

Nawar, L., C. B. Lloyd and B. Ibrahim (1994) 'Women's Autonomy and Gender Roles in Egyptian Families', paper presented at the Population Council Symposium on Family, Gender and Population Policy, Cairo, 7–9 February.

NCRFW (National Commission on the Role of Filipino Women) (1995) *Filipino Women: Issues and Trends,* NCRFW and Asian Development Bank, Manila.

NDHS (Nigeria Demographic and Health Survey) (1992) Lagos: Federal Office of Statistics and Columbia, MD: Institute for Resource Development/Macro International, Inc.

Nelson, B. J. and N. Chowdhury (eds) (1994) *Women and Politics Worldwide,* Yale University Press, New Haven.

New Woman Research and Study Centre (1996) *The Feminist Movement in the Arab World: Intervention and Studies from Four Countries,* New Woman Research and Study Center, Giza, Egypt.

New Woman Research and Study Centre and El Nadim Centre for Rehabilitation of Victims of Violence (1995) *Violence Against Women: Results of a Fieldwork in Preparation for the Fourth World Conference on Women, Beijing,* New Woman Research and Study Centre, Giza, Egypt.

Ng, C. (1989) 'Women in Development: Malaysia', Asian Development Bank, Country Briefing Paper, Kuala Lumpur.

Ng, C. and Chee H. L. (1996) 'Women in Malaysia: Present Struggles and Future Directions', *Asian Journal of Women's Studies,* Vol. 2 (May).

Norani Othman (1994) 'The Sociopolitical Dimensions of Islamisation in Malaysia: A Cultural Accommodation of Social Change?', in Norani Othman (ed.), *Shari'a Law and the Modern Nation-State : A Malaysian Symposium,* Sisters In Islam, Kuala Lumpur.

Norazah Zulkifli, S. *et al.* (1996) 'Country Report on Gender, Sexuality and Reproductive Health: Malaysia', paper presented at the Asia and Pacific Regional Network on Gender, Sexuality and Reproductive Health, Cebu City, Philippines, 8–13 January, Social Development Research Centre, De LaSalle University, Philippines.

Nunes, M. J. R. (1994) 'De Mulheres, Sexo e Igreja', in A. Costa and T. Amado (eds), *Alternativas Escassas: Saúde, Sexualidade e Reprodução na América Latina,* Ed. 34, São Paulo.

NYCDCP (New York City Department of City Planning) (1992a) *The Newest New Yorkers: An Analysis of Immigration into New York City during the 1980s,* Publication No. DCP 92–16, NYCDCP, New York.

NYCDCP (1992b) *Total Population by Selected Hispanic Origin or Descent: New York City, Boroughs and Community Districts,* NYCDCP, New York City.

NYCDOH (New York City Department of Health) (1993) *Family Planning: Creating a Public Policy Agenda for New York City*, Proceedings of a Symposium Sponsored by the New York City Department of Health and the Columbia University School of Public Health.

Obermeyer, C. M. (1992) 'Islam, Women and Politics: The Demography of Arab Countries', *Population and Development Review*, Vol. 18, No. 1.

Obermeyer, C. M. (1994) 'Religious Doctrine, State Ideology, and Reproductive Options in Islam', in G. Sen and R. C. Snow (eds), *Power and Decision: The Social Control of Reproduction*, Harvard Center for Population and Development Studies, Harvard University Press, Cambridge, MA.

Obermiller, P. J. (1994) 'The Question of Appalachian Identity', in *The History and Culture of Appalachia and Appalachian Ohio: A Resource and Training Manual for Directors and Teachers of Adult Basic and Literacy Education Programs*, Part I, edited by Gini Coover and Bruce Kihre, Rural Action, Inc., Athens, OH.

Okafor, C. and R. Rizzuto (1994) 'Women's and Health-care Providers' Views on Maternal Practices and Services in Rural Nigeria', *Studies in Family Planning*, Vol. 25, No. 6 (Nov./Dec.).

Okagbue, I. (1990) 'Pregnancy Termination and the Law in Nigeria', *Studies in Family Planning*, Vol. 21, No. 4 (July/Aug.).

Olusanya, O. (1989) 'Biosocial Factors in Maternal Mortality: A Study from a Nigerian Mission Hospital', *West African Journal of Medicine*, Vol. 8, No. 3.

Omran, A. (1992) *Family Planning in the Legacy of Islam*, Routledge, New York and London.

Ong, A. (1987) *Spirits of Resistance and Capitalist Discipline: Factory Women in Malaysia*, State University of New York Press, Albany.

Ong, A. (1994) 'State versus Islam: Malay Families, Women's Bodies and the Body Politic in Malaysia', in *Women's Reproductive Rights in Muslim Communities and Countries: Issues and Resources*, Women Living Under Muslim Laws, August, Cairo.

Oni, G. A. (1985) 'Effects of Women's Education on Postpartum Practices and Fertility in Urban Nigeria', *Studies in Family Planning*, Vol. 16, No. 6 (Nov./Dec.).

Oni, G. A. and J. McCarthy (1990) 'Contraceptive Knowledge and Practices in Ilorin, Nigeria', *Studies in Family Planning*, Vol. 21, No. 2 (March/Apr.).

Ortiz Ortega, A. (1996) 'The Feminist Demand for Legal Abortion: A Disrupture of Mexican State and Catholic Church Relations (1871–1995)', PhD thesis, Yale University, New Haven, CT.

Orubuloye, I.O. (1995) 'Patterns of Sexual Behavior of High Risk Populations and the Implications for STDs and HIV/AIDS Transmission in Nigeria', in R.G. Parker and J.H. Gagnon (eds), *Conceiving Sexuality*, Routledge, New York.

Orubuloye, I.O. (1996) 'Sexual Networking in Nigeria: Its Social and Behavioural Context', paper presented at Conference on Reconceiving Sexuality: International Perspectives on Gender, Sexuality and Sexual Health, Rio de Janeiro, Brazil (April).

Orubuloye, I.O. *et al.* (1992) 'Sexual Networking and the Risk of AIDS in Southwest Nigeria', in T. Dyson (ed.), *Sexual Behaviour and Networking: Anthropological and Socio-Cultural Studies on the Transmission of HIV*, Editions Derouauz-Ordina, Liège, Belgium.

Otto, D. (1995) 'Linking Health and Human Rights: A Critical Legal Perspective', *Health and Human Rights*, Vol. 1, No. 3.

Oyebola, D.D.O. (1980) 'Antenatal Care as Practiced by Yoruba Traditional Healers/ Midwives of Nigeria', *East African Medical Journal*, Vol. 57, No. 9.

Oyebola, D.D.O. (1981) 'Yoruba Traditional Healers' Knowledge of Contraception, Abortion and Inferility', *East African Medical Journal*, Vol. 58, No. 10.

Pamplona, F. *et al*. (1993) 'Marginación y desarrollo social en México', *Demos*, No. 6.

Parés Pombo, M. D. (1990) *Crisis e identidades colectivas en América Latina*, Universidad Autónoma Metropolitana, Mexico City.

Parker, R. and R.M. Barbosa (eds) (1996) *Sexualidades Brasileiras*, Relume Dumara, ABIA, IMS/UERJ, Rio de Janeiro.

Patai, D. (1991) 'US Academics and Third World Women: Is Ethical Research Possible?', in S. Gluck and D. Patai (eds), *Women's Words: The Feminist Practice of Oral History*, Routledge, New York/London.

Pateman, C. (1988) *The Sexual Contract*, Stanford University Press, Stanford, California.

Paxman, J. M. *et al*. (1993) 'The Clandestine Epidemic: The Practice of Unsafe Abortion in Latin America', *Studies in Family Planning*, Vol. 24, No. 4.

Pearce, T. O. (1995) 'Women's Reproductive Practices and Biomedicine: Cultural Conflicts and Transformations in Nigeria', in F. Ginsburg and R. Rapp (eds), *Conceiving the New World Order*, University of California Press, Berkeley.

Perez, A. (1995) *Family Planning Survey*, Department of Health, Manila.

Pessar, P. (1990) 'Dominican International Migration: The Role of Households and Social Networks', in R. W. Palmer (ed.), *In Search of a Better Life: Perspectives on Migration from the Caribbean*, Praeger, New York.

Petchesky R. P. (1981) 'Reproductive Choice in the Contemporary United States: A Social Analysis of Female Sterilization', in K. Michaelson (ed.), *And the Poor Get Children*, Monthly Review Press, New York.

Petchesky, R. P. (1987) 'Fetal Images: The Power of Visual Culture in the Politics of Reproduction', in M. Stanworth (ed.), *Reproductive Technologies*, Polity Press and the University of Minnesota, Cambridge and Minneapolis.

Petchesky, R. P. (1990) *Abortion and Woman's Choice: The State, Sexuality and Reproductive Freedom*, 2nd (revised) edn, Northeastern University Press, Boston.

Petchesky, R. P. (1995a) 'From Population Control to Reproductive Rights: Feminist Fault Lines', *Reproductive Health Matters*, No. 6, November.

Petchesky, R. P. (1995b) 'The Body as Property: A Feminist Re-Vision', in F. Ginsburg and R. Rapp (eds), *Conceiving the New World Order*, University of California Press, Berkeley.

Petchesky, R. P. (1997) 'Spiralling Discourses of Reproductive Rights', in J. Tronto, K. Jones and K. Cohen (eds), *Women Transforming Politics*, New York University Press, New York.

Petchesky, R. P. (forthcoming) 'Sexual Rights: Inventing a Concept, Mapping an International Practice', in R. G. Parker , R. M. Barbosa and P. Aggleton (eds), *Framing the Sexual Subject*.

Petchesky, R. P. and J. M. Weiner (1990), *Global Feminist Perspectives on Women's Reproductive Rights and Reproductive Health*, Reproductive Rights Education Project, Hunter College, New York.

Peters, J. and A. Wolper (eds) (1995) *Women's Rights, Human Rights: International Feminist Perspectives*, Routledge, New York/London.

Philippines DECS (Department of Education, Culture and Sports) (1995) *Research and Statistics*, DECS, Manila.

Philippines DOH (Department of Health) (1991), *Philippines Health Statistics*, DOH, Manila.

Philippines NSO (National Statistics Office) (1989) *Functional Literacy Education and Mass Media Survey*, NSO, Manila.

Philippines NSO (1991) *Survey of Overseas Workers*, NSO, Manila.

Philippines NSO (1992) *Labor Force Survey 1991*, NSO, Manila.

Philippines NSO (1994a) *National Demographic Survey 1993*. NSO, Manila.

Philippines NSO (1994b) *National Safe Motherhood Survey 1993*, NSO, Manila.

Pitanguy, J. (1994) 'Feminist Politics and Reproductive Rights: The Case of Brazil', in G. Sen and R. C. Snow (eds), *Power and Decision: The Social Control of Reproduction*, Harvard School of Public Health, Boston.

Pitanguy, J. and R. Petchesky (1993) 'Women and Population: A Feminist Perspective', *Conscience*, Vol. XIV, No. 3 (Autumn), Catholics for a Free Choice, Washington, DC.

PMMN (Prevention of Maternal Mortality Network) (1992) 'Barriers to Treatment of Obstetric Emergencies in Rural Communities of West Africa', *Studies in Family Planning*, Vol. 23, No. 5 (Sept./Oct.).

POPCOM (National Commission on Population) (1994) *The Philippines: Country Report on Population*, prepared for the International Conference on Population and Development, POPCOM, September 1994.

Population Council (1993) 'Prevention of Morbidity and Mortality from Unsafe Abortion in Nigeria', Report of a meeting held in 1991 by the Robert H. Ebert Program on Critical Issues in Reproductive Health and Population, Population Council, New York.

Population Reference Bureau (1996), *Country Profile: Philippines*, PRB, Washington DC.

Portella, A. P. (1993) *Relatório de Pesquisa: Perfil da Trabalhadora Doméstica no Brasil*, Sindicato das Domésticas/SOS CORPO, Recife.

Quarles, B. (1989) *The Negro in the Civil War*, DaCapo, New York.

Quintas, F. (1987) *Sexo e Marginalidade: Um Estudo sobre a Sexualidade Feminina em Camadas de Baixa Renda*, Ed. Vozes, Petrópolis.

Rashidah A. (1993) 'Changing Population Policies and Women's Lives in Malaysia', *Reproductive Health Matters*, No. 1 (May).

Rashidah A. (1996) 'The Women's Movement in Malaysia', unpublished communication.

Rashidah A./ARROW (1995) 'Challenges After Cairo', *Arrows for Change*, Vol. 1, No. 1, April.

Rashidah A., R. Raj-Hashim, and G. Schmitt (1995) *Battered Women in Malaysia: Prevalence, Problems and Public Attitudes*, Summary Report of Women's Aid Organisation, Malaysia's National Research on Domestic Violence, Kuala Lumpur.

Ravindran, T. K. S. (1993) 'The Politics of Women, Population and Development in India', *Reproductive Health Matters*, No. 1, May.

Ravindran, T. K. S. (1996) 'Factors Contributing to Fertility Transition in Tamil Nadu: A Qualitative Investigation', Report prepared for UNDP Project on Strategies and Financing for Human Resource Development, unpublished.

Renne, E. (1993) 'Gender Ideology and Fertility Strategies in an Ekiti Yoruba Village', *Studies in Family Planning*, Vol. 24, No. 6 (Nov/Dec).

Renne, E. (1995) 'Houses, Fertility, and the Nigerian Land Use Act', *Population and Development Review*, Vol. 21, No. 1 (March).

Reproductive Health Matters (1993–97), Nos. 1–10, London.

RHM/WHO (Reproductive Health Matters for the World Health Organization) (1997) *Beyond Acceptability: Users' Perspectives on Contraception*, Reproductive Health Matters, London.

Ribeiro, L. (1994) 'Anticoncepção e Comunidades Eclesiais de Base', in A.O. Costa and T. Amado (eds), *Alternativas Escassas: Saúde, Sexualidade e Reprodução na América Latina*, Fundação Carlos Chagas, São Paulo.

Richburg, K. (1995) 'The Philippine Economy: Can Success Be Trusted?' *Washington Post*, 17 October 1995.

Rivas, M. and A. Amuchástegui (1996) *Voces e historias sobre el aborto*, Population Council/EDAMEX, Mexico City.

Rodrique, J. M. (1990) 'The Black Community and the Birth Control Movement', in E. C. DuBois and V. L. Ruiz (eds), *Unequal Sisters*, Routledge, New York.

Rollins, J. (1985) *Between Women: Domestics and Their Employers*, Temple University Press, Philadelphia.

Romany, C. (1994) 'State Responsibility Goes Private: A Feminist Critique of the Public/Private Distinction in International Human Rights Law', in R. J. Cook (ed.), *Human Rights of Women*, University of Pennsylvania Press, Philadelphia.

Rosaldo, R. (1991) 'Cultura y verdad', *Nueva propuesta de análisis social*, CNCA/ Grijalbo, Col. Los Noventa, No. 77, Mexico City.

Ross, J. A., W. P. Mauldin and V. C. Miller (1993) *Family Planning and Population: A Compendium of International Statistics*, UNFPA/Population Council, New York.

Ross, L. J. (1996) 'African American Women and Abortion: 1800–1970', in S. M. James and A. T.A. Busia (eds), *Theorizing Black Feminisms: The Visionary Pragmatism of Black Women*, Routledge, New York.

Roziah Omar (1994) *The Malay Woman in the Body: Between Biology and Culture*, Penerbit Fajar Bakti, Kuala Lumpur.

Ruddick, S. (1989) *Maternal Thinking: Toward a Politics of Peace*, Ballantine, New York.

Rudie, I. (1994) *Visible Women in East Coast Malay Society: On the Reproduction of Gender in Ceremonial, School and Market*, Scandinavian University Press, Oslo.

Safa, H. and F. C. Butler (1992) 'Production, Reproduction and the Polity: Women's Strategic and Practical Gender Issues,' in Alfred Stepan (ed.), *Americas: New Interpretative Essays*, Oxford University Press, New York and Oxford.

Sagrario Floro, M. (1994) 'The Dynamics of Economic Change and Gender Roles: Export Cropping in the Philippines', in P. Sparr (ed.), *Mortgaging Women's Lives: Feminist Critiques of Structural Adjustment*, Zed Books, London.

Sanday, P. R. (1981) *Female Power and Male Dominance: On the Origins of Sexual Inequality*, Cambridge University Press, Cambridge, London.

Scheper-Hughes, N. (1992) *Death Without Weeping: The Violence of Everyday Life in Brazil*, University of California Press, Berkeley.

Schuler, M. A. (ed.) (1995) *From Basic Needs to Basic Rights: Women's Claim to Human Rights*, Women, Law and Development International, Washington, DC.

Scott, J. (1990) *Domination and the Arts of Resistance*, Yale University Press, New Haven, CT.

Secretaría de Salud (1994) *Mortalidad 1993*, Secretaría de Planeación, Dirección de Estadística e Informática, Mexico City.

Seif El Dawla, A. (1996) Personal communication regarding observations in the psychiatric clinic in Ain Shams University Hospital, Cairo.

Sen, A. (1981) *Poverty and Famines*, Harvard University Press, Cambridge, MA.

Sen, A. (1984) *Resources, Values and Development*, Harvard University Press, Cambridge, MA.

Sen, G. (1997) *Women and the New World Economy: Feminist Perspectives on Alternative Economic Frameworks*, Zed Books, London.

Sen, G. and R. C. Snow (eds) (1994) *Power and Decision: The Social Control of Reproduction*, Harvard University Press, Cambridge, MA.

Sen, G., A. Germain and L. C. Chen (eds) (1994) *Population Policies Reconsidered: Health, Empowerment and Rights*, Harvard University Press, Cambridge, MA.

Shapiro, Thomas M. (1985) *Population Control Politics: Women, Sterilization and Reproductive Choice*, Temple University Press, Philadelphia.

SIDA, ETS (1995) *Boletín*, Vol. I, No.3, CONASIDA and Secretaría de Salud, Mexico City.

SIDA, ETS (1996) *Boletín*, Vol. II, No. 1, CONASIDA and Secretaría de Salud, Mexico City.

Singh, S. and G. Sedgh (1997) 'The Relationship of Abortion to Trends in Contraception and Fertility in Brazil, Colombia and Mexico', *International Family Planning Perspectives*, Vol. 23, No. 1 (March).

Singh, S. *et al.* (1997) 'Estimating the Level of Abortion in the Philippines and Bangladesh', *International Family Planning Perspectives*, Vol. 23, No. 3.

Soares, V. *et al.* (1996) 'Brazilian Feminism and Women's Movement: A Two-Way Street', in A. Basu (ed.) *Women's Movement in Global Perspective: The Challenge of Local Feminisms*, Westview Press, Boulder/San Francisco/Oxford.

Souza, J. (1980) 'Paid Domestic Service in Brazil', *Latin America Perspectives*, No. 7.

Sparr, P. (ed.) (1994) *Mortgaging Women's Lives: Feminist Critiques of Structural Adjustment*, Zed Books, London.

Srinivas, K. R. and K. Kanakamala (1992) 'Introducing Norplant: Politics of Coercion', *Economic and Political Weekly* (18 July).

Stepan, A. (ed.) (1989) *Democratizing Brazil: Problems of Transition and Consolidation*, Oxford University Press, Oxford/New York.

Stephen, L. (1995) 'Women's Rights Are Human Rights: The Merging of Feminine and Feminist Interests Among El Salvador's Mothers of the Disappeared,' *American Ethnologist*, Vol. 22.

Sternbach, N. S. *et al.* (1992) 'Feminisms in Latin America: From Bogotá to San Bernardo,' *Signs*, Vol. 17, No. 2 (Spring).

Suárez, E. (1992) 'Desigualdades entre el varón y la mujer', *Demos*, No. 5.

Tahzib, F. (1983) 'Epidemiological Determinants of Vesicovaginal Fistulars', *British Journal of Obstetrics and Gynaecology*, Vol. 90.

Tambiah, Y. (1995) 'Sexuality and Human Rights', in M. Schuler (ed.), *From Basic Needs to Basic Rights*, Women, Law and Development International, Washington, DC.

Tan, P. C. and S. T. Ng (1995) 'Current and Emerging Family Patterns in Malaysia', paper presented at Bengkel Maklumat Kependudukan: Ke Arah Perancangan [A Population Information Workshop: Towards Planning], Pembangunan Berkesan, Port Dickson, 15–17 August.

Tarrés, M. L. (ed.) (1992) *La voluntad de ser: mujeres en los noventa*, College of Mexico, Mexico City.

Tervalon, M. (1988) 'Black Women's Reproductive Rights', in N. Worcester and M. H. Whatley (eds), *Women's Health*, Kendal Hunt Publishing, Iowa City.

Tey N. P. (1993) 'Patterns of Contraceptive Use and Policy Implications', in *Report of the Malaysian Family Life Survey – II, 1988*, National Population and Family Development Board, Malaysia and Rand Corporation, Kuala Lumpur.

Tey N. P. *et al.* (1995) *Contraceptive Choice in the Rural Areas of Peninsular Malaysia: Determinants and Change*, Faculty of Economics and Administration, University of Malaya, Kuala Lumpur.

Toubia, N. (1995) *Female Genital Mutilation: A Call for Global Action*, RAINBO (Research Action Information Network for Bodily Integrity of Women), New York.

Transparency International (1997) 'Corruption Perception Index', University of Goettingen, Germany, website [http://www.transparency.de] (July).

Trinh, T. M. (1990) 'Not You/Like You: Post-Colonial Women and the Interlocking Questions of Identity and Difference', in G. Anzaldúa (ed.), *Making Face, Making*

Soul/Haciendo Caras, Aunt Lute Foundation Books, San Francisco, CA.

Trottier, D. A. *et al.* (1994) 'User Characteristics and Oral Contraceptive Compliance in Egypt', *Studies in Family Planning*, Vol. 25, No. 5.

UN (United Nations) (1994) *Programme of Action of the International Conference on Population and Development*, Report of the International Conference on Population and Development, UN Doc A/Conf. 171/13, 18 Oct.

UN (United Nations) (1995a) Beijing Declaration and Platform for Action, adopted 15 September by the Fourth World Conference on Women, reprinted in *Women's Studies Quarterly*, Vol. XXIV, Nos. 1–2, Spring/Summer 1996.

UN (United Nations) (1995b) *The World's Women 1995: Trends and Statistics*, United Nations, New York.

UNDP (United Nations Development Programme) (1995) *Human Development Report 1995*, Oxford University Press, Oxford/New York.

UNDP (United Nations Development Programme) (1997) *Human Development Report 1997*, Oxford University Press, New York/Oxford.

UNFPA (United Nations Population Fund) (n.d.) *Quality of Family Planning Services*, Evaluation Report No. 8, UNFPA, New York.

UNFPA (1996) *Programme Country Profile, Philippines*. UNFPA, New York.

United States Women of Color Delegation to the International Conference on Population and Development (1994) 'Statement on Poverty, Development, and Population Activities', National Black Women's Health Project, Washington, DC.

Unuigbe, J. A. *et al.* (1988) 'Abortion Related Morbidity and Mortality in Benin City, Nigeria: 1973–1985', *International Journal of Gynaecolocy and Obstetrics*, Vol. 26.

US Department of Commerce, Bureau of the Census (1991) *Current Population Reports*, Series P-60, Washington, DC.

US Department of Commerce, Bureau of the Census (1993) *Income, Poverty, and Valuation of Noncash Benefits*, Washington, DC.

US Department of Commerce, Bureau of the Census (1996) *Current Population Reports*, Series P-60. Washington, DC.

US DOL (Department of Labor), Women's Bureau (1996) *20 Facts on Women Workers*, Washington, DC, September, 1996.

US State Department, Bureau of Public Affairs (1994) *Background Notes: Philippines*, Washington, DC, December 1994.

US State Department, Bureau of Public Affairs (1995) *Background Notes: Philippines*, Washington, DC. December 1995.

Ventura, S. *et al.* (1997) 'Births and Deaths: United States, 1996', *Monthly Vital Statistics Report*, Vol. 46, No. 1 (Supplement 2). Public Health Service, Hyattsville, MD.

Victora, C. (1995) 'As Imagens do Corpo: Representações do Aparelho Reprodutor Feminino e Reapropriações dos Modelos Médicos', in O.F. Leal (ed.), *Corpo e Significado: Ensaios de Antropologia Social*, Editora da Universidade/UFRGS, Porto Alegre.

Vieira, E. M. and N. J. Ford (1996) 'Regret After Female Sterilization Among Low-income Women in São Paulo, Brazil', *International Family Planning Perspectives*, Vol. 22, No. 1 (March).

Viqueira, J. P. (1984) 'Matrimonio y sexualidad en los confesionarios en lenguas indígenas', *Revista Cuicuilco*, No. 12.

Ward, M. C. (1986) *Poor Women, Powerful Men: America's Great Experiment in Family Planning*, Westview Press, Boulder, CO.

Wasserheit, J. N. and K. K. Holmes (1992) 'Reproductive Tract Infections: Challenges for International Health Policy, Programs and Research', in A. Germain *et al.* (eds),

Reproductive Tract Infections: Global Impact and Priorities for Women's Reproductive Health, Plenum, New York and London.

Wazir-Jahan, K. (1992) *Women and Culture: Between Malay Adat and Islam*, Westview Press, Boulder, Colorado.

Westhoff, C. F. (1994) 'Abortion Training in Residency Programs,' *Journal of the American Medical Women's Association*, Vol. 49, No. 5 (September–October).

Westoff, C. F. *et al.* (1994) *Marriage and Entry into Parenthood*, Demographic and Health Surveys, Comparative Studies, No. 10, Macro International, Calverton, MD.

WGNRR (Women's Global Network for Reproductive Rights) (1980–97) Newsletter, Nos. 33–56, Amsterdam.

WGNRR (1993) 'Population and Development Policies: Report on the International Conference "Reinforcing Reproductive Rights" ', *Newsletter*, No. 43 (April–June), Amsterdam.

WHO (World Health Organization) (1995) *Women's Health Profile: Philippines*. Woman's Health Series, Vol 7. Regional Office for the Western Pacific, WHO, Manila.

WHO (World Health Organization) (1997) *Health Alert*, Vol. XI, April 1-15, 1997.

WHO/UNICEF (World Health Organization and United Nations Children's Fund) (1996) *Revised 1990 Estimates of Maternal Mortality* (April), WHO, Geneva.

Williams, P.J. (1991) *The Alchemy of Race and Rights*, Harvard University Press, Cambridge, MA.

Women Against Fundamentalism (1995) *WAF Journal*, No. 7, November.

Women in Nigeria (WIN) (1991) 'Maternal Health Project', unpublished findings from focus group discussions in Zaria, Nigeria.

World Bank (1995) *World Development Report 1995*, Oxford University Press, Oxford/New York.

World Bank (1997) 'Women in Agriculture Project, Nigeria', The World Bank Website, [http://www.worldbank.org/html/edi/sourcebook/sbxw0701.htm].

Younis, N. *et al.* (1993) 'A Community Study of Gynaecological and Related Morbidities in Rural Egypt', *Studies in Family Planning*, Vol. 24, No. 3 (May/June).

Yuval-Davis, N. (1997) *Gender and Nation*, Sage Publications, London.

Yuval-Davis, N. and F. Anthias (eds) (1989) *Woman–Nation–State*, MacMillan, London.

Zaalouk, M. (1985) 'The Impact of Male Labour Migration on the Structure of the Family and the Women Left Behind in the City of Cairo', paper presented to the First International Conference on Arab and African Women, Cairo, 25–28 February.

Zeidenstein, S. and K. Moore (eds) (1996) *Learning About Sexuality: A Practical Beginning*, Population Council, New York.

Zulficar, M. (1994) *Women in Development: A Legal Study*, UNICEF, Amman, Jordan.

Zulficar, M. (1995) *The Egyptian NGO Platform Document to the Fourth World Women's Conference in Beijing*, National Committee for Population and Development, Cairo.

Index

79, 186, 206, 226, 305; *prenatal care* 9, 35-6, 56-7, 118-19, 206, 226, 268, 283-4; *primary health care* 5, 9, 118, 226; *public health services* 4, Brazil 35-6, 56-65, Egypt 71, 77-9, 99, 104, 105n, Malaysia 115, 117-19, 138, 141, Mexico 147, 155, 169-73, Nigeria 182, 184-7, 206-7, 210, Philippines 219, 222, 226, 228-9, 232, 247, 251, US 266-8, 276, 280, 282-4, 291, comparative analysis 298, 300, 306, 310, 313-17, 321-2; *reproductive health services* 14, 22, 35-7, 56-65, 70-1, 77-9, 115, 141, 155, 169-73, 184-6, 206-7, 210, 226, 232, 247, 251, 268, 280, 282-4, 298, 300, 314-15; *reproductive tract infections (RTIs)* 9; *sexually transmitted diseases (STDs)* 2, 16, 35, 37-8, 50-1, 59, 174, 185, 193-7, 212, 267, 269-70, 285, 311, 314, 319

hierarchy 21, 79, 104, 113, 188, 211, 311, 321

hilots 226

Hinduism 5, 108, 111, 220

human rights 2-3, 5-6, 10-12, 25, 73, 80, 113, 147, 173-5, 187

hysterectomy 56-7

Ibibio people 190

Igala people 190

India 3, 113

Indians 108-44 *passim,* 311

individualism 6, 15

Indonesia 226-7

industrialization 33, 42, 109-10, 114, 221

infant mortality 32, 58, 77, 115, 182, 185, 187, 200, 225-6, 263, 268, 297

infertility 35, 95-6, 131, 136, 200, 202, 204-5, 208-9

informal sector 32-4, 45, 71, 120-1, 151, 192, 223, 226, 264, 275

information 2, 10, 14, 21, 45, 47, 48-50, 60, 63, 65, 70, 78, 83-4, 98, 104, 136, 146-7, 160, 162-3, 167, 169, 171, 184-5, 191, 193-4, 197, 212-13, 245, 276, 285, 298, 301, 305, 312-14, 319, 321-2

Institutional Revolutionary Party (PRI) 150, 175

Interamerican Convention on Women's Civil Rights (1948) 65n

Interamerican Convention on Women's Political Rights (1948) 65n

International Campaign on Abortion, Sterilization and Contraception (ICASC) 27n

International Centre for Research on Women 28n

International Conference on Population and Development (ICPD) (1994) 3-6, 74, 79, 104n, 187, 189, 229, 320-2; *Programme of Action* 10, 28n, 34, 111, 155, 187, 320-2

International Covenant on Economic, Social and Cultural Rights (1967) 10

International Monetary Fund (IMF) 71, 221, 226

International Planned Parenthood Federation 66n

International Reproductive Rights Research Action Group (IRRRAG), *in Brazil* 32, 43; *comparative analysis of studies* 295-318; *conceptual framework of* 6-20; *in Egypt* 70, 80; *in Malaysia* 116; *in Mexico* 147-50, 155; *in Nigeria* 189-90, 213, 214n; *origins and global context* 1-6; *in Philippines* 217-18; *process and methodology of* 20-7, 39-43; *recommendations* 318-22; *in US* 258-9

Ipoh 117

Iran 110

Isis International 28n

Islam 3-5, 69, 72-6, 80-1, 83-4, 86-90, 92, 94, 97, 102-4, 104n, 108, 110-12, 114, 124, 135, 140, 182-5, 189, 191, 200-4, 206-7, 209, 214n, 218, 220, 224, 306-7, 310-11

Jews 262

Johnson, Cora Lee 257, 273, 289

Joint Action Group Against Violence Against Women (JAG) 113-14

Kaduna state 18

Kalinga sa Kalusugan ng Kababihan 232

Kampung Liri 117-20, 132

Kampung Pulau 117-20, 124-5, 127, 135

Kataf people 190, 196

Katipunan ng Bagon Pilipina (KaBaPil) 229

Katipunan ng Kalayaan para sa Kababihang (KALAYAAN) 228-9

Kelantan state 118

IRRRAG International and Country Coordinators' Offices

Brazil
Ana Paula Portella
SOS-CORPO Gênero e Cidadania
Rua Major Codeceira, 37
07 Santo Amaro CEP 50.100
Recife, PE Brazil
Tel: 55-81-423-3044
Fax: 55-81-423-3180
E-mail: soscorpo@elogica.com.br

Egypt
Aida Seif El Dawla
5 Khan Yunis Street
Mohanesseen
Cairo, Egypt
Tel: 20-2-570-1733
Fax: 20-2-344-4429
E-mail: hosams@intouch.com

Malaysia
Rashidah Abdullah
Asian Pacific Resource and Research
Centre for Women (ARROW)
2nd Floor, Block F, Anjung FELDA
Jalan Maktab 54000 Kuala Lumpur
Malaysia
Tel: 603-292-9913
Fax: 603-292-9958
E-mail: arrow@po.jaring.my

Mexico
Adriana Ortiz Ortega
Rio Elba 59-1, Col. Cuauhtemoc
Mexico D.F. 06500
Mexico
Tel and fax: 52-5-655-0435
E-mail: adriortiz@laneta.apc.org

Nigeria
Grace Osakue
2 Hudson Lane
off Akpakpava Street
Benin City
Edo State, Nigeria
Tel: 234-52-245345
Fax: 234-52-250668 or 252-497

Philippines
Mercy Fabros
WomanHealth Philippines, Inc.
16 Cabanatuan Road
Philam Homes 1104
Quezon City, Philippines
Tel and fax: 632-928-3276
E-mail: womanhealth@phil.gn.apc.org

United States
Eugenia Acuña
Women's Health Empowerment and
 Training (WHEAT)
Box 613
Hunter College
425 East 25th Street
New York, NY 10010, USA

International Coordinator
Rosalind P. Petchesky
Hunter College – c/o Women's Studies
695 Park Avenue, Room 1713 West
New York, NY 10021, USA
E-mail: rpetches@shiva.hunter.cuny.edu